The Sustainability
Dilemma

The Sustainability
Dilemma

Essays on British Columbia Forest and Environmental History

Robert Griffin and Richard A. Rajala

Published by the Royal BC Museum, 675 Belleville Street,
Victoria, British Columbia, V8W 9W2, Canada.

Pages and cover designed and produced by Lime Design Inc.

Main body typeset in Legacy Serif 9.5/13 and 8/12 with heads, subheads,
introductory copy, captions, and tables set in Benton Sans.

All images are from the Royal BC Museum and Archives except for those credited
otherwise in the captions. Some content in Chapter 4 has previously appeared in
Richard Rajala's article, "This Wasteful Use of a River: Log Driving, Conservation,
and British Columbia's Stellako River Controversy, 1965–72." *BC Studies* 165
(Spring 2010). Maps on pages 338 and 339 © Province of British Columbia.
All rights reserved. Reproduced with permission of the Province of British Columbia.

All images and text excerpts reprinted with permission.

Details on the cover and title page images can be found on page 64 and 135, respectively.

Printed in Canada by Friesens.

MIX
Paper from
responsible sources
FSC® C016245

Library and Archives Canada Cataloguing in Publication

Griffin, Robert Brian, 1951–, author
       The sustainability dilemma : essays on British Columbia
forest and environmental history / Robert Griffin and Richard
A. Rajala.

Includes bibliographical references and index.
ISBN 978-0-7726-6974-2 (paperback)

       1. Forests and forestry—British Columbia—History—20th century.
2. Forests and forestry—British Columbia—Management—History—20th
century. 3. Forests and forestry—Environmental aspects—British Columbia—
History—20th century. 4. British Columbia—Environmental conditions—
History—20th century. I. Rajala, Richard Allan, 1953-, author II. Royal
BC Museum, issuing body III. Title.

SD146.B7G75 2016   333.7509711   C2016-905803-4

About the Royal British Columbia Museum and Archives

2016 marks the 130th anniversary of the Royal BC Museum and 125 years since its first publication—*Check List of British Columbia Birds*—was published by the museum's first curator, John Fannin, in 1891. Since then the Royal BC Museum's many publications have contributed greatly to the public knowledge of British Columbia and the museum's reputation as a world-class institution, bringing the history and nature of our province to life in exciting, innovative and personal ways.

Acknowledgements

ROBERT GRIFFIN

The completion of my part of this book would not have been possible without the help, patience and support of my wife Donna. I would like to thank the Weston Family for their financial support, which was of great assistance in the completion this project. And I would also like to express my appreciation to the Records Management Centre of the Ministry of Lands, Forest and Natural Resource Operations and, in particular, Penny Newton and Lorraine Skinner.

RICHARD A. RAJALA

I wish to thank my wife Jean for her very important contributions to the preparation of chapters four and five. My portion of the book is dedicated to her. Many thanks also to Keith Moore for his cooperation, insights and the provision of images.

The authors join in expressing their gratitude to Michelle van der Merwe for her support and skill in bringing the manuscript to publication and thank Amy Reiswig for her fine editing work.

Contents

RICHARD A. RAJALA

4

Come Hell or High Water

Log Driving, Resource Politics and Conservation in British Columbia's Stellako River Controversy, 1950–75 **119**

5

The Battle of Riley Creek

Clearcuts, Salmon and Multiple Use on Haida Gwaii, 1970–1985 **239**

Introduction

ONE OF THE MORE CONTROVERSIAL ISSUES British Columbians have faced over the past 60 years is how our forests have been and are being managed. Government policy regarding forest management is routinely attacked by industry, by those concerned about environmental degradation, by First Nations and by many other groups. At times, seemingly everyone in the province, as well as many outside British Columbia, has—at the very least—an opinion on the subject. Forest policy and regulation in British Columbia has been intermittently responsive to these pressures given the inertia of large bureaucracies, resulting in almost continuous policy revision.

By the 1930s it was apparent to British Columbia's forest community and the BC Forest Service that how British Columbia approached its forests had to change. Professional foresters believed that British Columbia's forests, and forests worldwide, couldn't just be harvested but had to be actively managed. The concept that inspired them was sustained yield. BC's chief forester, E.C. Manning, and the subsequent chief forester, C.D. Orchard, were both strong proponents of sustained yield and both proposed its implementation during the 1930s and early 1940s.

But sustained yield was a policy that rarely stayed fixed for long. Sometimes the changes were minor regulatory adjustments while others appear to be major redirections. For instance, the shift from a 46-centimetre (18-inch) to a 33-centimetre (13-inch) diameter at breast height for cutting seems at first glance to be simple fine-tuning, but consider that change over thousands of felled trees. Suddenly a significant

---

Facing page: Log sorting area at Swanson Lumber Company's sawmill, 1953. NA-08627.

amount of new wood or fibre was available and new technology was required to process it. From inventory figures to allowable cuts, logging methods, log utilization and even organizational structure, everything changed—including timber allocation. The development of Public Working Circles (later called Public Sustained Yield Units) and Pulp Harvesting Areas stimulated changes among industry operators as well. For example, the implementation of close utilization policy in 1966 was a major innovation discussed with considerable fanfare in the press, but in some districts the industry began introducing it even before formal adoption by the BC Forest Service.

Of course, the BC Forest Service wasn't able to respond to changing social attitudes with a speed that met the many competing needs of British Columbians—a situation not improved when the minister of forests was frequently working toward a different agenda. The Forest Service regularly found they only learned about policy changes when the ministers announced them through the media. The result was that individuals or groups blamed the visible presence that seemed to be exacerbating the issues—the BC Forest Service.

We will not repeat the often-told story of the Sloan Royal Commissions and their role in the gradual implementation of British Columbia's sustained-yield policy—or, as one company executive put it, shifting 'the forests to being managed instead of mined.' We begin with the fact that, after a rather faltering start, by the late 1940s a sustained-yield policy was in place and thought to be functioning somewhat satisfactorily. How this occurred is examined in some detail in Chapter 1.

Chapter 2 looks at how industry responded to sustained-yield policies, presenting an in-depth study of one major company in BC's central interior. As that case study shows, the implementation of a seemingly straightforward policy such as that offered by early sustained yield proved an overwhelming task, one that sparked innovation as well as frustration. Chapter 3 then examines one of the major policy changes more closely, looking at how it affected both industry and the BC Forest Service. Caught between the pressures of the government, industry and popular movements, the Forest Service remained the target of opportunity. This is not to suggest that they did not adhere to and work from their own view of how things should be managed, but theirs was often a view that did not mesh with that of groups seeking competing objectives.

If forests have been contested ground in British Columbia history, perhaps no issue has proven more consistently contentious than the industry's impact on freshwater ecosystems. From the turn of the twentieth century to the passage of the 1995 *Forest Practices Act*, fisheries interests have condemned forest managers for the abuse of streams and harm to the fishes that inhabit them for all or part of their life cycle. Forest and fisheries managers both spoke the language of wise-use conservation and expressed faith in the wisdom of rational management to maximize sustained yields of their respective resources, and both groups also spoke a common language of multiple-use management. But that rhetoric did not translate into agreement on how best to capitalize on the revenue potential of one industry without compromising that of the other.

As chapters 4 and 5 show, that conflict generated some headlines but mostly played out in settings not subject to widespread public scrutiny. Competing land-use objectives were largely a matter of negotiation among professionals and politicians, those responsible for fish pressing their forestry counterparts for reforms in cutting practices and log transportation methods. The final two chapters therefore provide insight on the complex jurisdictional, political and scientific context that shaped conservationist discourse among the professionals and the public by focusing on two fish-forestry conflicts that *did* capture province-wide attention.

The controversies surrounding the Stellako River log drives of the mid-1960s in the central interior and the Riley Creek/Rennell Sound landslides over a decade later on Haida Gwaii brought to light systemic problems in multiple-use resource management. Both disputes erupted in the context of simmering intergovernmental tensions, pitting Victoria's authority over forests against Ottawa's apparent dedication to upholding federal jurisdiction over salmon habitat. Both situations helped fuel a conviction that the forest management regime needed not just tinkering but serious reform to bring industrial forestry into a more respectful relationship with those whose livelihoods and outdoor recreational pursuits demanded greater balance. The Haida people would make similar arguments, rooted in the region's long history of colonialism, in the campaign for Gwaii Haanas National Park and their claim to the lands and waters of Haida Gwaii.

The book's final chapters also examine how established and nascent environment-focused groups interpreted events from a critical ecological perspective that would come to distinguish environmentalism from more traditional conservationism. By the end of Chapter 5 we see opposition to clearcutting gaining widespread traction in a province experiencing an environmental awakening.

From the outset, BC Forest Service officials considered the mission given to them by government and by the legislation under which they operated as their primary guiding principle. This mission was to act as a revenue-generating agency for government and administer the forests as a perpetual crop. But as time went on the closed policy-making nexus of sustained-yield forestry—which had bound the provincial state, timber capital and unions together in resource allocation decisions —faced mounting criticism over excessive cutting rates and a host of forest practices that prioritized short-term profit and revenue considerations over sustainability and multiple-use balance.

In the chapters that follow we examine many of the issues that faced the Forest Service, industry and British Columbians in general. Our goal is to provide several alternative views as to how the BC Forest Service managed our forests and why events took the shape they did. While some of the historical events we recount have been largely forgotten by the public and largely unexamined by scholars, they reflect an understanding of larger power dynamics that goes beyond the practice of sustained-yield and multiple-use forestry to touch upon important themes in the province's social and cultural history—themes still relevant today.

ROBERT GRIFFIN

1

Implementation

THE IDEA OF SUSTAINED YIELD was not new to the BC Forest Service in the 1940s. Long used and well established in parts of Europe, the practice was widely accepted by trained foresters in North America. But it was still an approach reflecting the era from which it emerged. At that time sustained yield was not about preservation; rather, it treated the forest as a perpetual crop from which to derive revenue. Trees were to be harvested, turned into logs and used to create wood products. As Chief Justice Sloan wrote in his report:

> I would define "sustained yield" to mean a perpetual yield of wood of commercially usable quality from regional areas in yearly or periodic quantities of equal or increasing volume.[1]

Facing page: In 1945 and 1956 Chief Justice Gordon Sloan (shown here in 1937) chaired two Royal Commissions on forestry for the provincial government. His report was instrumental in the implementation of sustained-yield policy in British Columbia. B-07947.

The forest was, in effect, a farm. Such was the accepted view of most foresters when C.D. Orchard, chief forester of the Forest Service, began drafting his approach to managing British Columbia's forests. Orchard was determined to make British Columbia a leader in sustained yield. While his first goal was to manage the forests for economic reasons, his vision was not limited to harvesting, for he also viewed the forest as belonging to all British Columbians. Orchard's support for parks and the preservation of recreation areas showed that even when concerned with creating business opportunities and an overall stable economic situation, he sought to promote other values inherent in our forests.

Getting Started

THE FOREST SERVICE'S INTENT was to provide the forest industry with adequate timber in perpetuity and to create an economic environment that would sustain economic growth and community stability. Work began quickly following both the Royal Commission's report and the subsequent legislation and by 1948 the Forest Service began implementing their plans for sustained yield. Davis Carey and three assistants worked out of the Forest Service's Victoria office but, without adequate information, they faced an immense task. In order to establish a Public Working Circle (PWC), as the Forest Service's administered managed units[2] were initially called, a set of baseline data was required, especially the type of timber within a region and how fast it was growing. This information was necessary to set up the timeline and quantities for a perpetual harvest. Realizing that its first steps were rather tentative, the Forest Service initially refused to publish maps outlining managed unit boundaries and announced that allowable cuts within the managed blocks were preliminary and dependent on better future data.

Work started in two coastal forests: Sayward and Sechelt. By the end of 1950 preliminary cutting plans were in place for the Sayward forest and work was scheduled to begin in several other areas, especially in the interior, for 1951. The growing demand for housing lumber in the United States dramatically increased production in BC's interior wherever railway connections to major markets were established, although markets remained cyclical.

Throughout the central and southern interior demand for timber grew at an amazing rate. Lumbermen sought the most accessible timber first, which often did not meet the Forest Service's planning objectives for best-practice sustained yield. It also meant that some areas were overcut prior to being established as managed units. Several of these areas were initially left out of the management units but, once the logging was completed, these lands were then incorporated into a nearby management unit. In four instances areas were declared special sale areas (SSAs)[3] and, while not put on a sustained-yield basis right away, some controls were implemented. The two largest such areas were located around Prince George, extending south of Quesnel and around Kamloops. These each held a considerable amount of private land and were also being rapidly overcut. Placing the overcut areas under sustained yield would have meant a considerable cut reduction and the government was not prepared to face the fury from multiple operators. In addition, it was believed that much of the land in the Quesnel–Prince George SSA was arable and that it could be converted to agricultural use once logging was completed.

Another problem the Forest Service faced in beginning to implement sustained yield was how to monitor individual cutting licences within the managed areas so that the total cut matched the allowable cut. The decision in this case was to control the harvest through the use of cut control ledgers to be maintained in Victoria, at the various forest district offices and at the ranger offices. Even this was no simple task. What information was required? How was it to be handled? And who maintained what part of the volume? In the end it became primarily the responsibility of the district offices, with Victoria updating its copy twice a year to ensure accuracy. Each timber sale contract was to be entered into the ledger and the cut prorated over the years of the contract. This would then be charged against the yearly allowable cut. The ledger was also for monitoring applications for timber, which made part of the approval or rejection task easier, as Forest Service personnel could readily see if the application would result in exceeding the allowable cut.

Applications were disallowed for a variety of reasons, not only when they exceeded the allowable cut. As the demand for timber greatly exceeded the available supply, the Forest Service soon brought in a policy of only approving applications from established operators—that is, loggers already working in the Public Sustained Yield Unit (Public Working Circle and Public Sustained Yield Unit, or PSYU, were essentially the same, and the terms will be used

KAMLOOPS MANAGED UNITS

Name	Annual Allowable Cut (MM c.f.)	Total Commitments to Mar. 31, 1957		
		1957	1958	1959
Barriere	1.80	1804	1235	827
Niskonlith	2.35	2201	1399	1262
Quesnel Lake	5.76	5500	4532	2571
Salmon Arm	1.52	961	602	262
Similkameen	3.00	1216	969	758
Spallumcheen	9.70	9344	7694	5722
Williams Lake	6.30	5616	3893	1844
Big Bar S.Y.U.	12.00	11,805	8944	5922
Botanie Creek S.Y.U.	4.60	4444	3858	3007
Lac La Hache S.Y.U.	12.00	5510	5366	2118
Nicola Lake S.Y.U.	3.90	3390	2508	1809
* North Thompson S.Y.U.	3.00	1032	816	527
Stum Lake S.Y.U.	3.00	3168	2764	535
Taseko River S.Y.U.	4.20	4180	4177	3774
Yalakom S.Y.U.	3.00	540	519	406
Proposed Adams River S.Y.U.	1.50	no control ledger set up		
Proposed Bridge River S.Y.U.		"	"	
Proposed Eagle River S.Y.U.	2.50	2275	1831	712
Proposed Nehalliston S.Y.U.	2.00	1988	1914	1211

Record of cut from control ledger for Kamloops district showing future commitments, March 10, 1957. Lands, Forest and Natural Resources, Public Working Circles, Supervision File 0187119 Section 1.

interchangeably throughout the volume). Applications were also refused for a variety of silvicultural reasons, such as terrain issues or an overabundance of immature timber. On rarer occasions refusals were based on economic reasons—for example, if it was evident that the cost of proper road-building would mean the logger could not profitably log the area. Past experience had shown that in such cases the road would be badly built or the logging would not take place. And since the Forest Service sought to have the complete allowable cut harvested each year, a company not logging due to road-building cost would skew their calculations.

Organizational Challenges

PROBLEMS REGULARLY AROSE with the new plans and simple communication between Forest Service divisions and branches was not always successful. A 1950 memo to Chief Forester Orchard, for example, noted that the cutting budget for the Sechelt PWC could not be established until a decision was made on two forest management licence applications.[4] In another memo from that same year, the Vancouver district forester rather pointedly observed that he could not monitor the allowable cut in the Sechelt forest unless he was informed what the cut was to be, nor could he notify local operators of the allowable cut without this information.[5] Orchard's reply provided the allowable cuts but also made it clear that the information had actually been sent earlier.

Even between offices within Victoria communication was not always as it should have been. W.G. Hughes, forester in charge of working plans division, wrote to the management division saying it was "embarrassing" when other divisions made requests for information which working plans division did not have, so "in future we would appreciate receiving copies of any information supplied to other divisions concerning Public Working Circles so that we can keep our records up to date."[6]

The differences between Sayward and Sechelt revealed some of the perennial problems the Forest Service would face in setting up and dealing with existing conditions in the various PWCs. One problem highlighted in the Sechelt forest was the difference between theoretical values and the actual harvest. On paper it appeared that during 1950, 3.09 million cubic metres (109 million cubic feet) would be harvested, slightly over the allowable cut of 2.66 million cubic metres (94 million cubic feet). But analysis of past practice showed that the actual cut tended to be well below that figure, rarely exceeding 962,772.8 cubic metres (34 million cubic feet) and with about half of the operators not active in any given year.[7] While this lower actual cut might seem to solve the overcut problem, it only created additional problems. Even when not harvesting their full cut, no logger was going to accept anything less

Loading a logging truck near Sechelt, 1948. I-29108.

than what he deemed his full share of the potential harvest and so continual demands for additional timber by both established and new operators exacerbated the problem of harvest amounts.

The new and expanded Forest Service organization that emerged following the royal commission also faced difficulties in terms of where authority resided. There was no doubt that Chief Forester Orchard kept a tight rein on all decisions, but some authority had to be given to other staff within the Forest Service hierarchy. For example, F.S. McKinnon, the assistant chief forester, informed Carey that it was not possible to maintain a fully up-to-date ledger of all cutting applications in Victoria and that, therefore, decisions relating to applications meeting allowable cut had to be made by the district forester.[8]

In addition, the district foresters were starting to push for faster delineation of PWCs. The Prince George district forester, for instance, noted that two areas had complete inventory figures and that they should move on putting these into regulation of the harvest. He felt that one of them might already be in an overcut situation while the other could be soon. As he pointed out, "The longer we delay the more overcutting will aggravate the problems of necessary regulation."[9]

The districts were often impatient with the pace of decisions from Victoria. One example can be seen when the Prince Rupert district sent a proposal to the management division in Victoria outlining six proposed PWCs for the district, with boundaries marked on a map, and a question as to what assistance might be expected in developing these Working Circles.[10] The answer was, in effect: none. One solution that the Victoria office thought would help was the placement of sustained-yield foresters in the district offices. As early as February 1951 Carey had proposed that working plan division foresters be placed in certain areas to work on a variety of local projects; this would greatly speed the process of implementing sustained yield.[11]

Loaded logging truck near Smithers, 1971. NA-26718.

The transfer of these foresters to the district offices meant that considerably more responsibility for establishing PWCs devolved onto the districts, although final approval and control remained with Victoria. For example, A.L. Parlow, who had been posted to the Nelson district in 1952, was able to report that he had initiated work on four Kootenay PWCs and undertaken some minor work on three Arrow Lakes PWCs.[12] But Victoria's continued involvement in even the smallest details is evident from a district forester's reply to a request for information from the Nelson office on the St. Mary River Valley. The valley had been extensively cut over by the Crow's Nest Pass Lumber Company starting in 1904 and, as a result, it was believed that insufficient timber remained for the valley to be included in a managed area. For specifics about this area the Nelson office was referred to the Victoria management office where the requested information was more readily available.[13] This was clearly information that should have been available in the district without having to go through Victoria.

The Bigger Problems: Boundaries and Access

Assistant Forester A.L. Parlow in Nelson, 1959. NA-19316.

IN ADDITION to internal organizational challenges, the Forest Service faced problems with PWC boundaries. Boundary reviews continued to be of concern over the next decade but during the creation of the initial PWCs the boundaries were almost always in some flux. Volumes and cut figures in the districts and Victoria were often out of sync as either office would propose boundary changes and adjust the figures accordingly. As Parlow wrote in the early 1950s, the rangers still did not even have boundary maps for the PWCs they were supervising, and industry remained somewhat uncertain as to which PWC they were operating in. Parlow saw this as a not insurmountable obstacle, though, as the boundaries tended to follow heights of land between river drainages.[14]

Crow's Nest Pass Lumber Company loggers near Wardner, 1906. D-03541.

Procedures for establishing PWCs had also become somewhat haphazard and in early 1953 Orchard decided it was time to clarify them. The earlier shifting of foresters to the districts meant that much of the work and most of the proposals for establishing PWCs were now expected to start with a district and then be negotiated out with the Victoria-based working plans and management divisions. In a memo dated March 4, 1953, Orchard informed his staff that the initial step was to obtain approval from the chief forester—i.e., Orchard—and to then provide a working plan. The idea was for the district to assemble all the data, analyse the area, determine industry use and future use, provide information on the amount of timber available and then propose a boundary for the managed area. If no issues arose, the working plans division would approve the plan and it could be submitted to the management division. If there were issues of concern, such as an existing overcut, then a proposed remedy also had to be submitted to the management division, along with the overall plan, for that division's approval.[15]

Although the procedures Orchard outlined seem fairly straightforward, there was considerable pressure on the districts to get managed forest units in place as quickly as possible—not always an easy task. As one assistant forester noted: "I have your note of tribulation that you want all Working Circles under sustained regulation. So I offer my apologies and for the next ten months I'll grow arms like an octopus and do everything at once!"[16]

Despite an immense demand for timber in areas near to planers and saw-mills and along transportation corridors, the information needed to properly manage the forest on a sustained-yield basis was still largely unavailable in 1953, and the management plans and logging plans could not be prepared with any surety. In Nelson, Parlow decided that in order to at least make some progress he would cruise and map the more urgent drainages in each PWC and then proceed to work drainage by drainage until maps for all were completed. In 1953 he was responsible for seven PWCs, which was far from placing the whole of the Nelson district under management.[17]

Those in the Victoria office also sought to understand the issues facing the field men, and in March 1953 W.G. Hughes—at this time the forester in charge of the working plans division—went on a tour of three forest districts: Prince Rupert, Prince George and Kamloops. Here he encountered some good practices but also saw some of the problems. The Smithers PWC, for example, illustrated a growing concern in the interior that the Forest Service could only partially control. That is: how was cutting in excess of the annual allowable cut to be dealt with?

In the interior most of the timber remained under provincial jurisdiction and in several managed areas the overcut issue had become critical. Forest Service officials sought to control it at the local and middle management levels but the reality of politics quickly intruded and senior ministry officials recognized that no minister was going to accept a policy resulting in significant political pressure. Hughes, for example, recommended that cuts in the Smithers PWC be reduced over the next four years to match the existing allowable cut (although for local staff this cut was still too high). When Hughes discussed this with assistant chief forester F.S. McKinnon and J.S. Stokes, the forester in charge of the management division, they decided that the high cut would continue, with limited short-term timber sales, until a revised allowable cut was available. Then the allowable cut to each operator would be revised. Part of the problem was that 80 operators fed rough lumber into three planer

Seymour Lake Lumber Company's portable sawmill near Smithers, 1913. NA-03480.

mills and the local chamber of commerce worried about those loggers. What McKinnon and Stokes engaged in was a practice that played a critical role in shaping those Forest Service actions with potential political consequences: the tactic of delay. (This was also a tactic that Lands, Forests and Water Resources minister Ray Williston would use to his advantage on numerous occasions.) Experience had shown that many of those 80 operators would disappear over the next several years and although the demand for timber would continue, fewer, if stronger, voices would need to be answered.[18] This delay also allowed time, as McKinnon noted, to inform and convince the chamber of commerce "of the objectives of sustained yield and the necessity for the same." Senior officials felt it was critical that they not get mixed up "with political meetings" and lay the Forest Service "open to criticism."[19]

One issue that did prove useful in managing the forest was the road system being planned and built by the Forest Service. The layout of the roads was essential to directing the flow of logs—and impacted which communities benefited. For example, in the Big Valley PSYU an acrimonious fight broke out in 1958 between Quesnel and Prince George operators over the road program leading into block 2 of the unit. Quesnel controlled block 1, while Prince George

Clearing the Willow River access road, 1956. Roads were an important tool for the Forest Service, to direct logging into preferred areas. NA-16011.

lumbermen were eager to gain control of block 2, which they eventually did. The issue revolved around where the Forest Service was to build its access road.

Road construction could alleviate other problems as well. When Weldwood first developed its limits in the Quesnel Lake PSYU, logs were moved to the mill by driving them down the Quesnel River. As such practices became less and less acceptable as their ecological impacts became more widely known (see chapters 4 and 5), the issue of road-building, including cost and location, became significant.

Roads didn't just help manage operator concerns; they also helped manage the forest itself. During his tour through the Public Working Circles in 1953, Hughes found that on timber sales where careful attention had been given to road construction there was a greater potential for better logging practices. In a sale logged by Ferguson Sawmills in the Crooked River PWC Hughes noted they had done an excellent job of logging, which included minimal destruction of young growth and properly piled slash. He credited this largely due to proper road construction. Conversely, when reviewing the Naver PWC Hughes found that a badly located road contributed to poor logging. Road placement was only a contributing factor, though, as the Forest Service still did not have enough data to ensure that the best logging regulations were included in the timber sale contracts. For instance, the Naver contracts were based on tree diameter, but such criteria did not suit the stands being logged.[20]

Naver was actually in danger of being alarmingly overcut, a situation prevented only by the quick action of Prince George staff. Completion of the rail link between Quesnel and Prince George in 1950–51 suddenly made the Naver area very accessible and sawmillers and loggers immediately began applying for timber. Lorne Swannell, the district forester, saw the area as having significant forest production potential, so the Forest Service moved quickly to establish control over harvesting. But no surveys of the region had been undertaken since the 1920s and even this basic information was minimal. Already, five sales had been awarded to five different operators and another

Lord Lake Sawmills operation in the Naver Public Working Circle, loading a truck on the Naver access road, 1958. NA-17300.

eight were in the process of being cleared. Within months of the completed rail link to Prince George, Swannell requested the area be designated a PWC and was prepared to meet with all of the operators to inform them of the basis on which the Forest Service was prepared to recognize sales within the area. Swannell wrote to Chief Forester Orchard on July 9, 1951:

> It is felt that as this area is a new area, as yet relatively untouched, and the region should be managed on a sustained yield basis even though there is as yet no forest surveys for the greater part of the area.[21]

By July 31, 1951 the area was designated as the Naver Creek Provincial Forest. The district then began informing operators that a limitation of three years was being imposed on timber sales while the Forest Service established the appropriate annual allowable cut and prepared development and management plans.

Although Assistant Chief Forester F.S. McKinnon commended the district for its work, not everything went as smoothly as hoped—the demand for timber in the area was intense. As Assistant Forester Eric Robinson politely described the issue, "The annual allowable cut in each compartment had to be increased in order to get this forest off to a sound working unit"—that is, to satisfy the demands of the loggers.[22] To compensate for this demand he therefore suggested to extend the boundary "so that the forest was not in an over cut position," and McKinnon agreed. Such tactics only worked as long as there was additional unallocated nearby forest, which would not be the case for most of the tree farm licences and the PWCs.

One solution tried by the Prince George forest district in 1951 was to advocate for an extra-large initial cut that would then be reduced over the next 20 years to a sustainable annual cut on those PWCs where applications for timber already exceeded the allowable cut. Much of the forest here was considered mature and over-mature and the district felt a rapid cut was the best silvicultural practice. But the Victoria office quickly expressed dissatisfaction with this view. While it might look good on paper, the operators would establish themselves based on the existing allowable cut and would not be willing to take a reduced cut later on. In his response Orchard clearly expressed that he thought this was a bad idea, based partly on previous experience:

Lord Lake Sawmills, truck unloading at the mill log pond, 1958. NA-17302.

We have many illustrations in the past of this type of utilization; as for example in the East Kootenay's, where in 1910 we had six or eight large saw-mills; in 1920, the number had shrunk to three; in 1930, to two; and today, we have a very few small mills struggling for existence on the difficult and inac-cessible fringes.... The probabilities are that there is seldom any net profit at the end of a liquidation operation.[23]

Orchard's stated objective was, rather, to have a lower initial annual cut; to then increase it, should that prove warranted once the necessary information was accumulated; and then to implement regulated management from a sil-vicultural best-practice model. He wrote: "The personal problems to be solved are bound to increase with passing years and seldom will be easier of solution than at the time the Forest is first put under a Working Plan."[24] The reality of working with multiple aggressive loggers, many with significant political influence, meant that successful sustained-yield management required careful organization and forethought.

Victoria managers and the districts did not always agree on the best approach to managing, whether it was operator conflict, cut allowances or access to timber. If neither side was willing to yield in their arguments the matter was then referred to the chief forester for his decision, which was final unless overruled by the minister. One illustration of having to deal with differing management options that shows the problem of differing opinions can be seen in an inquiry from the Powell River Pulp and Paper Company in 1951.

Powell River Pulp and Paper was one of the few coastal pulp and paper mill operators who were seriously interested in securing pulp wood from the central interior at this time and arranged for the firm of Yorston & Rice of Quesnel to act as their agents. Larger-scale enterprise was also beginning to take root in the region around Quesnel with the establishment of Western

Winding newsprint off a paper machine at the Powell River Pulp and Paper Mill, 1949. The company unsuccessfully sought to expand operations into the BC interior. I-28845.

Plywood's plywood plant. The district forester thought this activity offered a good opportunity to improve silvicultural practice with thinning. McKinnon in Victoria disagreed, pointing out that such an operation would require the use of horses or small tractors and needed close supervision. McKinnon's concern was that area loggers were currently using tractors that were too large and were causing unnecessary damage to the younger trees. He expressed his opinion to the chief forester:

> For some time now our timber sale supervision has been very poor, in fact almost negligible. How then can we justify initiating new activities that demand close supervision for success until such time as our timber sale supervision has reached minimum standards?[25]

Although the Prince George district agreed with McKinnon's issues, they argued that the establishment of the Canyon Creek ranger district meant such supervision could be provided.[26] Orchard agreed with McKinnon that no industry thinning would take place. Both Orchard and McKinnon believed that if the Powell River Company was serious about obtaining pulp wood from the Quesnel area, sufficient salvage remained on sawlog timber sales to meet this need.[27]

Special Concerns: Implementing in Individual Regions

AS THE FOREST SERVICE moved to place each area under management, unique situations arose in different regions. In the Hixon Creek area in 1954 District Forester W.C. Phillips strongly recommended that the area be divided into three operating areas and that three timber sales of seven years each (the norm at this time was three years) should be allocated. Soon longer timber sales cycles evolved into a norm of 10-year sales, although these time frames continued to depend on the timber, the operator and the harvesting conditions. In the end, after considerable discussion, Victoria agreed to the seven-year sales as long as Phillips also secured agreement from the three operators involved.

The Forest Service had to move on each individual issue at the right moment, as no situation was completely straightforward. When Phillips made the proposal for the longer-term licences, four loggers were working in the area, but Phillips believed that only three needed to be consulted due to some

R.G. McKee following his appointment as deputy minister of forests, 1958. NA-17389.

industry changes happening at this time. As assistant forester (silviculture) Dennis Glew wrote to John Stokes, the forester in charge of the management division, the area had originally been developed by L.H. Zogas operating as the Columbia Spruce Company. After purchasing a timber sale in 1951, he interested three other companies to work with him to finance a road: Neals Lake Logging, Continental Lumber Company and S & D Lumber Company. Neals Lake sold their interest to the Basin Lumber Company who subsequently also purchased the interest of Columbia Spruce. Columbia Spruce disposed of another part of its interest to the Hixon Lumber Company so that, by the time the Forest Service suggested dividing the region into three sectors, the interested loggers were the Basin Lumber Company, Hixon Lumber Company and S & D Lumber Company. The district decided that a fourth logger, who was operating in the Hixon Basin, would be directed into an adjacent area.[28] As word of this plan spread to other operators working in other PSYUs, they began seeking similar assurances as to length of timber sales. The Forest Service remained firm, however. They would always meet immediate needs but such licences would only be issued as the areas came under proper management—basically, once they were able to establish areas of interest without creating undue turmoil among the operators. The proposed Hixon long-term licences did not ultimately come to fruition as the operators involved opposed them and the Forest Service dropped the idea for the time being. Two years later Basin Lumber tried to revive the idea as they sought to acquire the assets of S & D Lumber and Hixon Lumber, financed by the Swanson Lumber Company of Edmonton. They proposed to install a gang saw and create a more efficient operation.[29] R.G. McKee, the assistant chief forester in charge of Forest Service operations, wrote to the district forester for resolution but indicated he was prepared to support implementation of the previous plan of longer-term sales. The annual allowable cut, however, was to remain the same.[30]

The Forest Service generally held the line on timber sales, although with difficulty. The situation of L. Knudson illustrates the point. Knudson owned a sawmill at mile 370 on the Pacific Great Eastern Railway and was seeking additional timber. At the time of his inquiry in 1954 he was logging outside the nearest Working Circle and seeking timber just over 19 kilometres distant from his operation. He therefore proposed to build a road. Part of the Forest Service's concern was whether the road was economically viable, and they worried it might take as long as 45 years for Knudson to recover his costs. District forester Phillips wrote a rather ambiguous reply when Stokes requested more information so Stokes told him exactly what he wanted answered and what the policy was in this regard:

> The specific answer we require, therefore, is in view of the above, can the Abhou-Lodi Lake area be opened up and how much timber per year can be sold from this area. We do not consider that we would be guaranteeing Mr. Knudson an annual cut but we believe he has a perfect right to know how much timber we are prepared to offer for sale from this area each year. We do not guarantee that someone else will not bid against him nor will we put for sale any additional timber if he is bid out of a sale.[31]

The quandary the Forest Service faced in every Working Circle was how to accommodate established operations in balance with newcomers and

Typical load of logs on the Stone Creek access road near Prince George, 1958. NA-17294.

move the harvest to areas considered as priority harvesting areas—i.e., those with over-mature timber. When it came to securing rights, companies would use multiple arguments, playing their cards to the fullest. Strom Lumber of Prince George, for example, argued for cutting rights based on their long-term commitment, expansion plans and plans for continued harvesting in the area, fearing that the creation of the Naver forest would place them in a precarious position. To support their case, they outlined their activities. Strom had begun small operations in the 1930s, and by 1953 was operating a planer in Prince George and two sawmills within 40 kilometres of Prince George. In addition, two companies operated by Strom's sons, Tabor Creek Sawmill and Lord Lake Sawmills were closely linked. The company had built a new sawmill in 1948 and reorganized. They undertook extensive planning to utilize timber in the Stone Creek watershed that was now part of the Naver PWC. The main problem from Strom's perspective was that the current forest road construction program would exclude them from the timber. As well, only Lord Lake Lumber Company held a timber licence in the area under development, which would also severely limit the amount of timber that Strom could apply for in the new managed unit.[32] The Forest Service heard such arguments regularly and decisions had to be made on who to support and how, and who not to support and why.

The Forest Service regularly faced considerable disagreement over how best to bring each managed area into a proper sustained-yield situation. Loggers continued to seek the more accessible areas, even when these did not necessarily reflect best practice, and access problems meant the Forest Service frequently felt compelled to grant the requested timber sales. But every option proposed both internally and from industry was given serious consideration. For example, when A. Groner of the Kamloops forest district office made a proposal to W.G. Hughes that would, at least in his view, help rectify the access situation, he was answered by John Stokes, the assistant deputy minister. Stokes noted that while the ultimate goal was for the Forest Service to plan and lay out the timber sales, it was not yet time to change from allowing the loggers to make applications—applications which, while occasionally not approved, frequently were. Stokes thought that each PWC still had its own specific problems and that no overall policy was therefore feasible. He was very aware of the political reality that any attempt to forcibly move the loggers to where the Forest Service thought they should be logging would meet with resistance and political interference (although, as shall be shown later, this was sometimes the approach adopted). Instead, Stokes' hope was to use the Forest Service's road construction to induce loggers to move into the areas the Forest Service wanted them to log.[33] In their efforts to introduce sustained yield, senior administrators always had to be wary of the political influence operators possessed. A simple thank-you note from the Coast Small Operators Association reinforced this concern when they mentioned their upcoming meeting with the Minister of Forests, R.E. Sommers, and one of W.A.C. Bennett's more trusted lieutenants, P.A. Gaglardi.[34]

By the end of 1953, 25 PWCs were in operation: eight in the Vancouver forest district, three in Kamloops, two in Prince Rupert, seven in Prince George and five in Nelson. Of these only one was actually in an overcut position; that of Salmon Arm in the Kamloops forest district. Another area of concern, one which continued to cause problems, came under scrutiny in late 1953 as well: the lower Fraser River Canyon area. Orchard's initial solution was to establish a Fraser Canyon PWC, but he was well aware that this proposal to the minster was going to be somewhat of a stop-gap measure and that pressure would increase significantly in this area. Orchard argued that something needed to be done quickly, however. Not only had the cut quadrupled between 1950 and 1952, but there were also numerous forest management licence (FML) applications covering the area. Taking into account the extensive cut occurring on private land in the area it was estimated that the area was already significantly overcut, perhaps the worst in the province.[35] The proposal came back to Orchard with a number of deletions based on government's desire to not include selected areas that were under FML application. Orchard revised the plan accordingly.

Stroms Sawmill, 1953. NA-14510.

In early 1954 Walter Lessing of the working plans division began visiting the various districts to help staff understand the inventory and survey information being sent to them, and to talk about how to deal with problems. For example, the Prince Rupert district had, by this time, five PWCs in place, but the Smithers unit was now in an overcut situation and district staff were uncertain how to correct it. As Lessing noted:

> The District staff feel they are not holding the line in their timber sale policy, and wish to know they can formulate a practical method of regulation to stay within the sustained yield; especially in the light of too sketchy field data, which in their opinion is not sufficient to regulate the cut closely.[36]

As was often the case, the issues here were quite unique, and Lessing further noted:

> In the Smithers region the over mature hemlock presents a problem in that there is no demand for these stands because there is not enough spruce to make an economic logging unit. The site appears good and the problem of regeneration presents a controversial problem.[37]

By the end of 1954 the situation in many districts could be described as almost desperate. How were the overcut forests to be managed, and how to prevent those still undercut from becoming overcut? In the Kamloops region, as the Kamloops district forester wrote to Hughes, "The present regulations measures are inadequate." He reported his estimate that of the seven managed units in the Kamloops district, all but one would be overcut in 1954. Although he expected some of the units could be brought back into line, several of the regional sawmill companies were expanding their operations and he expected further demand on timber resources. The forest situation around Kamloops was considered especially difficult, not even considering the overcommitted special sale area that was also in place.[38]

By the end of 1954 the Forest Service had 36 PWCs established and had awarded 17 management licences.

PWCs and Management Licences, 1954

PWC	Name	ML	Company
1	Arrowhead	1	Columbia Cellulose Company Limited
2	Babine	2	Elk Falls Company Limited
3	Barkley	3	Passmore Lumber Company Limited
4	Barriere	4	D. Morrison
5	Broughton	5	Western Plywood Company Limited
6	Cape Scott	6	Alaska Pine & Cellulose Limited
7	Cariboo	7	Salmon River Logging Company Limited
8	Carp Lake	8	Boundary Sawmills Limited
9	Chilliwack	9	S.M. Simpson Ltd.
10	Cottonwood	10	Timberland Development Co.
11	Crooked River	11	Olinger Lumber Co.
12	Edgewood	12	Bendickson Logging Co.
13	Fraser Canyon	13	Galloway Sawmills
14	Gardner Canal	14	Cranbrook Sawmills Limited
15	Kettle Valley	15	Oliver Sawmills Limited
16	Kyuquot	16	Ponderosa Pine Lumber Company Limited
17	Morice	17	Evans Products Company Limited
18	Nakusp		
19	Naver		
20	Nicola Lake		
21	Niskonlith		
22	Purden Lake		
23	Redonda		
24	Rivers Inlet		
25	Salmon Arm		
26	Sayward		
27	Sechelt		
28	Similikameen		
29	Slocan		
30	Smithers		
31	Spallumcheen		
32	Stuart Lake		
33	Upper Kootenay		
34	West Creston		
35	West Lake		
36	Willow river		

The BC Forest Service sought to place areas under sustained-yield management prior to extensive logging when possible, which made the implementation of regulation somewhat simpler. But a lack of accurate up-to-date information created problems, resulting in boundary changes and sometimes overcommitment. Difficulties sometimes also arose from the loggers, who did not always understand the ramifications of sustained-yield implementation, and nearly all areas of the province had at least one interested operator by the time the Forest Service could consider imposing sustained-yield management on an area.

J.S. Stokes, a key player in the implementation of the sustained-yield policy, 1958. NA-17829.

Balancing Act

SEEKING TO CONTROL a worsening timber demand and potential overcut situation, the Forest Service introduced several policies intended to give established operators greater security in the PSYUs and provide them with a somewhat more assured timber supply.[39] In 1960 the Forest Service introduced the licence priority system for fully committed PSYUs. Under the terms of this policy an operator's quota or allowable cut within a managed unit was calculated, and applications for more timber could only be made by operators having a quota within that unit. As an added protection, the applicant could choose bidding by sealed tender, a process in which the applicant could match any bid made and thus secure the timber sale.[40] As well, the Minister of Forests could disallow any sale that exceeded double the upset price, and the operator could then reapply for the sale.

One critique of sustained-yield policy—and it has been the most contentious—is the accusation that the Forest Service manipulated the forest management system to favour larger operators and that this resulted in concentration of the industry into fewer and fewer hands that controlled more and more timber. While the needs of large operators were certainly a factor in planning and process, the Forest Service was also well aware of the smaller industry players' needs and sought to meet them. In 1951 several coastal PWCs were proposed for just this purpose. For instance, the Rivers Inlet PWC was specifically established to allow the smaller operators access to timber, as were several other, more southerly coastal Working Circles.[41]

Refinements in the management of the PWCs and PSYUs continued to be introduced as the process of sustained yield unfolded, sometimes in direct response to industry competition. Some operators, though, continually sought to at least partially circumvent the rules and find ways to secure their timber supplies far into the future. This was especially true as more and more of the PWCs became fully committed. One industry approach was to submit applications for timber well in advance of future years' need. Both the district and Victoria staff agreed that such applications should be disallowed and the operator advised to reapply at a more appropriate time.[42] But other operators also now saw the establishment of PWCs as working to their advantage rather than as simply a roadblock in their exploitation practices. In 1955 Blackwater Timber, for example, petitioned the ministry to establish a PWC in the 100 Mile area. The result of establishing three PWCs to the north was that every newcomer who wanted to become a logger was now trying to secure timber in the 100 Mile area, to the detriment of the established operators. Blackwater Timber therefore sought to limit the emergence of new operators and considered the area as already being overcut.[43] The Forest Service agreed, and in the next year the Lac La Hache Sustained Yield Unit was created, although it too became immediately overcut.

While problems remained, by 1955 a large part of the province was being managed on a sustained-yield basis. The Forest Service was aware that greater control was necessary for proper management and that it was not just a case of needing better inventories and moving as many operators as possible into over-mature timber areas. Rather, the Forest Service now realized they had to begin looking at species distribution and cut as well, appreciating that if non-merchantable species were included in the allowable cut calculations, excessive cutting of in-demand species occurred to the detriment of the overall inventory.[44]

Conscious of the difficulties operators had in adjusting to the idea that they could not just go in and get whatever timber they decided was in their best economic interest, the Forest Service implemented many of their

G.E. Meents, the ranger at Quesnel who pointed out that the rules need to be enforced, 1950. NA-10006.

policies gradually and were often quite forgiving of operator errors. But they made it clear very early on that the rules were to be enforced, especially in terms of silviculture and fire protection. One area where enforcement had been lax was around the allowable cut on timber licences. By 1971, though, deputy minister Stokes, with agreement from minister Williston, decided it was time to become more rigorous in enforcing cutting levels as outlined in the timber licences. The original idea was that each licensee would cut a certain amount from the licence each year and, in theory, would be penalized if they did not meet this obligation. But penalties had rarely been applied. Stokes now decided that such penalties should be enforced, although some flexibility was still allowed. Excess timber cut, for example, was now to be considered a breach of the licence and operators would be charged accordingly.[45]

Throughout the 1950s the rangers had begun enforcing as many of the timber sale contract clauses as possible. As the Quesnel ranger G.E. Meents noted in 1955, "there is no point in selling timber, putting a lot of clauses in the contracts, etc. and then forgetting about them."[46] As Meents also pointed out, the job continued to increase in difficulty: "all phases of the job have become more compacted with an entirely new approach to timber cruising, requiring a considerable amount of detail and more and longer report forms."[47]

By 1956 the Forest Service had established what they viewed as their essential criteria and responsibilities in any managed area. Assistant forester H.G. Bancroft wrote to the Victoria management section that he understood that the Forest Service's first responsibility was to "make available for timber sale purposes an amount equivalent to the allowable annual cut," and second, "to see that such timber is harvested under the best silvicultural practices in order to keep the land productive."[48] Late that year the Forest Service had implemented standard procedures and criteria for the evaluation of timber applications. Essentially, basic information was collected and then key Forest Service staff met in a roundtable to evaluate each application. A list of nine factors, ranked in order of importance, was to guide the evaluation.[49]

1. Applications from operators with more than five years' supply will be turned down.
2. When necessary to reduce the volume applied for, applications from parties not operating in the areas should be disallowed.
3. If still more volume needs to be eliminated, applications in areas reserved for future development will be disallowed.
4. Low priority areas should be avoided.
5. Silvicultural considerations may be used to disallow applications.
6. On occasion, two sales may be joined if they make an economic unit.
7. If protection plans require an area be set aside, applications in the area are to be disallowed.
8. If still too much timber volume is requested, then the years for an operator's supply can be reduced to three and even two years.
9. Finally, if volume still needs to be reduced, use the application date as a criterion.[50]

In 1957 N.A. McRae, a BC Forest Service forester, proposed eliminating cut restrictions in PWC contracts, arguing that the working plan now required by the Forest Service within the first year of the award of a timber licence would satisfactorily control the cut.[51] D.B. Taylor, district forester for the coast district, then had McRae forward his memo to J.S. Stokes, who was in charge of management in Victoria and who then discussed it with the assistant chief forester. Both agreed, and approval was given to implement the change. Such revisions occurred on a regular basis and, while improving procedures, were probably confusing to the smaller loggers.[52] By 1959 the Forest Service was seeking to create an even more precise formula for determining allowable cuts, especially in the interior. District foresters were being asked for greater detail on stand treatments in an effort to understand what constituted an acceptable cutting practice. However, as Hughes in Victoria acknowledged:

Driver marking logs before loading, 1958. NA-17311.

We are a long way from having a precise and intimate knowledge of the major forest types in each SYU, nevertheless it is important that we relate, as best we can, our allowable cut estimates to the methods of cutting and the objectives we are striving for under different stand treatments.[53]

Although a number of large tree farm licences (TFLs) had been allocated on the coast, those in the interior were fewer and smaller and eventually ceased to be an option for the interior operators. In the Prince George forest district a series of small TFLs were designated.

These TFLs were all linked to existing large sawmills except Western Plywood's, which was linked to a proposed and subsequently built plywood plant.

Prince George Forest District TFLs

Western Plywood (later Weldwood)	No. 5
Shelley Development Limited	No. 28
Eagle Lake Sawmills Limited	No. 29
Sinclair Spruce Lumber Company Limited	No. 30
Upper Fraser Spruce Mills Limited	No. 31
Church Sawmill Limited	No. 34

Seeking a balance between TFLs and PWCs was not a simple task. By 1956 the Forest Service had 23 TFLs in place and were reviewing a further 157 applications and 30 letters of intent. Few were without some problem or opposition, and almost all covered lands that were being considered for PWC management. It was trouble over a TFL that eventually led to the only jail sentence handed out to a BC MLA and cabinet minister, Robert Sommers.[54] In the case of the Prince George district TFLs, Victoria was very concerned by how these proposals, except Western Plywood's, were located along the rail line such that more distant timber had considerably reduced accessibility. Their location gave every appearance of intentionally blocking access to these timber resources, effectively tying up larger blocks of additional timber that would only be accessible to the TFL holders.[55]

The Forest Service was not only concerned with the allocation of large TFLs to large companies. Early on Orchard, at least, hoped that the smaller loggers would take up small TFLs to meet their future logging requirements indefinitely. When small operator M.C. Carrol, who had been logging on Blind Channel, applied for a small TFL on West Thurlow Island in 1949, Orchard followed the application with great interest. Despite an objection from the Canadian Western Lumber Company (as it impinged on their Duncan Bay tree farm application and pulp mill proposal) the Forest Service decided to go ahead with Carrol's application and even offered him help not provided to the larger companies in getting the TFL organized. TFL 4 was approved July 12, 1949 and awarded May 15, 1950.

It did not work out as the Forest Service had hoped. In late 1953 Carrol advised the Forest Service that, due to doctor's advice, he could no longer continue logging and so requested permission to sell his TFL to Minstrel Island logger D.A. Morrison. In late 1956 Morrison, as the result of a bad back,

Log dump and log raft, Thurlow Island, 1938. Logging was conducted on West and East Thurlow Island for many years prior to Carrol applying for his management licence. NA-10898.

requested permission to transfer the licence to a somewhat larger logger, I.W. McDonagh. In 1964 McDonagh moved the TFL into the name of his logging company, Fourmax Logging Limited, and in 1966 assigned the TFL to F & R Logging Limited, which operated TFL 36 and was, in effect, a subsidiary of BC Forest Products. BC Forest Products eventually amalgamated TFLs 4 and 36. Amalgamations such as this were happening around the province, against the Forest Service's aspirations of using the TFLs to support mid-sized logging companies. As Orchard wrote to the minster on November 6, 1956:

> From the start of the Management Licence program we had envisioned that there would be a good representation of small units producing about one million board feet a year in addition to the larger units necessary to sustain the large integrated industries that have been established in the coastal region.
>
> It was therefore somewhat of a surprise to find in the course of time that few of the so-called small operators were interested enough to submit

an application for a Forest Management Licence, and in the case of those that did we went out of our way to try and work out a practical proposition.[56]

Certainly by the late 1960s the frameworks of British Columbia's timber allocation policies were moving into place—many of which continue to influence how timber is allocated today. These policies included close utilization,[57] to increase the timber supply and support the pulp mills; bidding practices to protect existing loggers; and allocating areas to specific companies. Outside of the TFLs and in the PWCs, areas were now being considered effectively delineated for a certain operator's primary use. In a letter assessing the Ainsworth Lumber Company's 1968 application to hold a timber sale harvesting licence (TSHL), the Forest Service referred to zones of influence and to the operating territories of the various surrounding companies.[58]

In 1967 the Forest Service undertook several experiments in close utilization before fully implementing the policy. One experiment was with Jacobson Brothers of Williams Lake in the Kamloops forest district. A second was undertaken with BC Forest Products at Port Renfrew, and a third at MacMillan Bloedel's Franklin River division in the Vancouver forest district. The critical element from the MacMillan Bloedel study related to scaling and stumpage payments. MacMillan contended that the formula in place worked for net cubic scaling and foot board measure (FBM) scaling but not for gross cubic scaling, and therefore an adjustment factor was required.[59] A fourth experimental program carried out with Kamloops Pulp and Paper highlighted additional scaling problems, this time over the two scaling methods then in use. The large difference between the district scale and the inventory scale caused reviewing Forest Service officers considerable concern and created enough of a furor in Victoria that E.L. Young, the forester in charge of inventory, instructed George Allison to prepare a summation that would be less controversial than the detailed report.[60]

Scaling remained the most contentious issue before implementing close-utilization standards in 1967, and detailed studies of how to determine scale continued to be undertaken. The most thorough study appears to have been by Kamloops Pulp and Paper at their Lumby sawmill. The logs were separated and then scaled by both the company's scaler and tallyman and by a BC Forest Service scaler and tallyman. A five per cent selection was made for further study and these were then again scaled at their hauled lengths and rescaled when cut to length for optimum mill usage, in an effort to determine a fair method of scaling the smaller timber.[61]

Special Sale Areas

ACHIEVING SUSTAINED-YIELD MANAGEMENT was much more difficult in certain areas, such as the Kamloops and Prince George SSAs. Establishing a PSYU was not just about good forest management but also about politics. If the larger operators were in opposition, the department was well aware that political interference would likely occur. Sometimes even the smaller operators could marshal sufficient support to raise political concerns. Obtaining some form of consensus was critical in these areas before sustained yield could be introduced.

Douglas fir and balsam removed from a road in Weldwood's Management Licence Number 5, 1950. Ian MacQueen, Weldwood's chief forester and logging manager at Quesnel, is standing near the photo's centre. NA-10387.

The Kamloops area was particularly sensitive, as several moderately sized sawmillers were active and each held very definite opinions, often in disagreement with one another. The government decided it would not go ahead with sustained yield in this area unless the operators were in agreement. Williston made this very clear to a number of the region's operators in 1964, writing to Joe Frolek, the Ponderosa Pine Lumber Company and BC Interior Sawmills Ltd., saying:

> I am still in hopes that the established licensees of the Kamloops Region will come to some agreement which will enable a sustained yield unit to be established. Unless this occurs, then for the present I intend administering the Kamloops Region as in the immediate past.[62]

Williston had been presented with a petition from 21 of the region's operators requesting that certain policies be adopted and a new inventory undertaken immediately. His response was basically that they must agree to sustained yield or the answer was no, but as he noted:

> I hope, however, that the firms and individuals, who have established a record of production in the Kamloops region, will get together and request that the area be put on Sustained Yield. I realize that this will mean that their right of application—the so called quota right—will decrease. Being on Sustained Yield, however, would have the definite advantage that the recognized applicants would have the protection of the bidding fee recently made law and, further, the right to match any higher bid made under sealed tender.
>
> It would further mean that my department would re-inventory the area as soon as finances and other priorities permit. This might, I admit, still mean several years of delay.
>
> A copy of this letter is being sent to all established licensees as per the attached list. I would strongly urge you to get together and request that the area be put on Sustained Yield. The advantages of protection in bidding, not to mention the long term advantage will surely overcome the reduction in cut necessary for the immediate future.[63]

The Kamloops forest district had, in fact, proposed that the area be made a Sustained Yield Unit in January 1961 but, to achieve this, logging in the area would have been reduced by 60 per cent. The decision to delay was based on concerns that such a drastic cut reduction might have created problems for the then proposed pulp mill at Kamloops, as well as generated opposition from the established operators.[64] Even as early as 1957 Forest Service rangers were pointing out to districts and Victoria that the area was being severely overcut and that some regulation was necessary. The issue was brought to a head by 20 applications from the Halston Lumber Company for 60 million FBM. The local rangers saw this as timber speculation, as Halston already had a two-year supply and other companies were still only applying for their normal amounts to maintain their operations.[65]

The Forest Service was inclined to not regulate those areas in which severe overcutting was taking place unless these areas could be incorporated in a way that would not result in significant industry or political problems. Kamloops was late in being looked at for conversion to a managed area, mainly due to the varied tree farm applications that had been made, of which only two—that of Ponderosa Pine and BC Interior Sawmills—were eventually allocated. Once the government had clarified how it was going to handle the varied FML applications in the interior, most being disallowed, concern focused on how to manage the Kamloops region.

The Kamloops situation was complicated by the great distrust that the older, long-established operations—BC Interior Sawmills in particular, with a long-running sawmill in Kamloops, and the Ponderosa Pine Company, with a sawmill at Monte Lake—had for several of the newer concerns that were using portable sawmills. One of the newer operators, Terrace Forest Products, had been creating havoc with the timber sales by bidding sales up beyond the possibilities of economic return in order to gain control of timber supplies. As far as the older companies were concerned, these newer operations were securing timber without concern for the industry's future and were primarily responsible for the extensive overcutting happening within the region. In the controversy over sustained yield the older firms saw the upstarts as ravaging the forest for short-term gain and as being supported by Forest Service policy in these efforts. Williston and the Forest Service, however, were determined to force the lumber companies to resolve their differences themselves and, until operators reached a wider consensus as to the best solution, Williston was unwilling to take action to bring the region under management. As deputy minister R.G. McKee noted in 1963, if the Forest Service undertook action "it would reduce the pressure on industry…to solve their own problems."[66] To some extent, allocating TFLs to Ponderosa Pine and BC Interior Sawmills reduced the anxiety of these two leading operations.[67]

By the mid and late 1960s Williston was moving to resolve the problems in the Kamloops region, although his solution would be detrimental to some of the smaller operators. It was clear by this point that the Kamloops region's industrial players were never going to agree. Williston used the newly formulated close utilization policy to force out several small operators, as there was simply insufficient timber of the appropriate type to supply their operations. Long & Son wrote to the minister in 1968 that the decision to stop their operations in 1972 came as a "shock." Long pointed out that they had been operating at the same location for over 20 years, and he supplied production figures to support their claim that they were fully utilizing all materials brought to the sawmill.[68] A number of other mills were in a similar situation. Several of these smaller mills had not immediately been able to convert to close utilization, and by the time they realized that it was necessary for survival and could finance such a proposition, the close utilization supply had already been allocated to other sawmills.

In 1967 Drew Sawmills was advised by Ray Williston that there was no point in converting their sawmill to close utilization as the supply was committed.[69] Similarly, Frolek attempted to convince the minister to provide them with additional timber based on close utilization. They, in turn, were advised not to base their plans on the expectation that they would receive any timber beyond their present five-year commitment.[70] Frolek operated a long-established ranch near Kamloops, having first homesteaded in 1906. In 1946 they began logging and sawmilling using portable mills and set up their own planer at Halston, just north of Kamloops. They became closely associated with the Charlie Bennett group of sawmills (Terrace Forest Products, Halston Lumber Company and Punjab Lumber Company). This association worked somewhat to their detriment, as several of the larger stationary mills viewed the Bennett group with disdain and argued that they were using poor forest management practices. As well, when Balco purchased the Bennett operations they did not purchase Frolek's mills, which left Frolek isolated from the bulk of the Kamloops region operators. When the region began shifting to the Forest Service's close utilization standards in 1967, the death of two of Frolek's principals—first the major shareholder in 1967, and then the founder

Waste pile at Frolek's sawmill, 1952. NA-14649.

in 1968—resulted in the company being unable to participate in the first distribution by constructing the necessary facilities to engage in close utilization.
When Frolek tried to get back into the game in 1969, it was too late; the timber
had been allocated. Although Frolek went to considerable effort to change
the minister's mind, it was to no avail. There was simply no more timber to be
allocated. Williston had warned Frolek that building a new, modern sawmill
would not change the government's position, and it did not. By 1973 Frolek
Sawmills was out of business.

The Kamloops forest district had more than its fair share of problems. A
number of the PSYUs were being overcut and many had numerous operators.
Co-operation amongst industry was not happening as it was in other forest
districts. In the Prince George district most Sustained Yield Units were operated through industry associations where the members agreed on the allocation of timber, while in the Nelson area a jointly owned company frequently
acquired the cutting rights and farmed these out to member companies.
Kamloops, by contrast, was still faced with excessive bidding and operators
who acquired sales in order to cut off a competitor's future supply.[71]

The Williams Lake, Lac La Hache and Shuswap PWCs were also problem areas. Williams Lake PWC was created in 1955 when a large PWC called Cariboo East was divided into the Williams Lake and the Quesnel Lake PWCs. Unfortunately the area included in the Williams Lake PWC was already in an overcut position. The management approach the Forest Service applied here was much more hard-line than in the Kamloops region. A memo from Victoria noted: "It is obvious, however, that the present actual cut cannot be sustained and the working circle must be brought into balance."[72] In effect, operators would be made to conform to the allowable cut established by the Forest Service.

As evidenced in Kamloops, each special sale area posed unique problems for the Forest Service in trying to impose their approach to sustained yield. Issues in the Prince George special sale area (PGSSA), for instance, exemplify problems that the Forest Service faced in tenures around the province. The PGSSA was not considered a sustained-yield area, but the Forest Service did seek to impose limits on harvesting so that some activity could continue over the years. It was also an area where as soon as any decision was made, new conflicts arose.

When the pulp harvesting areas were established (see Chapter 3), the Forest Service asked Northwood and Prince George Pulp and Paper, who both had rights in the special sale area, to delineate their zones of operation. After months of negotiation, no decision could be reached, and the BC Forest Service then imposed Prince George Pulp and Paper's proposal. New problems arose as a result, as Prince George Pulp was the most active pulp mill engaged in harvesting and they applied for timber in an area that Lloyd Brothers considered as their operating area. In addition, the logging they undertook was unsatisfactory to the area's ranchers who claimed land-clearing was harder after Prince George Pulp had logged a timber sale. The ranchers requested the company log and do land-clearing at the same time.

The official reason that the PGSSA had been created was the Forest Service's belief that much of the land had economic value for more than just forestry—i.e., it was suitable for agriculture. Conflicts reached such a difficult point that in 1968 several public meetings were held and a land use special study was undertaken by the Ministry of Lands, Forests and Water Resources with the hope of determining optimal agricultural versus forestry land use, partly so the Forest Service could more easily recognize when applications for

Kamloops Pulp and Paper's scaling study played a significant role in how smaller logs should be scaled, 1966. NA-22876.

farmland were made mostly to acquire timber (as the land in question was not considered arable).

While certainly influenced by the issue of agricultural land use, and while that may have been the official reason for its creation, the PGSSA was primarily created for much the same reasons as Kamloops: too many operators logging too little timber. Two disputes quickly surfaced. First, the area loggers greatly feared a reduction in cut if they were moved into a PSYU. Second, there were so many loggers—over 250—that the Forest Service was uncertain how to allocate them to a PWC. Unlike Kamloops, the PGSSA was soon placed under regulations that provided existing loggers protection similar to that in the PWCs.[73] This was not the end of controversy, however, as the creation of the pulp harvesting areas, which included much of the PGSSA, exacerbated small loggers' concerns around their wood supply.

Sawmill at Kamloops, 1966. I-22374.

In addition, in his statement of March 17, 1965, the minister assured mills established as stud mills that they would receive a guaranteed supply of logs of smaller diameter than sawlog[74] mills. A stud mill was defined as a mill having the specialized equipment to handle smaller logs and that mainly produced 38 x 89 millimetres x 2.43 metres (2 x 4 inch x 8 foot) lumber.[75] At the time of the minister's statement there were three such operations in the region: Lloyd Brothers and Clear Lake sawmills of Prince George, and Tubafour of Quesnel. Of these, Tubafour was most persistent in seeking extra privileges that they considered their just due and wrote extensively to Williston with their concerns about timber supply. Initially, Tubafour had only a small quota in the special sale area, but as they sought to establish their presence they quickly began buying quota from many of the area's small loggers and significantly improved operations, to the point that minister Williston privately assured them that "this mill will not be allowed to shut down through lack of raw material."[76]

Although the ministerial assurance of timber supply reduced the troubles between the stud mills, it did not solve the issues between the stud mills and the pulp and paper companies who were looking at the same timber stands. In this dispute the Forest Service adopted their preferred approach, which was to force industry to arrive at a solution themselves. After extensive negotiations between Prince George Pulp, Intercontinental Pulp, Northwood Pulp and the stud mills, led by Tubafour, two plans were drawn up, one by Prince George Pulp and one by Northwood Pulp, as they could not agree on certain points. Both plans were presented to the Forest Service, who chose Prince George Pulp's plan. This plan effectively divided up the appropriate stands in areas so that only the designated mill could apply for timber in that area. Meanwhile, the Forest Service would undertake an extensive survey of the stands over the next five years in order to determine whether additional areas could be allocated to any of the parties to the agreement.

Williston initially decided that this was one place where government could hold the line. Under the terms of the agreement with Intercontinental Pulp and Paper, stud mills were eligible to apply for additional timber. But there were several stud mills in the PGSSA that were utilizing private timber and had not recently held a Crown timber sale. Williston decided these mills were not eligible for the additional timber—although eventually, in the case of two additional mills, he deviated from this decision and allowed them the extra timber.[77] Williston and the Forest Service agreed, therefore, that only two additional mills would be eligible under the terms of the sales, bringing the total number of stud mills to five instead of three.[78]

Government's decision did not prevent other mill owners from trying to become part of this select group. The Atlin Sawmill Ltd., based in Hixon, wrote to the minister requesting consideration.[79] Williston responded with a qualified no, saying that if one of the other operations failed to meet their obligations, then Atlin Sawmills Ltd. would be in the running for their timber position.[80] In addition, Tubafour immediately protested the decision designating the Ernst Lumber Company at Quesnel as a stud operation. They mainly objected because including Ernst meant that his timber would come from the reserve zone closer to Quesnel, providing Ernst an unfair advantage in Tubafour's view. Tubafour had also previously applied for and been denied timber in the area. They were having access problems with their present supply and argued that access to the Whittier Creek timber, now granted to Ernst, was easier. Tubafour indicated to Ray Williston that upgrading the Quesnel River road to an all-year road would solve their problem. This option was investigated, but Williston eventually decided to give them access to other timber in the Forest Service reserve area near Quesnel.

Tubafour were not the only objectors to granting the Ernst sawmill timber in the Whittier Creek area. A.L. Patchett & Sons had already developed the area for sawlogs and argued that they had not recovered the funds expended in road construction and that the grant to Ernst would cut them off from the timber needed to recover this cost. Additionally, they noted to the minister that Patchett also had the capability for stud production. They requested

Ponderosa Pine Lumber Company's sawmill at Monte Lake, 1965. NA-22537.

Adams River Lumber Company's sawmill was built at Chase in 1907. The company had extensive timbers limits in the Shuswap area but closed the mill in 1925 when timber quality did to meet their expectations. F-09184.

rights similar to the stud mills but received the same answer as Atlin Saw-mills: if one of the existing stud mill operations defaulted, they would be in line to take over the quota. Of course, those benefitting from Williston's decision most lauded his judgment. For instance, John Ernst of the Ernst Lumber Company wrote in regard to their acquisition of the Whittier Creek timber, "we would like at this time to express our appreciation and to commend your wisdom in such progressive thinking", and further stated: "Since first estab-lishing an operation in the Quesnel area 16 years ago, I have never faulted in my belief that the answer lay in smaller stems. It is gratifying to see that dream become a reality."[81] It should be noted that Ernst Lumber Company was the first sawmill, in 1964, to install a Chip-N-Saw for small-diameter lumber pro-duction.[82] Despite zoning the Whittier Creek area to Ernst, Williston listened to Patchett's arguments and granted them additional timber in the Whittier

Creek area.[83] Ernst Lumber Company, of course, immediately protested this allocation, and Williston's response was to suggest there was adequate timber for both companies and that Ernst should work out a suitable division with Patchett so that "destructive competitive bidding" did not occur.[84]

More than any other operator, Tubafour sought to provide the Forest Service with options that, if approved, would give them the timber they needed on a sustainable basis. The company had timber holdings in both the PGSSA and the Narcosli PSYU. Unfortunately, the holdings were too far apart to manage as a single unit but Tubafour sought to improve their situation in the Narcosli area by moving to a cutting permit system, which meant they had an assured timber supply and only needed to submit a cutting plan to get the authorization to proceed. The four loggers in the Narcosli area had agreed on zoning within the PSYU. Within the PGSSA Tubafour prepared a plan in 1967 to place their zone under sustained-yield management, but minister Williston was not amenable to this idea at the time. Rather, he saw the special sale area as operating on a liquidation basis to support the various pulp mills, with the situation to be reviewed in 1970.[85] In further correspondence Williston indicated his appreciation of Tubafour's input, noting that he had asked the Forest Service to begin their study of the special sale area in 1969 rather than 1970.[86] In response, Tubafour pointed out that the zoning, instead of creating stability, had in fact decreased it, largely due to Williston granting harvesting rights to other sawmills from the Forest Service reserve area in the special sale area.[87] Tubafour remained especially concerned about the special sale area because, despite also having rights in the Narcosli PSYU, it was the source of over half their logs. They again reiterated their desire to operate their special sale area zone on a sustained-yield basis and even suggested incorporating it into the adjacent Cottonwood PWC.

Williston continued to receive substantial pressure regarding the PGSSA timber. The Weirs sawmill at Quesnel went so far as to enlist the aid of Alex Fraser, then mayor of Quesnel, and Robert Bonnar, the attorney general, in a desperate quest for more timber. The pressure was so intense that in May 1968 a public hearing was called to discuss the area. Although ostensibly to discuss land use policy, the meeting soon deteriorated into an attack on forest policy within the special sale area. In large part, this dissension was between the smaller loggers and ranchers and the large pulp and paper companies who had obtained extensive rights throughout much of the special sale area. The

Jacobson Brothers sawmill at Williams Lake, 1979. I-04926.

sawlog loggers had by this point mostly harvested the areas having trees designated by the Forest Service as producing sawlogs, and the sawlog loggers wanted to be able to move into cutting the timber designated for the pulp and paper companies and the stud mills—that is, younger trees of smaller diameter. Based on contracts between the government and the pulp companies, the Forest Service was refusing to grant permission for the sawlog quota holders to log these stands. At the public meeting considerable concern was also expressed that speculators would tie up the forest under the guise of an agricultural lease.[88] But as the meeting chairman recorded, "Farmers and ranchers in the Quesnel area cannot sustain themselves on a strictly agricultural economy." Another source of income was necessary and logging was the sought-after source of that income.[89]

Sinclair Spruce Mills' portable three-man sawmill near Prince George. F-06050.

Following the public hearings, Tubafour sent a long letter to Williston outlining their beliefs about why their position in the special sale area had deteriorated over the years despite their leading the way in the processing of small logs and their developing the use of pine, previously not considered commercially viable. After listing their extensive initiatives and improvements to their sawmill, they observed: "we stand prepared to do more if only we can get some stability into our long term timber position."[90] Tubafour believed itself particularly deserving because of their efforts at fully utilizing their allocated timber supply. As company president E.A. McRae wrote:

> For over three years we have cooperated as much as we could in trying to make CU (close utilization) work in this area. We have made our contribution to proving two things. The first is that good use can be made of small wood and the second is that sawmill waste can feed the pulp mills with a

higher percentage of their chips requirements than was imagined in 1965. We have not "camped on your doorstep" asking for special treatment but we have reached the point, however, where we must ask for some specific commitment. The pressures are building in the SSA and it should be our turn now to get something "on the line."[91]

Tubafour's request for more timber resulted in two inquiries: first, an investigation as to whether or not Tubafour's claims to improved utilization were justified, and second, what the effect would be of close utilization standards being applied to the two nearby PSYUs, Narcosli and Cottonwood. The studies found that, indeed, Tubafour was engaging in the best utilization out of all similar mills in the district, but not to the extent claimed in their letter, and that much additional timber would be available if the close utilization standard was applied to the two PSYUs.[92] The Forest Service proposed that Tubafour's supply problems could be alleviated through their position in the Narcosli PSYU when it was placed on a close utilization standard, as that would increase the harvest and Tubafour, as the largest quota holder, would gain the most. As a result, the Forest Service proposed to shift Tubafour's production from the PGSSA to the Narcosli PSYU. As well, a further temporary supply, as needed, would be allowed in the Ten Mile Lake area near Quesnel.[93]

Looking southwest toward Quesnel from Tabor Lookout, east of Prince George, the view shows the region's typical terrain and forest, 1946. I-73604.

The transition did not go as smoothly as Tubafour and the Forest Service hoped, nor was Tubafour happy with the idea that once they received their additional quota in the Narcosli PSYU, the Forest Service expected them to move right out of the PGSSA. Upon learning this, company officials immediately visited the Prince George district office in an effort to retain their position in PGSSA by arguing about the problem of obtaining logs during breakup. Unfortunately, from their perspective, they did not receive much support from the district forester, who informed them that any allocation in the PGSSA would result in a reduction of Tubafour's position in the Narcosli PSYU.[94] Bad weather delayed logging in the Narcosli, resulting in Tubafour asking for an extension of their operations in the PGSSA.

The timber situation in the PGSSA was becoming desperate. When Pinette and Therrien, a Williams Lake sawmiller that Williston had previously supported with additional timber, asked for more, Williston responded:

> It may well be that we have reached the point in your area where those mills that wish to expand will have to do so by purchasing the wood supply of one of the other mills. It is quite possible that the wood supply consumption requirements of the mills in Williams Lake may be greater than the wood that is available particularly since it seems that inevitably the mills must expand their capacity in the face of rising costs so as to take advantage of economies of scale.[95]

Upon learning that he was, similarly, no longer going to be able to log PGSSA timber, John Ernst protested, arguing that their Narcosli allocation was not economic to process. Williston lent a sympathetic ear but was not prepared to give in. He wrote:

> It is my opinion that the problem that you now face is more a result of depressed market than change in the quality of the log input to your mill. This is not to say that the phasing out of your SSA operation has had no effect on profitability but surely any disadvantage is more than compensated by the increased wood supply that has been made available to you.[96]

Shifting these previously established companies from the PGSSA into the managed areas was not so simple, though. The Forest Service did agree that

Sawmills at Quesnel on Two Mile Flat, 1970. Weirs, Tubafour and Ernst were all located in this area. NA-25575.

forcing Ernst to only use the allotted Narcosli PSYU timber would cause disruption to his operations so, to compensate Ernst, the Forest Service allowed him to initially log a better area than that assigned. The other four licensees in the Narcosli PSYU, of course, immediately objected, arguing that this would establish Ernst in an area they considered as their "sphere of influence."[97] Part of the issue was that the other licensees did not think Ernst had been building his fair share of the roads in the PSYU. The Forest Service had been working at having small industry associations solve these kinds of problems, but in this instance officials had to intervene. By limiting the sale to one year and creating a road use agreement that satisfied the road-builders, the Forest Service averted a stalemate that would have resulted in a breakdown of co-operation in the PSYU.

The 1968 public hearing had clearly shown that the forest industry and the rancher-farmers were on a collision course in the PGSSA. On his staff's advice, Williston decided that the only way of approaching the problem was to set up a technical study team that could suggest changes to current land use policies. The team submitted a 33-page report suggesting numerous changes, especially in the way the Lands Department administered land use processing. The

Threshing at the Australian Ranch south of Quesnel. Farming was frequently a marginal activity in the Cariboo and logging brought in much needed income. I-21222.

main recommendations included setting up a settlement reserve and allowing farm woodlots in the settlement reserve. Williston chose to implement these policies. In response, the forest industry began fighting back against the idea that agricultural land use had a higher use value than forestry. Hugh Goodman, a Weldwood forester, sent a memo to the minister and wrote an article in *The Forestry Chronicle*, both of which stated:

> The misguided concept by agriculture that agriculture is the best land use for forest land has led to all kinds of grief across Canada and it is timely to reverse that polarity of thinking.[98]

The Forest Service had promised a review of the PGSSA would be done in 1970. That review was conducted by assessing the inventory and examining the operations of each licence holder in the area. Part of the Forest Service's objective became to move licensees out of the SSA, which was achieved, when possible, by meeting sawmill needs out of the third-band timber uplift in the PSYUs.[99] Thus, the pulp mills retained their zones of operation in the SSA while only one of the stud mills, Clear Lake, was allowed to retain quota in the SSA. The sawlog operators would find it even more difficult to locate timber and were expected to soon disappear, as few stands meeting the sawlog definition of 140 years or older were still available in the SSA. As well, anyone who had not operated under a timber licence in the previous three years was to be eliminated from the list of approved licensees in the PGSSA.[100] As deputy minister J.S. Stokes wrote to the minister:

> In the distribution of third band wood in adjacent sustained yield units, we have endeavoured to provide cut allotments to meet the capacities of licensee mills, where adequate cut at CU (close utilization) level was available. On this basis the cut allotment of some licensees in the SSA should now terminate except for an emergency allotment in some cases, to carry operations until third band sales can be developed.[101]

Even so, considerable anxiety persisted about the PGSSA. The Prince George district forester wrote to Victoria:

> The SSA is being depleted at an alarming rate and will not stand unlimited expansion. The industry's "build now and get your timber later" attitude must be changed to a more realistic approach of matching capacity with available timber supply.[102]

The district forester further noted, the following year:

> As discussed earlier, we are getting pressure from all directions for re-instatement and new quotas in the SSA (i.e., Ernst, West Fraser, Lloyd Bros, etc., etc.). We trust you will continue to support us in this matter.[103]

By 1971 the Prince George forest district office was also pressuring Victoria that the PGSSA should shift to being managed using silvicultural standards and that the forest lands should be added to adjacent management areas.[104]

Weiers, Tubafour, Earnest and West Fraser were the main sawmills operating on Two Mile Flat at Quesnel; only the Patchett sawmill was south of town, 1967. I-21215.

In the major reorganization of the Forest Service following the 1976 Pearse Commission, British Columbia's forests were designated as Timber Supply Areas (TSAs). Each TSA was created to support the industry in a specific place. For example, the timber areas supporting the Quesnel sawmills were generally combined into one management area—the Quesnel Timber Supply Area—and the annual allowable cut was based on the resources of this area. One would expect that developing a comprehensive analysis and allocation would end the dissension over wood supply, but such was not the case.

In order to support government's Small Business Forest Enterprise Program, established in 1978, the Forest Service reduced the allocated cut for companies still operating in the PGSSA by 50 per cent, but converted the other 50 per cent still held by the companies into permanent allowable cut, whereas it had previously been issued as a temporary allocation. A few protests immediately flowed in but were rejected. In 1989 West Fraser proposed building a board plant at Quesnel and asked for a return of the removed 50 per cent. They enlisted the support of Neil Vant, the Minister of Transportation and

Highways and MLA for the Cariboo, but despite a strong appeal, the Minster of Forests, Dave Parker, held firm. While supporting construction of the new plant, Parker was not willing to provide additional timber except by competitive bidding.

Though a special case (and presenting more issues than most other managed areas), the history of the PGSSA underscores the continual pressure the Forest Service faced to supply industry with additional timber, and it reveals some of the complexities of trying to manage a timber supply that did not fully meet the needs of the established industry.

The Forest Service did, under government direction, seek to meet the established industry's needs, from small loggers to large sawmillers, while striving to also maintain sustained yield as their guiding principle. Caught between various community interests, they sought to balance the demands, often with inadequate information and occasionally conflicting direction from government or even between their own various offices. While always adapting and responding to unique regional concerns, Forest Service policy continued to be influenced by the idea that the forests were a major revenue source for the provincial government and that they should be managed as such. Administering a vast land base also highlighted the difficulty of shifting policy and procedures quickly enough to meet rapidly changing community expectations.

ROBERT GRIFFIN

2

Industry Responses to Government
Western Plywood in the Central Interior

BRITISH COLUMBIA'S FOREST INDUSTRY responded strongly to the Forest Service's goal of implementing sustained yield as the central principle of forest management. This was especially true of the larger companies who realized that a sustained forest could mean long-term industrial growth. But industry's coping mechanisms varied from region to region and business to business. Some operators simply increased their mill size and then demanded additional timber; others, realizing such a tactic generally would not work, chose more manipulative approaches. Occasionally, though, operators in some regions emerged as leaders in seeking to mitigate the impact of sustained yield on their timber supply. Throughout the Cariboo this role was partly filled by Western Plywood (later known as Weldwood and then West Fraser).

Western Plywood's move into the region and their application for a forest management licence in 1947 created considerable controversy among other operators, but once in place they became a vital part of the region's forest economics. Western Plywood was the largest single player in the developing central interior forest industry after 1949 and until the establishment of the

---

Facing page: Building the Western Plywood Company's plywood mill near Quesnel, 1950. NA-10398.

Prince George pulp mills in the mid-1960s. Operating a major plywood plant in Vancouver, Western opened a second plant in Quesnel in 1951. They originally invested in the Quesnel area to secure cottonwood logs for their Vancouver operation, but the potential for a plant was quickly realised and work began in securing the necessary resources. Prior to the decision to build a plant, logs were purchased through timber sales and logged under contract by Garner's, A.L. Patchett & Sons and other contractors. The sawlogs were then sold locally, primarily to Patchett. In part, the decision to build was to protect this log supply, as in order to acquire a forest management licence the company had to build a plant. As far as Western Plywood was concerned, though, the plant would only be built if the management licence was obtained. The company estimated that approximately 609,600 metres (2 million feet) for the mill could be obtained by the purchase of logs from local settlers, sawmillers and loggers, most of which would be hauled by truck to the plant. The remainder and bulk of the materials would either be floated or towed down the Fraser or Quesnel rivers or moved over the Pacific Great Eastern Railway from the forest management licence.[1]

The company was both innovative—with the first softwood plywood plant to open in the interior—and intent on expansion.[2] Initially, Western's log supply at the Quesnel plant depended on forest management licence No. 5 and on logs from private purchases. Through necessity they soon became extensively involved in Forest Service timber sales. The location of their plants (in Vancouver and Quesnel) and their need for a certain type of log (peelers) resulted in company activities in more Public Working Circles and timber sales than any other individual firm in the area. Another result was more interaction with more firms than other area operators.

Western Plywood's activities also illustrate other conditions of the region's industrial development. These include the differences between establishing a plywood plant and a sawmill; new industries' dependence on securing appropriate raw material resources; and the role that a company, much larger than its competitors could engage in to solidify its position within that industry. The leadership role taken by Western Plywood in some ways mitigated both the Forest Service's control over the natural resource and the smaller operators' tendency toward individualism. That Western could successfully undertake this role is primarily due to the structural characteristics of plywood production. First, the minimum plant size for plywood was larger than that required by the average sawmiller. This meant that the company

Western Plywood was also manufacturing cottonwood plywood at this time; these Quesnel area logs are destined for Vancouver, 1950. NA-10428.

had more employees, a larger capital investment and also needed considerably more timber than the average area operator, a requirement not satisfied by the acquisition of the forest management licence. Second, the nature of the raw material needed—larger and better quality logs than those required by the sawmills—meant that special arrangements between operators could be negotiated for the mutual benefit of all the parties involved.

Although Western's activities are not typical, that fact in itself also means that studying their actions will shed more light on industry response to sustained-yield policies than looking at any other company.

Expansion Plans

AS MENTIONED, Western's entry into the interior industry hinged on the BC Forest Service providing a forest management licence near Quesnel. The application was initiated in 1947, with the plant to come on line four years later. But that licence supplied just a small part of the total timber resources needed. In 1960, for instance, the forest management licence was only supplying 17 per cent of the total requirement, with the remainder coming from private purchases and timber sales. At the time, the company could not secure enough timber from the management licence for its needs—especially after 1950 when the PWCs were established in the area, thereby ensuring Western would be unable to obtain additional timber under a forest management licence and imposing limits on what timber could be secured. As well, the Forest Service initiated programs that exerted greater and greater control over cut and harvesting rights, intending to reduce speculation and to ensure sustained yield in areas harvested by multiple operators. For several of the key players, such as Western Plywood and West Fraser in Quesnel or Lignum's in Williams Lake, expansion was a chief goal. But it was obvious that timber was going to be more difficult to obtain, as such Forest Service controls reduced the opportunities for businesses wanting to expand. Since Western aimed to expand their Quesnel operations, they had to actively seek additional timber sources and implement other changes as well.

In terms of organizational change, Western set up a supervisory structure in the Quesnel area (where most of Western's early effort was focused) in order to deal with their forest management licence and to regulate the contract loggers. Ian MacQueen was placed in charge as logging manager and he had a staff of six to assist with various tasks such as log purchasing. Several additional employees were also made available when needed. The initial start-up of the plywood plant in 1951 had gone relatively smoothly but the logging situation was not as satisfactory, with logging rapidly falling behind schedule.

They also had to implement some on-the-ground operational changes. In 1950 the company's logging camp in the forest management licence was located almost 26 kilometres north of the mill site on the Fraser River. They proposed to move some 2.4 million metres (8 million feet) a year down the Fraser River using three boats, so radios were installed to control boat movements. In about 1952 the 30-man camp was to move another 22.5 kilometres

Western Plywood logging using a swinging boom jammer NA-10249.

north to Marvin Creek. Radio control was thought essential as Cottonwood Canyon was quite hazardous.[3] An extensive booming ground was built at the mill site. (The lack of log storage had been a factor in deciding against building the plywood plant closer to the village of Quesnel.) As well, a pocket in the river, covering about 1.5 hectares and with a 15-metre-wide channel, was constructed and a 1.5-metre dam was built across the river from the riverbank on the mill side to Rich Bar.[4]

Although the BC Forest Service engaged in an extensive road-building program to target areas they wanted opened up, most companies also built roads to suit their logging needs. Western Plywood began construction of what became called the Garner road in 1953, building sections to shorten logging hauls as they acquired timber sales. They wanted to avoid public roads as they intended to use four-metre (14-foot) bunks on their trucks. There was also concern about road-building costs and who should build the road. In the end, Western decided to have their primary contractor build the road at $2,000 per mile. Investigation had shown road-building costs varied between $1,000 and $5,000 per mile,[5] although some of the costs could be recouped by charging other loggers for the use of the road. Companies also used roads to cut off other loggers from timber. For example, in 1955 Western Plywood wanted to cut Patchett off from some timber so they met with their contractor, Garner, to discuss options:

> We discussed a potential road program for 1956 and are both in agreement that a further southerly extension should take place an approximately similar distance. This further extension is in view of Patchett's activities in the Maquoi lake area and along the public highway between Macalister Ferry and Mackin Creek we have no time to lose in positioning ourselves for the future in this area.[6]

The relationship between contractor and contractee, though, could become quite convoluted. As E.E. Gregg, the senior Western Plywood timber supply manager, noted to John Bene, the company president:

> We set out at first to do our own logging in the Cariboo. Then on the premise that contracting was the solution for cheaper logs, we went completely in that direction. Our experience is that at the outset of dealing with a contractor we seem to get a good competitive figure. Once the contractor is established on the logging area there is tendency for extraordinary contingencies to increase the log cost. With the contractor established we have lost the protection of competition, with the result that in the case of every contract we have had the contract price has crept up.[7]

Tractors skidding logs on Western Plywood Forest Management Licence near Quesnel, 1952. NA-12911.

In 1955, for example, Western supported the purchase of two new trucks by their contractor, Garner Brothers, but threatened cancellation of the contract unless Garner could achieve "a higher efficiency" as distances increased.[8] In response Garner began experimenting with ways he could reduce truck time, mainly by using other equipment to move loaded trailers to more advantageous turnaround points.[9] Western also began experimenting with contracts. One proposal was to divide each logging situation into three parts, using three contractors. Ken Boyd would fall and do some bucking and skidding;[10] Bill Eastman would do additional bucking and would deck and load the logs onto the trailer, then move the trailers to the pickup point; and Garner would haul the logs to the plant.[11]

Discussions with contractors could get quite acrimonious at times. In 1956 one frustrated teletype arrived at Quesnel: "As background information to forthcoming discussion with Joe Garner, Please advise your views if we tell Garner to go to H—."[12] MacQueen's reply was equally pithy: "annually Garner becomes more difficult and dependent on us while [he is] resident in Duncan." The Garners originally lived in Duncan and the implication is that Garner was therefore not able to properly supervise the contract. "Also he must pay more to sub-contractors to hold them—which he does not want to do. In my opinion only a matte[r] of time before we tell him off. Only alterative being increased log cost to hold him. I would have no opposition to your suggestion."[13] Finally, after considerable discussion and argument over various details that included responsibility for slash disposal and payment for bridge I-beams, Western and Garner renewed the contract, which remained in effect until 1960.

The actual methods of logging also changed gradually over the 1940s and 1950s. In the early 1940s much of the logging was still being done with horses but the rapid advance of sawmilling and greater hauling distance meant hauling shifted to trucks. During the later 1940s the development of truck arches[14] greatly improved the movement of logs from the woods to mill. But by 1950 loggers were generally shifting to cat yarding[15] operations and they were also yarding in tree lengths rather than bucked lengths. The smaller operations had shifted from horses to farm tractors for yarding logs, although horses were still sometimes used in winter.[16] By 1955 the truck arches came back into vogue in certain places, as hauling distances to the small sawmills became greater and the cats and arches were found to be too slow.[17] The technology used varied from area to area. In the Quesnel district in 1955, the ranger reported no truck arches in use, noting that of the sawmills in his district 19 were using cats exclusively; 9 used a combination of wheeled tractors and cats; 19 used wheeled tractors exclusively; 2 were using horses; and 13 mills were using a combination of methods.[18] Logging methods eventually settled to primarily cat and arch with truck haul, and the cats and arches were eventually largely replaced by timber skidders as the small portable mills located on the timber sales were phased out.

By 1955 Western Plywood was exerting every effort to secure increased log production. As far they were concerned, the situation was critical if operations were to be maintained and grown. Their initial problems in peeling comparatively small logs were under control, if not completely solved, and the plywood market was expanding by leaps and bounds. Increased capacity at Quesnel was therefore clearly desirable. Local sawmill operators opposed such a move, concerned that Western might tie up too much inventory with their aggressive log buying and timber sale acquisition initiatives.[19] The Forest Service initially kept timber sales small and within reach of the smaller operators,[20] and many of the PWCs were soon loosely controlled by voluntary associations. All these factors slowed Western's expansion, forcing them into an approach of accommodation and partnership. The need for Western to establish themselves in new cutting areas and overcome the opposition of already established sawmill operators caused MacQueen, Western Plywood's logging manager and chief forester, to cautiously suggest a limited expansion into the Horsefly area for Western Plywood's long proposed pulp mill at Quesnel. He expected log quality to be marginal and costs to be exorbitant. The Quesnel River was not considered drivable (although eventually, Western did drive the river) due to a canyon and the difficulty of catching the logs at Quesnel. This meant that without suitable roads the costs of construction and log hauling were going to be high, while Forest Service regulation prohibited any timber sales sitting idle for lengthy periods. There was also considerable local agitation over Western's intentions by groups such as the Cariboo Lumbermen's Association. This association argued that Western was a "deterrent to Industry" and contended the company was "forcing the small operator out of business in the Quesnel area by openly competing for his timber sales."[21]

The company saw MacQueen's recommendation for immediate expansion into Horsefly as necessary, though, in order to obtain a quota for future needs, even though it meant initial losses. It was also a means of demonstrating to the local small operators that they could, if not benefit from Western's participation, at least feel comfortable with their presence. MacQueen made specific recommendations of areas that should be acquired. He believed that even though pulp and peeler logs were growing on the same sites, the company should continue to seek timber sales rather than another management licence. He also recommended the company relinquish a previously established pulp reserve. MacQueen was reacting to the attitudes of both the smaller operators in the area and the BC Forest Service. The company had faced considerable opposition to their earlier forest management licence and, given the industry's subsequent expansion, a new one to supply Western's proposed pulp mill would create even more opposition. As well, a considerable commitment to

Peeler-grade Douglas fir logs destined for Western Plywood at Quesnel, 1950. NA-10246.

capital investment would be required even prior to building the pulp mill. The only way that the licence might succeed was for the company to build a sawmill at Horsefly or Likely, where sawmills already existed.[22]

The situation was critical. Only three years after Western's Quesnel plywood plant went into production, as MacQueen phrased it, "the timber fight is now on." Some of MacQueen's suggestions were radical, especially the relinquishment of the pulp reserve, which would make the pulp mill largely dependent on waste from sawmills and the plywood plant.[23] MacQueen argued that if Western continued the pulp reserve, they would meet significant local opposition to all their activities: "[At] this time the planer mill industry is not only many fold the capacity of 1947 or 1950, but to-day has its back against the wall with <u>no timber available</u> in the very near future."[24] His proposal to drop the pulp reserve was, however, disregarded by the company's head office, as Western hoped that negotiations would soon bear fruit for the pulp mill construction. They wanted to take no chance that might jeopardize this development.[25] This decision proved unfortunate. Dropping the reserve could well have increased local goodwill and ultimately it was cancelled by the BC Forest Service before Western Plywood could make use of it.

Despite this setback MacQueen moved quickly to secure a large block of timber, some 566,336 cubic metres (20 million cubic feet), which they estimated would require 20 years to log. The block was adjacent to the Quesnel River and comprised some 3,116 hectares. At this time Western was logging in the forest management licence and on timber sales X54014, X50707, X50799 and X50801, and they were proposing to start logging on sales X59197 and X57537.[26] In his appeal to the Forest Service MacQueen detailed Western's situation. They needed approximately 169,902 cubic metres (6 million cubic feet) for the Quesnel operations, of which slightly less than half had to be peelable. The forest management licence was providing 42,475 cubic metres (1.5 million cubic feet); timber sale X54014 was providing about 28,317 cubic metres (1 million cubic feet) and was expected to last for 10 to 12 years. Most of the rest was made up of purchases from small operators and he expected this source to dry up soon. The remaining timber licences sent most of their logs to the Vancouver plant. It was anticipated that a Soda Creek timber sale would temporarily fill this lack but MacQueen claimed that if the company hoped to keep Quesnel in operation, the situation was desperate. He informed the district forester that once Soda Creek was exhausted, "we must have additional raw material in order that these plants shall keep operating."[27] Western very much saw their plants at Quesnel as an integrated operation and believed they must have the log supply to continue this development.[28]

Interestingly, there was no effort to manipulate the Forest Service by threatening to discontinue the pulp mill project. Western merely insisted that "the plywood mill <u>must keep on functioning without fail</u>." There was no suggestion that the pulp project would be cancelled if the plywood plant shut down. The implication was that they needed a short-term allocation until the

Weldwood's Lac La Hache sawmill, 1968. NA-24052.

pulp project was underway, at which time the pulp harvesting area would supply sufficient peelers.[29] Although the Forest Service refused to give in to this
pressure, they made certain that the Quesnel mill continued to receive a large
enough allocation to keep operating.

Responding to Policy

THE FOREST SERVICE soon made Western Plywood aware of its plans to privilege maintenance of the forest resource above production, as per the principle of sustained yield. Although Forest Service policy was to assist the local
operators as much as they could, it was not to be to the detriment of the forest. Western Plywood's top forester made it clear to his management that the
Forest Service would not accept increased production to overcome a log shortage at the Quesnel plywood plant if it was at the expense of the forest.[30] This
was also evident in the Forest Service's dealings with the several Public Working Circle associations that emerged to negotiate with the Forest Service over

allowable cut and individual operator quotas. In the Naver PWC, for instance, the Ahbau Forestry Association was informed that their proposed quota and cutting plan would not be changed except when it conflicted with forest principles and that they would be consulted about such changes.[31]

Unable to increase log production through indiscriminate acquisition, Western sought other avenues to alleviate their log shortage. This included efforts to influence Forest Service policies, clearly hoping that their size and their proximity to Victoria would exert some pressure. But the company's ability to have any direct effect was limited. Outside of the forest management licences the Forest Service favoured the smaller operators, and regulations did not take into account special needs such as peeler logs. Western Plywood's size did not always work to their advantage. As MacQueen wrote: "In this present political situation, the Forest Service must treat all operators alike and that consequently, if anything, a larger company would receive less favourable treatment than a small one."[32]

Some success was, however, achieved through government intervention, such as when Western asked Minister of Railways Ralph Chetwynd for help. In that case the Forest Service did proceed with four timber sales to satisfy Western.[33] Fortunately for Western, the area they were interested in had only two other operators working there; otherwise, even ministerial involvement would probably not have resulted in extra consideration. In the end, being close to Victoria, along with the company's size, did provide Western Plywood's senior management a small advantage in the provincial capital, especially when they were having trouble with local authority. In attempting to secure additional timber adjacent to their main logging road but located in the Kamloops district, they experienced considerable difficulty as the Kamloops district forester simply refused Western any timber rights in his area.

> So far Swannell has rigidly stood upon refusing our applications in a Unit of his Forest District. He forgets that we are still British Columbian's with a plant in Quesnel, BC which has to be provided with raw materials from the vicinity, whether that vicinity remains in the Fort George District or spills over into the Kamloops Forest District.[34]

Working through R.G. McKee and J.S. Stokes at the chief forester's office in Victoria, Western was able to circumvent the Kamloops forester. Western's correspondence with the district forester was quite conciliatory but, when communicating with Stokes and McKee, the company pointed out that they were "face[d] with a situation which for us is an impossible one." They assured Victoria that these sales were necessary for the company to continue operating.[35]

MacQueen was very critical of Forest Service policy. He found the situation in 1955 to be "very confusing indeed" and thought that it would turn into a "dog eat dog situation for the next few years" as the Forest Service tried to stabilize management of the area's forests.[36] He considered the circumstances acute and urged Western's top management to use whatever political leverage was available to them to ensure an adequate log supply.[37] Western was very concerned they might be frozen out of bidding for timber, due to quotas and the Forest Service's perception of how best to stabilize the industry, even in an area where Western had the "biggest investment."[38] It was therefore necessary to overcome what was sometimes described as the district forester's "warped reasoning".[39] On numerous occasions Western reminded the Forest Service, both in their Victoria and district offices, of the company's lengthy and large-scale commitment in the Quesnel area. Yet Western's influence was only rarely effective, as E.E. Gregg made clear. He conveyed his displeasure to the district forester in Kamloops and the chief forester in Victoria but, as they had "no alternative but to submit", details of future timber sales were requested.[40] Interestingly, both MacQueen and Gregg were former senior Forest Service personnel.

In instances where Western failed to meet their obligations under Forest Service guidelines, however, they received no special consideration. For instance, Western's contractor, Netherlands Overseas Mills, failed to meet conditions on timber sale X67504. Netherlands argued that their subcontractor's reasons for this failure were legitimate as operations only started three weeks prior to expiry of the contract and only 45 cubic metres were removed. M.L. Kerr, the assistant forester, informed Western that "In view of the fact that bona fide operations were not carried out during the normal terms of this contract, the Department is not accepting your applications for extension or resale and the contract will close out on the merits of your performance to date."[41] Western's protests were to no avail and the response was an even firmer statement from the department:

Netherlands Overseas operated sawmills in various locations before finally setting up their main base of operations in Prince George, 1978. NA-34588.

At no time has such a delayed and minor operation on a three year sale for an estimated 538 cu ft been considered a bona fide effort by this department and we could, therefore, see no good cause for allowing either an extension or a Resale. I assure you that the forfeiture is in accordance with our general policies.[42]

Throughout the 1950s Western Plywood used every means possible to secure additional timber. They could not approach the forest as operators had prior to World War II, and they could only rarely influence Victoria or the local offices. It was therefore important that they become deeply involved in the logging operations and the acquisition of timber sales in the area surrounding Quesnel and to the south, where the company concentrated its operations.

New Approach: Involvement

AS MENTIONED, the management licence could not completely supply Western's plywood mill and the company was forced to increase its activities in the PWCs. The area surrounding Quesnel supplied logs to the Quesnel plant, while extensive logging operations at Williams Lake and 100 Mile House were largely directed to Western's Vancouver mill. When shortages occurred at Quesnel, such as in 1955, the company kept their coastal plant operating even if it meant closures at Quesnel.[43]

Their strategy was therefore to involve themselves in a wide number of PWCs. Western Plywood and Lignum, in Williams Lake, were the only

Lignum sawmill at Williams Lake, 1978. Lignum's owner was one of the more vocal area lumbermen and was frequently critical of Forest Service policies. NA-34765.

Loaded logging truck near Quesnel, 1970.

NA-25531.

operators to do this on a broad scale, but these two firms adopted completely different approaches to timber control. Lignum set up a series of companies, each generally operating in separate or adjacent PWCs, which virtually acted as independent operations under the same owner. For instance, Lignum mainly operated in the Cariboo East PWC while their subsidiary firm, Quesnel Sawmills, operated in the Cottonwood PWC to the north and the Narcosli PWC to the west. Their Hush Lake firm operated even further north in Naver.[44] Each of these operations had their own sawmill and planer mill. In contrast, Western's strategy was to operate from a central plant while becoming directly involved in various Working Circles. The timber was acquired in Western's name, or through an agreement with a local operator, and was then separated into peelers and sawlogs. The peelers (logs that a veneer lathe was able to peel into veneer, with size variations depending on the lathe) were shipped out of the Working Circle to Quesnel or Vancouver, while the sawlogs were either sold locally or transported to Quesnel and, later, to 100 Mile House, when a sawmill was acquired there.

Western's specialized plywood operations and its need for peeler logs forced this widespread involvement in different PWCs. Their sphere of activity included a vast region extending south of 100 Mile House and nearly to Prince George, as well as a considerable distance east and west of Quesnel. The ability to move the southern logs to either Vancouver or Quesnel explains why Western emphasized areas south of Quesnel rather than northern regions closer to the forest management licence.[45]

The need for log supply controlled the direction of company development, which for Western meant working with other operators and associations. Early problems at the company's forest management licence included equipment breakdowns and procedural issues, and the method of handling logs at the landing had to be reorganized.[46] The Forest Service's decision to increase the allowable cut at the forest management licence helped, but it was not until 1955 that a systematic flow of logs from the forest management licence reached the Quesnel plant. In that year an agreement was reached with the firm of Sword and Kerr to undertake this logging contract while, at the same time, the company attempted to increase its allowable cut in the licence by 25 per cent. Certain hauling would continue to be subcontracted outside Sword and Kerr, and Garner would also continue contract logging for the company, especially on the west side of the Fraser.[47] Sword and Kerr Logging replaced the earlier contractor Scheller Logging (although this does not seem to have completely soured their relations with Scheller as he was employed to log a timber sale in the Chilliwack Lake area in 1958).[48]

Western Plywood was much happier with the work of Sword and Kerr Logging. Using fewer men and less equipment, they achieved higher production than the previous contractor. Sword and Kerr were skidding with a cat and using four trucks and eleven men, delivering seven to eight loads daily and averaging slightly over 283 cubic metres (10,000 cubic feet) a day. While this production was slightly lower than that of Scheller Logging, the haul was longer and, because Sword and Kerr used fewer men with less equipment, Western decided it more than balanced out. This was also prior to an expected manpower increase of four or five men that moved the operation into full swing.[49] This improvement is not to suggest that all went completely as planned over the next few years. A collision between two trucks caused considerable difficulty, and the death of a scaler also put a crimp in operations.[50] Lloyd Sword, who was actually running the operation, ran into other difficulties as well. Production costs had been higher than expected and there had been road problems, among other setbacks. As a result, Sword wanted a higher contract price. Western instead advanced him some operating funds and went over the situation with him, demonstrating that under the new system and by logging both from the management licence and at Woodpecker, the situation would improve.[51] They were extremely pleased with Sword's operation and, although determined to maintain the contract price, wanted Sword to be as happy as possible.[52] Western therefore agreed to write off a portion of Sword's debt against road maintenance as conditions had been severe over the 1955–56 winter, which seems to have been what Sword was hoping would happen.[53] But it didn't solve the problems. When Sword re-examined his situation, he found he had taken a $17,000 loss and could not afford to continue in this manner. With the banks tightening credit, Sword started to panic. MacQueen remained convinced that Sword could pull out of his difficulties in the next year, viewing Sword as equipment-rich, with equipment idle while awaiting the Woodpecker development. MacQueen emphasized that Sword had "continued operations throughout a tough winter season and gave us good production despite all his difficulties"[54] and made what was for him a strong suggestion to head office in Vancouver that some kind of "financial settlement concerning last year's production" was needed.[55] In order to reassure both themselves and Sword, Western made a detailed examination of Sword and Kerr Logging's annual financial statement for 1955. After considerable discussion an agreement was reached: "Last night we had a long session with S & K about the renewal of their contract. We have been able to convince them that the terms of their contract will enable them to make a very nice profit this year and they finally agreed (1 a.m.) to continue logging on the same terms."[56]

Despite this, Sword was still in financial difficulty, trying to meet heavy payments for equipment while keeping operations going. He took what steps he considered necessary, which included, partly, beginning to use Western Plywood as his banker—something Western quickly became disenchanted with. He was also slow to develop the new logging site at Woodpecker and instead focused on extracting as much as possible from the already established forest management licence operation. Western was not happy with any of these developments but MacQueen continued to support Sword, convinced that he would not go broke and that they were the loggers Western needed.[57] This seemed to resolve the situation and Sword and Kerr went to work under a logging plan they agreed to with Western Plywood and the BC Forest Service in 1956. Within months, though, Western discovered that Sword and Kerr might have been intending to cancel the contract at the end of the next season and that . their investment in the company was largely unsecured. Steps therefore had to be taken.[58] Finally, after some manoeuvring, Western decided to forestall any pre-emptive action on Sword and Kerr's part and terminated the agreement in December 1957.[59] Western held, however that the termination was based on new conditions—primarily a shift to river-driving the logs rather than truck haul-ing. Western also made it clear they were prepared to negotiate a new agree-ment with Sword and Kerr,[60] but the relationship continued to deteriorate. Clearly, Sword and Kerr had decided that Western failed to appreciate their concerns and they sought every opportunity to obtain the maximum amount of cash from Western that it could. Western was in a tight spot. Sword and Kerr Logging were logging far in excess of what could be delivered by the end of the contract and refused to stop even at Western's request. It was necessary for Western to proceed carefully as "it wud [sic] appear that by...arbitration award (as per contract) S & K wud [sic] take a lot of cash."[61] In the end, the settlement was amicable but still not to Western's satisfaction, as Sword and Kerr com-pleted their contract and only partially paid off their debts to Western.

Logged area in the Naver Public Working Circle, 1968. NA-24522.

Western Plywood typically issued logging contracts to specific operators for a general area.[62] With the exception of Garner Brothers, who Western had persuaded to move from the coast to become their main contract logger, Western Plywood contracted the logging of all timber sales to local operators. For instance, in the Canim Lake area they contracted with Netherlands Overseas Sawmills, who operated a sawmill at Macalister.[63] But Western did not hesitate in seeking alternatives, should the need arise. As an example, they had an agreement with Pinette and Therrien (P&T)[64] to saw logs in the Williams Lake area, but when times became difficult, especially in Williams Lake, P&T were not prepared to give Western the price they wanted and Western investigated trucking the logs to Quesnel. Some of the timber was already cut, though, and the need for a quick decision forced them to accept P&T's offer.[65] It also meant rejecting a higher offer from Chilcotin Sawmills, who could not take the logs for several months. In October 1958 Western reached a more extensive contract with P&T to take the sawlogs from certain other sales. The problem of disposing of sawlogs in the more southerly timber sales, from which peelers were shipped to Vancouver, continued to be acute, and on several sales the logging contractor arranged the sawlog sales.

Western saw the implementation of sustained-yield policy as the biggest obstacle to securing adequate timber supplies. Except the forest management licence and a small area of special timber sales, most of the surrounding forest was either in a PWC or a forest reserve, or in the process of being placed in one. While it had become clear to Western Plywood that they had to acquire timber sales and become established operators in the various Working Circles, it was also clear that the Forest Service was not prepared to allocate any special rights to Western Plywood in the PWCs. Thus, Western not only had to become established operators, but they had to maintain this status if they wanted to gain advantages within the PWC environment. Although bidding for timber sales was open to anyone, the system favoured established operators and it could be very expensive for outsiders to acquire a quota within a Working Circle. The Forest Service program of cut control and harvesting rights was intended to eliminate speculation and ensure sustained yield in areas harvested by multiple small operators. A large company like Western Plywood hung balanced between their own efforts to secure supply and the Forest Service's efforts to limit supplies of timber.

Log sorting area at Swanson Lumber Company's sawmill, 1953. NA-08627.

Once a timber quota was acquired, it had to be used or was lost.[66] In the Cottonwood PWC, for instance, Western acquired an early sale but lost their status as established operator when their contractor failed to exploit the licence to the Forest Service's satisfaction. The Forest Service emphatically noted that, despite this licence, they did not consider Western an established operator. Western's response was to increase their quota and retain their rights through the acquisition of another operator. If they had failed to act they may have lost their rights to any timber in this PWC. In this case Forest Service policy led directly to the company's expansion and to consolidation of timber under one operator.

The gradual concentration of harvesting quotas in most Working Circles worked to Western's advantage. The quota in the Cottonwood PWC was reduced from 27 to 3 holders for the whole Working Circle by 1965. Brownmiller Brothers held the largest share, while the remainder was divided between Beaver Planer Mills and Western Plywood (by this time Weldwood of Canada).[67] Each operated in their own areas within the PWC, not infringing on the other operators' timber supply. This reduced number made it easier for the operators to control who had what timber and which timber was being exploited. Such arrangements were based either on association agreements or individual agreements between the operators. Association agreements, such as existed in Cottonwood, were much easier to maintain in those Working Circles that had fewer operators. They were also supported by the Forest Service, who preferred to deal with the association.

Competition for Timber: Open Bidding

THE FOREST SERVICE'S POLICY of open bidding might seem to have encouraged chaos, but competitive bidding at timber sales was rare. Generally, any threats and manoeuvring happened before the sale and resulted in the sale being sold at the upset price established by the Forest Service. There are cases, though, where competition did occur (especially in the Kamloops forest district), and in others cases it was only narrowly avoided. Sometimes an operator became desperate and undertook bidding at any price, as Pacific Western Planers did on several occasions.[68] The approach to and reasons for bidding varied considerably, and abuses pointed out by critics of the system certainly did exist. For instance, one operator attempted to pressure Western Plywood into letting them have the timber sale, but as soon as Western put in a bid above the upset price, the operator withdrew.[69] Western also faced competition from

Falling timber, 1953. I-29410.

Lignum sawmill, Williams Lake, 1958. NA-17618.

loggers trying to force the company to hire them to log the timber sale. In one case they reached agreement with the logger, but in another the logger, upon refusal, "left before the sale opened."[70] Bidding occasionally resulted from difficulties over the initial application. Western applied for the area first but confusion at the Forest Service resulted in another operator's application being allowed over Western's. The sawmiller placed his bid at upset and, when Western raised this bid, he did not proceed further. The sawmiller later indicated he would not have gone forward with the application had he known Western had a prior claim.[71]

Breaking ranks was risky for an operator when it came to bidding. During the late 1950s an operator backed by one of the Williams Lake planers began to bid up sales, and then Western bid until they acquired the sale at considerably above the upset price. The other operator also bid at a number of sales where established operators counterbid until they secured the sales; thus the rogue bidder was effectively excluded from acquiring timber, though at some cost to the established operators. The larger companies were angered by these actions and intended to bid at every sale the operator's backer tried to acquire. This same backer had previously been allowed to acquire two sales unopposed in what was considered his area of interest.[72]

Competition didn't just come from rogue outsiders, though. More often it came from established operators. On timber sale X78596, Buck Ridge Planers tried to oppose Western Plywood but could not meet the bids. Prior to the sale, Western had tried to discourage Buck Ridge from participating by threatening cancellation of a contract Western held with one of Buck Ridge's suppliers on several First Nations reserves. This did not deter Buck Ridge as they believed the contract secure.[73] At the same sale, Western was also threatened by another planer operator who believed Western should leave it for him. This planer operator merely put in his cheque and "then sat back." In this case Western also threatened to bid on the planer operator's sales, but apparently without deterring him.[74] Western believed they had to take this sale to maintain their position within the PWC and so bid until any opposition was removed. Their objective had been to "try to eliminate the competition prior to auction" but, as seen above, they were not always successful.[75] In part, this balancing act shows the fine line Western felt compelled to follow in securing their timber supply without alienating the smaller local operators. In one example, Western did not bid on an applicant's sale even though, prior to the sale, the applicant was part of a conspiratorial group that had worked to deny Western several sales.[76]

The Loggers Control Timber Acquisition

WHILE A KEY SOURCE of both conflict and accommodation, the Forest Service's bidding process was not what usually controlled timber sale acquisition; rather, it was the various agreements between the loggers.[77] Established operators, competing for limited resources, developed a series of agreements that they believed would further their individual and mutual interests. Given this fact, Western was keenly interested in the activities and potential of local loggers and compiled reports of local log users and producers. To do this they maintained close contact with the Forest Service to learn who was making applications for what timber.[78] If Western was to survive, they "should leave no stone unturned in putting forth [their] case."[79]

Truck arch working at Clearwater Timber Co., 1951. Truck arches were developed to speed movement of logs to portable sawmills or to a place where they could be loaded for road-hauling to the sawmill. NA-12353.

The objectives of each operator could differ considerably and so agreements between operators ranged widely, from Western's with Savona Timber to log a specific timber sale that the two firms jointly controlled, to the actual takeover of specific operations, such as that of JB Martineau & Son. This takeover included not only several timber licences but also a logging operation and a small sawmill at 100 Mile House.[80] In this instance Western also made an agreement with Northern BC Lumber Limited, a subsidiary of Allfir of Washington State. Under this agreement Northern BC Lumber would take all the sawlogs in the Williams Lake area and purchase the portable sawmill acquired from JB Martineau & Son.[81]

Individual agreements also often existed in the Working Circles that had associations, especially where the association had many members. In the Narcosli PWC, Western had an individual agreement with Lignum (Quesnel Sawmills). This agreement initially resulted from one of Lignum's captive sawmillers wanting to acquire a timber sale Western was determined to purchase. The negotiated result was that Leslie Kerr, owner of Lignum, "will let you [MacQueen of Western] buy this sale."[82] Discussion continued, each side making their timber objectives clear, and the final agreement established that Lignum "will work with us rather than oppose."[83] One potential problem with such agreements was that when conflicts occurred, the Forest Service did not recognize the boundaries established by the companies, but operators often managed to settle these issues amicably. For example, MacQueen noted: "I had agreed…with Leslie [at Lignum] that we would not extend south of the height of land between Hawks Creek and Soda Creek whereas, he had agreed not to push into our territory."[84] When two timber sales set up by the Forest Service crossed this boundary, both were purchased by Lignum, and one was subsequently turned over to Western for sawlogs.[85] The only way to secure increased production was to mitigate the competitive process through agreements. The acquisition of timber became a politics of manoeuver, collusion and collaboration by established operators in opposition to Forest Service regulations and to new entrants.

Western's 1957 purchase of a number of timber sales in the Williams Lake area illustrates a different approach. They neither wanted to log these sales nor mill the sawlogs, instead reaching an agreement with Northern BC Lumber who milled the timber felled by another of Western's contractors, J & W Logging.[86] In 1958 Western offered to sell this timber to Northern BC Lumber but the market was poor and Northern rejected the offer, which meant Western had to continue their own logging operations.[87]

This network of agreements related to both harvesting and the securing of timber. At stake was the vital need to control timber sale acquisition and the larger operators were forced to work together and coerce the smaller operators into co-operation. In at least one instance Garner, Western and Lignum joined forces to acquire timber sales in Western's name, using this combination to stop several other major bidders from trying for the timber.[88] Agreements as obvious as these represent only the surface layer of this underlying network of operator interactions, where agreements ranged considerably in

A D6 cat stacking logs on Savona Timber Company limits in preparation for hauling to sawmill, 1955. H-03798.

nature and direction. Often these relationships were informal, occasionally even without signed agreements, but all had the same objective: the purchase of timber at the Forest Service's upset price.

The potential complexity of these widely ranging agreements is illustrated by Western Plywood's interest in timber sale X58149. Application for this sale was made by Cascade Spruce Mills in 1953. Western seriously considered acquiring the sale because it joined timber sale X51600, which they already owned. The sale was also adjacent to Cascade Spruce's logging and sawmill operation, with Cascade Spruce arguing that they must have the sale to continue operations. Timber acquisition required co-operation among established operators if they were to maintain control and Western decided not to try and acquire the timber sale, noting: "we are not able to buy this sale with Mr. Crick's concurrence." Clearly, Western was going to adhere to the unwritten rule that generally left the acquisition of the timber sale to the company making the application. Crick, one of the owners of Cascade Spruce, also agreed to supply peelers to Western, and so Western decided that "we don't see any alternative but to let him buy it."[89]

Communications with Leslie Kerr of Lignum/Quesnel Sawmills illustrates other complicated aspects surrounding this sale. Kerr had mixed motives during the negotiations over timber sale X58149. He initially tried to argue Western Plywood out of any involvement in the Cottonwood PWC, where this particular timber sale was taking place. When Western replied that they were already in the Working Circle and intended to stay, Kerr tried to get them to undermine Cascade Spruce's acquisition of the sale. Cascade was proposing to construct a planer mill near Quesnel; Kerr wanted to prevent this. Kerr also told George Kibblewhite of Western that he would keep another planer operator, Matheson Planers, from becoming involved in the sale.[90]

Matheson's involvement added several more complicating factors to the sale—factors that Kerr was only partly aware of. Matheson wanted to recoup losses from a previously proposed sale in the area that they had failed to obtain (it was rejected because they were not an established operator in this Working Circle). They also hoped to get agreement that Cascade would purchase a planer mill Matheson had at Quesnel rather than for Cascade to build a new mill. Western Plywood's role became that of an intermediary between all these parties, even though they had already decided they would not buy the sale for themselves. Western had offered to buy the sale on behalf of Cascade but Cascade felt it would make them too dependent on Western.[91] In the end, Western negotiated an agreement on Matheson's behalf in which Cascade supplied the Matheson planer with 56,633 cubic metres (2 million cubic feet) of rough lumber, and a supply of logs was arranged to satisfy Kerr and "alleviate their present log shortage."[92] Western also confirmed that no other planers intended to bid on the sale.[93] In return, Western obtained many of the peeler logs from the sale.

The timber sale was held on June 27, 1953, and was attended by Bert Crick of Cascade, Emil Tushak and Russell Coulter from Quesnel Sawmills (Lignum) and George Kibblewhite of Western Plywood. Only Cascade bid and the sale was purchased at the upset price of $2.50 per cubic metre.[94] At this time Western entered into an additional agreement with Cascade that the two

Gardner's Sawmill on Horsefly Lake, 1960. NA-20029.

companies would alternate in the acquisition of timber sales in the area, with the sawlogs going to Cascade and the peelers to Western Plywood.[95] In 1956 Western acquired this sale along with several others when they purchased Cascade's timber sales and quota in the Cottonwood PWC to bolster their own operations.

In effect, the larger operators, with the co-operation of the smaller operators, subverted the bidding process to minimize the problems of open bidding. Yet the above examples still only partially illustrate the complexity of this agreement system. In another example, a small sawmiller, Tattinger and MacDonald, operated a sawmill capable of producing about 5 million cubic metres annually but were out of timber. The Forest Service therefore allowed them to apply for a special timber sale. Difficulty arose as the sawmill operator was backed by Allfir of Williams Lake and they were moving into an area which Matheson Planers of Macalister regarded as their territory. Matheson proposed that Western Plywood purchase the timber sale, as they had done prior, and split the logs between Matheson and Western. This case was not so straightforward, though. One of Western's contractors in the Williams Lake area was using an Allfir site to load logs onto the Pacific Great Eastern

Railway and Western did not want to risk losing this site.[96] The solution in this case was for Matheson to purchase the timber sale, Tattinger and MacDonald to cut the logs for Matheson, and Western to receive the peelers—a situation Western noted was in line with "our agreement with Matheson in September 1953 wherein we agreed to work in conjunction with him in this area."[97]

Another variation is shown in Western Plywood's 1957 discussions with Netherlands Overseas Mills concerning a timber sale in the Soda Creek area. Western had had extensive dealings with Netherlands over the previous several years, but in this case they decided that Netherlands was asking too much for the peelers and would have to come down in price or Western would buy the sale.[98] Some concern was raised over the effect this might have on their relationship with Netherlands. But Netherlands was supporting several operators Western did not approve of and, therefore, Western decided that their agreement with Netherlands was no longer of much use.[99] Western also discovered that the sawmiller on whose behalf Netherlands wanted to purchase the timber was a particular nuisance and, if that sawmiller lost Netherlands' support, it would be to Western's advantage to eliminate him.[100] Netherlands proceeded to negotiate with Western, unbeknownst to Netherlands' sawmiller, although the end result was mutually beneficial to all. Western purchased the sale and sold the sawlogs to Netherlands who, in turn, had their sawmiller mill the logs.[101] Thus, even though an opportunity existed for Western to undermine Netherlands' position and rid themselves of a nuisance competitor who had started stepping outside the rules, they did not take advantage of the situation. Such collaborative action seems fairly typical of most operators, with counter-action only being taken against operators who seriously disrupted the agreement network.

Still, each operator in an area continuously manoeuvred against the others, despite their various agreements. If the action only misled but did not break an agreement, all was fair. In a timber sale south of Quesnel, near Alexandria, Quesnel Sawmills spread the rumour that it had a "well-heeled" operator who "could give us [Western Plywood] trouble." Quesnel Sawmills claimed that they could put him off if Western agreed to share the logs. On investigation, Western found that the operator in question had a small sawmill at McLeese Lake and was certainly not well-heeled, nor even very interested in the sale, but rather very much in debt to Quesnel Sawmills.[102] After Western purchased the sale, Quesnel Sawmills, in a further effort, claimed they had put the operator off and deserved some compensation, a tactic Western rejected.[103] At the same time that Quesnel Sawmills was trying to manipulate Western on this sale, they had a timber-/area-sharing agreement with Western in another PWC and Lignum, the owner of Quesnel Sawmills, had log-sharing agreements in place at Williams Lake. As well, despite the misleading actions, Quesnel Sawmills made no effort to actually bid against Western. It was all a bluff to try and gain some advantage.

In addition to agreements, a network of exchanges also operated among the larger operators. Timber sale X62851 was acquired on February 11, 1955 by Quesnel Sawmills, who then transferred it to another subsidiary of Lignum, Cariboo Fir Co. Ltd., on July 12. Some logging and sawmilling was conducted on the sale during 1955 and then Western Plywood acquired the sale from Cariboo Fir in March 1957. In July 1957 Western Plywood transferred this sale to the Martin Sawmill Company, along with three other timber sales.[104] The network of agreements and exchanges between operators was so varied that it's impossible to cover all of their diversity here. But it was these operator-to-operator agreements that truly managed the timber sale process, not the Forest Service's bidding practice.

Working with the Forest Service

AGREEMENTS AND ASSOCIATIONS were also at play in managing who secured what timber in the Public Working Circles. The Forest Service placed most timber in the central interior into PWCs, and in order to support local operators the Forest Service only permitted established operators within a Working Circle to apply for timber. This gave established operators the ability to control the location of the timber to be exploited. Access roads were partially put in by the Forest Service who controlled most of the rights of way for those roads they did not put in. Thus, they had some control over who had access to what timber. Timber sales were generally kept small and short-term to discourage large operators who were not established from coming in and taking over.[105] The Forest Service also had a variety of reasons for disallowing applications, including simply their view that the operator already had enough timber. Through these measures the Forest Service used a variety of mechanisms to promote stability within the Working Circles. What they had no control over during this period was the fact that once an application was approved,

Log scaler working on a Savona Timber Company licence, 1955. NA-15302.

the bidding was open to anyone. Power then fell to the Working Circle associations and the established operators.

In some Working Circles these associations worked out the proposed quota for individual companies and even sometimes where and when to make applications for new timber. The Forest Service, in turn, co-operated with association activities to further the Working Circle stability. Not all of these efforts were cordial. A group from the Narcosli Working Circle intended to meet with the Minister of Forests in 1954 in an attempt to meet their goals. The Forest Service felt it essential they be in attendance to counter the "partial statements and twisted interpretations" that may otherwise be given.[106] Co-operation was thus mixed with each side trying to further their own objectives. But by and large, in most Working Circles the Forest Service and the associations worked together to control the harvest.

When it came to the aforementioned agreements, Western's objectives coincided with the smaller operators more often than with those of other large operators, and this gave them a fairly persuasive voice in the operator councils. Their economic power and specialized logging interests also made them attractive partners. Agreements thus became the most common way of controlling cutting rights. Collusion, in effect, became a way of managing under sustained yield. But it was collusion within very specific limits, controlled either by the larger operators or the PWC associations. Nor was such collusion unusual in the forestry sector. When the Swedish sawmill industry began expanding into Russia during the 1890s the timber was owned by the government, so the Swedish industry established cartels to reduce competition at the auctions.[107]

Intended by the Forest Service to be a free and equitable means of supplying timber to operators at a price shaped by actual market value, most timber sales were acquired at the upset price without competition. Those loggers that did not get the timber they sought argued against the system, which suggests cutthroat competition. But this does not seem generally to have been the case, nor was the system as ineffective as has been suggested.[108] The process largely worked to the advantage of established operators, even with the open bidding, due to Forest Service favouritism of those with immediate needs for wood. This also gave the Forest Service breathing room to assess the situation in each PWC. Any potential for unregulated and indiscriminate destruction of the resource base was limited by both the operator's and the Forest Service's actions. The operators, through agreements and associations and with the co-operation of the Forest Service, controlled exploitation, and this kind of operator activity to regulate the cut was a direct response to the Forest Service policy of maintaining a reasonable sustained annual harvest. In that sense, the Forest Service and the operators co-operated to provide a comparatively equitable and stable distribution of the limited forest resource. This is not to suggest, of course, that all was fair or that things always worked smoothly. But given the conditions under which it was implemented, the BC Forest Service's Public Working Circle policy created an environment in which sustained yield was possible.

The launch of the PWC system acted as a major check to the expansive, destructive tendencies of lumbermen and helped the Forest Service to further a major objective of government policy, that of community stability. Community stability has been defined in various ways, but in this case the central goal

Tractor and arch logging at the Kelly Sawmill at Summit Lake, 1956. NA-16018.

was to give established lumbermen a chance to continue business on the same footing they had previously enjoyed. The side benefit, it was agreed, would be a stable economic base for overall community growth. Thus the Forest Service's approach balanced the individual lumberman's opportunity to remain operating and the policy objective of managing the forest in the best interests of the province as a whole. Within the context of this activity, if a businessman chose to sell their business to someone else—either to an established operator in order to increase their capacity or to a new player—under Canadian business philosophy, that was their prerogative. Given this attitude there was little the Forest Service could do to counter an economic situation that tended to favour concentration, but the Forest Service was doing everything it could to ensure the survival of the smaller operators.

If the Forest Service wanted to ensure government got the best price possible for its timber while protecting local established operators in the interest of a stable and economically sound community, an examination of the timber sale records suggests, by and large, that they succeeded. Blame for timber shortages can be placed on operator greed and government policy, not Forest Service incompetence as has sometimes been suggested in other studies. Greater Forest Service resources could likely have mitigated the situation but would still not have solved the problem. Operators complained strenuously about Forest Service and government policy but developed a system that frequently worked. That system's major failing, like many voluntary, collaborative efforts, was that it involved large numbers of individual businesses; therefore, on occasion, it broke down.[109] Success depended on the larger firms, the industry leaders—in this case Western Plywood—acting as intermediaries. As we have seen, Western's actions had a large impact on other industry players. Their special interests supported the local industry by creating an additional supply of sawlogs on many of their sales and, aware that the Forest Service would not tolerate uncontrolled destruction of the forest, they worked as part of operator-formed associations and reached agreements that met the needs of most established operators. Those

Sawmills near Quesnel at Two Mile Flat, 1970. NA-25572.

operators who were not big enough bought out other operators. Development within the forest industry as a whole suggests that this was the future trend regardless of any impediments to concentration that the Forest Service could have imposed. Overall, the industry continued to grow significantly. In 1951, 2,052 cars of lumber were shipped from Quesnel while by 1956 the area was shipping 4,398 cars of lumber.[110] This rose further to 5,177 by 1959.[111]

Minister Ray Williston in his office, 1966. NA-22402.

This chapter has shown that forest management underwent considerable change following the 1948 *Forest Act*. It was a period of almost continuous transformation as both the Forest Service and industry responded to new laws and regulations. A kind of equilibrium had been reached by the 1970s but more changes were in the works, and new players wanted their share of the forest. Some of the future was highlighted in a draft letter intended for all licence holders:

> In his address, the Honourable Ray Williston, outlined some of the new responsibilities the forest industry must be prepared to accept if it wishes to continue its success as a prime user of British Columbia's prime natural resource. A major responsibility, outlined by the Honourable Minister, is acceptance of the need for maintaining an environment satisfactory and suitable to the needs of all British Columbians. He noted that we have reached the stage where our forest lands must be managed to achieve the greatest overall benefits associated with forest and must seek a balanced use of forest land. This requirement commits us all to preventing exclusive dedication of forest land to the unreasonable restrictions of any single-use demand.
>
> In addition he went on to say that "It must be recognized by all of us that, in addition to the basic consideration of timber, we must be fully aware of the overall public interest in the use of this land and of the need to hand over the land in an acceptable state to succeeding generations of British Columbians."[112]

Times would again be changing for the Forest Service and the industry.

ROBERT GRIFFIN

3

Behind Closed Doors
Managing Forest Policy and Economic Development

AS MINISTER OF LANDS, FORESTS, AND WATER RESOURCES Ray Williston
developed forest policies to further the provincial government's objective of
northern development. In particular, he used legislation to reshape the interior
forest industry by encouraging the construction of pulp and paper mills. British
Columbia has had three waves of pulp mill expansion, largely induced by government policy. Provincial legislation passed in 1901 (although repealed in 1903)
stimulated the building of a series of coastal mills, with the first coming on line
at Swanson Bay in 1909. Some 40 years later the introduction of sustained yield
and tree farm licences saw a second surge in pulp mill construction, with new
mills being built first at Port Alberni and then at Prince Rupert, Harmac, Elk
Falls and Crofton.[1] The third boom occurred in the early 1960s when government legislation sparked pulp mill expansion into British Columbia's interior.

As one of the few Social Credit cabinet members that premier W.A.C.
Bennett actually trusted, Williston was one of the key players throughout this
later period. What Williston sought above all else was to finish implementing
the sustained-yield policy begun decades earlier and to push utilization even

---

Facing page: The Prince George Pulp and Paper mill, 1965. NA-22565.

Ray Williston signing the first pulp harvesting agreement with Prince George Pulp and Paper, 1962. NA-21630.

further through integration of the interior forest industry. Integration for Williston meant building pulp mills that would consume the waste products from sawmills and plywood plants and thereby use as much of the forest fibre as possible. The method Williston chose to achieve his objective was an amendment to the *Forest Act*, section 17A, which was passed in 1961. This amendment allowed him to allocate Pulp Harvesting Areas (PHAs). In these areas, each of which covered a number of Public Sustained Yield Units (PSYUs), the Forest Service gave the designated pulp mill the right to secure all pulpwood harvested in the region, the right to contract to secure all waste wood and chips from the region's sawmills and plywood plants and, should this waste wood be insufficient, the right to secure a timber licence to harvest roundwood in order to ensure a sufficient fibre supply for the mill. However, prices had to be equitable, and if the pulp mill did not meet the going price, the chips could be sold to another mill.

The story goes that not long after assuming his place as minister, following the rather tawdry Sommers affair[2], Williston was horrified by the amount of waste at interior sawmill operations. Many sawmills were small bush mills that processed logs into lumber on the individual timber sales. These mills used circular saws and cut for maximum profit. Sawmill waste was therefore considerable, and not only in solid wood. The relatively large kerf (that is, the slit made by cutting) of the heavy circular saws produced piles of sawdust. Williston was determined to do something about this waste and generally adopted two approaches. First, Forest Service policy was directed toward the gradual elimination of many of the small bush mills in order to shift log processing to large, centrally located sawmills. This was achieved partly by regulation and partly by economies of scale. Williston realized that a second solution was increased utilization of the available fibre, which could be accomplished by integrating logging and sawmilling and by encouraging the production of pulp from the residues.

The idea for the PHAs came from a variety of sources, but Williston especially credited two: the owners of a company called National Forest Products, based in Prince George, and the widely respected Ian Mahood who had worked for MacMillan Bloedel for some years but left in 1959 to set up as an independent. It was perhaps Mahood that Williston listened to the closest. Mahood had little respect for the pulp mill operators, almost considering them a blight on the forest, and certainly saw them as in dire need of regulation.[3]

Williston's approach gave the mills' financial backers a sense of security by assuring them that a sufficiently large fibre supply existed and was guaranteed to a mill. At the same time he retained government control over the forest base. Williston's intent appears to have been to keep the pulp mill operators out of the forest unless they were integrated and to develop those pulp operations that were totally reliant on sawmill and plywood mill waste product. If

Portable tie mill in the Kamloops area, showing some of the waste these small mills produced, 1941. NA-07712.

he could induce sawmills to chip their waste product, he believed a series of centrally located pulp mills could be built throughout the province's interior that would be supported through sawmill-produced chips. The PHA concept was one of Williston's tools to reach this goal.

Public and Private Goals

IMPLEMENTATION OF WILLISTON'S PLAN required a mechanism to issue the licences as well as the operators' willingness to apply for the licences and fulfil their obligations under the terms. Achieving this part of the objective followed two distinct avenues, those of private meetings and public hearings. The process went like this: Ray Williston and his ministry formulated a policy, had it authorized in the *Forest Act* and then followed through with implementation. The forest companies, with this legislation as a catalyst, became more aggressive in seeking to increase their wood utilization and produce the required documentation to show their intent. The two sides then met in private meetings with premier Bennett, minister Williston and ministry officials, and in the public hearings that Williston held throughout the province (although most frequently in the Prince George area and Victoria).

On one hand, the PHA approach was perhaps the clearest demonstration of Williston's intentions to implement two government- and industry-supported objectives. That is, first, in keeping with premier Bennett's general goals, he wanted to promote economic development—in particular, economic development along the Pacific Great Eastern Railway line and especially in the northern sector. The second goal was elimination of wood waste being produced by the small gypo[4] (or independent) mills cutting on the timber licences. But on the other hand, the legislation and policy Williston developed to implement this program was vague and confused many of the loggers. Whether he did this intentionally or simply implemented the program before the policy was fully developed is unclear, and we may never solve this riddle.

Weldwood noted that the first three public hearings were relatively uncontroversial; they believed this resulted from the smaller operators not understanding the potential consequences of the applications. Applicants at the second hearing were the better-informed major operators, while at the third, Weldwood noted, Northwood, which already held a substantial part of the quota, sought local approval and undertook a comprehensive public relations campaign both in Prince George and to the concerned sawmills and loggers.[5] As Williston received no opposition or counterproposals at these hearings, they were quickly awarded.

At a fourth hearing, for Bulkley Valley Forest Products, the policy's vagueness began to show itself. The minister now came under some critical questioning of the policy's implications and his responses were pointed, if somewhat obscure. Clearly, no applicant was willing to risk offending the minister by debating the policy in these open forums. In answer to a general question, for example, he said: "anytime anyone seems to think that there are a hard and fast set of regulations at this time, should be assured such is not the case".[6] He further stated: "I think in fairness…our standards of utilization are changing almost daily".[7] When asked to define what pulpwood was under the agreement he again evaded the question, saying this had not yet been defined.

Williston did have certain objectives in mind, though, and he made this clear in private meetings with the companies—although they, too, sometimes seemed to get a blurred message.[8] But Williston reassured each potential applicant that "if we finally license you for a given size of mill, then we stand ready [to] guarantee you that supply of material from the area." He also clarified that he was not going to coerce any mill owner to co-operate: "I state as a matter of policy the Forest Service has not required the installation of barking and chipping facilities, and we should use the 'carrot' approach rather than the 'big stick' approach in the matter of utilization."[9] This was not always the case, as was seen in the Kamloops region where a number of sawmills were driven out of business as a result of not upgrading in time to get in on the timber boom (see Chapter 1). In the private meetings Williston also encouraged applicants to ask for more than they could use. In light of his final decisions, he was probably seeking leeway with which he could manoeuver a compromise (see table 2, below).

Aside from his two major goals with the PHA program, Williston had a number of expectations that he hoped to get each applicant to satisfy. A senior Weldwood[10] employee, Bob Wood (their chief forester), met with Williston in 1964 and obtained an outline of what the minister was looking for from applicants. Williston expected all proposals to include a comprehensive engineering study demonstrating that the pulp mill was feasible, complete with a timeline for construction, and he wanted acknowledgement that the financing was in place—in effect, proof that the pulp mill could be built. The report had to

Chipper at a Kamloops sawmill, 1960. Williston and the BC Forest Service required all sawmills that were to receive third band timber to have small-wood facilities in operation, including chipping machines. NA-19977.

delineate the source of the wood supply and show that the harvesting area was required to support the project. He also looked for regional support, meaning that there was no significant opposition from the major quota holders in the area. Finally, he wanted evidence that pollution would not be a problem; at this time he appears to have been primarily concerned about water pollution.[11]

At the meeting with Bob Wood, Williston learned that the major English pulp and paper firm of Bowater was to be Weldwood's partner. Wood also indicated that Bowater greatly favoured a site at Union Bay on Vancouver Island. While generally making his views known, Williston was still somewhat cagey and noncommittal and the key element to emerge from this meeting with Wood was that Williston favoured an interior, or at least a Squamish, location for Weldwood's application. Bowater, however, somehow interpreted the meeting as providing support for building a pulp mill at Union Bay.[12] But as events progressed, Williston made it clear that he was not going to allow interior wood to be used to supply a coastal mill. This was reinforced to Gene Brewer, president of United States Plywood (owners of Weldwood), in an August 1964 meeting when Williston advised him that there would be little chance of supplying Union Bay with timber from the Cariboo. Williston's intent was to "grant first refusal of pulpwood harvesting rights to parties willing to undertake to build new pulp capacity in undeveloped areas of the province and to locate the pulp harvesting areas strategically throughout the Province so as to create markets for chipable sawmill residues and pulpwood grade timber."[13]

Industry Participation

Supervisory staff at the Prince George district office, 1952. Seated from left: E. Robinson, L.F. Swannell, W. Henning, I. Burrows. Standing from left: R. Robins, F. Nelson, L. Willington. NA-12524.

IF WE LOOK AT THE PHA POLICY from a results point of view, it appears that the government put a successful policy in place, one that created a whole new industrial network. This is certainly the tenor in the published media and even in industry discussion around Ray Williston and his policy changes. But if we look at Williston's initiatives from an alternative perspective, we see that the outline often presented in the literature does not fully capture the circumstances surrounding forest policy evolution in the 1960s. This is particularly evident when policy-making is represented as government simply giving in to industry pressure.

The industry, especially the larger operators, and the Forest Service were also deeply concerned about sawmill waste. Studies by both the federal government and industry in the 1930s had clearly identified waste as a

Chip car destined
for a Prince George
pulp mill, at the
Ernst sawmill near
Quesnel, 1970.
NA-25576.

significant issue and Bloedel, Stewart and Welch built their Port Alberni pulp mill in order to increase utilization and reduce waste (the mill was planned prior to 1939 but was delayed until 1946 by World War II). This major company initiated research and development to solve the critical problem of an efficient whole-log barker to permit the economic use of slab wood (residue left from squaring the logs) and sawmill fibre residuals. The barker developed by Bloedel, Stewart and Welch became an industry standard on the west coast. Similarly, the H.R. MacMillan Export Company worked with Simons Engineering of Vancouver to develop a barker, which was also used in several sawmills on the coast. By the time Williston initiated his integration policy in the 1960s, the North American forest industry had solved enough of the technical difficulties so that a pulp industry based on chips from sawmill residues was feasible.

The larger companies already believed integration and complete utilization were key to business success. Following the establishment of his company in 1945, Western Plywood's president, John Bene, immediately began investigating ways to use waste from plywood manufacturing. He initially investigated hardboard manufacture and visited Germany to learn about a newly developed process but, on hearing rumours that MacMillan was about to build a similar plant, he switched his attention to pulp manufacturing. Less than two years after his plywood plant began production, Bene was publicly stating that waste had to be utilized, writing in 1947: "I am quite certain that no company can be successful in the future unless they find a profitable utilization for the high percentage of wood volume which is to-day wasted".[14]

Various operators began to look at wide-ranging possibilities. Partnerships were investigated, new sources of raw materials examined and every aspect of utilization was scrutinized. The market for pulp was strong and growing and for most operators and the government it was seen as the solution to the wastage problem. Bene wrote to the Canadian Pulp and Paper Institute in 1948: "A number of BC sawmills and plywood plants are investigating the possibility of establishing a jointly owned kraft pulping unit to utilize economically their pulpable by-products."[15] Many such aspirations fell by the wayside as coastal production expanded rapidly, but new plants were built following Bloedel, Stewart and Welch's lead. Columbia Cellulose at Prince Rupert, Harmac near Nanaimo and Elk Falls and Crofton all came on stream. The older mills also increased production as Powell River, Port Mellon and Woodfibre modernized and expanded. Production in BC's interior was also being considered and, while the implementation of PHAs undoubtedly sped up this process, an interior pulp industry would likely have emerged regardless. The first interior pulp mill to go on-line in 1961, for example—Celgar at Castlegar—initially based its fibre supply on a tree farm licence rather than a PHA licence to secure its wood supply.

Celgar pulp near Castlegar, 1976. I-06182.

Between 1965 and 1975 the number of interior pulp mills grew from one to nine and production rose from 570 tons per day to 5,960 tons per day, from what was once generally considered sawmill waste. When Williston initiated his policy no one anticipated such quick response. Williston and the industry both believed that considerable amounts of roundwood would be required to meet the needs of these new pulp mills. In all, between 1962 and 1966 Williston granted seven PHAs to support seven pulp mills.

Table 1. Pulp Harvesting Area application awards, 1962–66

Pulp Harvesting Area	Company and mill location	Overlapping applications and protests
PHA 1 (1962)	Canfor, Prince George	No overlaps
PHA 2 (1963)	Weyerhaeuser, Kamloops	No overlaps
PHA 3 (1964)	Northwood, Prince George	No overlaps
PHA 4 (1965)	Bulkley Valley Forest Products, Houston	Overlaps from MacMillan Bloedel (Kitimat) and Columbia Cellulose (Prince Rupert); Ben Ginter (Prince George) protested but withdrew
PHA 5 (1965)	Weldwood, Quesnel	Overlap with United Pulp (Squamish); protests from Canfor and Northwood
PHA 6 (1965)	United Pulp Partnership, Squamish	Overlaps with Weldwood (Quesnel) and Rayonier (Woodfibre)
PHA 7 (1966)	Canfor, Prince George	No overlaps; opposition from northern operators

By 1964, following the granting of the first three PHAs, Williston was faced with a series of overlapping proposals covering much of the province's interior, from Squamish to the Peace Country, as industry mobilized to try and take advantage of the new opportunity. Little rancour was apparent, even in the later public meetings; they gave the appearance of a relaxed and friendly debate, with considerable humour on the part of the minister and company representatives. When opposition arose from two of the larger companies during the discussion around the Bulkley Valley proposal, only a few rather pointed comments from MacMillan Bloedel about serving the best interests of the community suggested any underlying tension. In that case the major allocation went to local interests—the Bulkley Valley sawmill consortium, with MacMillan Bloedel and Columbia Cellulose receiving an additional allocation as compensation. But that was insufficient to induce MacMillan Bloedel to build their proposed Kitimat pulp mill (although Columbia Cellulose did complete their new kraft mill).[16] Williston was not a fan of MacMillan Bloedel's tactics. In 1960, for example, he was most annoyed with them when they secretly financed opposition to a tree farm licence application by Powell River.[17]

The Bulkley Valley award seems to reflect Williston's desire to accommodate each application. In effect, Williston guaranteed each applicant sufficient timber to meet their needs, but with a slight favouring of local enterprise.[18] The most difficult decision Williston faced over the PHAs were the proposals by Rayonier (proposed mill at Woodfibre on Howe Sound), United Pulp

Woodfibre on Howe Sound, 1945. Woodfibre was one of the six original pulp mills built in British Columbia between 1910 and 1912. During the post-World War II period they, as were many other mills, were expanding and seeking addition fibre supplies. I-22341.

Intercontinental Pulp mill at Prince George, 1968. NA-24362.

(proposed mill at Squamish on Howe Sound) and Weldwood's counterpro-
posal at Quesnel. Rayonier was granted wider authority to compete for additional fibre to support their expansion at Woodfibre. United Pulp requested a
PHA that included full rights over the Soo, Yalakom, Big Bar, Lac La Hache,
Williams Lake, Quesnel Lake, Cottonwood, Stum and Teseko PSYUs. Instead,
they received rights in fewer PSYUs and only 40 to 50 per cent of PSYU production. Some wood would be directed toward their operation from the Soo
PSYU but the remaining percentage of pulpwood was directed to the current
quota holders who could sell it on the open market. Weldwood requested full
rights over the Big Bar, Cottonwood, Lac La Hache, Narcosli, Quesnel Lake,
Stum, Teseko and Williams Lake PSYUs. They already held quota in all of the
PSYUs in which they received rights and also held quota in several of those now
partially allocated to United Pulp, which could be used to supplement their
award—an award that was considerably less than they requested. Intercontinental (Canfor) asked for four PSYUs and received rights over "the two less

attractive ones."[19] Williston not only looked at the applications but also at proposed plants and existing quota, and he then allocated to ensure that all the proposed plants had an adequate supply of fibre for their successful operation.

These hearings did make clear one decision about PHA policy: no coastal PSYU would be included in a PHA. This maintained the status quo on the coast and, as a coastal chip market was already developing, Williston saw little need to provide further incentives. As well, only the proposals at Squamish and Kitimat involved new coastal pulp mills.

What these hearings and the subsequent decisions also demonstrated was that Williston was not only focused on developing the interior pulp network, but that any reasonable proposal for a mill would be guaranteed an adequate fibre supply even if it meant harvesting roundwood. [In addition, the minimum diameter to be cut in the interior was reduced from 27.94 centimetres (11 inches) to 17.78 centimetres (7 inches).] The allocation decisions were a compromise, with each applicant getting only part of what was asked for but receiving enough to ensure the successful operation of the proposed mill. Future expansion would be dealt with later on.

The hearing transcripts and news reports give the impression that these were open hearings in which each party was armed with similar information and competed openly during the proceedings. In reality the minister generally knew what each applicant had prepared and how they were going to

Table 2. PSYUs awarded

United Pulp	Weldwood
New Stum PSYU – 40%	Narcosli – 50%
Williams Lake – 40%	Cottonwood – 50%
Lac La Hache – 40%	Quesnel Lake I – 50%
Big Bar – 50%	Quesnel Lake II – 100%
Yalakom – 50%	

make their presentation before the hearings started. He was in regular discussion with each applicant, advised them on their applications and sometimes revealed his opinion of the other applicants. For example, Williston informed Weldwood on several occasions that he did not think the United Pulp mill proposals would ever be completed, even if they were able to get an application in place. Although he was probably uncertain about some of the minor objections or what support each applicant had marshalled, Williston no doubt had a fairly complete picture of how each hearing would go and who would attend.

Building a Pulp Mill

IN ORDER TO DEVELOP A CASE STUDY of corporate response to the PHA program, we will again focus on one company as an example—Weldwood, formerly Western Plywood—and look at how they eventually came to build a pulp mill at Quesnel. Western/Weldwood is the firm for which the most information is available and their negotiations are probably among the most complex of any of the applicants, including the sawmill consortiums of Bulkley Valley Forest Products and United Pulp, neither of which ultimately built a pulp mill. These two consortiums quickly came under the general control of larger pulp companies; Bulkley Valley became associated with Bowater of England, and United Pulp with Price Brothers from eastern Canada. Interestingly, both Bowater and Price Brothers were also associated with Weldwood at various times during their venture.

Western Plywood, the predecessor company of Weldwood of Canada, was formed by the Hungarian immigrant John Bene. Bene had worked at Pacific Veneer during World War II, and by 1945 was ready to go out on his own. He purchased the assets of the BC Veneer Works in Nelson and moved these to Vancouver, where he opened a cottonwood panel plant on Kent Avenue. Over the next 15 years, two major issues preoccupied Bene's plans for company growth. First, he needed a more secure timber supply, and second, he believed integration and improved utilization were essential for industrial success. He expanded by building a plywood plant at Quesnel and another in Edmonton, Alberta, and he ultimately acquired the plant of J.R. Murray in Vancouver for its timber holdings. His final goal was to add a pulp mill at Quesnel.

Weldwood's Cariboo Pulp and Paper mill at Quesnel, 1973. NA-30001.

Western Plywood embarked on an extensive program in their efforts to establish a pulp mill in the interior. But in the 1940s and 1950s Western was not alone in this interest and was only one of several larger companies intent on such expansion. Western Plywood's interior operations were close to Quesnel and it was here that Bene looked, but it would take some time.

As early as 1947 one of his vice-presidents, Geoff Tullidge, had visited the Rubberoid Corporation in New Jersey to organize a test run of popular chips.[20] Bene arranged for a number of firms and organizations to test chips and pulp, including extensive testing by Bulkley Dunton of New York and further tests by International Paper at their research laboratory in New York.[21] Tests were also made in Sweden, at the Fernstrom Paper Mills in California and at the Pulp and Paper Research Institute in Montreal, and two small rolls of pulp were produced by the Rubberoid Corporation at Gloucester, New York.[22] Once a small stock of paper was in hand, Bene arranged with Canadian Boxes of Vancouver for a test run to produce corrugated paper, which Canadian Boxes reported to be of excellent quality. Following this trial, a vice-president of Pacific Mills at Canadian Boxes suggested that Western Plywood not go into pulp manufacture but rather sell their chips to its parent company, Crown Zellerbach.[23]

Bene continued his investigations, shifting into a more comprehensive approach. He found that Sidney Roofing in Victoria was chipping cores from Murray, although these were fir and hemlock. He then studied Westminster Paper's harvesting and chipping of cottonwood. Eventually, Western Plywood reached an agreement with Westminster Paper over the cottonwood that grew along the Fraser River and decided to co-manage a number of stands.[24] Two of Bene's vice-presidents visited Sweden, and additional visits were made to the eastern United States and Canada. Bene participated in the wide-ranging discussions being held amongst the smaller operators, although these were mainly aimed at the coastal industry. As Bene noted to the Canadian Pulp and Paper Association in 1948: "A number of BC sawmills and plywood plants are investigating the possibility of establishing a jointly owned kraft pulping unit to utilize economically their pulpable by-products."[25]

The project went as far as completing an engineering study and acquiring pulp harvesting rights in the Quesnel Lake area before Western Plywood's failure to meet its commitments caused cancellation of the licence in 1960. The Forest Service cited failure to meet established goals as the reason, but Western Plywood blamed the problem on the Forest Service's failure to provide adequate long-term fibre.[26] In reality, as Western Plywood secured its coastal timber position the company was probably unable to commit enough of their own capital to interest a partner in the Quesnel project. This was also a major reason why in 1961 Bene sold his company to United States Plywood and created Weldwood of Canada.

The advent of the new Weldwood of Canada completely changed Bene's range of possibilities. He was now in charge of a Canada-wide organization that could draw on the resources of United States Plywood, but Bene himself could only act as a subordinate partner, not as an equal. Company decisions now rested with New York and, in particular, in the hands of United States Plywood's president, Gene Brewer. Still, Bene's approach corresponded with that of the parent company and the New York executives seemed to like and respect him and his abilities. Fortunately for Bene, it was also a time when United States Plywood was expanding its operations and had the resources to achieve this expansion. It all happened very quickly, with a new company being formed that merged two distinct organizations. Decisions were also made to acquire Canadian Collieries and secure that firm's coastal wood supply and, at John Bene's urging, commit to the construction of a new pulp mill.

Bene apparently saw his opportunity when Williston announced the new policy in regard to pulp harvesting, as by May of 1963 he was pushing Brewer to consider establishing a pulp mill in British Columbia. He also foreshadowed later developments when he suggested partnering with a Japanese pulp buyer.[27] Given the turn of events it seems unlikely that John Bene seriously considered establishing a pulp mill anywhere but near Quesnel, but the acquisition of Canadian Collieries brought Weldwood a significant coastal timber resource and they also acquired an excellent site for a pulp mill near Union Bay on Vancouver Island.

United States Plywood was conservative in its approach to business, as was John Bene. Their views on business meshed.[28] A risk-taker would have had the pulp mill at Quesnel Lake up and running but Bene waited for better circumstances. United States Plywood had little experience in the area of pulp and, though convinced by Bene, they moved cautiously. But time was of the essence. Even before Williston had fully formulated his policy, applications were coming in and the timber of the central and southern interior was rapidly being committed, with tentative moves also being made ever northward. Probably critical to United States Plywood's decision was that everyone seemed interested in British Columbia. In the late 1950s and early 1960s BC was the hot spot for developing forest resources in North America, especially as a producer of kraft pulp. Bene was quick to reinforce this notion in New York: "The pulp, lumber and plywood industries in BC, are now riding the crest of a boomlet and there is hardly a day in which no substantial expansion project is being announced."[29]

During the 1960s United States Plywood, like many other North American corporations, had entered a period of aggressive growth. The company had made some inroads into their traditional area of building products, especially panels, through acquisitions such as Western Plywood. But senior executives were starting to see their only option, one that had been widely adopted, as integration. Such integration, in the view of one United States Plywood senior researcher, would not only increase sales revenue but would provide opportunities for increased timber resources and additional peeler logs for their plywood mills. To a growing company, the researcher highlighted, one of the major advantages of moving into pulp production was that, once established, these mills were places of large cash flows, even when return on investment was below expectation. In turn, this large cash flow and capital stock could be used to leverage funds for further expansion. United States Plywood initially investigated three expansion options—British Columbia, California and Oregon—and by 1965 had narrowed down to two options, which they pursued. Quesnel, British Columbia and McCloud, California became their focus, since it was at these locations that the company controlled "two of the cheapest sources of softwood suitable for pulping in all of North America."[30]

Convincing New York of Quesnel's value took considerable manoeuvring on the part of John Bene. He had to persuade company executives that a rapid move was required, even though they were still organizing the Canadian operations and had just invested considerable resources in the acquisition of Canadian Collieries. Despite the occasional caution about the future of the kraft pulp market, the worldwide attention on British Columbia's forests had paved his way and he had little difficulty in convincing New York that this was an opportunity that should be investigated. Events moved ahead quickly. Plans were facilitated when United States (US) Plywood's former president and board chairman, Tony Antoville, discovered during a London meeting with Bowater that they were very interested in British Columbia pulp production and, more to the point, interested in partnering with US Plywood in British Columbia.[31] But the Bowater partnership soon deteriorated. Bowater's representative strongly favoured the Union Bay site on Vancouver Island and would not even consider Quesnel. At US Plywood's head office it also became clear that to Bowater the term "partnership" meant Bowater operating the pulp mill and controlling the timber, which was not acceptable to US Plywood in either British Columbia or New York.[32] Immediately upon termination of the agreement, New York began making use of its extensive contacts to discuss other partnership possibilities, including Weyerhaeuser, Mitsubishi, Gotteman & Company, Bukley-Dunton and St. Regis.[33]

The prospect of outside capital encouraged US Plywood to give Bene the authority to go ahead with negotiations for a Pulp Harvesting Area and

Stand of cedar at Quesnel Lake in the area where Weldwood initially secured pulp harvesting rights, 1913. NA-03750.

finally, on June 15, 1964, the company president, Gene Brewer, gave the official go-ahead to prepare and present a proposal.[34] But US Plywood head office was still not completely convinced they should proceed. As their senior scientist'wrote:

> A pulp mill for the production of nothing but market pulp, to be sold on the world market, is a rough business which we should stay out of unless we have strong competitive advantages in the fierce struggle for markets for bleached sulphate pulp. I don't know of any such advantages available to Weldwood of Canada or US Plywood, except maybe for the supply of pulp chips and pulpwood here in BC but that situation is far from unique.[35]

Weldwood adopted a three-stage process, pursuing all stages simultaneously. First, the company had to determine what Williston and the ministry wanted to see. Second, they began closely monitoring what other companies were doing to secure PHAs. Third, they had to prepare a technical package that would be acceptable to government before a licence would be granted. Clearly the linchpin in this process was Ray Williston, and it was he they handled with greatest care. Regular meetings were held, which sometimes included premier Bennett and sometimes ministry staff. It should be noted that other applicants were going through the same process. In Weldwood's case they brought out United States Plywood's president on several occasions to meet with both premier Bennett and minister Williston, and it was in these meetings that they fully determined what Williston expected of each application.[36]

Weldwood had considerable advantage over their major competitor, United Pulp, in the process. United Pulp was a consortium of coastal sawmill operators who, backed by Price Brothers, sought additional wood supplies to supplement their chip production. Many of the areas United Pulp was trying to obtain rights over were areas in which Weldwood already held quota. This gave Weldwood a legitimate reason to attend the public meetings held by United Pulp. It also meant Weldwood had close contact and relationships with many of the quota holders of the timber areas coveted by United Pulp.[37]

Weldwood's shift from Union Bay and Squamish locations was a gradual one over the months prior to the applicant's hearing on January 5, 1965. Not only was New York initially fixed on the two coastal locations but Bene faced opposition within Weldwood as well. The former general manager of

It is timber such as this stand of fine fir near Union Bay that United States Plywood corporation, owners of Weldwood, hoped to use in their new pulp mill, 1938. NA-11210.

Canadian Collieries, Roly Ellison, also greatly favoured the coastal locations, especially Squamish. He did not hesitate to make these views known directly to New York.[38] Quesnel was, for much of this period, only a distant second choice, due for consideration in 10 or 15 years' time.[39] Bene was able to sidetrack Ellison and then gradually ease him out of the company with Gene Brewer's assistance.[40] As the site engineering studies progressed, Bene convinced New York to include Quesnel in the studies.[41] When the final reports were presented, it was clear that Quesnel was the more viable location. Although some costs were higher at Quesnel the considerably reduced cost of fibre, along with the local support and regional nature of the project, outweighed any advantages of the other sites.[42]

Weldwood rallied local government and community support for their application: the local MLA, William Speare, was outspoken in his support for the project[43]; the company announced programs similar to those made by other applicants, including financial assistance to build chipping facilities at regional sawmills; and they reassured potentially troublesome operators, such as John Ernst, that they would not encroach on their operations.[44] Their

Gangsaw at the Dunkley Lumber Company, one of the various sawmill operators competing with Weldwood for timber, near Quesnel, 1971. NA-26212.

political manoeuvring was so effective that their only significant opposition came from their opponent United Pulp. Some complaint also came from Northwood and Canfor, whose self-interest was evident and who feared that Weldwood would forestall their expansion plans, but these objections were based on possible expansion sometime in the future so had little impact on Williston's decision. A few operators did raise concerns about what was considered pulpwood, as they were already exceeding close utilization standards. What also helped Weldwood was that at the hearing the mayor of Squamish expressed concerns about the odour produced by pulp mills, while the mayor of Quesnel, Alex Fraser, said that a little thing like odour was of no concern. Fraser, a future Social Credit minister of highways, stated: "They are worried about the pollution from pulp plants. I would like to say that the Town of Quesnel is not a bit worried about air pollution from pulp plants. We want the air pollution from pulp plants (laughter and applause). To us it is the smell of dollar bills."[45] It is also interesting to note that at this time Weldwood donated land valued at $22,000 to Quesnel for a park.[46]

Weldwood went to considerable effort to ensure their success, even placing an option on their proposed mill site, but they were basically in a winning position. They were also prepared to force Canfor and Northwood to withdraw their objections, should it have been required.[47] They found Williston to be someone they liked dealing with and Williston appears to have favoured working with them. Brewer wrote to a Williams Lake operator after the hearing: "it is comforting that in Mr. Williston we have an unusual public servant, who seems dedicated to working out equitable solutions."[48] Weldwood was also aware that Williston did not respond well to external pressure, as he complained to Weldwood when United Pulp tried to use the minister of industrial development to influence his decision. Weldwood had generally found Williston to be very reasonable, despite occasional differences with the Forest Service over timber limits. Internally, they considered him a good friend of the company.[49]

Williston, despite providing timber to United Pulp, did not believe that the Squamish enterprise would succeed, a view he expressed to Weldwood several times. Nor did United Pulp have Williston's full support, as he had expressed a number of times that a pulp mill at Squamish using resources from BC's interior did not match his or the government's objectives. Weldwood was of similar opinion; they had actually been a member of United Pulp, a relationship that they, along with several other mills, only severed when US Plywood decided to commit to a separate application in June 1964. Some of the remaining United participants seemed less than optimistic. Sandwell Engineering, who were providing the engineering for United Pulp, met several times with Weldwood and, while not revealing any confidential information, were clearly positioning themselves to seek the Quesnel project contract. Price Brothers also held several meetings with Weldwood. The companies' top executives met in Montreal and New York[50] and Price eventually replaced Bowater as Weldwood's partner in the Quesnel project.[51]

Despite the propitious signs and all the elements seemingly in place, it would take another seven years before Weldwood's pulp mill finally began operation. In fact, it was one of the last to go on line in the interior. There were two main reasons for this start-up delay. First, Weldwood was, as mentioned, a fiscally conservative company. Reports in 1964 and 1965 estimated that demand for Canadian pulp would exceed mill capacity as late as 1975.[52] Within a year this optimism had changed and dire warnings of overcapacity were appearing. Within three years the market was glutted with Canadian pulp; sales were slow and difficult and Weldwood delayed completion of the plant.[53] Second, Champion International and US Plywood merged in 1967. Over the next year, Champion decided that it was not in the US company's best interest to continue the partnership with Price Brothers. Brewer wrote on April 5, 1968:

> This will advise you that we have severed our partnership arrangement with the Price Company on the Caribou [sic] Project. The decision to take this step was reached after long and serious consideration of the very likely conflict of interest between our two companies in the future and we felt keenly that we should promptly inform the Price people of our thinking....[54]

Weldwood's pulp plant finally came on line in November 1972—later than initially hoped but still in the range of what Weldwood considered as meeting the Forest Service's deadlines. Williston publicly applied pressure for completion, but even by 1965 he considered that some delay was appropriate so that the new pulp mills did not all come on stream at the same time (although he probably would have preferred completion to have been in 1969 or 1970).[55] He was not prepared to go to cabinet and request such a delay, though, and his advice to Weldwood was to begin construction and carry it out slowly until they were prepared to start production.[56]

Weldwood held a number of discussions with other companies and began actively exploring options before finally forming a partnership with two Japanese firms: Daishowa Paper Manufacturing Co. Ltd. and Marubeni Corporation. The Quesnel mill today remains a partnership pulp producer despite repeated assurances to Williston that they intended to eventually include newsprint production. As Brewer said to the minister in 1968: "the ultimate goal for the Caribou [sic] project is the manufacture of paper."[57] West Fraser Timber Mills Ltd. now owns the 50 per cent once held by Weldwood.

As we have seen in this chapter, change continued to be at the core of BC forest policy. Williston's introduction of the PHAs helped shape not just the interior pulp industry but furthered government objectives of better utilization, less overall waste and new industrial growth in the northern and central part of the province. The minister's involvement in both public hearings and

Sawmills at Quesnel, 1974. NA-25574.

Alec Fraser, Minister of Highways and Transportation and MLA for the Cariboo, 1984. I-68028.

private meetings influenced industry response in terms of exploring new technologies and partnerships as they sought to get in line with the principle of integration—and secure new timber supplies in the process.

The example of Western Plywood/Weldwood of Canada/United States Plywood and their long process of establishing a pulp mill at Quesnel brings all of these concerns together, allowing us to see the inner workings of industry manoeuvring and dynamism in response to one example of new policy. As the next chapter shows, individual case studies shine a light on one of BC's most valuable—and sometimes volatile—industries.

RICHARD A. RAJALA

4

Come Hell or High Water

Log Driving, Resource Politics and Conservation in British Columbia's Stellako River Controversy, 1950–75

"LOGGERS FIRED UPON," read the title of one newspaper story. "Gunfire Heralds Stellako Drive," read another. Additional reports mention "night riders" and "sabotage".[1] These accounts, dating from 1967, refer to a relatively short, relatively obscure river in north-central BC. How did the Stellako River come to provoke such tensions in the heady days of BC's postwar boom? It was a time when resources still seemed limitless. And given massive development schemes on the Columbia, Peace and Nechako rivers, the fate of one short river might seem more or less inconsequential. But clearly, emotions ran high along the Stellako's banks in the mid-1960s, this chapter aims to shed light on an underappreciated series of events in BC's environmental and political history shaped, in part, by the BC forest industry and its policies.

The Stellako River does not rank as one of British Columbia's great rivers in terms of length or grandeur. Just under 13 kilometres long, it flows in a northeasterly direction from its source in Francois Lake through a narrow, forested valley for about 6.5 kilometres before the valley widens. As E.H. Tredcroft noted in a 1943 survey of the river's hydroelectric potential, two islands formed

---

Facing page: Fly fishing on the Stellako, 1948. I-20883.

"minor disturbances"[2] in this canyon stretch, which ends with a 1.5 metre fall. The river then meanders through low-lying bench lands, some of which had been put into cultivation, before joining the Endako at a lagoon and emptying into Fraser Lake. A number of channels, gravel bars, rapids and small islands mark the lower half of the river, which turns and bends through its most productive salmon spawning grounds. Fraser Lake, in turn, fed the Nechako which, at the time of Tredcroft's report, flowed eastward into the main stem of the Fraser River at Prince George. Tredcroft was unenthusiastic about the Stellako's power-generating capacities, so the river would be spared the kind of development that a decade later reversed the Nechako's flow and put it to use in powering the Aluminium Company of Canada's Kitimat smelter. That story, unlike the Stellako's, is well known.[3]

The Stellako's gravel beds were, and remain, an important component of the Fraser River Sockeye run. Not until about two weeks after entering the Fraser's mouth do the spawners reach Prince George then turn into the Nechako. Another five or six days of struggle carry them through Fraser Lake and into the Stellako itself, where those Sockeye that manage to avoid the commercial fishermen and fight their way past the Fraser's many obstacles finally spawn and die. Smaller populations of Chinook Salmon and Kokanee also inhabit the river.

The Stellako's waters were productive for human use as well and, while some of that story has been documented by local historians, for most of the twentieth century the river has gone largely unnoticed by those who live outside the north-central interior. Yes, fisheries biologists knew of the Stellako's contribution to the Fraser's Sockeye runs; the region's residents knew the river as a fine stretch of Rainbow Trout habitat; and, as access increased, its reputation as a splendid fly-fishing stream grew among outdoorsmen. And for centuries before that, the Stellako's Sockeye provided the Carrier people with a source of subsistence. That would all change in the early twentieth century. Federal policies banned the use of traditional fishing weirs and the Fraser's Sockeye run collapsed due to obstructions caused by Canadian Northern Railway construction at Hell's Gate in 1913–14.

Usable Energy versus Conservation

OUR FORESTRY-RELATED STORY really begins with the building of another railway, the Grand Trunk Pacific (GTP), which created another interaction with the Stellako. The GTP's enormous demand for forest products in the form of ties and other construction materials, and its enticement to settlement, gave rise to the region's forest industry. A mixed economy developed, linking homesteading with wintertime woods work, with settlers and the Carrier cutting timber for local building materials and for railway ties. Here is where the Stellako's energy came into play as a cheap, if not always reliable, way of moving ties and logs. The timber was cut along the shores of Francois Lake and moved down the Stellako to sawmills on Fraser Lake, where the GTP turned up the Endako River to the Burkley and the Skeena. Between around 1914 and 1948, with an interlude until 1965, the rising waters of the late spring freshet gave the Lakes District residents an opportunity to take part in one of the grandest and most destructive traditions of North American lumbering—the river drive. Shaped by seasonal rhythms that meshed agriculture and lumbering, the annual drive drew brief mention in lumbering journals but captured no headlines.

Then, in the mid-1960s, the resumption of the Stellako River log drive suddenly became news. Each spring and summer between 1965 and 1967 events on the Stellako were the subject of heated local, provincial and even national debate, heightening tensions between Victoria and Ottawa, between provincial resource agencies, and between those with a stake in fisheries (both commercial and recreational) and the forest industry. The Stellako controversy, in short, provided a glimpse into the future of competitive land use debate, practice and policy in BC. Yet it has drawn little attention from historians. Mentioned but not explored in recent treatments of environmental politics and left out of forest histories, the Stellako incident has been only briefly considered by some fisheries historians. Yet the story of the Stellako River log drives deserves more attention than it has received.[4]

For British Columbians, the story's meaning depended on where one lived, what one did for a living and how one viewed the relationship between forest exploitation and a well-used but beautiful and productive stretch of water. Perhaps most importantly, the Stellako story reveals, as Arn Keeling shows in his work,[5] a province experiencing a profound sense of unease and doubt about the supposed benefits of modernization. But the Stellako does not fit the familiar

Stellako River, 1945. Courtesy of Pacific Salmon Commission.

narrative; this conflict was not rooted in the ecological consequences of a massive hydroelectric project, a gigantic smelter or a new pulp mill (although it was connected to the structural changes pulp and paper production brought to the central interior forest industry). Rather, this controversy arose over the use of a technology as old as lumbering itself, employed to feed a relatively small but recently modernized sawmill. Nor were the economic benefits particularly high except on a purely local scale and, many argued, these did not compensate for potential losses to the salmon fishery and tourism.

Indeed, for the province as a whole, the Stellako's importance was primarily symbolic. To many, log drives symbolized misuse, waste, federal-provincial bickering and the forest industry's power to ride roughshod over other resources—and over nature itself. Also significant, though largely unmentioned in any reports about the drives, were the effects on the inhabitants of the Stellako Indian Reserve, located at the river's juncture with Fraser Lake. Along with logging and mining in Strathcona and other parks, broader pollution concerns linked to urbanization and industrialization and a society's emerging demand for unspoiled spaces for recreation and renewal, the Stellako incident confronted British Columbians with some disturbing realities.

How, many came to wonder at that time, could 'progress' so heavily dependent upon forest industry expansion be reconciled with the habitat needs of salmon for the commercial fishery and the trout prized by an increasing number of recreational fishers? Conservation, defined as the wise use of natural resources, suggested that science could be joined with the regulatory power of governments to ensure balanced and sustainable practices. Timber would be cut, processed and put into world markets in accordance with the principles of sustained-yield forestry, and conflicts would be resolved through sustained yield's philosophical cousin—multiple use. Priorities could be weighed, this credo held, in a way that met society's diverse needs. That did not imply an equality of uses, however. The BC forest industry's pre-eminence as a generator of investment, profits, revenues and jobs meant that its requirements often ranked first in the hierarchy of uses.[6]

Therein lay the problem, as author-conservationist Roderick Haig-Brown saw it in the early 1950s. He saw an industry free to devour forests with marginal attention to renewing that resource, one that paid none at all to "preservation of soil or water resources." He saw multiple use as a convenient disguise for a single-minded approach to resource exploitation driven by what he called "the false urgency and outdated sanctity of progress." Genuine conservation, he believed, required more science and better coordination in planning to achieve a proper balancing of interests. Fish and forests were still resources subject to human use, but their interdependence demanded recognition and understanding, lest the former be needlessly sacrificed to the plunder of the latter. Haig-Brown was far from alone in drawing this conclusion, although he expressed it with greater vigour and sophistication than most of his contemporaries.[7]

Haig-Brown and other defenders of Pacific salmon and trout looked to government for the scientific and regulatory capacity to achieve the potential of multiple-use planning, but economic realities and the structure of Canadian federalism left them frustrated. The federal *Fisheries Act* was extended to BC in 1876, legislation containing clauses prohibiting the pollution or alteration of fish habitat. By 1930 a series of court rulings had confirmed the federal government's jurisdiction over sea coast and inland fisheries, extending Ottawa's claim to salmon and other anadromous fish into the non-tidal portions of rivers. But provincial jurisdiction complicated matters in several ways. First, in non-tidal waters the provinces exercised jurisdiction over property and civil rights, affording BC an indirect say in fishing. Second, BC had possession of the beds of rivers and their surface waters after entering Confederation. Water use fell under the provincial *Water Act*, administered by the Water Rights Branch after its creation in 1911. By 1950 some 10,000 water licences had been issued, most for mining and irrigation but some for log transportation purposes. Stream flows within BC's boundaries were a provincial resource, a source of both industrial and agricultural development, and licence revenue for the provincial Crown.[8]

BC also played a part in the commercial salmon fishery, having named John P. Babcock as fisheries commissioner in 1901 in order to spearhead hatchery development. Six years later Babcock's Fisheries Office became the Fisheries Department, which attained full ministerial status in 1947. In 1937 BC reached agreement with Ottawa to take over enforcement of regulations for the conservation of non-tidal sport fish. That responsibility fell to the province's Game Department, which in 1957, now known as the Fish and Wildlife Branch, became part of the new Department of Recreation and Conservation. In that reorganization the Department of Fisheries was relegated to branch status in the new department.[9]

BC advised Ottawa on commercial fishing regulations, sharing responsibility for enforcement of the *Fisheries Act*, but in matters of forest management the province reigned supreme. Under the *British North America Act* the provinces controlled the sale and use of public lands and forests. BC followed tradition by disposing of cutting rights through various forms of licencing. Returns from water and sport fishing licences were inconsequential compared to revenue from forests, and the province drew little direct benefit from the commercial fishery despite gaining the right to licence canneries in 1908. Ottawa retained its jurisdiction over tidal fisheries, where the courts decided that no property rights to fish existed, and the *Fisheries Act* remained a potentially powerful tool in making regulations to protect salmon habitat. In actuality, though, federal authority was applied loosely even when the law clearly prohibited certain forest industry practices like the dumping of sawdust in rivers, and that authority stopped at the edge of fish-bearing streams, where provincial power kicked in.[10]

The two levels of government squabbled over loggers' tendency to plug streams with debris, thereby obstructing fish passage to spawning grounds, throughout the early twentieth century. Neither the BC Forest Service (BCFS) nor Water Rights Branch showed much interest in impairing the performance of such a key industry in order to protect a resource of lesser economic importance that fell under federal jurisdiction. Indeed, the Fish and Wildlife Branch and Commercial Fisheries Branch lacked the power to do so. A 1932 amendment strengthened the *Fisheries Act*, making it illegal for those engaged in logging or land-clearing to place logs, slash, stumps and other debris into salmon streams, but strict enforcement would have brought logging to a virtual halt. Staffing levels permitted no more than occasional inspections and post-logging cleanup requirements took precedence over prosecutions. The *Fisheries Act* itself dictated caution, since damage to the resource had to be proven in court. Rather than resort to costly and uncertain prosecution of scores of offenders, federal fisheries officers initiated legal proceedings from time to time, campaigned for greater care in logging, pleaded with the BCFS to take on an enforcement role and documented the destruction in annual reports.[11]

The lack of regard for fish habitat shown by provincial authorities and the forest industry, and Ottawa's reluctance to offend a major industry, became more alarming after World War II. Healthy world demand, a still-abundant forest resource, and W.A.C. Bennett's industry-friendly Social Credit government drew investment capital into the province. Logging to supply sawmills and a new generation of pulp and paper plants endangered more streams, at the same time as hydroelectric dams built to power factories threatened to extinguish some fish populations altogether. Provincial parks were opened to dams and industry. Much of the ensuing outcry came from the inhabitants of rural communities, from commercial fishermen along the coast and from hikers, campers, hunters and fishers throughout the province, all of whom were disturbed at the degradation of local environments. Haig-Brown, in this sense, was an eloquent spokesman for a much wider conservationist impulse that questioned the pace and ecological consequences of modernization and of traditional industry as well.[12]

Shaping up for Protest

IN THIS ATMOSPHERE of localized and province-wide contemplation of the costs of progress, the political and economic elites continued to defend their authority with assurances of sound policy and practice. Maximum sustained yield, wise-use conservationism and multiple use were terms of legitimization, but the rhetoric failed to square with reality. Industrialization and unionization raised living standards, increased leisure time and promoted purchasing power—of pickup trucks, campers, boats and fishing gear to experience nature. But in opening up the countryside, logging roads brought more people face-to-face with massive clear-cuts, crumbling streambanks and sediment-filled waters.

These processes were part of what Haig-Brown termed a pattern of "silent erosions" that too often went unnoticed because neither the causes nor the remedies were readily apparent. Haig-Brown made these remarks in Prince George at the May 1966 convention of the BC Wildlife Federation (which will be discussed in greater detail). The Stellako log drives had not gone unnoticed. They had the potential to capture and focus the attention of a public prepared to question the easy exchange of a river and its fish for a sawmill's profits. Between 1965 and 1967 the Stellako drives did just that, contributing to the erosion of support for wise-use conservationism.[13]

The lesson many drew from the Stellako log drives was that conservation as practiced by economic and political elites was at best inadequate to address an array of human needs going beyond profits, revenues and wages, and at worst a mere cover for a business-as-usual development agenda. The BC Wildlife Federation (BCWF), which led the protests against the 1966 Stellako drive, arrived at this conclusion and called for a social base of activism that encompassed more people than just fishers and hunters. That objective was realized; within three years the establishment of the Sierra Club of BC and the Society for Pollution and Environmental Control (SPEC) signalled the arrival of a new social movement that would reshape the province's political culture.

Had those organizations been in existence during the period of the Stellako drives, things might have turned out differently. Perhaps the opposition would have achieved sufficient dimensions to prevent the log runs. But provincial and federal decision-makers did not face this sort of pressure in the mid-1960s. In 1966, however, the Canadian Broadcasting Corporation's "This Land of Ours" series did produce a documentary on the 1966 drive. Shown nationally the following year, the film presented a series of themes: the era of frontier exploitation had passed; nature's interconnectedness must be acknowledged; resources had limits. The final scene featured host John Foster listening to high school students at the Vancouver Aquarium express their views on the need for higher standards of environmental protection. The teenagers' remarks reflected both the contemporary importance attached to the Stellako and the part the drives played in building support for environmentalism.[14]

The Stellako drives represented an example of what could go wrong, but the voices of dissent were too few and the region too isolated from major population centres to move the issue from the arena of debate and change expressions of disgust to actual protest. The developing ecological perspective did not take hold in time but the Stellako's influence in shaping that outlook should not be discounted.

A Story Bigger than Logs

WHILE MY ACCOUNT is less concerned with policy than with the perceptions that brought attention to the Stellako, it's appropriate to provide some explanation, beyond the need to move timber, of why the drives took place. At the most basic level, the Stellako drives reflected a multi-dimensional search for power in pursuit of control. Fraser Lake Sawmills sought control of the river's power to reduce the costs of moving logs from the forests around Francois Lake to its mill. But that simple cost consideration involving a single sawmill was embedded in a larger struggle over the uses to which rivers should be put. Expansion of the north-central interior forest industry, and the emergence of Prince George as the single largest centre of pulp and paper production in the province, raised the stakes. Those plants generated an enormous demand for fibre, in the form of both logs and the chips that area sawmills would produce in cutting lumber. A new, integrated industrial structure was in the making (see Chapter 3) and the needs of other mills, both actual and planned, had to be considered as well. At Prince Rupert, Columbia Cellulose had made the Nass and Kitsumgallum rivers central forces in its transportation system. Quesnel, already the destination of river-driven logs, and Houston were prospects for new pulp enterprises, raising the stakes still higher.

BC's Minister of Lands, Forests and Water Resources Ray Williston was the architect of interior forest industrialization, and for him provincial control of rivers was both a means to an end and an end in itself. Rivers supplied the energy for province-building, whether for hydroelectric power or log transportation. Interference from the federal Department of Fisheries could therefore not be tolerated. Forests drew more investment capital, created more jobs and captured greater revenue than salmon, and the disparity was widening. In 1950 forestry activity produced almost $400 million in wealth versus the commercial fishery's $63 million worth of products. By 1965 forestry generated $980 million in annual wealth, well beyond the fishery's mere $52 million. But the Stellako's value as a Sockeye salmon stream, relative to its worth as a corridor for log movement, generated a quite different set of numbers. Along with the Adams, Chilko and Horsefly runs, the Stellako was one of the main contributors to the Fraser River Sockeye catch.[15]

With the larger balance sheet in mind, Williston fought to keep his, BC Hydro's and the forest industry's options open. The Stellako's significance to forest productivity may have been minor when measured in purely financial terms, but as events unfolded it became a prize in the larger arena of federal-provincial conflict. In 1966 Williston went so far as to defy a federal order prohibiting the Stellako drive, seized the logs for non-payment of stumpage fees and engaged Fraser Lake Sawmills to conduct the operation on the province's behalf. Here was a variation on the development strategy that had seen W.A.C. Bennett take over the Black Ball Ferry Line and the BC Electric Company earlier in the decade. When private capital would not—or, in the sawmill company's case, could not—act in accordance with the Social Credit agenda, the government found a way. In this instance, Williston and the Fraser Lake enterprise shared a common objective—use of the Stellako's energy. But the company would also become a pawn in the minister's provocation of a constitutional showdown.

Ottawa's timid response to the challenge is easy to document but more difficult to explain. After agreeing to permit a 1965 drive on a one-time-only basis, federal Minister of Fisheries H.J. Robichaud appeared ready to flex his muscles the following year. An exhaustive federal-provincial study of the 1965 drive had produced clear evidence of damage to spawning grounds and public opinion favoured resistance. In the end, though, Robichaud wilted in the face of Williston's pressure. Denying the validity of the 1965 findings, Williston engaged the BC Research Council to study his 1966 drive. That investigation was sufficiently inconclusive in its report to justify his 'multiple' use of the Stellako River, Williston claimed. The fact that few outside of forest industry circles agreed mattered less than the scientific uncertainty he had created, in a few minds at least. Robichaud's officials remained committed to the self-evident fact that log drives on shallow streams like the Stellako were bad for salmon, but in 1967 Robichaud continued his retreat. Rather than confront Williston in the constitutional arena, he now joined his provincial counter-part in the quest for scientific understanding. A third study would be con-ducted of the final log drive, this one a controlled exercise conducted in an atmosphere of federal-provincial co-operation.

Alan George Phillips argues that the explanation for Robichaud's com-mitment to compromise lies in the uncertainty of Ottawa's jurisdiction in matters of habitat protection. Other scholars agree that intergovernmental power relations in natural resource management were marked by considerable ambiguity. It wasn't until a pair of 1980 court cases involving prosecutions of loggers under the *Fisheries Act* that the Supreme Court provided clarity on the scope of federal power in relation to forestry. In the mid-1960s the Stellako episode boiled down to a question of will. While Williston seemed prepared, even eager, to have the question of jurisdiction settled, Robichaud took the path of least resistance at every opportunity.[16]

In the end the Stellako mattered more to Victoria than it did to Ottawa, par-ticularly during a period of expanding provincial authority and persistent pres-sure from premier Bennett for greater autonomy and a larger return of federal tax dollars to BC. In Ottawa's view the Stellako River salmon, in this context, were an acceptable price for avoiding more squabbles with a provincial govern-ment determined to demand a greater share in the benefits of Confederation.

In the course of this project I came to view the Stellako River conflict as a three-act drama and, in constructing the narrative, sought to resist the temp-tation to cast the major players as heroes or villains; the latter as despoilers of nature and the former as defenders of ecological integrity. Some actors of prominence in the fray are actually more notable for their absence than their words or actions. For instance, BC's Minister of Recreation and Conservation, Ken Kiernan, stayed mum relative to the powerful Williston. Howard Paish of the BCWF was the most prominent conservationist voice, but place exerted a heavy influence on how members of rod and gun clubs treated the Stellako log drives. In 1967 local resort owner Doug Kelly moved to centre stage and carried out a personal and very public campaign against the drives that threatened the river's fly-fishing destination status. The Stellako, too, along with its salmon and trout, had a character that shaped the events. More difficult to control than its forest industry users would have liked, the Stellako also proved more resilient than its defenders thought it to be.

A Brief History of a Short River and the Context of Controversy

DESCRIBING the wonderful sport fishing opportunities in central BC in 1946, F.W. Lindsay cautioned that the region was "not a land of milk and honey." Rather, the trappers, loggers, sawmillers, farmers and ranchers inhabited a "primitive land of hard work", one where the pursuit of a "small measure of independence" took precedence over wealth accumulation. [17] Lindsay's characterization captured the essence of a hardscrabble existence that developed earlier in the century, when the Grand Trunk Pacific Railway opened new settlement possibilities and connected the region to forest and agricultural product markets. Tie cutting to meet the GTP's construction needs provided homesteaders with a source of cash income, with much of the cut destined for a small sawmill on Fraser Lake that brought the surrounding forests into contact with the railway.

The Stellako River became an essential link in this chain by the 1920s, an era when horses still provided the power for the initial stage of log transportation. Completing the process, the drives of logs and ties were an annual rite timed to make use of the late spring freshet produced by the melting snowpack. At the mouth of the Fraser, meanwhile, another industry faced a crisis brought on by a different railway. Canadian Northern construction activities in 1913–14 had blocked the upstream passage of spawning Sockeye, an impediment not eliminated until 1946. The Stellako drives drew little attention in the interim and the river's usefulness to the forest industry declined after a postwar surge in portable sawmilling decentralized regional processing.

In the mid-1960s, innovation in tenure policies gave rise to massive pulp and paper investment at Prince George and the Stellako's flows once again became vital to the functioning of a new industrial order. A modernized Fraser Lake sawmill would cut logs drawn from the forests around Francois Lake, but fishway construction on the lower Fraser had revived the Stellako's

Sockeye runs and a postwar boom in outdoor recreation now gave its Rainbow Trout prominence for sport fishers. Knowledge of log driving's destructive effects on fish populations in BC and elsewhere, inexact but persuasive in qualitative terms, contributed to critical scrutiny of a practice associated with the worst abuses of the North American lumbering frontier.

The Stellako entered the production sphere as a 'working' river during GTP construction. Newcomers, some genuine settlers along with many speculators, pre-empted land during an early twentieth-century boom, but the outbreak of World War I coupled with the end of GTP construction prompted an exodus. The holdouts settled in, cutting ties, trapping and homesteading. The floundering GTP, taken over by the federal government in 1920 and folded into the Canadian National Railways system, issued annual tie orders to contractors such as Olaf Hanson, Silvert Anderson, the Prince Rupert Logging Company and Jack Stanyer during the 1920s. They, in turn, sublet the work to settlers and Carrier loggers who hewed the region's Lodgepole Pine timber by hand, hauled it to the banks of Francois Lake with horses and boomed the wood for towing down the lake. Stanyer, from Southbank on the south shore of Francois Lake, introduced a steam-powered side-wheeler to the lake in 1923 for towing the booms to the mouth of the Stellako. In 1919 Dan Webster and Bert Black had established a steam sawmill on the shoreline of Fraser Lake, below the village. The mill burned in the summer of 1922, but over 1,000 men cut ties that winter between Prince Rupert and Fraser Lake. The operation reopened a couple of years later as Fraser Lake Sawmills Ltd., with a new partner in local merchant Mark Connelly. The mill cut 4,719.47 cubic metres (2 million feet) in 1925, doubled that the following year and also supplied the CNR with 25,000 ties annually.[18]

The hewn-tie industry, which may have produced over six million ties in the area between Prince Rupert and Endako from 1919 to 1930, entered a decline by the late 1920s. There were three main reasons. First, the opening of a creosoting plant in Edmonton in 1926 demanded that ties be peeled to accept treatment, a time-consuming procedure that the CNR did not reward with higher prices. Second, mill-sawn ties accepted creosote just as well as the hewn variety, prompting the proliferation of portable tie mills. Finally, creosoting tripled the lifespan of ties, reducing CNR demand. Tie-cutting, nevertheless, remained an important means by which settlers secured cash in the late 1920s and 1930s despite reduced orders. Logs as well as ties continued to come down the Stellako in these years; Fraser Lake sawmills took out

Top: Nechako Valley homesteaders. D-00465. **Middle:** Harvest time on ranch near Francois Lake, 1920s. I-52642. **Bottom:** Ties for Grand Trunk Pacific Railway construction, 1913. E-02782.

Top: Webster and Black Mill, 1923. NA-05436.
Bottom: Start of Stellako River log drive, 1929. NA-05726.

11,798.69 cubic metres (5 million feet) of logs from around Francois Lake in 1928, a record cut. When Dan Webster died in 1933, Mark Connelly and Bert Black became the chief Fraser Lake Sawmills shareholders, enduring the Depression by sawing a wide variety of building materials for the local market.[19]

The central interior's economic pattern went fundamentally unchanged during World War II. Despite a sharp increase in the number of portable bush mills and the introduction by larger operators of tractors and trucks to cope with longer hauling distances, logging remained a winter activity, with sawmills running from the summer until freeze-up. At Fraser Lake, Connelly, having taken sole ownership, sold out to Louie Dahlgren and a group of investors in 1946. By that time the company operated a planer as well, finishing lumber cut by smaller bush mills in the area. Dahlgren eventually acquired all the shares and two years later, no doubt anxious to take advantage of stronger markets, Fraser Lake Sawmills embarked on a project to 'improve' the Stellako. Log jams had always been a problem on the shallow, fast-flowing river. "The logs would jam up," drive foreman Harvey MacDonald recalls, especially on the rapids, at corners and at points where large rocks created obstructions. "Sometimes they'd jam up clear across the river and there'd be a lake behind. In front, there would be hardly any water at all." Breaking such jams was the most hazardous part of any log drive, a task requiring sure judgement and quick feet. "When you got the key log everything went!" MacDonald explains. "You had to head for the back end because you'd get ground up in front."[20]

Hoping to eliminate one such impediment, in 1948 Fraser Lake Sawmills undertook to create a new and wider channel around the south side of an island at Little Lake, where the Stellako met the Endako River (the two rivers then flowing together into Fraser Lake). They used heavy equipment to allow logs to pass unobstructed but they did so without first gaining approval of the federal Fisheries Department, which exercised jurisdiction over salmon habitat on the Fraser system. This created what local historians termed "a few uncomfortable moments" for Fraser Lake Sawmills. Prior to this the drives took place without federal interference, but by 1948 fisheries officials had new reasons for heightened concern over the Fraser's spawning habitat. That's a story that needs a brief consideration of the river's broader history.[21]

For millennia the Fraser's Sockeye runs had peaked every four years, with a dominant cycle yielding perhaps 30 times as many fish as intervening runs. So great was the run during these 'big years' that canneries at the mouth of

Top: Rock slide at Hell's Gate, 1914. A-04680. **Bottom:** Salmon weir at Fraser Lake, 1909. G-03743.

the Fraser could not hope to process all the available fish during the season. That pattern held until 1913 when the Canadian Northern Railway dumped tons of rock into the river at Hell's Gate, narrowing the channel and increasing the river's flow and turbulence at that point. A rockslide the following year worsened the problem and, while the 1913 Sockeye catch produced 2.4 million cases, neither the fish from that dominant cycle nor the next were able to pass the obstruction that closed off the up-river spawning grounds.[22]

Excavation efforts seemed at first to remove the impasse but 1917, the next anticipated peak year in the Sockeye's four-year life cycle, produced only about 500,000 cases. The numbers fell further during the 1920s, rarely exceeding 200,000 cases. By this time fisheries biologist Charles Gilbert, working for John Babcock of the BC Fisheries Department, had produced conclusive evidence that the Fraser River runs consisted of discrete races, each tied to a specific spawning river and nursery lake. Gilbert's confirmation of the home-stream theory had important long-term implications for fisheries management, but it provided no immediate solution to problems on the Fraser. Neither did debate over the relative impacts that over-fishing and the obstructions had on the Fraser River run decline. During the 1920s, though, engineering studies suggested that turbulence at Hell's Gate remained a significant barrier to fish passage. But no action was taken, as Matthew Evenden documents, with massive consequences for both Aboriginal economies and the commercial fisheries. As the fishing industry turned its attention increasingly to the Skeena, Nass and Rivers Inlet Sockeye runs and to the smaller coastal streams that supported Pink and Coho stocks, the Stellako runs declined with only "slight escapements" recorded between 1917 and 1937. Prior to this time Aboriginal catches in the years of dominant runs had been in the neighbourhood of 60,000 Sockeye, but by the time of the McKenna-McBride Commission in 1915 the Fraser Lake Carrier captured too few salmon for winter consumption. In 1938 some 3,077 Sockeye spawned in the river, raising hopes of a revived dominant run but, having been deprived of their traditional food source, the Carrier people had altered subsistence patterns by fishing at Babine Lake, trapping, moose hunting and undertaking seasonal labour. A federal clampdown on weir fishing at Fraser Lake and Stewart Lake only worsened their situation.[23]

Salmon canners responded to the crisis by calling for more hatcheries in addition to tighter restrictions on Aboriginal fishing methods. The hatchery solution to declining fish populations pitted fish culturalists against research findings accumulated during the 1920s that questioned the efficacy of artificial propagation, culminating in the Biological Board of Canada's 12-year Cultus Lake study on the lower Fraser River. That inquiry raised sufficient doubts about hatchery production, relative to the costs of the facilities, to prompt closure of all 10 federal installations on the Pacific coast in 1937. That same year, the newly established International Pacific Salmon Fisheries Commission (IPSFC) initiated thorough studies of the entire Fraser River watershed. As part of that program, the Stellako River's spawning populations were surveyed on an annual basis. The Hell's Gate question also came under rigorous investigation, leading to the construction of fishways in 1945-46 that opened up-river passage to spawners. That success prompted further fishway construction at other problematic areas, with the entire cost over the 1944-66 period coming to over $2 million.[24]

Top: Hell's Gate fish ladder, 1957. I-27808.
Bottom: IPSFC staff conducting studies on Stellako River. Courtesy of Pacific Salmon Commission.

Top: Fly fishing on the Stellako, 1948. I-20883.
Bottom: Plowman's cabins, Francois Lake, 1948. I-26303.

The results on the Stellako were evident immediately, with Sockeye escapement reaching 245,200 in 1946, the largest ever recorded. An IPSFC estimate put the Stellako's average annual contribution to the Fraser River commercial fishery at a value of $1,188,500 between 1952 and 1966, with perhaps 10 per cent of the Aboriginal catch along the Fraser originating from the Stellako. As mentioned, the river also gained renown as a sport fisher's paradise. BC Game Commissioner A. Bryan Williams described the Stellako as "an excellent fly fishing stream" in 1935, its swift waters yielding trout from one to three pounds in weight. When big-game guides Clarence and Enid Plowman opened the first tourist resort—Poplar Lodge—on Francois Lake, W.F. Pochin listed the Stellako in his 1946 guide to hunting and angling in BC. Eric Rudlam established Glennanon Resort near the Stellako's outlet that same year. By 1950 John Kost's Nithi Lodge operated at the east end of Francois Lake and in 1965 Doug and Betty Kelly purchased the Stellako Lodge. The lodges, along with the Menard Resort, offered amenities ranging from cabins to trailer courts, boat rentals and stores. "Visiting fishermen...love this stretch of territory," declared F.W. Lindsay, in describing the central interior's Lakes District, "for the lakes and creeks abound with trout." Bruce Hutchison considered the lakes west of Prince George to hold the "largest accessible reservoir of trout in America," Francois Lake being "invaded annually by Americans."[25]

Neither the sport nor Aboriginal fishery overly interested federal managers when Fraser Lake Sawmills embarked on their river 'improvement' in 1948, but the Fraser's recovery as a system for the production of commercial fish placed their actions in a new light. Fortunately, the 1948 log drive was one of the last for a time. Peeled ties continued to move down the Stellako until 1957, but in much smaller amounts than in pre-war years. After World War II road improvements encouraged the proliferation of smaller bush mills, with operators trucking rough lumber to the Fraser Lake Sawmill's planer for finishing and rail shipment. "It is a mystery to me why the small mills do not do their own shipping," the local ranger reported, "but they appear to be satisfied with the present arrangement." Truck transportation of logs to the mill also became more feasible. The company's main sawmill was dismantled by 1956 in favour of two smaller plants on Fraser Lake, with respective capacities of 20,000 and 15,000 feet. Two other 10,000-foot capacity mills also operated along the lake. As Ken Drushka relates, the portable bush mill came to characterize the interior forest industry during the 1950s, a development inspired by a healthy North American lumber market accessible by rail, the exhaustion of large stands of spruce and fir timber, and a remaining supply of smaller trees. Cobbling together a circular saw and log carriage powered by an automobile or truck engine allowed anybody with a small financial stake, "a bit of ambition and no fear of hard work" to acquire a timber sale and enter the lumber business.[26]

The frantic pace of activity in the central interior saw the Prince George forest district's cut increased seven-fold during the 1945–59 period, while total provincial production doubled. By the mid-1950s, as Lawrence A. De Grace noted, a "shift of the centre of balance from the coastal region to the interior forests" was very much in evidence, with structural changes also apparent in the Fraser Lake–Francois Lake district. Depletion of timber accessible to the small farmer or portable-type operator pointed to greater control by larger concerns able to afford costly Caterpillar tractors. BC Forest Service timber auctions became increasingly competitive as the province shifted toward a

Portable mill near Francois Lake, 1944. NA-08450.

sustained-yield policy under the 1948 *Forest Act*. In 1960 Minister of Lands, Forests and Water Resources Ray Williston sought to impose order by adopting a quota system, giving preference in timber acquisition to operators with a history in a particular Public Sustained Yield Unit (PSYU). Quotas quickly became commodities, with wealthier planer mill operators buying the timber rights of the bush mill men in a pattern of acquisition and concentration of logging rights. Fraser Lake Sawmills took this approach, acquiring several quotas along the west shore of Francois Lake. By 1960 the company had achieved dominant status in the Fort Fraser ranger district, described as a region of generally small operators and having a "generally penurious aspect."[27]

More sweeping structural changes were in store that would bring the bush mill era to an end. Anxious to promote pulp and paper production in the interior, Williston used a recent study of sawmill and logging waste in the Prince George region to lure corporate investment. MacMillan Bloedel expressed mild interest but declined to go ahead without assured access to timber beyond the fibre that might come from waste. The PSYUs had been established on a sawlog basis, leaving Williston to devise a new tenure arrangement capable of superimposing a pulp economy on the existing lumber industry. Canadian Forest Products, more enthusiastic about the prospect of operating a pulp mill on sawmill waste, ultimately entered a partnership with the Reed Paper Company of England. Toronto-based mining company Noranda was also contemplating diversifying into pulp production at Prince George.[28]

The ultimate solution came from forester Ian Mahood. While investigating timber supply for Noranda, Mahood came up with the idea for a new kind of tenure targeting the interior's mature timber considered too small for lumber manufacturing. Granting the new pulp mills access to this timber would, he reasoned, eliminate all fibre supply concerns when coupled with the abundance of sawmill and logging residues. That concept provided the basis for Williston's tenure innovation, the Pulpwood Harvesting Agreement (PHA), which he developed to meet the fibre requirements of interior pulp mills (see Chapter 3). The first went to the Canfor-Reed group's Prince George Pulp and Paper Company, which began construction in 1964. Noranda, after buying several small sawmills, partnered with the Mead Corporation of Ohio to obtain another PHA and launched Northwood Mills Ltd. in 1964. Northwood began buying chips shortly thereafter, completing a storage area as the first phase of its construction program. By early 1965, with its plant under construction, Prince George boosters had further reason for excitement as the prospects for a third mill looked good. Premier Bennett himself inspected the Prince George Pulp and Northwood sites in April 1965, just before the former company joined forces with the German firm Feldmuhle to secure a third PHA for their planned Intercontinental Pulp and Paper mill.[29]

The prospect of supplying chips from slabs and edgings to the new Prince George pulp mills, and perhaps another planned for Houston, promoted further consolidation and modernization in the sawmill sector. Area sawmill operators began 'tooling-up,' installing chippers and barkers. Fraser Lake Sawmills, situated at the eastern edge of PHA No. 1 in the Nechako PSYU, centralized its sawing, planing and chipping operations at the original mill site on the lakefront. Dahlgren and partner L. Strom invested in a new 35,000-foot capacity plant, planning to revive the river drive from their Francois Lake holdings. A gravel road ran from the eastern end of Francois Lake to the southern shore of Fraser Lake, providing a link to the sawmill, Highway 16 and the CNR line. But that would involve taking yarded logs to Francois Lake, placing them on trucks, hauling them to Fraser Lake and watering them again for booming. Drawing its logs from the lake with a conveyor, Fraser Lake Sawmills decided that the river's energy offered a cheaper means of log transportation than trucking.[30]

They were not alone in arriving at this sort of conclusion. Despite an aggressive government forest access road-building program, general maintenance and snowplowing problems made some operators reluctant to use them. Lack of capital on the part of the company's Francois Lake logging contractors may also have played a part in the decision to rely on the river, for that method removed truck maintenance and fuel expenses. Weighing the alternatives, Fraser Lake management opted to pay drive crew wages for a week or so rather than cut into the profit margin by footing a higher bill from contractors.[31]

By July 1964, when Fraser Lake Sawmills advised the Department of Fisheries of its intention to resume Stellako River log driving the following spring, fisheries officials were battling development on many fronts. The commercial salmon catch had doubled over the past two decades, but over 7,000 boats competed for the fish, with over 300 sophisticated purse seiners steadily increasing their share. Despite the surge of previous decades, the total annual catch weight was now in steady decline, from about 390 million kilograms (860 million pounds) in the 1951–55 period to about 284 million kilograms

(625 million pounds) in the years 1956–60. Tensions rose between recreational and commercial fishers over catch allocation. The overall impact of logging practices on fish habitat had become pressing, as the rate of cut expanded in all areas of the province. A referral system had come into effect in the late 1950s, in theory permitting federal fisheries managers to consult on the inclusion of stream protection clauses in cutting rights along the coast. But fisheries agencies lacked the necessary staff, and the Forest Service the enthusiasm, to make the process effective. As well, real and proposed hydroelectric developments had inspired a vigorous fish-versus-power debate. The federal Department of Fisheries and IPSFC responded with new technologies of salmon reproduction on several Fraser River tributaries, building spawning channels to boost their productivity. Reasonably successful but expensive, they represented no generally applicable solution to what Haig-Brown saw as "the continuing damage of bad land management."[32]

With the swing to truck logging well underway, fisheries managers now confronted a renewed interest on the part of interior operators to make use of rivers as transportation corridors. The practice, as noted previously, had a long and contentious history going back to the colonial period on the eastern seaboard of North America. By the late nineteenth century the logging frontier had shifted west to the Great Lakes region, where splash dam technology made the use of even shallow streams practical. Great Lakes lumbermen continued driving well into the twentieth century, over the protests of some fishing and sporting clubs, taking advantage of what William Rector calls "one of the cheapest means of transportation mankind has ever devised." The spring river drive, central to eastern Canadian lumbering as well, played a certain but unquantifiable part in the decline of the Atlantic salmon.[33]

On the west coast, California, Oregon and Washington streams proved just as important in the process of industrialization. In the Grays Harbor region of Washington State alone, loggers constructed at least 95 dams as aids to log transportation in the late nineteenth and early twentieth centuries. Most were splash dams: carefully engineered structures behind which a head of water backed up until the sluice gates were opened, sending logs downstream in the torrent of released flow. Few rivers in BC's south coastal region provided the proper size and flow to make effective log transportation routes. Frequent rapids and waterfalls disrupted efforts made on the Cowichan, Comox and Bella Coola rivers. Logs were left stranded along the banks and gravel bars,

Adams River Lumber Company, Chase, 1920s. F-09173.

with huge jams on the Cowichan requiring frequent use of dynamite. Splash dams were the most tangible manifestation of the conflict between forestry and fisheries. "There is no time of the year when sluicing or flood gate dams can be operated, without injury to the fishing interest, unless supplied with fishways," observed a Department of Marine and Fisheries officer in 1911.[34]

That danger of damage became tragically clear in southeastern BC where logging followed traditions set in the east. "Eastern methods of logging prevail," wrote a Golden observer in 1908. "We cut our logs in winter when the snow is on the ground, and haul them to the river's edge and in the spring they are floated." At Chase, the Adams River Lumber Company established a modern mill and townsite in 1908, cutting timber along the shoreline of

Shushwap Lake and towing the logs down the lake to the plant with stern-wheelers. By 1912, however, with the shoreline timber exhausted, the company engaged engineer W.D. Starbird to construct a 17.7-kilometre (11-mile) flume to bring the logs from the Bear Creek valley to the lower Adams River. Water from a small lake was diverted into the flume, carrying up to 353.96 cubic metres (150,000 board feet) of logs a day down to the river in just 15 minutes. A splash dam at the mouth of Adams Lake would, C. Heather Allen explains, "maintain a flow of water roughly equal to that of the spring freshet," with a system of gates being used to flush the logs downriver. When closed, the gates deprived the river of water for several months.[35]

The 1913 and 1914 Adams River Sockeye run survived in spite of the Hell's Gate slides, arriving after partial clearing of the obstruction, but the dam and the drives it powered now blocked all spawners from reaching their upper Adams River grounds. The lower Adams run felt the effects of the drives and the Hell's Gate blockage but survived in sufficient numbers to provide for a gradual recovery. Above Adams Lake, however, the Sockeye vanished despite the provision of a fishway in the dam. During the mid-1940s, 20 years after the mill had closed, the dam remained in place, although in a "bad state of repair". Its fate was determined in the context of the company's 1944 application

Adams River Dam. I-62756.

for renewal of its water licence and the prospect that the dam would be rebuilt for a resumption of drives down the lower Adams. Fisheries organizations, including the IPSFC, federal Fisheries Department, United Fishermen's Federal Union, the Salmon Canners' Operating Committee, Native Brotherhood of British Columbia and sportsmen's clubs opposed renewal and demanded the dam's removal. At hearings in Kamloops the Interior Lumber Manufacturers' Association supported the company's application, claiming that the most economical way to bring nearly three billion feet of Adams River watershed timber to market was down the river. The Kamloops Board of Trade, envisioning future power development on the Adams, also supported licence renewal. But pending construction of the Hell's Gate fishways tipped the scales in favour of the fisheries' interests. As *The Fisherman* put it, "it seems absurd that the [IPSFC] has been empowered to spend two million dollars upon the construction of fish ladders at Hell's Gate to allow sockeye greater opportunity to reach the upper Fraser River spawning grounds if such valuable spawning beds as those in the Adams River are allowed to be destroyed by logging or other interests." Denial of the application represented a rare victory in the fishing industry's struggle against habitat destruction but the dam left a legacy of genetic extinction that biologists only began to overcome in the 1990s.[36]

Fisheries managers had good reason to be concerned, then, when Fraser Lake Sawmills announced its intention to begin driving the Stellako again. Abundant evidence from BC and beyond showed the practice's destructive effects, despite the absence of rigorous studies. While the company made no mention of a splash dam, other river 'improvements' such as the removal of obstructions, straightening of bends and bulldozing of new channels would drastically alter the stream's ecology. Describing the effects of such modification in eastern North America in 1962, University of New Brunswick wildlife biologist Bruce Wright observed that the stream became "an efficient sluice, but a biological desert." Erosion of riverbanks, gouging of spawning beds and accumulation of bark deposits caused deterioration that persisted for many years. The University of Ottawa's Varim D. Vladykov estimated in 1959 that pulpwood drives deposited several million tons of bark in Quebec rivers annually, smothering both spawning and food production areas and releasing tannic acid which depleted the water's oxygen content. In Newfoundland, chief forester Ed Ralph estimated that each cord of pulpwood deposited

127 kilograms (280 pounds) of bark, with accumulations of perhaps nine tons on many rivers over the previous 30 years. Department of Fisheries official A.L. Pritchard presented a similarly grim estimate of the destruction of spawning grounds, eggs and fry in the maritime provinces. "One would find it almost impossible to assess absolutely the damage from this source," he concluded, "but it has been heavy and the productive capacity of the rivers has suffered."[37]

Fishery managers on the Pacific coast, aware of such reports and of the Adams River catastrophe, were justifiably wary. The Adams River situation had been described, for example, by the University of British Columbia's J.T. Pennell as "an outstanding example of what log driving can do to a river and its fish." Department of Fisheries Pacific Area Director A.J. Whitmore expressed cautious approval of what he considered improved industry practices at the 1955 Royal Commission on Forestry hearings held by Gordon Sloan. Progressive clearcutting had given way to patch logging, leaving more forest cover in place, and coastal operators made much less use of streams as yarding roads. But Whitmore also expressed concern about the growing interest in log driving, especially on shallow streams. Prince George mill men were using the Nechako, despite lower water levels caused by the Kenny Dam. Columbia Cellulose had been unsuccessful in driving the Skeena but persisted in its efforts on the Kitsumgallum, with plans to 'improve' the river for transportation purposes. Disturbing, too, were developments down the Fraser, where Western Plywood had begun towing logs to supply its new Quesnel mill. Further downriver, Martin Kester and the River Towing Company were driving log bundles through the Fraser canyon to Yale. One forest industry enthusiast envisioned the Fraser as a "potential access road 500 miles long from Vancouver to Prince George." While fishery officials in eastern Canada were welcoming a gradual transition to truck hauling, their BC counterparts had new reasons to worry about an old practice.[38]

Royal Commissioner Sloan, believing that Whitmore had underestimated the growing use of rivers for log transportation, recommended that the subject receive serious study as a basis for possible legislation. The IPSFC took a more tolerant view, during the 1950s at least. Only in the case of the Adams River dam had the timber and fisheries resources come in direct conflict in the Fraser watershed, and throughout North America splash dam technology was disappearing. "Lumber and sockeye need have no conflict in the years to come," the IPSFC declared in its 1952 annual report. The optimism held even as the pace of logging picked up in the central interior. Modern conservation practices allowed timber harvesting to be conducted without harming the sockeye's reproductive environment. Far more threatening to the IPSFC was the development of hydroelectric power, with its dams, reservoirs and river diversions. The 1960 Sockeye run, one of the best 'big years' in recent history, only seemed to confirm the two industries' compatibility.[39]

By 1962, however, logging of the Weaver Creek watershed near Harrison Lake on the lower Fraser had disrupted that stream's water regime. Low flows alternated with floods, producing erosion and dumping tons of earth and gravel on spawning beds. The annual catch value of the Weaver Creek run fell from $420,000 in the mid-1950s to $230,000. The IPSFC responded in 1965 with a $200,000 spawning channel, installing pumps and pipes to regulate flows from the creek and laying in gravel of the ideal size to maximize egg-to-fry survival. The Weaver Creek initiatives succeeded in boosting survival rates over the stream's natural productivity, but by 1965 the concerned IPSFC ranked logging alongside high dams and pollution as potentially disastrous in their collective impact on the salmon resource.[40]

If the wide-ranging impacts of logging of fish habitat merited increasing concern, industry's new enthusiasm for river driving in the northern part of the Fraser watershed proved mildly disturbing as well. Penny Spruce Mills began driving the Slim Creek tributary in 1954 rather than trucking logs to the Fraser for its main river drive. LeBoe Brothers used the Fraser to carry logs to their Crescent Spur mill. And Canadian Forest Products' chief forester Tom Wright predicted in 1959 that the interior's large lakes and rivers would come into increasing future use. After 40 years of operation, Cornell Sawmills initiated a Fraser River drive in 1956 as an alternative to truck hauling over muskeg. The company supplemented its mill supply by driving 1.2 million metres (4 million feet) of logs the next year and planned to bring in its entire annual cut, of 2 to 2.4 million metres (7 to 8 million feet), by water within four years. Cornell and similar operations were rediscovering the river to "beat the bugaboo of rising production costs," one *British Columbia Lumberman* reporter observed, adding: "no road building headaches, no hauling costs, no equipment depreciation." Sinclair Mills, one of the companies acquired by Northwood, also ran logs down the upper Fraser. Shelley Sawmills, one of the 'East Line' mills stationed along the CNR east of Prince George that had driven logs on the Fraser for decades, modernized by adopting high-speed boats to patrol the river and clear jams.

In the southern Cariboo, Western Plywood was said to be "eyeing the Quesnel and Fraser Rivers" as transportation routes; towing log barges and bundles had worked "after a fashion" but not well enough to satisfy managers.[41]

Western Plywood manager Don McColl's new 'modern scientific approach' involved installing a system of fin booms along the banks of the Fraser to prevent hang-ups. Rather than build an expensive network of truck roads on the west side of the Fraser on its Quesnel-based tree farm licence, the company inaugurated a 104-kilometre (65-mile) log drive in 1958, reducing transportation costs by a reported 25 per cent. "Determined men, with probing, answer-seeking minds," had turned the Fraser into an ally, declared reporter Joseph Des Champs. Confident that drives on the wide, deep, slow-moving main stem of the Fraser posed no serious problems, the Department of Fisheries allowed the drive to continue for many years. Of somewhat greater concern was Western Plywood's decision to begin driving the Quesnel River in 1963, but that also received approval (over Quesnel Rod and Gun Club protests), subject to Department of Fisheries restrictions on timing. The company used bulldozers to reshape channels for more efficient log movement, and over time large bark deposits and the scouring of the riverbed damaged spawning grounds.[42]

Richard Wright visited the Quesnel River in 1969, describing it as a "sluice box" in the process of ruin. "River banks are sliding into the water, gravel bars are disappearing, trees being uprooted," he observed, "and what river is left being solid with bark, branches, broken wood and debris." Despite booms and gravel dykes, at some points logs hung up on the banks and, as Wright noted, "worked away at the gravel bars, scouring and scouring and eroding with every movement of the water." Jet boats brought bulldozers placed on barges to clear logs from the bars. "Gradually the river is, in fact, being straightened out," Wright concluded. Wright's report in *Western Fish and Game Magazine* drew a swift response from Weldwood's public relations manager (having acquired Western Plywood in 1964). The Fraser and its tributaries were, like the Quesnel, in a constant state of change, W.D.G. McCauley retorted, their flows carving out new paths and eroding banks and gravel bars in a centuries-old natural process. At most, the drives had "a minimal effect on the total erosional process of these rivers" and constant monitoring by the Department of Fisheries ensured protection for the Quesnel trout and Sockeye populations. "Desecration of rivers" was not a company policy and differences of opinion could best be resolved by "a factual, rational and direct approach."[43]

A similar pattern is evident in another watershed, far to the north, where Columbia Cellulose began massive year-round log drives on the Nass River in 1959. The firm undertook an aggressive program of river 'improvements', using heavy equipment to clear new channels past islands and gravel bars and linking sloughs to produce clear pathways for log movement. As Western Plywood had done on the Fraser and Quesnel, Colcel installed a system of booms to prevent hang-ups on the banks and sandbars. Bulldozers constructed coffer-dam-like ridges at points to force the stream into more efficient paths. In late 1964 the Department of Fisheries tightened its authority with a regulation requiring the company to obtain a permit before releasing logs into the Nass. The measure also specified the time when logs could be placed in the river at certain points, and made further stream alterations subject to the agency's authority.[44]

Initial misgivings on the part of commercial fisheries' interests and the Nisga'a turned to outright opposition by 1968. Guy Williams of the Native Brotherhood of BC and New Democratic Party MLA Frank Calder, also speaking as head of the Nisga'a Tribal Council, expressed deep concern over the Fisheries Department's ignorance of the drives' impacts on salmon and oolichan populations and criticized the lack of co-operation between provincial and federal officials. Colcel responded with an admission that the 1968 drive had left many logs strewn along the banks of the Nass. However, a further round of 'improvements' would correct all the problems encountered in "bringing the river under control." The United Fishermen and Allied Workers Union (UFAWU) prepared a special report on the drives, calling for the establishment of a citizens' oversight committee and further independent research. "Many people feel that a 'snow job' has been done on this question," the union declared. The federal Fisheries minister and his Pacific coast staff defended their supervision, promising that Colcel's new measures would prevent a repeat of the jams and hang-ups. Their answers fell flat with the fishermen. "To many people in this part of the country the Nass River log drive…epitomizes how a large company appears to ride rough-shod and largely scot-free over a fishery resource where survival can be a highly delicate thing," wrote Richard Morgan. Colcel's drives represented "the inexorable closing-in of one resource's development over another."[45]

These late 1960s controversies over log driving on the Quesnel and Nass Rivers developed after, and were no doubt influenced by, the Stellako debate, but they merit consideration here both for what they reveal about the broader nature of industrialization in these watersheds and the public's increasing scepticism about what the provincial government advertised as a multiple-use approach to resource management. During the 1950s the UFAWU, individual commercial and recreational fishers, local rod and gun clubs and their provincial organization, the BC Federation of Fish and Game Clubs, had become more and more vocal in their criticism of industrial forest practices. It had become clear that the Department of Recreation and Conservation provided no counterweight to the power exercised by the Department of Lands, Forests and Water Resources. Moreover, its very creation had cost the commercial fishery its ministerial voice in government, with fisheries now a mere branch of the new department. A storm was beginning to brew as log driving returned to the rivers that drained into central interior lakes in the early 1960s.[46]

Logs piled on banks of Nadina River, 1965. Courtesy of Pacific Salmon Commission.

This Wasteful Use of a River: The 1965 Stellako Drive

THE STELLAKO APPEARED SAFE IN EARLY 1965. The federal Department of Fisheries had recently assumed new powers to prohibit or control log driving, the Sockeye run had recovered thanks to the Hell's Gate fishways and trout fishing drew increasing numbers of tourists to the Francois Lake resorts. Moreover, a road, albeit a rough one, connected Francois and Fraser lakes. Jeopardizing the commercial and recreational fishery for the sake of a sawmill's profits would be illogical. Or so it seemed, until H.J. Robichaud bent to provincial and industry pressure and approved the 1965 log drive as a concession to Fraser Lake Sawmills. A single drive, subject to federal restrictions and rigorous analysis, would enable the company and its log suppliers time to achieve satisfactory returns on the forest harvest.

The decision prompted a good deal of grumbling from the resort owners and local fish and game clubs; even the Prince George *Citizen* registered disapproval over seeming favouritism shown the company. But no massive outcry developed, although Howard Paish and other sportsmen had their suspicions about the industry's long-range plans for the Stellako and other rivers. Parks had been opened to development, clearcutting posed an ever-increasing threat to fish habitat, and the Prince George pulp and paper firms were poised to launch major operations in interior timberlands. Ottawa's capitulation on the Stellako did not bode well for the future.

But from the outset the controversy did not conform to a simple 'big industry versus the river' confrontation. Fraser Lake Sawmills, a mid-sized operation that served an important regional processing and shipping role, did not quite fit the stereotype of a greedy, uncaring multinational. Very quickly, log drive supporters in industry and the provincial government framed the issue in a way that actually shifted Fraser Lake Sawmills to the edge of the picture. Placed squarely in the centre were the small operators of Francois Lake, depicted as a group of hardy, frontier individualists whose precarious existence depended upon use of the river.

The 1965 Stellako controversy began quietly enough in the late 1950s, when a small mill on Francois Lake began a log drive on the Nadina River, which drained into the lake's west end. The Tachie River, which emptied into Stuart Lake to the north, was the site of a similar operation. Federal fisheries officer John Tuyttens visited both sites to set timing conditions for the drives to ensure that water levels would be sufficiently high to prevent scouring of spawning beds and so the logs would not interfere with the movement of Sockeye fry from the rivers to the lakes. The IPSFC noted that the "uncontrolled driving of logs" might damage eggs or young salmon in northern rivers, where the spring driving season coincided with their emergence from spawning beds.[47]

The Nadina and Tachie river drives proceeded over the next couple of years without raising great alarm and then, in the summer of 1964, Fraser Lake Sawmills submitted its notice of intent to drive the Stellako the next spring. That was in accord with a May amendment to the Department of Fisheries BC regulations giving the minister the authority to prohibit or regulate the driving, towing or booming of logs where such measures might pollute or obstruct spawning streams. Colcel's drives on the Kitsumgallum River had proven both inefficient and destructive. A new channel cut in 1949 had redirected the river's flow, producing scouring in several areas. Stranded logs piled up on spawning beds, requiring the use of bulldozers and dynamite and resulting in the "breakdown of river banks, gouging of bed, [and] disturbance and death of fish and eggs." Now the firm wished to construct a splash dam to improve efficiency. Horrified at the prospect of a repeat of the Adams River catastrophe and concerned about the recent increase in driving, federal officials took new authority to regulate the use of rivers.[48]

Discussions followed, with both the federal agency and the IPSFC registering strong objections to a resumption of the Stellako drive. Since 1948 the Stellako salmon runs had recovered to satisfactory levels of abundance, although the relative contributions of the Hell's Gate fishways and the lack of log driving were unknown. Moreover, the Stellako, a shallow river even during spring freshets, was particularly vulnerable.

The sport fishery also demanded some consideration. Postwar affluence, coupled with new technologies, led to an outdoor recreation boom. The replacement of bamboo with fibreglass after World War II reduced the cost of a fly rod by a third and the widespread use of outboard motors and aluminum boats increased angling on large lakes such as Francois. Over 185,000 licensed anglers frequented BC's non-tidal waters by the early 1960s and estimates put their value to the province's tourism industry at about $30 million annually. A wide variety of truck-mounted campers and travel trailers, available for rental or purchase, also contributed to the summer influx to the Lakes District. Poor fishing on the Stellako had prompted area rod and gun clubs to discuss closing the river in 1959, but angling improved over the following years along with the tourist trade for Francois Lake resorts. Although the increasing number of 'fisherman tourists' arriving in campers and trailers worried lodge owners, crowded government campsites on Francois and Fraser Lakes pleased storekeepers and restaurant owners. "The addresses are representative of almost every state below the border, and all the provinces in Canada," a Burns Lake newspaper observed in the summer of 1964.[49]

By early 1965 it seemed that the fisheries officials had made their case. Tuyttens referred to his department's "vital concern" in keeping central interior waters safe for fish production. Worries over pollution from the new Prince George pulp mills contributed to water quality issues in the region, despite Williston's promise that all possible protective measures would be taken to control effluents. "Will salmon returning to spawn still find the waters acceptable as 'home?'" asked Dick Phillips of Prince George. Yes, Williston assured worried fishermen. A failure to catch fish on the region's many fine rivers should not be blamed on the loggers, the mills or the tourists.

Preliminary reports that the log drive application had been denied pleased outdoors writer 'Salmo', who admitted to rushing the season after a late March 1965 visit with friends to the Stellako, "their favourite stream". The real trout action would not begin until May, when the young Sockeye began moving from the river to Fraser Lake. July and August were the best months for fly fishers but in September the abundance of salmon eggs provided a natural food source for trout, which frustrated anglers. During September one fisherman explained, "some people swear by the Stellako, and others just swear at it." At any rate, given long-accepted findings that bark and wood chip deposits hindered the development of salmon and trout eggs and could be fatal to fry, Salmo praised the apparent decision to prohibit the drive.[50]

It came as something of a surprise, then, when the federal government passed an order-in-council approving the drive in early June. What a Prince George *Citizen* reporter called "effective lobbying" by Fraser Lake Sawmills in Ottawa persuaded cabinet that running logs down the Stellako was the only practical transportation method available. The company had consolidated control over Francois Lake timber holdings and modernized the mill on the basis of cost estimates involving a drive, not the more expensive trucking alternative. Unspecified circumstances had overruled Fisheries Department objections, John Tuyttens explained, without going into detail.[51]

Cariboo Social Credit MP Bert LeBoe championed the company's cause in Ottawa. A prominent 'East Line' lumberman, LeBoe had entered the business at Loos, about 160 kilometres east of Prince George, with his brother Wilfred in 1939. They rebuilt the mill after a 1943 fire and in 1952 LeBoe moved to Prince George, becoming president of both the Northern Interior Lumbermen's Association and the Fort George Social Credit Association. Elected to parliament the following year, he quickly gained a reputation as "MP for the Cariboo mill man." A user of the Fraser's energy to supply his own mill, LeBoe defended Fraser Lake Sawmills' right to the Stellako in 1965, arguing that the potential for harm was exaggerated and that the company should not be forced to subsidize the fishing or tourist industries. Rather, Fraser Lake Sawmills should be given a government subsidy if denied use of the river.[52]

Log jam on the Stellako River, 1965. Courtesy of Pacific Salmon Commission.

Federal approval for the 1965 drive as an "interim measure" came with the assumption that there would be no repeat, and with strings attached. Logs would not be permitted in the Stellako until June 4, after Sockeye fry had emerged from the gravel, and the run should end by July 20, allowing spawning adults to enter without interference. Conditions as to jam clearance, including a ban on explosives, were imposed, along with limitations on the extent of stream improvements. The drive would also be subject to the first serious study of a North American log drive, a co-operative venture by the IPSFC and Department of Fisheries, in collaboration with the BC Fish and Wildlife Branch. By this time Stellako surveys had identified the major spawning grounds and, in addition to these nine areas, four sites were selected for detailed examination of the drive's effects. The provisions satisfied some interests. Fisheries Association of BC spokesman Ken Campbell considered the Stellako "well looked-after", but noted that "some of the new pulp mills going in undoubtedly will consider using the rivers." As Campbell observed, "It's certainly the cheapest transportation." He therefore rightly anticipated that the controversy might be the first of many.[53]

The drive began on June 6, with the release of 1,888 cubic metres (800,000 board feet) of logs. Over the next two days 5,899 cubic metres (2.5 million feet) entered the Stellako. These releases produced 26 major jams; 11 of them, the report noted, "on or adjacent to major salmon spawning grounds", with consequent erosion. The worst jam involved an estimated 4,719 cubic metres (2 million feet) of timber and extended from bank to bank, altering the structure of the riverbed sufficiently to practically eliminate one spawning bed. Two sets of brick or stone markers placed in the river to help determine effects were swept away or destroyed by high water speeds and shifts in the stream bed, by jams and by efforts to free the logs. Severe scouring and bank erosion occurred in several areas. On June 9 trays placed in the riverbed to estimate bark and wood fibre accumulations were removed. Their contents revealed that a tremendous amount of bark had been deposited on spawning grounds.[54]

By June 9 members of the East End Francois Lake Resort Association —representing Stellako Lodge, Nithi Lodge, Poplar Lodge, Menard's Lodge, Glennanon Lodge and Scott's Snug Bay Resort—had seen enough. They met that evening and decided to contact a Vancouver lawyer about a legal remedy. "It looks as if someone has dumped about ten barrels of turpentine into the river," said Association president and Nithi Lodge owner John Kost. "The bottom of the river is covered with bark." Campbell's "well looked after" remark elicited Kost's scorn: "We've been here a lot longer than he has. What does he know about it? We know the river is being poisoned by those logs." Cyril Shelford, member of a prominent Lakes District ranching family and a "rough-hewn logger-farmer" himself who had served as Social Credit MLA for Omineca since 1952 and was now chair of the legislature's Select Standing Committee on Forestry, downplayed the drive's negative potential. The logs were smaller than those driven during the late 1930s and Francois Lake salmon populations had not been harmed by those drives. Besides, Shelford said, this was mainly a federal issue. Skeena NDP MP Frank Howard agreed, if only on the jurisdictional question, when the *Citizen* informed him of the drive via telegram. He would ask the Department of Fisheries to investigate. Bert LeBoe also wanted facts. Fisheries officials believed that the drives would harm salmon but belief fell short of proof. "I said you've got to know," LeBoe told the *Citizen* in a story that credited him with prompting the current study.[55]

After a respite to clear the initial jams, driving continued on June 16 and 17. An additional 1,416 cubic metres (600,000 board feet) of logs entered the river, bringing the total to 9,203 cubic metres (3.9 million feet). Another two-week interlude followed before a smaller drive of 3,776 cubic metres (1.6 million feet) over the period July 3-7. Debris analysis continued until the end of July and biologists remained on the Stellako into the fall, seeking insight into the drive's effects on spawning distribution. During that month, then, the Stellako's energy moved 12,979 cubic metres (5.5 million board feet) of logs to the Fraser Lake Sawmills plant. A year would pass before the report appeared, however. Whatever the long-term consequences for the Sockeye might be, in the spring and summer of 1965 no one could dispute the damage to the sports fishery. Massive amounts of bark and wood fibre fouled lines, making the river "practically unfishable." The logs themselves, of course, threatened wading fishermen and kept the resorts' rubber drift-boats off the river.[56]

While the lodge operators fumed over lost revenues and fishermen contemplated the deterioration of a productive stream, developments outside the north-central interior helped shape the drive's meaning. Between 1948 and 1961 the provincial government removed 1.9 million hectares of land from the provincial park system, opening these areas to resource exploitation. Strathcona Park on Vancouver Island—BC's first provincial park—had been marred by the flooding of Buttle Lake in the 1950s for hydroelectric development. Over a million acres in Tweedsmuir Park were given over to Alcan's Kenny Dam project. Establishment of the Department of Recreation and Conservation in 1957 saw Strathcona lose its special status, becoming a class A park, in theory closed to resource development. Recreation Minister Ken Kiernan later reclassified a third of the park to class B status, opening that portion to mineral development by Western Mines.[57] Then, in early 1965, Kiernan went further and announced amendments to the *Parks Act*, allowing the government to reclassify any provincial park without debate. Kokanee Glacier Park immediately went from class A to class B status. An editorial outcry ensued. The new *Parks Act*, declared the *Victoria Daily Times*, was "little more than a convenient instrument to enable Recreation Minister Kiernan to wrest every cent of revenue from the parks, to treat them as sources of industrial raw material." Around the province, logging's threat to fish habitat had, by 1965, inspired a demand by sport fishers and the UFAWU for leave strips along streams. The BC Federation of Fish and Game Clubs wanted a major research project launched into the effects of deforestation on watersheds.[58]

The Stellako, its waters temporarily free of log releases as crews cleared the jams in late June, may have been on Roderick Haig-Brown's mind when he delivered a well-publicized speech to the Canadian Authors' Association convention at Victoria's Empress Hotel on June 21, 1965. Embittered by the damage to Strathcona Park and increasingly cynical about government and industry multiple-use claims, Haig-Brown declared his hatred for "practically everything British Columbia stands for." He went on to express disdain for the "shoddy, uncaring development of our natural resources, the chamber of commerce mentality which favours short-term material gains over all other considerations, the utter contempt for human values of every kind." Throwing in a reference to a "trivial provincial mentality that denies Canada's national heritage," Haig-Brown left many delegates shocked. "Downright rude," one listener remarked, and the association's Victoria president, James Audain, quickly disassociated himself from the critique, saying Haig-Brown was "living in the past" and unwilling to "make way for progress." For others, Haig-Brown's remarks captured BC's postwar development culture perfectly. While Arn Keeling and Robert McDonald are likely correct in claiming that most British Columbians, like Audain, embraced the "ideology of progress", Haig-Brown was far from alone. Tofino fisherman Roland Arnet, for example, thought the "I hate BC" speech expressed a sense of loss felt by many. So deep was the province's "infatuation with pulp mills, with growing cities, with accumulation of 'wealth' through the exploitation of nature," Arnet remarked, "that we are failing to see that the real 'gold' is slipping from our grasp."[59]

The Prince George *Citizen* gave brief coverage to Haig-Brown's speech and a guest editorial a week later attributed the Stellako drive and recent *Parks Act* amendments to meddling by misinformed elected officials. Without naming names, the writer chastised Kiernan and LeBoe, a former lumberman who had "suddenly developed a flair for fishery research", for overriding the advice of experts in their fields. In mid-July the *Citizen* denounced the absence of firm government policy on the Stellako, saying that the bar had been lowered for the sawmill company and treating the dispute as a simple forestry-fishery fight ignored the fact that *both* resources belonged to the people. "When transportation of logs can be achieved at a profit by other means than running rivers," the *Citizen* concluded, "then logs should not be run, if they damage fisheries."[60]

The region's sport fishers agreed wholeheartedly. The Prince George Rod and Gun Club, North-Central Zone of Rod and Gun Clubs and the resort owners, among other groups, were infuriated by the log drives and lodged protests with Ottawa. BC Federation of Fish and Game Clubs director and *British Columbia Digest* contributor Dick Phillips wondered: how, given the unanimous opposition of federal and provincial fisheries agencies, could the interests of a relatively small logging operation have taken precedence over those of the sport and commercial fishery and the river itself? Interior firms were now trucking logs up to 10 times as far as the 17.7 kilometres (11 miles) separating the Stellako's outlet; the mill and a road running south of the river connected the two lakes. The wisdom of employing experts to manage resources in the public interest only to have "short sighted and expensive political expediency" defeat the whole effort, escaped Phillips.[61]

The only consolation in "this wasteful use of a river," Phillips concluded, was that the episode had generated sufficient opposition that it would likely not be repeated in future. Others, mindful of the appeal river driving held for the forest industry, were not so sure. BC Federation of Fish and Game Clubs secretary-manager Howard Paish spoke at regional public meetings that autumn, as the organization shifted its focus from fishing and hunting regulations to ecological issues, taking a more militant response to depredations such as the Stellako drive. Next spring could bring a "test of strength" he said, perhaps a court battle if the drive went ahead again in the face of strong scientific evidence of its destructiveness. Paish's words, summarized by Geoff Warden in the *Quesnel Rod and Gun Club Bulletin* and then in *British Columbia Digest*, contextualized the Stellako incident in broad terms—as a function of headlong postwar industrialization that required a more effective lobbying response by recreationists. "It's like Paish said," Warden explained, "we outdoor buffs are resource-users without an industry to look after our interests." Going into land and water use disputes "hat in hand" with a desire to appear reasonable merely played into the hands of the hydro, logging and mining interests. Warden's assertion that "some lunkhead in Ottawa" had approved the 1965 Stellako drive raised the question: how could one rule out the same result in 1966? Paish's speech left Warden pondering not only the proper role of rod and gun clubs but the Stellako's broader significance. Industrial use of the river was not just a "local problem to the guys who saw some of the best fishing going down the drain," Warden concluded. "It turns out it's really a national issue."[62]

While some sought to achieve a broader perspective in this first round of the Stellako dispute, local economic effects could not be discounted. The Stellako might yield pleasure for fishermen, food for First Nations and returns for resort owners, but it was also part of an industrial structure that blended elements old and new. Joe Leslie presented what would come to be the dominant forest industry view in a *British Columbia Digest* letter, describing Phillips's Stellako article as a "hysterical outburst," either ignorant of the facts or "poison-pen reporting at its worst." Giving his address as Fort Fraser but failing to mention his position as Fraser Lake Sawmills' logging superintendent, Leslie set out his version of the facts.[63]

First, Leslie asserted, water transportation was an inalienable right, although he was ignoring both the province's *Water Act*—administered by the Water Rights Branch, which exercised provincial jurisdiction over the flow of water in BC streams—and Ottawa's recent amendment to the fishery regulations. Second, Fraser Lake Sawmills and others had driven logs and ties down the Stellako since 1920, in some years from the early spring runoff until September, with no regard for salmon fry or spawning runs. Far from declining, populations had increased over the past 40 years, Leslie argued, making no mention of the lower Fraser fishways. Third, aware of new interest in fish conservation, in 1964 the company had initiated discussions with the Department of Fisheries which resulted in conditions being set on the 1965 drive's start date and duration to avoid interference with fry or spawners.[64]

Finally, Leslie turned to the question of financial benefits. It was not the company that reaped the lion's share of the rewards, he explained. Fraser Lake Sawmills could survive for a good while without the Francois Lake logs. But the Stellako offered the only means by which 40 or 50 small operators in the Francois Lake–Ootsa Lake region could bring their logs to market. Closing the Stellako would not only deny them economic opportunity, "hundreds of millions of feet of timber would mature and die." Running the Stellako, on the other hand, meant the use of an otherwise inaccessible resource with considerable financial reward to the province through stumpage payments. The commercial fishery, by contrast, contributed little in direct revenues to provincial coffers. Even if one accepted estimates that placed the Stellako's Sockeye run at an annual value of over $1.5 million, the Prince George forest district generated $200 million worth of forest products in 1964. Leslie concluded that neither industry should suffer at the hands of the other as Phillips would have it; through co-operation both could "make use of our God-given resources."[65]

Leslie's retort tapped into some important currents in BC's postwar political culture. Conservation of resources, it was widely held, involved not their preservation but wise use, especially in the case of forests. Left standing, they would reach maturity, stagnate and fall victim to insect attack and disease. Sound forestry practice conducted on sustained-yield principles, according to this view, called for the removal of trees as they matured, to be replaced by fast-growing young stands. And while Fraser Lake Sawmills was far from an industry giant, in shifting the focus from the company to the small Francois Lake operators, Leslie crafted a populist argument with broad appeal. A Social Credit stronghold, the Lakes District west of Prince George remained committed to what Gordon Hak calls populism's idealized "egalitarian social order made up of independent, small producers." In depicting the Stellako conflict in terms of making life even more difficult for those who combined farming, ranching and seasonal logging while the main benefits flowed to the coastal commercial fishery, Leslie expressed regional social and economic tensions in a way that resonated.[66]

Leslie would not have the last word. Phillips fired back, saying that his opinions were based on consultation with Department of Fisheries, IPSFC and BC Fish and Wildlife personnel. His knowledge of themes that later appeared in the IPSFC report support this assertion. The federal order-in-council authorizing the 1965 drive was a matter of record, Phillips began. Nor could one accept Leslie's use of history in discounting the fisheries impacts of previous drives. The drives between 1940 and 1957 principally involved ties that were smaller than logs and therefore less damaging to stream banks and spawning beds. Cut fairly clean, the ties also introduced less bark and debris to the river. Any possible increase in fish populations could be attributed to better management, including the Hell's Gate fishways, and to the complete absence of drives between 1957 and 1965. Phillips also expressed doubt that all of the salmon fry had hatched before the 1965 drive and the trout, hatching later, would certainly have suffered.[67]

Turning to the troubles of the small operators, Phillips asked why their logs could not be cut at a Francois Lake mill, presumably the small Nicholson operation, or trucked to one of the many Burns Lake or Houston mills. Driving the Stellako was, he wrote, "not a life-or-death matter" to the Francois Lake loggers, nor was there any apparent danger of millions of feet of timber maturing and dying. Phillips claimed that Leslie had also erred in estimates of the region's forest production values and in giving the impression that the industry's vitality hinged on the Stellako. Only a small fraction of the region's total log output came down the river, and a more telling comparison would balance their value against that of the Stellako as a producer of fish. The logs could be trucked around the river; the fish had no alternative. "To survive, fish must have the river to spawn."[68]

Having learned that trucking would cost between $40,000 and $80,000, Phillips pointed out that the logs could still be processed at a price competitive with raw material trucked from other areas. The savings represented "an increase of net profit over and above normal profit," a clear case of "one industry profiting at the expense of another." The log drive had only a single, if dubious value, Phillips observed: creating the opportunity for a rigorous study of its effects on a small river. That, at least, should produce the "hard, cold facts" needed to assess future applications so that decisions could be evidence-based rather than made for political expediency. Leslie was correct in calling for co-operation in the use of natural resources, Phillips concluded, but if one accepted the dictionary definition of the term as 'to work together', the Stellako River log drive hardly qualified.[69]

The need for better coordination among resource agencies could hardly be denied. A Federal-Provincial BC Fisheries Committee had been established in 1964, facilitating consultation between fisheries officials from both levels of government and the BCFS, but the agencies pursued their respective agendas with little commitment to collaboration, as one biologist asserted in June 1965. That October, representatives of the provincial Bureau of Commercial Fisheries, the Fish and Wildlife Branch and BCFS met with federal Department of Fisheries staff to consider areas of conflict between the two industries. Topics included deposition of logging debris in streams, extension of the referral system from the coast to the entire province, and river driving.[70]

The BCFS had no jurisdiction over rivers, forester W.G. Hughes pointed out, and fisheries agencies could prohibit log driving as they saw fit. A Department of Fisheries official replied that federal policy was to prohibit the practice on salmon spawning streams and, where necessary, to regulate the use of those serving as migration routes. Shown a copy of the May 1964 BC Fishery Regulations amendment, Hughes acknowledged the department's opposition to the Stellako drive and asked if damage had resulted. With the IPSFC report still months from release, biologist F.C. Boyd explained that jams had caused major shifts of spawning gravel. Discussion then turned to the cost implications of a prohibition on log driving and it was agreed that the BCFS required early notice, since that "could result in adjustment of stumpage rates to compensate for increased log transportation costs." That prospect offered hope for compromise, but would the province be willing to make the required financial sacrifice? Stumpage payments were calculated on a profit-sharing principle and an increase in transportation costs for the operator cut into the province's share of the logs' market value. That made the BCFS—its role as a forest industry regulator compromised by its revenue-generation function—a less than enthusiastic partner.[71]

The revenue issue had come up a decade earlier, in the context of Colcel's plan to drive the Kitsumkalum. The company calculated that trucking logs would cost from 20 to 25 cents per thousand board feet, compared to just three cents or less for the companies driving logs on the Fraser. Driving the river would pay, Colcel manager C.B. Dunham informed federal fisheries officials, but BC stood to boost its take as well. Since the stumpage rate was based "on the difference between the actual cost of the logs delivered to the mill and their value at this point"; he continued, "the province was anxious that they decrease their hauling costs in order to increase the spread and consequently increase the stumpage."[72]

Dunham's explanation of the profit-sharing principle prompted Department of Fisheries Pacific Area Chief Supervisor A.J. Whitmore to seek a clarification from G.J. Alexander, BC's deputy minister of Fisheries. Was the Forest Service insistent on reducing transportation costs, as Dunham stated? Accepting the part of middleman, Alexander posed the question to his Department of Lands, Forests and Water Resources counterpart. It was true, he then advised Whitmore, that Colcel's lower costs would boost government stumpage revenues. But the deputy minister was emphatic that the Forest Service "does not in any way interfere with, nor dictate to the holders of various management licences, as to how they should conduct their affairs."[73]

Alexander came away from the conversation with the sense that while the province welcomed any boost in revenue, foresters "would not want increased revenue at the expense of fisheries." Dunham, then, had misrepresented the Crown-industry relationship in implying that the pressure to drive the Kitsumkalum came from government rather than the company. But BCFS insistence that it followed a policy of non-interference with regard to industry practices cut both ways. If the agency was innocent of pressing operators to reduce logging costs, with damaging consequences for fish habitat, it also could not be counted on as an ally in the campaign to improve or change those practices.[74]

That became evident in the early 1960s when coastal operations abandoned their short-lived experiment with patch logging as an aid to natural regeneration. The smaller clear-cuts that had drawn Whitmore's approval at the second Sloan Commission now expanded in scale as engineering factors overruled forest protection and renewal considerations in logging plans. Nor did fisheries interests make any headway in convincing industry and government foresters that they should adopt the practice of leaving strips of timber along streams to minimize debris loads, sedimentation and water temperature increases. "As long as the Province is supported chiefly by a forest products economy," explained one executive, "the needs of the timber user must be the principal consideration in the integrated use of all forest lands."[75]

Such pronouncements did not augur well for an easy solution to fish-forestry conflicts as pollution concerns assumed an increasingly prominent role in public discourse. Fouled streams and the loss of trout and salmon might seem inconsequential or even necessary to an expanding economy, BC Commercial Fisheries Branch Director R.G. McMynn wrote early in 1966, but to others the tendency to write clean water off in the name of progress was "unnecessary and an affront to human decency." McMynn made this observation while introducing an informed discussion of pollution issues for *British Columbia Digest* readers, mentioning the damage attributable to log driving but making no direct reference to the Stellako or any other river in his section on logging. McMynn had considered the subject more fully in a report tabled in the legislature in February 1966, describing log driving in shallow streams as a "constant threat to salmon production."[76]

The Stellako's symbolic importance figured prominently in other settings as British Columbians pondered the price of modernization. Delegates to the December 1965 Conference on Water Pollution at the University of British Columbia heard BCWF director Ted Barsby talk about the dangers of pulp mill pollution and increased logging before he turned to the Stellako as an instance of government-sanctioned logging pollution. The decay of bark on the riverbed deprived the water of oxygen, he explained, killing organisms and severing the food chain. In rendering spawning grounds unusable, "the fish is killed just as dead as it would be if it received a dose of poison," Barsby declared. In a province of such abundance, he asked, why should one resource be used to subsidize another? Commercial fisheries interests, with no provincial minister directly responsible for their industry, asked similar questions.[77]

Federal and provincial fisheries managers had their hands full with the log driving issue in early 1966. The Wannock River, running from Owikeno Lake into Rivers Inlet, had also been driven in 1965, bringing criticism from the UFAWU. Howard Paish spoke at the union's early spring convention, stressing the common interests of sport and commercial fishermen in bringing attention to the "general absence of integrated resource management" on the Stellako. Wildlife Federation protests had produced a short-term furor in 1965 and promised that, should another attempt be made in 1966, more would follow. The UFAWU followed up by taking out an honorary membership in the federation, the first labour union to do so. Federal Fisheries Department Regional Director W.R. Hourston appeared as well, conveying his department's determination to eliminate log driving on spawning streams in the interior, where the pulp mill boom promoted their increasing use.[78]

The 1965 Stellako drive had serious ecological consequences. Almost 1.8 million metres (6 million feet) of logs were released into the river without controlling their entry, producing enormous jams and the consequent scouring of spawning beds. Grinding against each other, the logs were stripped of their bark, which accumulated in huge deposits on the river bottom. Simple observation left no doubt that the drive had been destructive and, while the final report's release lay months ahead, provincial officials had been made aware of the situation. Angered by the drive and concerned that another might be in the offing, sport and commercial fishers hoped for more stalwart support from Ottawa should the river be placed at risk again.

Multiple Use or Wanton Destruction?: The 1966 Stellako Drive

THE 1965 STELLAKO DRIVE had alarmed conservationists and fishery interests but it had also come with the assumption that it wouldn't be allowed to happen again. That assumption proved unfounded. The spring of 1966 saw another run of logs, as Ottawa capitulated once more in the face of BC's insistence on control over provincial waters. The events of June 1966 stunned some observers, angered others and undermined the credibility of multiple use. Many felt the term had become simply a label for policies that sacrificed rivers, salmon and trout to constitutional one-upmanship in the service of provincial power and forest industry profit. Ray Williston would emerge as the dominant figure in this part of the drama, his cabinet colleague Ken Kiernan and federal Fisheries minister H.J. Robichaud taking roles as not-so-innocent bystander and overmatched sparring partner, respectively. Williston's victory would come at some cost to his reputation, though, and to that of federalism's capacity to produce a balanced resolution to resource conflict.

No one knew for sure in the early spring of 1966 whether the Stellako would be put to use as a log transportation corridor again that year. Seeking clarity in late April, representatives from the Department of Fisheries, IPSFC and BC Fish and Wildlife Branch met with Fraser Lake Sawmills' Joe Leslie. Hourston opened discussions by reminding Leslie that the 1965 drive had received "conditional authorization" only because the company had no immediate alternative method of moving logs from the western end of Francois Lake to the mill. Unfortunately, the BCFS had said no to possible lower stumpage rates on that timber, eliminating one easy solution. Nevertheless, the previous year's documented damage to fish spawning and rearing areas left Hourston's department no choice but to recommend that Fisheries minister Robichaud prohibit further log driving on the Stellako.[79]

Leslie admitted that the company could have devoted more attention to fisheries aspects but he emphasized—as he had in his *British Columbia Digest* exchange with Phillips—that the long record of pre-1965 drives had elicited no complaints. An IPSFC official countered, as Phillips had, that the Hell's Gate obstructions had made it impossible to calculate their effects. The subsequent recovery of Stellako salmon populations, coinciding with the cessation of drives and construction of the fishways, contributed to the difficulty of establishing "reliable cause-and-effect relationships." A swap of timber involving Fraser Lake's holdings in the eastern section of the Ootsa PSYU for blocks in the Nechako and Burns Lake PSYUs held by Quality Spruce Mills Ltd. of Topley might allow his company to truck some logs to the mill, Leslie said, but the Stellako remained the only outlet for logs cut along the western portion of Francois Lake. Moreover, over 14,158 cubic metres (6 million feet) of logs now sat in Francois Lake. Having recently acquired the Nicholson mill, some of the larger logs might be sorted out for sawing there, but that would leave 7,079 to 9,439 cubic metres (3 to 4 million feet) to be driven this year.[80]

Getting to the heart of things, Hourston asked how the company would react in the event of a prohibition. Fraser Lake "would be forced to fight elimination of the log drive," Leslie replied, and the imposition of a stop order would "necessitate a very critical examination of the company's position." With the threat of a suspension or curtailment of operations attributable to federal meddling on the table, Hourston turned to the 1965 jams. Leslie conceded that inexperience had resulted in "some operational difficulties." Could jams be prevented, asked E.H. Vernon of the Fish and Wildlife Branch? Many, Leslie replied, and the company would install booms to protect key areas if assured that driving could continue for several more years. Even in the unlikely event that the barter arrangement with Quality Spruce Mills came off, three or four years of driving remained. Trucking from Francois Lake to Fraser Lake was simply uneconomical, he explained. Steep grades demanded that loads be reduced in size to the point where trucking costs rose to $5.25 per 2.36 cubic metres (1,000 board feet), in contrast to the 75 cents-per-thousand figure of driving logs down the Stellako. Fraser Lake Sawmills had no desire to damage the commercial or sport fishery but could see no real alternative to the log drive.[81]

Ray Williston. I-32635.

Leslie's declaration of his company's position is important both for what it included and for what it did not. Absent was any expression of concern for the small operators of Francois Lake who would, as time went on, become more prominent in the public statements of log drive defenders. But clarity had been achieved at the meeting. The company was disinclined to consider trucking, and the province's refusal to make stumpage adjustments dimmed hopes for a compromise. When the quota transfer negotiations fell through, the ball was in Hourston's court. He informed Fraser Lake Sawmills of his department's ruling on May 4. Enclosing a summary of the soon-to-be released technical report on the 1965 drive, Hourston conveyed its "entirely valid" conclusions on the loss of salmon and trout habitat due to scouring and bark depositions. As well, Leslie had not convinced the agency that the road connecting the east end of Francois Lake to Highway 16 was unsuitable for trucking. The department's initial conclusion that the Stellako should not be used for driving was "unalterable," and the company's proposal to continue the river drive was "clearly unacceptable." A truck-hauling operation must be introduced, Hourston concluded. Upon receiving a copy of Hourston's letter, R.G. McMynn expressed his branch's full agreement with the federal stance.[82]

The Stellako issue was a topic of much concern when BCWF delegates gathered in Prince George for their annual convention on May 4, the same day Hourston communicated his department's decision to Fraser Lake Sawmills. The featured speaker, BC Minister of Lands, Forests and Water Resources Ray Williston, emphasized the need for "multi-use" resource development that gave prime consideration to outdoor recreation. Fortunately, his department and that overseen by provincial Recreation and Conservation Minister Ken Kiernan had the most co-operative relationship in Canada, one of "complete co-ordination." Over and above that, the two agencies had what Williston described as a close relationship and liaison with the federal Department of Fisheries. Within a couple of months Williston would turn down Kiernan's request for a stronger say in fish and wildlife habitat management on tree farm licences, but the Prince George convention gave Williston an opportunity to celebrate the achievements of multiple-use forest and water administration, not discuss the mounting contradictions.[83]

Also at the convention, Roderick Haig-Brown addressed that subject in a wide-ranging talk that touched on competing land use interests: the soaring demand for outdoor recreation, the commercial exploitation of parks, the need for better forest and wildlife management and a desire among commercial and sporting interests for strong fisheries. "The public mind has been dulled—often deliberately," he asserted, by assumptions that the province's fish, wildlife and recreational resources were of sufficient abundance to "withstand almost any abuse." Despite excellent federal research there was neither the imagination nor enthusiasm for proper fisheries management. A new provincial fisheries department would help, along with a closer "interlocking" of federal-provincial responsibilities, but both levels of government must take stronger action. Aside from its responsibility for negotiating international agreements, Ottawa provided research capacity and much-needed "remoteness from local commercial pressures." For its part, the province needed to introduce better planning processes and step up protection from pollution and a host of poor logging practices to curtail the "silent erosions" of stream productivity.[84]

Salmo considered Haig-Brown's speech the highlight of the convention. Published soon after in *British Columbia Digest*, the text was accompanied by an image of the Stellako River, its bed plugged with logs during the 1965 drive as a classic example of abuse. But Ottawa had not proven immune to commercial pressure on the Stellako in 1965 and the issue focused attention in a way that hundreds of dispersed, isolated logging operations did not. Fixed in time and place, observable and perceived as damaging to a range of interests, the Stellako log drives were about to leave the category of 'silent' erosion. They would do so not because of the Stellako's measurable economic importance, although that would play a part, but because of what the river came to represent in the context of north-central interior industrialization and a particularly contentious period of Victoria-Ottawa relations.[85]

Having muscled his way to victory in negotiations with John Diefenbaker and Lester B. Pearson over the Columbia River Treaty in a way that legitimized

Peace River hydroelectric development, W.A.C. Bennett was bullish on the central interior's economic prospects. Support from the mining and pulp and paper industries had helped confirm his vision for the simultaneous harnessing of both rivers' power. Prince George was the scene of frantic growth, inspired by Williston's tenure innovations and the new BC Hydro Corporation's capacity to generate cheap power for the three new mills. Having been elbowed out of the power picture on the Peace by Bennett and with the Pacific Great Eastern Railway pushing north from Prince George, Axel Wenner-Gren had surrendered control of a Peace River pulp mill to BC Forest Products in 1964. That firm undertook planning for the 'instant town' of Mackenzie, incorporated in 1966 as the base for a new sawmill and pulp mill that opened in 1972. This was province-building on a grand scale, implemented by Williston under Bennett's firm guidance.[86]

At the same time, and driven by the same commitment to provincial development without federal interference, the premier pushed at the perceived constraints of postwar co-operative federalism. "BC has been badly dealt with by the national government," he declared in May 1965, denying he had any wish to secede while bemoaning the Pearson administration's efforts to widen the gulf between Ottawa and Victoria. Bennett urged Ottawa to relinquish control of income taxes to the provinces, challenged federal banking authority with his Bank of BC scheme, asserted his right to make trade deals with other countries and took the occasion of the 1965 Dominion-Provincial Conference to assert his right to control off-shore oil reserves. No step by a national administration had caused more concern since BC's entry into Confederation, Bennett responded, than when Pearson referred that last matter to the Supreme Court. Provincial jurisdiction over natural resources was not a matter to be debated on the grounds of legal technicalities. Highways minister Phil Gaglardi put it more bluntly, warning Ottawa to "keep its cotton-picking fingers off all our resources."[87]

Conservationists like Haig-Brown found such political posturing, and the accompanying denial of national vision and authority, distasteful. But while BC accepted Ottawa's jurisdiction over that other offshore resource—salmon —either because of the fishery's lacklustre revenue potential compared to forestry or because its defence demanded restrictions on a more lucrative sector, the Stellako controversy occurred during a serious struggle for advantage in natural resource issues on the west coast. In this context the short Stellako

River's fate took on great significance in the summer of 1966 as a kind of test case in the shaping of resource policy. Precedents might be set, with implications for forest practices and intergovernmental relationships around the province.

Such issues were specifically raised at the BCWF's Prince George convention, where Williston and Haig-Brown set out their quite different perspectives on the state of resource management. With the support of other sporting groups, a Prince George Rod and Gun Club Stellako River resolution expressed concern that a repeat drive would "lead to the establishment of another precedent which will be difficult to dispose of." Use of rivers by the new pulp mills threatened to become a widespread practice, especially in the interior where log driving was a ready and cheap alternative to expensive roads. Having learned that studies of the 1965 drive indeed confirmed the original objections, delegates approved the resolution, which sought strict federal and provincial control on the running of smaller rivers and streams. Major rivers such as the Skeena, Fraser and Columbia would be subject to looser regulation.[88]

It would be "interesting indeed" to see the dispute's outcome as June brought the annual rise in the Stellako's waters, Salmo observed. In the convention's aftermath, interests staked out their positions. Hourston said the IPSFC study, still over a month from release, showed that drives were "pretty hard on the fish." LeBoe reaffirmed his support for the company; trucking was too costly, and a ban on the drive would constitute a subsidy of the commercial fishery by the timber industry. Dick Phillips, now a Wildlife Federation vice-president, hoped that the Department of Recreation and Conservation would play a role in defending the sport fishery.[89]

By early June 1966, however, all expectations of federal-provincial cooperation on the Stellako vanished. Minister of Fisheries Robichaud gave official notice to Williston, Kiernan and Fraser Lake Sawmills that he would not issue a permit for another Stellako River log drive. Research had proven beyond doubt that the 1965 drive had "immediate and accumulative adverse effects on the river's productive capacity." Robichaud then informed the *Citizen* of his decision, soon after Williston went on record endorsing log drives as an efficient method of moving logs from Francois Lake to Fraser Lake. Demanding further study, Williston said that if the drives conducted over the past decades were so detrimental, the Stellako should be empty of fish. More study was needed.[90]

That set the stage for a shocking June 9 announcement by Williston: the company was unable to pay stumpage on some of the logs in Francois Lake.

His department had, therefore, seized the logs, which would be driven down the Stellako by the company under the provincial government's authority. Once in Fraser Lake the logs would be scaled to determine their value. When the government had claimed its share to cover the stumpage fees owing, the remainder would revert to the company. "Rivers are a provincial resource and a provincial responsibility," Williston told the *Citizen* in a telephone interview, explaining his defiance of Ottawa. His agency had co-operated fully with the Fisheries Department, but it had failed to reciprocate—a full copy of the report on the 1965 drive had yet to be received.[91]

If Williston had not yet seen the report in full, he certainly knew enough about its findings to deny their validity. So did Bert LeBoe. Holding tenaciously to the principle that no logging operator should be forced to subsidize the fishing industry, but defending the company's right to compensation for increased transportation costs if denied use of the river, LeBoe described the 1965 drive study as "almost entirely pure nonsense." Williston's seizure of the logs, in any event, placed the prospect of a 1966 Stellako drive in an entirely new light. A conflict involving a small company and a federal bureaucracy had become a direct test of wills between Victoria and Ottawa. Williston seemed to be spoiling for a fight, a point Dick Phillips drove home in expressing amazement at the frightening speed at which the minister's typically slow-moving department had acted.[92]

Phillips did not need to see a scientific report. Any Stellako fishermen could attest to the results of log driving: "the bottom in many areas covered with inches of decomposing and decomposed bark, chips and such residue, bank gouging, gravel removal, and similar destructions." The Francois Lake resort owners, fish and game clubs and conservationists were disturbed at the direction and pace of events, but it was the lodge operators who had the most to lose in the short-term. Prospective visitors who had lost fishing time the previous year, they claimed, had communicated their intention to cancel reservations if the drive went ahead. Preparations were underway for the drive to begin when members of the East End Francois Lake Resorts Association met on Sunday, June 12 to discuss a course of action. Enid Plowman expressed the group's bitterness best, saying, "We don't even have a government when something like this takes place." Some favoured going the legal route and seeking an injunction but Doug Kelly wondered if a successful court action might result in the group being held liable for the company's trucking costs. "What have we got to lose," another lodge operator replied. "If we back down now they've got us beat."[93]

Direct action, including a 'halt or hamper' strategy also came up for consideration. The resort owners might all gather at the Stellako's mouth in their boats and go fishing when the logs were set for release. "Let them arrest us," one told an interviewer when asked about the possible implications. "If we go to jail, all the better." The Stellako First Nation also had a stake in the outcome. Both the river and the road to Fraser Lake ran through their reserve and in the past the band had charged fishermen a toll as they motored west to Francois Lake. Chief Moise Isadore now hinted that the band would attempt to stop the drive if not compensated for use of the river. Isadore recalled that payment was to have been made the previous year but did not think that the money had been received.[94]

Just what action Ottawa would take remained a mystery. Hourston was under instructions to simply report when the drive began; any decision on a response would come from the capital. A provincial conservation officer stationed at Burns Lake made the surprising announcement that, until told otherwise, he intended to challenge the drive on the grounds that no permit had been issued. As his crew made final preparations, Leslie described the controversy as both unfortunate and unanticipated. Omineca riding MLA Cyril Shelford asked why the Stellako had been singled out for a ban. Drives continued on some eastern Canadian rivers and Fraser Lake Sawmills had been targeted unfairly while operators elsewhere carried out the same practice.[95]

Ultimately, the lodge operators would join the BCWF in going the legal route, making only a token 'picket protest' by piloting their boats around the mouth of the river when the drive began just after eight o'clock on the morning of June 14. Neither tactic seemed to worry Williston, who in the preceding days had taken steps to define the drive as both a principled exercise of the province's jurisdiction over rivers and a scientific endeavour. Ottawa, seeking control over BC waterways by virtue of its mandate under the *Fisheries Act*, had presented no convincing evidence to support a ban. The province would pursue definitive answers, however, by engaging the BC Research Council (BCRC) to study the upcoming drive. Moreover, this would not be an uncontrolled drive such as those that had been carried out over the past 40 years, "without apparent ill-effect" according to Williston. The drive would be conducted under strict controls, with BCRC and Water Resources Branch staff on site to undertake rigorous study of its ecological effects. Evidence of damage would mean an end to the Stellako drives, Williston promised, even though the loss in stumpage revenue to the province might run into the millions over the following years. "This whole thing will straighten itself out," the minister told reporters, "but whatever is decided must remain for all time." Without indisputable evidence of damage to the fishery, log transportation would continue on the Stellako River.[96]

By the morning of June 14 the Stellako dispute had achieved more than regional significance. "A new battle between BC and Ottawa about federal-provincial rights began in this northern interior community today," the *Sun* reported from Fraser Lake as the first release of the drive's 18,878 cubic metres (8 million feet) of logs began moving down the river. But if the nature of the fight seemed clear, the *Sun* story went on to provide additional insight on the motivations behind the province's seizure of the logs. Fraser Lake Sawmills did owe stumpage fees, but an unnamed senior Forest Service official admitted that the real reason was to challenge Department of Fisheries jurisdiction. "The provincial government did not want to see the logging operators bound-up in a contest with Ottawa," he explained, "so it seized the logs." In effect, by daring Ottawa to take legal action under the *Fisheries Act*, Williston hoped to make the Stellako a jurisdictional test case. Hourston thought it "too bad" that the province would put the spawning grounds at risk once more, but Fraser Lake's sawmill manager again brought the Francois Lake loggers into play. Closing the river meant curtailing operations and throwing those 60 or so small operators out of work.[97]

"How much is a salmon worth?" the *Sun* asked in its editorial. With an International Woodworkers of America strike looming, the Bennett government's sermons about the need for a calm, rational resolution of labour-management conflict seemed "hypocritical," even "grotesque" given its handling of the Stellako dispute. Nor, with Strathcona Park recently opened to development, was the government's conservation record one to inspire confidence in its fisheries management skills. Williston's "pooh-poohing of federal objections" in favouring logs over salmon might be expected, but where was Conservation minister Kiernan? "Would it be too much to suggest that he voice an opinion?" the *Sun* asked.[98]

While Kiernan avoided comment, 8,000 logs went down the Stellako on the drive's first day, timed to take advantage of high water. Sockeye fry had not yet begun their migration downstream to Fraser Lake, nor had returning adults appeared. The resort owners and Wildlife Federation had gone ahead with an application for a writ of mandamus that, if granted, would force federal Fisheries Officer John Tuyttens to enforce his department's order under the *Fisheries Act*. Justice J.S. Aikens denied it on the grounds that neither Tuyttens nor BC Attorney General Robert Bonner had been served proper notice. With time running out, the drive opponents would press ahead on the legal front. Another two booms, totalling 11,780 logs, followed on Wednesday, June 15, bringing the two-day total to over 1,831 cubic metres (776,000 board feet). Ottawa, meanwhile, did nothing, although acting Fisheries minister J.W. Pickersgill assured the House of Commons that the government would take "appropriate action." Deputy minister Dr. S.V. Ozere provided more clarity, saying that no decision would come down before the end of the week, until after the receipt of field reports.[99]

As feelings escalated on the drive's second day the Prince George *Citizen* offered a sharp perspective on the role of experts, on the larger issues at play and on those who had been caught up in the Stellako affair. The fisheries experts may not be correct, the paper observed, but their conclusions should have been accepted until the weight of evidence proved them wrong. Understanding why they had been ignored demanded a recognition that the Stellako's run of salmon mattered little in the battle over the control of watersheds with hydro-power development potential. The current conflict, a year in the making, was "merely a detonator for a far larger explosion." It made little sense, then, to cast Fraser Lake Sawmills as the "villain in the piece," since its owners were mere middlemen in the federal-provincial struggle. Finally, the *Citizen* referred to the "cavalier treatment" of the Stellako people whose undisputed claim to the waters running through their reserve, along with their demand for compensation, had been disregarded entirely. They counted among the pawns in the Stellako game, along with the recreational and commercial fishermen, conservation officers, lumbermen and resort owners. "The arena in which the struggle is taking place could have been better chosen," the publisher concluded.[100]

His counterpart at the Burns Lake-based *Lakes District News* saw the controversy in much the same terms. Expressing regret at the hard feelings caused and hoping not "to add fuel to the fire", he emphasized that both the sawmill company and the resort operators were "caught in the squeeze" of two

First boom arrives at start, Stellako River. NA-23442.

governments determined to make a test case of the Stellako. Everyone in the region had known the dispute was coming to a head and a resolution should have been achieved before erupting into a full-scale stand-off.[101]

The dispute's divisive nature continued to play out in the voices of locals as well. Mrs. J. Riderley of Summit Lake, reading the *Citizen's* Stellako coverage with "regret and sorrow", asked how parents could raise their children with a proper respect for the law given Williston's defiance. If truly a matter of principle, control of the river should be referred to the courts. But the Prince George Rod and Gun Club, sponsor of the Wildlife Federation convention resolution, now retreated from the Stellako conflict. With Northwood Pulp just weeks away from entering production alongside Prince George Pulp and Paper, and the town in the midst of a boom that had more than doubled its population over the past decade, president Jim Slesinger said the club would take no further action until log driving had been proven harmful to fish. "It's people like him who come to the lodges and scream and holler if they can't catch a fish," an infuriated Resorts Association president John Kost responded in the *Citizen*. "But they won't take action beforehand." Williston's defence of his policy as one of principle, assertions that water levels were sufficiently high to prevent disturbance of spawning beds, and assurances that his officials exercised strict control over the drive contributed to Kost's disgust. No matter how high the water, pollution from acidic bark deposits was lethal to fish life, he maintained.[102]

Responding to Kost's blast, Slesinger accused the resort owners of putting their own private interests above public welfare. Kost, concerned only about a week of lost tourist revenue, had no regard for the much greater financial losses that the loggers would suffer if denied use of the river. His club's convention resolution had not been motivated by a desire to discriminate against anyone, he explained. Then, hinting at discord between the Prince George sportsmen and the Wildlife Federation, Slesinger added that the "organization and dispensation of that resolution has much to be desired." Caught up in the swirl of competing social and economic forces in his community, Slesinger restated the need for conclusive evidence of damage to the Stellako's spawning beds and fish stocks before disrupting Fraser Lake Sawmills' operation. If the effects were so severe, Williston should have received a full report of the 1965 study.[103]

More logs remained to be run and the 1966 Stellako drama was yet in its early stages. On Thursday, June 16, crews opened another boom containing 4,553 logs for release. On that day, another interest joined the fray when the UFAWU's general executive board decided to launch a vigorous protest campaign against the Socreds' contempt for federal fisheries law. The Stellako drive illustrated perfectly the sort of irresponsible management that contributed to the long decline of the salmon resource, the union asserted. The fishermen would make their views known to federal and provincial representatives, and explore the possibility of co-operating with the Wildlife Federation in the legal effort to halt the drive.[104]

As the logs swept down the river, Vancouver-Burrard Liberal MP Ron Basford rose in the House of Commons and drew a Speaker's rebuke by asking Robichaud what he intended to do about the BC government's "callous disregard for the welfare of our salmon industry." That same day Robichaud telegrammed his official disapproval to Williston, perhaps motivated in part by a large jam that had developed at the river's mouth which took tugs over four hours to clear. "They call them control problems," Kost remarked, but the drive was plagued by jams over the entire length of the river. Robichaud informed Williston that the provincial government's defiance was a "matter of serious concern". Even though there was clearly no lingering doubt about BC's challenge to Ottawa's jurisdiction over coastal and inland fisheries, Robichaud requested a wire clarifying the province's position.[105]

The Fisheries minister explained to the House of Commons that serious legal questions had to be answered before taking action, but conveyed his willingness to consider submitting the issue to the Supreme Court of Canada. He had done all he could for the moment; it would be improper for one level of government to seek an injunction against another. Peace River Conservative MP Gerald Baldwin saw the Stellako in the context of W.A.C. Bennett's disregard of federal authority in damming the Peace River, a navigable stream that crossed provincial boundaries. Would the minister consider launching an injunction and then go to the Supreme Court if unsuccessful? BC must make its position known before taking action, Robichaud repeated; in the meantime he would seek an opinion from the Justice Department. Robichaud may have been biding his time while awaiting the outcome of the private legal action launched by the East Francois Lake Resort Owners Association and BCWF. Acting on their behalf, lawyer Roland Johnson had arranged for Tuyttens to be served notice of their writ application on the evening of Wednesday, June 15, with Attorney General Bonner receiving his the next day. Johnson would not appear before Justice Aikens in Vancouver until the following Monday, however, which was destined to be the drive's final day.[106]

Friday, June 17 was a busy day on the Stellako, and on the political and legal fronts. With the previous day's jams cleared, over 17,000 logs entered the river, and Williston expressed delight at Robichaud's vague threat to take the Stellako issue to the Supreme Court. "Let's find out if the Fisheries Act permits the federal government to take unilateral action over a provincial resource that is not harming a federal resource," he declared. The burden of proof lay with Ottawa and it had not been met. Worse yet, federal fisheries policy was conducted on a "one-resource basis", unlike the province's multiple-use philosophy. Williston went on to dismiss drive opponents as "emotional"; his observers had seen no fish in the river and high water levels coupled with controls ensured that spawning beds went undisturbed. "Yet listen to the protests!" he said, apparently bemused at the lack of understanding. Undeterred, and despite knowing that court action would come too late to stop many logs from being driven, the Wildlife Federation and Francois Lake resort owners pressed on doggedly. Even if issued after the fact, the writ would serve a purpose. Giving up now would be an open invitation "to drive all summer, high water, low water or no water at all."[107]

By the end of the week Williston's efforts to cast himself in the role of principled defender of provincial rights had failed utterly to swing the tide of editorial opinion. But if the Stellako was the scene of a debacle, there was plenty of blame to go around. The *Victoria Daily Times* attributed it all to one of the Socreds' "self-inflicted disabilities." Kiernan had yet to be heard from and, in eliminating its fisheries department in favour of branch status within his ministry, the government had deprived itself of the public servants needed to offer wise counsel on an important economic sector. While some wondered about the province's ability to come up with a more reasoned policy than simply telling federal authorities "that they can whistle", others pointed the finger at Ottawa. "No wonder this country is falling to pieces," declared the *Citizen*. Why had federal fisheries officials "shuffled around" on the river for so long, doing little more than hoping for a private legal action to succeed? In Cold War terms, that was the equivalent of "being invaded by the Russians and sending the Boy Scouts to start fighting before the country declares war." Whether one accepted Williston's 'point of principle' argument or not, BC was destined to win without a fight, another failure of national leadership that saw Canada being cut into what the *Citizen* called "an unappetizing pie." Columnist Maurice Western held out hopes for a stronger stand by Ottawa. Robichaud had expressed some willingness to "meet Mr. Bennett in a judicial showdown", one attributable to the premier's "Jesse James approach" to co-operative federalism. Having ignored the federal government's interest on the Peace River, his administration had done so again on the Stellako. Only Ottawa, it seemed, had any responsibility to consult during this period of provincial government activism.[108]

The public commentary eased off over the weekend, but if anything the pace of activity on the Stellako picked up. On Saturday, June 18 over 17,400 logs went out and on Sunday crews unleashed three booms consisting of almost 23,900 logs. Reporting from Francois Lake, with the drive almost over, Larry Emrick foresaw the tiny community soon returning to its normal routine of "looking to the needs of its livelihood—the tourist." The drive's ramifications rippled widely, though, and aside from the main federal-provincial conflict, it had pitted two of BC's departments against each other. Or had it?

While Williston had defended the BCFS's interests and the Fish and Wildlife Branch sided with the feds, Kiernan had remained on the sideline. The minister had not yet spoken and a letter from the resort owners had gone unanswered. Howard Paish observed that "the minister of conservation as long as it doesn't interfere with logging, mining and all the rest", had "pulled the rug out from under his own department."[109]

The *Vancouver Sun's* Ian MacAlpine added to Kiernan's embarrassment with a column that imagined a meeting between him and Williston. In this scenario, Kiernan enters the latter's office with a report written by one of his staff and learns that Williston has the Stellako matter well in hand. "Fisheries chaps in Ottawa" were using the Stellako as a "gimmick to get their hands on our rivers." Just like in the offshore oil rights matter, Kiernan agrees but suggests that Williston look at the document. "Seen it," he replied, referring to McMynn's 1965 report on fisheries, which had been tabled in the legislature but not released to the public, but the document was irrelevant to the Stellako anyway. The river was running at peak flow and the chances of spawning bed gouging were "as remote as [NDP leader Robert] Strachan knocking over the Chief in the next election."[110]

Kiernan, his "brow furrowed" in MacAlpine's fictional account, admits it's none of his business, expresses a fervent desire to be left out of the dispute but refers again to the report, quoting a section that presents a generally alarming picture of the hazards posed by logging and river driving to fisheries. "Like what hazards?" Williston asks. "Listen to this," Kiernan responds, going over findings on the disruption of flow regimes, bark and debris deposits, and finally reading the report's conclusion that log driving was a practice inconsistent with wise resource use. "That's all very well Ken," retorts Williston. "But where's the proof?" Practicality demanded that a stand be taken on the Stellako. "If we knuckle under to a few guys trying to play nurse maid to a bunch of fish, we're leaving ourselves wide open to the same kind of guff from those who would say power dams are harmful to salmon." Expressing fervent agreement, Kiernan refers to his approval of Strathcona Park mining, along with a wish that the public leave such things in their hands. "People just don't understand, Ken," Williston says as Kiernan departs. "They just don't understand."[111] MacAlpine made all this up, of course, but the story seemed plausible enough in capturing the Socred cabinet hierarchy, the marginalization of fisheries science and the Stellako's place in the larger political scheme of things.

On the afternoon of Monday, June 20, the last of the logs entered the Stellako, "amid a confusing welter of legal technicalities and bitter protest", reaching Fraser Lake at about 10:30 that evening. Just over 25,000 logs, the largest single-day movement, concluded the 1966 drive. Over the seven days an estimated 106,728 logs, representing over 18,900 cubic metres (8 million board feet) of timber, had gone down to the mill booming grounds. But their passage had not been the smooth, controlled flow of raw material Williston had promised. A total of 29 jams, the largest involving some 2,500 logs at the Highway 16 bridge, had formed over the week. The consequences became a matter of debate the following year, with the release of the BCRC report. Leslie described the Highway 16 bridge jam as the only "serious misfortune", expressed his company's regrets about negative public opinion and explained that every effort had been made to keep booms clear of the Francois Lake resort areas.[112]

But if the drive was over, the controversy surrounding it was not. On Monday morning Roland Johnson appeared in a Vancouver courtroom on behalf of the Wildlife Federation and resort owners, still in pursuit of the writ of mandamus. The action stalled there, however, with Johnson and Crown lawyers agreeing to an adjournment until Friday so that cases could be prepared. In the interim, drive supporters and detractors kept the Stellako issue percolating in public discourse. That same day the Northern Interior Lumbermen's Association expressed support for Williston, protesting Robichaud's "arbitrary stand" and weighing in on the alleged ecological impacts of log driving on the Stellako. These were greatly exaggerated, said manager Bob Gallagher—misleading the public. High water and a swift current ensured that bark and other wood debris washed downstream rather than settling on spawning grounds, and that same natural process kept these areas in a constant state of change even without the presence of logs. Nor had the sport fishery suffered to any great extent, and the image of fishermen "lined up in droves" to fish the Stellako further distorted reality. Serious anglers avoided the river during the freshet. Controlled drives should be allowed to continue, Gallagher concluded. Area logger Ray Baxter's experience on the Stellako led him to contrast the practical wisdom of industry veterans who had driven the river for years, seemingly without harming the fishing, to the education of federal fisheries experts—"a mess of graduated youngsters from alleged schools of learning." He claimed the latter's' misguided efforts, instigated by the complaints of "money hungry" resort owners, constituted an unwarranted interference with the more important industry. [113]

BC First Nations had both local and province-wide reasons to offer a dissenting opinion. The Stellako flowed through a reserve and coastal First Nations still played a prominent if declining role in the commercial fishery. Guy Williams, president of the Native Brotherhood of British Columbia, expressed his organization's conviction that the Stellako case represented a threat to the incomes of hundreds of fishermen. First Nations would be particular losers if the province persisted in "making the salmon industry expendable in the financial interests of logging operators." Not only should the Francois Lake logs be trucked, Williams maintained, logging in general should be kept well back from the banks of productive rivers. [114]

Even though the last log had been run, all interests were well aware that the larger issues remained unresolved. Would the Stellako be subject to further drives? How many other rivers would be pressed into the service of the forest industry? More importantly, hydroelectric schemes for the Fraser, such as the Moran dam proposal, were still alive. Could fisheries interests count on Ottawa's support in challenging such developments? Would Kiernan ever speak out?

Additional fuel for the fire arrived on June 22, with the release of the 85-page IPSFC report on the 1965 drive. First providing data on the Stellako's commercial and sport fishery resources, valuing the former at $1,188,500 annually and noting that the latter was likely destined to take a major place in the local economy, the report went on to consider the "long record of unsatisfactory experience" in North American streams with characteristics similar to the Stellako. Thankfully the practice had come to an end in Washington, Oregon and California. Among rivers in the western United States, only the Clearwater in Idaho was still used for log transportation, but even there the drive avoided important steelhead spawning areas. Still, despite all the evidence—from Maine and New Brunswick to the Adams, Quesnel and Kitsumgallum (Kitsumkalum) rivers—that log driving "could only adversely affect" the Stellako's salmon and trout populations, permission had been granted in 1965. [115]

Focusing on the Stellako spawning grounds identified since the early 1940s, the co-operating agencies devoted considerable attention to the destructive effects of jams. At four critical sites selected for intensive study, scouring eroded 19.23 square metres (23,800 square yards) of "choice spawning grounds", representing 8.6 per cent of the river's total capacity. Less severe scouring occurred at numerous other sites, along with many points of bank erosion. Cumulatively, the researchers concluded, a significant amount of spawning ground had been lost to the 1965 drive, with effects that would persist for several years, and further driving would only worsen the deterioration.[116]

A second component of the study, involving estimates of bark and debris deposits, looked at the trays and other sampling equipment set out in the riverbed before the drive. Pre-drive collections found very little material but, when researchers repeated the procedure three days after the drive began, they found significant additions of fresh bark in the river. Another round of samples taken 21 days later produced similar results. Together with 28 days of final sampling, begun on June 30, these studies showed that the amount of bark and debris on the riverbed had "increased tremendously" since the drive began, remained higher than pre-drive levels in October, and the rate of decomposition would not eliminate the accumulations within a year. Future drives would add to the river's load of contaminants, threatening its natural ecology as decomposition increased carbon dioxide levels in the water. Water quality studies found little chemical contamination through the leaching of tannin from bark and wood, but the study warned that the "potentially dangerous consequences of increased organic decomposition are clearly indicated."[117]

The study team offered no firm conclusions concerning the drive's effects on Sockeye, Chinook and trout eggs and fry. Although the 1965 drive had been timed to allow most Sockeye fry to emerge from the gravel, some Chinook fry remained in the river during the drive period. As for the trout, their eggs would still have been developing during the drive. Field observations provided no real insight on their fate, although the report concluded that "those located in areas of severe scouring would have had little chance of survival." Moreover, Chinook and trout eggs and fry would continue to feel the drive's effects after its completion, as bark and wood deposits reduced the river-bottom organisms available for food. Finally, despite the fact that most salmon fry had emerged from the gravel beds, many had not made their way fully into Fraser Lake before the drive.[118]

Findings on the drive's implications for salmon and trout spawning were more definite, and more damning. Stellako Sockeye spawning counts had been conducted by area since 1938 and a detailed 1950 survey of the river had mapped the distribution of spawners by individual gravel bars. Since that time the annual counts had continued, determining that 22.3 per cent of the runs spawned in the lower Stellako. But in 1965 only 11.9 per cent of the Sockeye used that portion of the river, a smaller proportion than any previous year. The total number of spawners in the lower Stellako also declined relative to the average, reflecting a decrease in available spawning areas. Comparison of the 1965 spawning distribution with historical maps belonging to the same cycle, particularly that for 1953, supported this conclusion. The 1965 spawning distribution throughout the entire lower Stellako showed a marked reduction from that of 1953, particularly at the most severely scoured sites.[119]

Quantifying their findings, the research team calculated that the 1953 Sockeye run had been able to use 34.28 square metres (41,200 square yards) of spawning area. In 1965, by contrast, only 14.21 square metres (17,000 square yards) were occupied, a loss of 20.07 square metres (24,200 square yards) that had "apparently become unusable or at least undesirable to adult sockeye spawners." As much of this same area was subject to scouring or other damage during the 1965 drive, the report attributed the lion's share of the loss to that event. Some salmon likely found alternative areas upriver, but during dominant runs the much more numerous spawners would be forced to occupy less suitable breeding grounds.[120]

It was by no means certain, however, that Sockeye forced to spawn in marginal parts of the river would do so successfully, and a continuation of the drives could only further reduce the Stellako's productivity. The report had much less to say about the drive's impact on trout spawning, except to note that most Rainbow Trout used only two sites, and the sort of disruption noted for Sockeye might therefore have even more severe consequences. Only a few Chinook were observed in 1965, and the undisturbed spawning area seemed adequate to their needs, although increased competition among all salmon species during dominant Sockeye cycles could be expected.[121]

Some evidence also suggested that the Sockeye did not easily adjust to new spawning areas, even if they were available. Studies from the Karluk River in Alaska indicated that most spawned in the precise stretch of gravel from which they had emerged as fry. If unseeded during a run, such areas would yield no fish in subsequent years. The troubling history of the Nadina River, flowing into Francois Lake, supported that conclusion. Log driving and associated rechannelling over the previous 10 years had displaced the entire Sockeye population from its original spawning grounds in that river. Some had strayed to spawn in other areas of the Nadina, but the runs had been greatly diminished, and the returning Sockeye avoided several miles of apparently undisturbed gravel bars within the original spawning grounds. Increased deposits of sand, silt and organic material might explain such behaviour but, whatever the cause, displacement could only result in eventual overcrowding in alternative spawning beds.[122]

Concluding the most intensive study of a North American log drive ever conducted, the technical staff of the IPSFC, Department of Fisheries and BC Fish and Wildlife Branch advised that the spawning grounds supporting the Sockeye, Chinook and trout populations of the Stellako River should be protected from further damage. "It is recommended that the Stellako River should not be used for log driving," the report's final words read. It escaped no one's notice, of course, that the report's central recommendation appeared the day after the river *had* been subjected to another drive.[123]

The report received widespread press coverage, and some regretted its unfortunate timing. Wildlife Federation vice-president Dick Phillips thought an earlier release might have prevented the 1966 run. Issuing a summary of the report to the press, The Fisheries Association of BC agreed, arguing that policies subject to inter-agency tension and "political considerations" would negatively impact the commercial fishing and resort industries, sport fishermen and central interior Aboriginal peoples who relied on the Stellako as a food source. The *Nechako Chronicle* published the analysis and provided its own brief account of the findings, describing the breakdown in communication between governments as deplorable. These interpretations of the Stellako issue rested on the questionable assumption that an earlier release would have influenced Williston. Nor did they address the question of the report's delayed appearance, which hinted at Robichaud's lack of enthusiasm for a direct confrontation with Victoria. The findings were available, at least in summary form, for earlier release, but waiting until the drive's completion had preserved Robichaud's freedom of inaction. In the short term, however, the report placed Williston on the wrong side of the best science available. Williston had said that the provincial government needed sustained evidence of damage; the *Province's* Norman Hacking observed, "He now has the evidence."[124]

Williston asked why the report's release had been delayed for so long. Admitting on June 23 that he had not yet read it, he called the report inconclusive and "highly controversial." He himself had "lived beside the river for

21 years" and he claimed that apart from the selfish resort owners, local residents had shown no interest at all in the matter. Rather, the whole row had been "blown up by coast people." Dedicated to the quest for unbiased scientific knowledge, he hoped to have his BCRC report on the 1966 drive in a few days. But the first interim report did not arrive on his desk until September, and neither that document nor a second submitted in February 1967 were released. The final BCRC report only went public the following month. For the moment, Williston could only bemoan the lack of understanding that gave rise to such controversies. "Everybody," he remarked, "believes in the multiple use of resources except the one they are interested in."[125]

But was the 1966 Stellako drive an instance of multiple-use resource policy in action, the *Victoria Daily Times* asked, or a case of Williston ensuring that the province capitalized on its financial interest in the logs? What if the minister was wrong in his conviction that the drive caused no injury to the fish? Apparently confident in the BCRC's impartiality, the publisher predicted a highly embarrassing time for Williston if the report indicated otherwise. But if the IPSFC report caused Williston some initial discomfort, he showed no inclination to back down. The recent drive was justified, he informed the *Citizen*, in order to obtain independent findings on its fisheries impacts. The feds could not be trusted, he implied; the IPSFC report had been withheld not only from him, but even the BCRC had been denied a copy. He had finally obtained a copy from Kiernan and turned it over to the BCRC without reading it. Preliminary indications from field officers who had inspected the just-completed drive seemed to confirm the wisdom of his decision. "They can see nothing really damaging," he remarked, but added that if the BCRC turned up evidence of harm he would allow no further drives. The public could anticipate immediate release of the BCRC study upon its completion; he had "nothing to hide."[126]

Besides, Williston told Ian MacAlpine, if he was so determined to harm the Stellako's fish runs, sending the BCRC in to investigate would be "colossally stupid." Once again he issued assurances that, unlike the IPSFC findings that had been shaped by Ottawa's desire to discredit log driving, his BCRC study would generate unbiased conclusions. "If the report tells me I'm crazy, well I'm crazy. There it is," he declared. Conservationists remained decidedly skeptical about Williston's commitment to scientific rigour, and the as-yet-uncompleted report generated its own controversy. At a Wildlife Federation press conference Howard Paish observed that while the 1965 IPSFC study included six federal biologists, an equal number of its own experts and several engineers, the province sent one lone biologist to investigate the 1966 drive. Dr. Craig Walden, head of the BCRC's biology section, pointed out that technical experts from both levels of government were co-operating with biologist Ian V.F. Allen, whose independent assessment for the province would take several months to complete. This was neither a superficial exercise nor a matter of scientific competition. Unconvinced, R.G. McMynn would later characterize the BCRC effort as nothing more than an attempt to "disprove the original fisheries report."[127]

Through it all, McMynn's minister Ken Kiernan remained "conspicuously absent" from the controversy. "Missing: one minister of conservation" read the first line of a *Province* editorial. Even though his own Fish and Wildlife Branch co-authored the IPSFC study, Kiernan had done nothing to stop the 1966 drive. "Either uninterested, or ineffectual, or both," he bore the primary responsibility for damage done to the Stellako. Under fire for inactivity during the early summer of 1966, Kiernan's actions were found even more deplorable by many. Western Mines had just received his approval to establish a townsite in Strathcona Park and Tweedsmuir was to get a landing strip. In this context, the "conservation minister who does not conserve," as the *Victoria Daily Times* called Kiernan, earned ridicule for taking a stand against the contribution disposable bottles made to the litter problem. Even if one thought that the dangers to the Stellako's fish populations had been exaggerated, a position Victoria's Bert Dodd took in criticizing the *Province*'s coverage of that issue, the paper's essential critique of Kiernan seemed sound. Dodd even went further, citing the recent "selling, desecrating, and spoiling" of wilderness lands in characterizing him as the "most dangerous minister to have held that portfolio in my memory."[128]

Commercial fisheries interests agreed. Calling the recent drive a "crime against nature and against a large industry," *Western Fisheries* columnist Gerry Kidd implored Robichaud to make good on his threat of a possible Supreme Court case. The UFAWU, however, placed little faith in the federal minister who had demonstrated his disinterest by authorizing a 1966 log-towing operation on the Wannock River, by failing to take action against Japanese and American fishing fleets and by doing nothing to stop the Stellako drive. The UFAWU saw the industry consistently losing out as the province's modernization gradually eroded vital salmon spawning habitat. A massive campaign in defence of the resource's status "as a vital economic, recreational, and aesthetic part of British Columbia's heritage" was needed.[129]

That campaign would not involve a local legal battle, at least on the original terms. At the end of June 1966 the BCWF and resort owners withdrew their now pointless request for a court order to have the Stellako drive halted. Federation lawyer Roland Johnson would instead look into the possibility of laying a private charge against Fraser Lake Sawmills under the *Fisheries Act*. Meanwhile, Howard Paish kept up his attack on Williston, questioning the validity of the BCRC study. The minister responded by accusing sportsmen of using "scare techniques" and trying to cloud the issue. Paish countered that it was Williston who sought to confuse the public by refusing to accept the IPSFC report. How could a serious comparison be made between the two studies, Paish asked. Twelve biologists and engineers had taken almost a year to analyse the effects of the 1965 drive, an impressive array of expertise compared to the sole BCRC biologist assigned to the 1966 instalment. "It's high time the people of this province were scared occasionally at the wonton destruction of our natural resources," Paish asserted.[130]

W.A. James of Victoria, expressing outrage at Williston's "sheer gall", agreed. The minister knew of the IPSFC findings as early as May, when Hourston had addressed the Wildlife Federation's Prince George convention. Expert opinion was available from the province's Commercial Fisheries Branch, but Williston, rightly suspecting their negative stance on log driving, went to the BCRC instead. But Williston's "snow job" was not the worst of his sins, James observed. More disturbing was his lack of respect for federal conservation laws, saddening indeed for parents seeking to instil proper moral values in their children. Victoria fly fisherman P.B. Wrixon, who knew the Stellako, shared James's contempt for Williston's actions. "I wonder who he is trying to fool?" Wrixon asked. Having moved "foolishly and in a precipitous manner" to defy the federal ban, thereby "driving another nail into Confederation" and damaging a fine river, the minister had turned to the provincially funded BCRC to cover his bad judgement. Reporting on all this, Norman Hacking concluded that the fight between Williston and the conservationists was "just warming up."[131]

Just what sort of ally federal Fisheries minister Robichaud would make in the struggle remained unclear. On the west coast to attend the Steveston Salmon Queen Festival in early July, he spoke of Ottawa's heavy investment in spawning channel projects on the Fraser and Skeena rivers. The Stellako dispute had not been forgotten, he assured his audience; advice from the Justice Department on possible legal action could be expected soon. That statement, and a discussion with Paish, left the conservationist somewhat cheered but short of confident. The Wildlife Federation remained vitally concerned with the Stellako not just because of the intrinsic problems raised by the 1965 drive, he explained to Robichaud in subsequent correspondence, but because of the precedents involved. The organization's application for a writ of mandamus had been motivated in part by his department's failure to enforce his own order, and the federation remained dedicated to seeing the jurisdictional question resolved. As long as doubts persisted over the control of fisheries and water resources, habitat would continue to suffer in the face of industrial expansion. The option of taking further legal action by laying a private charge, a measure that would cast doubt on his department's competence, had been rejected. But the Federation had no intention of allowing the issue to be forgotten "only to erupt once again at a later date, or on some other river."[132]

Paish wanted assurances that doubts about Robichaud's willingness to show some spine in protecting the province's fisheries resources were unfounded. He would wait. The universally harsh media treatment of the provincial government begged fundamental questions about Robichaud's enthusiasm for his role as "guardian of the resource." At the very least, Paish wrote in a *British Columbia Digest* analysis, the Department of Fisheries should have been better prepared for the legal tussle. No one, at least, doubted Williston's resolve, and in Victoria the *Province*'s Ian Street sensed a federal bluff. "No one here seems to expect a showdown this time," he reported. Vancouver-Burrard Liberal MP Ron Basford hinted that Robichaud was made of sterner stuff, telling the UFAWU that Ottawa was prepared to take a stand. Williston had threatened the "whole constitutional basis" of an expensive federal fisheries program and a reference to the Supreme Court could be anticipated. Only one thing was truly clear, Street observed: the fish had become almost incidental in a test of strength that pitted Ottawa's jurisdiction over salmon against Victoria's power over forests and water rights.[133]

The 1966 Stellako affair also caused divisions within the conservationist camp and pitted local people against each other within Lakes District communities. At the end of June the directors of the BCWF met in Vancouver, expressing their extreme disappointment at the statements made earlier that month by Prince George Rod and Gun Club president Jim Slesinger. In conveying his own views rather than those of the club, Slesinger had acted inappropriately, Paish observed. But the Prince George group backed its president with a public statement of support for his "non-committal" position on the Stellako. Anxious to avoid becoming "embroiled in a political dispute or a scientific argument between various scientific bodies," the Prince George sportsmen would await the outcome of Williston's study. Given the nature of the community's emerging industry—one so dependent upon an uninterrupted flow of fibre—a place on the sidelines no doubt seemed appropriate.[134]

The same sort of tensions manifested at Burns Lake, but here the lines were drawn more boldly. Reports of two recent meetings appeared in the July 20 issue of the *Lakes District News*. Over 40 members of the Lakes District Sawmill Association had attended a special meeting, called the previous week, to discuss the Stellako drive. Expressing their unanimous support for Williston's defence of the multiple use of BC streams, the lumbermen appointed MLA Cyril Shelford, Joe Leslie and Alan Blackwell of Wistaria to draw up a letter of approval for Williston. Another letter, protesting discrimination against the industry, would go to Robichaud. "As logging is the main source of income for the area," the meeting resolved, "economic transportation of logs is essential." But members of the Tweedsmuir Park Rod and Gun Club had their own lively gathering that week, coming out with a unanimous denunciation of Williston. He, Shelford, Kiernan and other MLAs were all sent letters of protest.[135]

Perhaps the strongest and most thoughtful conservationist critique of the events of 1966 came out of Quesnel, a community not unfamiliar with river driving. A July Rod and Gun Club *Bulletin* piece, probably written by Geoff Warden, that was reprinted in the *Lakes District News* summarized the IPSFC findings and scorned Williston—"that eminent authority on fish and fisheries"—for declaring them inconclusive. That the minister had done so without first reading the report seemed, oddly enough, quite logical. "We believe him," the Quesnel group observed. "No man in his right mind who had read the report could with a clear conscience declare that it was inconclusive and should be ignored." In its "asinine arrogance" the provincial government had betrayed the trust of the public—the true owners of both the forests and the fish—in order to save Fraser Lake Sawmills a few thousand dollars and to assert its control over rivers. From Quesnel, the Stellako affair revealed a "crippling" absence of planning and co-operation among government departments, the power of Williston's ministry over Kiernan's and a fine example of "the way we rape a resource in good ol' Dynamic BC."[136]

Stellako log drive supporters responded to the criticism with a renewed effort to frame the dispute in a way that highlighted the plight of the small Francois Lake farmer-loggers. Fraser Lake Sawmills would purchase no more of their logs until the Stellako question was settled, Williston and Shelford reported in late July. Shelford, speaking as one of about 50 members of the Grassy Plains and District Small Loggers' Association, likened the federal government to a bully that picked on small operators while leaving the large pulp companies of Quebec and Ontario free to drive central Canadian rivers.[137]

Lakes District Sawmill Association secretary Alan Blackwell warned that loss of the log market would cripple the economy in a large area north of Francois Lake. Annual log sales to Fraser Lake Sawmills brought in about $200,000 annually but the operators had borrowed to acquire equipment. Joe Leslie's announcement of an end to log buying, pending a resolution, made for a bleak future of lost income and unpaid debts. Their logs were trucked up to 48 kilometres (30 miles) before being dumped in the lake, he explained, and the operators could not afford to lift them out for a second stage of trucking to the Fraser Lake sawmill. Blackwell's point was not entirely invalid. The road running west along the north side of Francois Lake from the Highway 16 juncture came to a dead end after several miles. But why, Cicely Lyons asked in her 1969 history of the salmon industry, did the provincial government not simply extend the road westward to the logging area and make it suitable for logging trucks? While that question hung in the air, some of the Lakes District operators announced their intention to go on welfare if denied their log market.[138]

Completion of the BCRC report would provide a potential break in the federal-provincial impasse, Shelford suggested. And September brought signs of intergovernmental co-operation, when the much-criticized Kiernan announced that truck hauling would replace log driving on the Homathko River, which drained into Bute Inlet about 225 kilometres (140 miles) north of Vancouver. Towing operations on the Wannock River would not be repeated in 1967 either, thanks to a new $280,000 Forest Service road connecting Owikeno Lake and Rivers Inlet. Clearcutting in that watershed remained a distinct threat and the Stellako drive represented a stark violation of the "rules of conservation and good sense," Norman Hacking remarked. But the Wannock development was nevertheless a welcome instance of "mutual understanding and compromise" between the salmon and logging industries. Or was it a glaring example of inconsistency? A *Citizen* editorial reprinted in the *Lakes District News* asked: if log driving threatened spawning on the Homathko, how could the same not be said for the Stellako?[139]

If conservationists held out any hope that Williston's BCRC study would contribute further scientific grounds for an era of co-operative good will, initial findings held out little promise. A September 29 progress report forwarded to Williston a few days later presented a carefully worded though generally supportive analysis of the 1966 drive. Tagging two per cent of the estimated 106,728 logs driven and recovering 714 of those logs in Fraser Lake for bark loss inspection, I.V.F. Allen determined that over half lost no bark at all. Losses from most of the rest varied from 10–30 per cent. Only 10 per cent lost 40–80 per cent of their bark, and none lost all of their bark. The total amount of bark deposited from the study sample would near two tons, and laboratory tests confirmed that the deposits represented a potential source of pollution to salmon eggs if they remained in the gravel after spawning. Water quality tests were inconclusive but indicated no significant changes attributable to the drive.[140]

Consideration of the hydraulic aspects of the drive, focused on the 10 or 11 log jams that had occurred at or adjacent to spawning areas, produced few negative observations. A large jam where the Stellako turned north after leaving Francois Lake caused "no serious disturbance of the river." Allen noted the possibility of some localized bank erosion and scouring, but no "substantial movement of bed material." Other jams further down the river left "little evidence of bank erosion or serious riverbed disturbance." Some localized scouring may have occurred where logs piled up against islands but Allen said it was difficult to distinguish the natural processes of bed movement and erosion in streams such as the Stellako from those caused by log driving. "From visual observations only," he concluded, "any detrimental effect of the 1966 log drive on the river regime appeared to be minimal." Scouring of the stream bed, "if it occurred", was confined to small areas; jams left no serious sediment deposits; and any wearing away of stream banks was "consistent with natural erosion."[141]

Allen would return to the Stellako to conduct further study of possible effects on spawning but the initial report must have pleased Williston. Robichaud was heading west to attend 'Salute to the Salmon' ceremonies on the Adams River and an October 24 meeting had been scheduled with Williston and Kiernan in Victoria. Responding to a series of questions from Vancouver Island NDP MP Tom Barnett before leaving Ottawa, he hinted to the House of Commons that a deal was in the works. "I am convinced in advance," Robichaud said, "that following discussions with the ministers concerned we will be able to come to some mutual agreement to protect the fisheries' interest." Howard Paish saw the meeting as a positive, if long overdue, development.[142]

The three ministers emerged from their discussion to report that the intergovernmental squabble over the Stellako had been cleared up. Instead of a jurisdictional showdown, steps would be taken to improve communication between Victoria and Ottawa. Provincial Deputy Minister of Water Resources Arthur Paget took up membership on the Federal-Provincial BC Fisheries Committee and his counterparts in the departments of Lands, Forests and Water Resources and Mines would take part in meetings when relevant issues arose. Williston termed it a useful gathering that laid the foundation for improved co-operation. A better "working arrangement" had been arrived at, Kiernan promised. Robichaud joined the chorus. The Stellako case was the result of poor communication, he told reporters, but meetings like the one just concluded would "probably prevent such incidents in the future."[143]

But the new administrative arrangements failed to generate much enthusiasm. Only Paget's place on the federal-provincial committee represented an innovation, and that seemed a small accomplishment after months of wrangling. The 'poor communication' explanation lacked real credibility, too, as Williston's words and actions had been very clear, leaving little room for confusion. Besides, Gerry Kidd pointed out, telephone service between Victoria and Ottawa was quite reliable and relatively inexpensive. It did not bode well for conservation, then, that the province's "flagrant act of senseless destruction" on the Stellako could be passed off with Williston's "what's past is past, we're looking to the future" explanation.[144]

The BCWF looked to the future as well, submitting a brief to the provincial cabinet one day after the ministers' meeting. Making no mention whatsoever of the Stellako, the document developed broad themes in a plea for more systematic planning in safeguarding fish, wildlife and outdoor recreation. The term 'multiple use' no longer had real meaning, the federation asserted, embodying both "unplanned simultaneous use" and the execution of single use policies, with the accommodation of other resource users only as an afterthought. Long-term priorities had to be established to achieve natural resource development without depriving British Columbians of the opportunity to enjoy a quality environment.[145]

Writing for a larger audience during the late summer of 1966, even before the ministers' discussions, Paish analyzed the Stellako's recent history in more argumentative terms. Multiple use had become nothing more than a "political platitude" that enabled the users of one resource to trample the legitimate rights of others. The problem lay not in a lack of understanding, Paish maintained; technical staff in the various departments had the knowledge to reconcile competing claims to the province's waters. The real problem was an absence of integrated planning, of applying "19th Century administrative machinery...under 19th Century resource development attitudes," to the modern dilemma of balancing the demands of production and consumption. While agencies continued to "wander along single-track courses," and the politicians and their senior civil servants squabbled over turf, public resources suffered.[146]

Paish was certainly not alone in drawing such conclusions. "The concept of conservation as wise use has proved to be extremely difficult to apply simultaneously to more than one resource," a 1966 BC Fish and Wildlife Branch report conceded. No single incident made that point more clearly than the 1966 Stellako River log drive and few were optimistic that the Robichaud-Williston-Kiernan get-together had produced anything more than a hastily conceived Band-Aid solution to a problem that would continue to fester.[147]

Mutually Acceptable: The 1967 Stellako Drive

THE SPRING OF 1967 saw the last of the Stellako River log drives. Like the previous runs, it subjected the river's spawning habitat to abuse but involved fewer logs and unprecedented efforts to minimize stream bed gouging and erosion. The measures aimed to legitimize the drive as an experimental undertaking designed to yield conclusive answers to the multiple-use question, and they came with Ottawa's approval. Now in full retreat, Robichaud rejected confrontation in favour of intergovernmental harmony. Co-operative federalism in action on the Stellako prompted more skepticism than support, but the interests that had protested the 1966 drive were less belligerent in 1967. The BCWF, its coffers drained by legal fees, restricted itself to rhetorical condemnation. The UFAWU grumbled but pursued no united front with sportsmen. Isolated, the Francois Lake resort owners, with one very significant exception, could only express their resentment and frustration.

Only Stellako resort owner Doug Kelly opted for a brief but well-publicized campaign of civil disobedience. But in the end, the logs went down the river, this time in the name of federal-provincial co-operation and scientific inquiry. Ray Williston's victory in this arena came at a cost, though, as conservationists and an emerging environmental movement pondered the meaning of the Stellako drives. Williston could control the river and Ottawa, at least enough to meet his immediate objectives, but he could not control the drives' symbolic legacy in a province fast losing faith in multiple-use platitudes.

The concluding act of the Stellako controversy opened with Cyril Shelford going to bat again for the Omineca farmer-loggers. Many of his constituents had been badly hurt financially, he informed Robichaud in late December. Having purchased small tractors and loaders on instalment plans, they were now two to three months behind on their payments because of Fraser Lake Sawmills' decision to curtail log purchases. Ottawa's determination to protect the fisheries had pushed them to the brink of bankruptcy and damaged the economic life of the communities around Francois Lake, Shelford explained when proposing a federal aid package. First, the region should be declared a disaster area. Second, the ban on driving the Stellako should be deferred for a year, enabling the small operators to hold off the finance companies and equipment dealers. Finally, a five-year public works program, funded to one-quarter of the annual value of the Stellako's contribution to the commercial salmon fishery, or $297,125 per year, would give the region time to adjust its economy. Shelford kept up his campaign in the legislature after the New Year, now calling for a two-year moratorium on any Stellako River log driving ban. Between $20,000 and $30,000 worth of new logging machinery had been idled in late 1966, he claimed, and the current healthy state of the salmon runs obviated the need for a federal decision made in "panicky haste."[148]

Shelford's proposal, printed in the *Lakes District News*, failed to elicit much in the way of sympathy for what Burns Lake's Tweedsmuir Rod and Gun Club called the "small farmers-cum loggers" of Francois Lake. Club president W.F. Ratcliffe suggested facetiously in a public letter to Robichaud, Shelford, Williston and Frank Howard that rather than spend almost $1.5 million over five years to relieve the small operators' hardship, Ottawa should make the equipment payments directly. At $30,000 for each of the "destitute farmers", taxpayers would come out roughly $285,000 ahead. Citing area firms that trucked their logs and lumber much farther than the 16 or 17 kilometres that separated the east end of Francois Lake and the Fraser Lake mill, Ratcliffe expressed doubt about that company's inability to survive trucking a small part of its log supply such a short distance. Certainly, the operation should not be "subsidized by the destruction of a fine recreational and monetary asset such as the fish life of the Stellako River." The BCFS valued the 18,878 cubic metres (8 million feet) of logs driven in 1966 at about $500,000, much less than the worth of the annual Stellako salmon run, a calculation that did not consider the financial contribution of the recreational fishery. Moreover, the company would experience no absolute loss by trucking the logs, only a slight increase in costs. Continued driving, on the other hand, would virtually wipe out the river's value. "The log drives on the Stellako must never again occur," the Burns Lake sportsmen concluded.[149]

Shelford took the letter in stride; Ratcliffe had expressed what Shelford called the "conservationist" view, but the Omineca MLA only wished to minimize economic disruption by giving those affected a chance to prepare for the future. The Tweedsmuir group, regrettably, did not share this concern. Nor did it grasp the benefits of his proposed public works scheme, which Shelford now envisioned as including boat launches on the area's lakes, improved road access to those sites and perhaps even a fish hatchery.[150]

For BC Commercial Fisheries Branch Director R.G. McMynn, the rhetorical battle obscured a more fundamental question: was all that new logging equipment around Francois Lake really idle? McMynn was worried that logs were being cut and stored on the lake, setting the stage for a replay of the events of 1966. At this point, there was no sign that relations between the Bennett and Pearson governments had become any sunnier. Social Credit cabinet ministers "needled Ottawa" routinely throughout the early 1967 legislative session, with Kiernan declaring that the province would be better off financially outside of Confederation.[151]

Nothing had changed at the administrative level either, a fact that concerned the UFAWU. In 1966 the salmon pack reached its highest level since 1958, and spawning channels had proven their worth. But BC still lacked a Fisheries minister to act on behalf of commercial fishermen. Kiernan had finally spoken, but only to explain that his department had no jurisdiction over fisheries. BC regulated the sports fishery by virtue of a gentlemen's agreement only; under both the *British North America Act* and terms of the province's entry into Confederation, constitutional authority rested with Ottawa. Facing forest industry expansion that brought the value of production to over $1 billion in 1966 (in contrast to the $86.6 million generated by salmon products) and with 14 pulp mills in operation and a further 16 either under construction or in the planning stage, the UFAWU had plenty of reason to worry about cutting practices, pollution and log driving. The union's opposition to the 1966 Stellako run had accomplished nothing, and they hoped that a minister responsible for the commercial fishery would provide a supportive voice in cabinet in the event of another drive attempt.[152]

The UFAWU plea met deaf ears in Victoria, but late February brought signs of a tougher stance from the federal Department of Fisheries. Protection Officer John Tuyttens warned central interior loggers to expect strict enforcement of *Fisheries Act* provisions against the deposit of sawdust and bark in rivers and lakes. Convictions of two Fort St. James loggers—for bucking logs on a frozen stream without cleaning up debris—followed soon after. A federal crackdown seemed to be in the works, as warnings gave way to prosecutions.[153]

Williston, however, was also positioning himself for the third and final round in the Stellako fight. Responding to the time pressure in early February, C.C. Walden, head of the BCRC's division of applied biology, sent a senior Department of Lands, Forests and Water Resources official a summary report of the council's study on the 1966 drive. The full technical report would not be complete until mid-March, but the summary of conclusions suited the provincial government's "immediate purpose." Publicly, Walden stressed that the study had been a co-operative effort by the BCRC, IPSFC and federal Department of Fisheries, but the findings were "our own," he explained to V. Raudsepp of the BC Water Investigations Branch. The key conclusion suited Williston's needs nicely. "Within the time limitations imposed by the project," I.V.F. Allen wrote, "the BCRC can demonstrate no detrimental effect of the 1966 log drive on the survival of embryonic salmon." No attempt had been made to determine effects on trout populations or fish food production, and, in an important qualification, Allen made it clear that the long-term consequences for salmon reproduction on the Stellako could not be assessed.[154]

The BCRC report's "no detrimental effects" conclusion would, nevertheless, be useful in challenging the IPSFC's critical analysis of the 1965 drive, and not just on the Stellako. The findings remained private for the moment, but by the second week of March newspaper stories emphasized the "very intensive" nature of the study and the BCRC's close working relationship with the federal Fisheries Department and other groups, including fish and game clubs. A confident Williston asserted that the study would be relevant to log runs on all salmon streams. Weldwood of Canada, he pointed out, intended to greatly expand its Quesnel River drive. Having obtained a PHA in the Quesnel Lake region in 1965 to supply its new Cariboo Pulp and Paper plant, scheduled to open in 1969, Weldwood was anxious to increase the flow of raw material for stockpiling at Quesnel. "It seems to make good sense to do so at flood time down the Quesnel River," Williston explained on March 10.[155]

Five days later he submitted the much-anticipated BCRC final report to the legislature. Field observations during the drive had focused on the potential effects of bark loss and erosion. A second phase of the study, from September 26 to October 4, looking at limitations in spawning bed use had investigated the behaviour of adult Sockeye spawners, and a final field examination over the period of November 21–30 analyzed egg development. Laboratory tests of water quality were also performed. Observations of the drive itself revealed a total of 28 jams, involving an estimated 12,325 logs or 11 per cent of the 106,728 logs driven. Half of the jams occurred "on or directly adjacent to spawning areas," and at the drive's conclusion, about 10 per cent of the logs remained in the river, tied up in jams.[156]

Despite these figures, the BCRC found little in the way of detrimental effects from bark loss and erosion. Bark loss findings presented in the September progress report were again set out, indicating that over half of the 714 logs tagged for analysis lost no bark at all. Others lost between 10 and 90 per cent, resulting in an estimated total bark loss of almost 4,000 pounds (1.8 kilograms). Assuming that the log sample was representative, the BCRC final report determined that total bark losses amounted to about 90,718 kilograms (100 tons). Some bank erosion occurred, but Allen repeated that the effects of the drive could not be distinguished from normal hydraulic processes accompanying the spring freshet.[157]

The BCRC final report was similarly inconclusive in assessing the drive's impact on Sockeye spawning. Using IPSFC data on the numbers of spawners in 1966 and relating those to figures for the period 1950–63, the BCRC concluded that about 26 per cent of the run in the years 1950–62 spawned in the lower reaches of the Stellako. The corresponding figure for 1966 was just 20 per cent but the BCRC compared this to 1963, when only 14.8 per cent of the spawners used those portions of the river. No drive had been conducted that year, or for several years previous. "Factors other than log driving may be implicated" in the lower than average numbers of spawners on the lower Stellako in 1966, the report concluded.[158]

Neither bark losses nor gouging and erosion appeared to have disrupted normal spawning patterns. "Spawning was not restricted due to lack of available spawning beds," Allen wrote, and the fish used beds in which some bark was present. Water quality tests were positive as well, recording oxygen content levels generally high enough to support egg development. Only in the deepest part of the river did bark deposit decomposition create potentially lethal conditions.[159]

While the BCRC report's concluding discussion did not endorse log driving on the Stellako, it did not quite condemn the practice either. Contrasting the controlled drive of 1966 to previous "slug" drives, Allen remarked that jams appeared inevitable without a system to keep logs away from shallows, islands and bends. Heavy bark deposits had occurred at points along the entire length of the river, but egg survival tests conducted under various conditions indicated no link between bark concentrations and mortality. Available gravel beds were sufficient to accommodate the 1966 salmon run, and egg survival and development did not appear to have been inhibited by any aspects of the drive. The ultimate finding—that given the time constraints, "no detrimental effect" of the 1966 drive could be determined—pleased Williston. But others would emphasize the questions that had not been asked, much less answered. As in the previous summary reports, the final report still did not consider the fate of the fry that emerged from the gravel beds or look at the drive's consequences for subsequent adult Sockeye populations. The report's final qualification, that it could offer no conclusions regarding the "long term effects on salmon reproduction, of log driving on the Stellako River", left some wondering about the study's worth. Drive supporters and opponents alike could find aspects of the report to support their positions.[160]

Williston saw enough in the BCRC conclusions to justify his decision to go ahead with the 1966 drive, but few commentators shared his certainty. Bob McConnell of the *Province* found the report "studded with question marks" and an accompanying editorial described it as a "classic in the art of non-statement." No answers were to be found on the effects of log jams, erosion and gouging on the Stellako's spawning beds, and even the bark deposit findings, the report's central point of inquiry, left "many questions unanswered." The *Sun* agreed, considering the report brief and inconclusive. Outdoors writer Dale Ethier, commenting in Quesnel's *Observer*, remarked on the "blinding speed" at which the government had moved in securing a hastily prepared but inconclusive report that served Williston's objectives. "As in the majority of these whiz-bang cases the end result is exactly what the government wants," Ethier declared. The highly regarded and "conclusive" IPSFC report, ignored because it did not suit the wishes of the Resources Ministry, had reached what Ethier saw as the only logical conclusion: log drives must be banned from the Stellako River.[161]

If the BCRC's report supported forest industry contentions that the 1966 Stellako drive was "not that bad," and enabled Williston to see justification for his decision, public opinion ran counter to both assumptions. So, too, did a March joint review of the BCRC report submitted by the technical staffs of the IPSFC, Department of Fisheries and BC Department of Recreation and Conservation. Complementing the BCRC researchers for the "credible job" they had done, considering the time constraints and narrow terms of reference, the critique went on to find fault with the report's failure to consider the cumulative effects of log driving on stream erosion and bark deposition. Several important errors and omissions had also been detected in a report that made some contribution to existing knowledge but failed to "provide a case for permitting future log drives."[162]

Addressing perceived errors first, the review found fault with the math skills of BCRC biologists. Using the BCRC report's tables on bark losses, which arrived at a total estimate of 90,719 kilograms (100 tons) of bark deposited, the review's calculations put this figure at 596,383 kilograms (657.4 tons). The BCRC had also underestimated the number of logs involved in jams, the critique argued. Instead of some 12,325 logs, or 11 per cent of the total, an independent one-day IPSFC estimate confined to just one stretch of the river calculated that at least 23,000 logs, or 21 per cent, had been tied up in major blockages. The BCRC's inability to differentiate natural erosion from that induced by the drive drew more criticism. Surveys showed that the Stellako experienced "major changes" in both 1965 and 1966, the reviewers countered, and visual evidence alone indicated a "marked increase in turbidity during active log passage." Other alleged errors included underestimating the effect of bark on egg survival and an invalid comparison of Sockeye spawning population distribution in 1963 and 1966. The 1963 run was atypical in a number of respects, the reviewers charged, with warm water temperatures contributing to a high mortality rate among spawners.[163]

Aside from errors, the reviewers felt several other BCRC findings required expansion or qualification. Bark deposited by the 1966 drive would have curtailed fish food production over several thousand square feet of the Stellako's bed, the critique maintained. Second, displacement of stream-bottom markers indicated that gravel shifts and scouring induced by the drive surpassed the "minimum effects" mentioned in the provincial report. The reviewers also found the BCRC's conclusions regarding the dissolved oxygen content of "subgravel" waters in spawning areas less than sound. While adequate for egg survival, oxygen levels were low enough to cause concern. Moreover, further introduction of bark particles into spawning gravel would disrupt subsurface flows and lower water quality as degradation of organic material consumed oxygen. Citing evidence that the amount of bark interspersed in spawning gravel had nearly doubled in 1966 over measurements taken after the previous drive, the reviewers expressed concern that this process could culminate in oxygen levels too low for survival.[164]

Wrapping up their analysis with a summary of gravel bed scouring, a factor given insufficient consideration in the BCRC report, the IPSFC and federal and provincial fisheries staffs made it clear that the BCRC study did nothing to alter the conclusion advanced in their report on the 1965 drive: "log driving on the Stellako River should be discontinued." Here, then, was a clear case of scientific disagreement, one that pitted the findings of fisheries organizations against those of the BCRC. But the critique had to be made public in order to have full effect, and it was never released. The IPSFC did refer to the dispute in its 1966 annual report, though, asserting that the 1966 drive "resulted in additional erosion of stream banks, further deposition of bark upon and within the gravel stream bed, further erosion of spawning grounds and continued displacement of spawners from the lower part of the river." All of this, the IPSFC declared, substantiated the previous year's findings, which were not contradicted by the BCRC study.[165]

While the IPFSC review was never made public, release of the BCRC report coincided, perhaps by design, with a March 14 meeting of the Federal-

Provincial BC Fisheries Committee. The gathering came to agreement on the need for joint study of the Stellako problem to be undertaken by a technical subcommittee. The urgency faded, however, when Deputy Minister of Forests F.S. McKinnon announced that no logs would be available for driving in 1967. The Stellako affair seemed to have come to a welcome, if temporary, end.[166]

The BCRC report and the apparent Stellako solution also coincided with passage in April of a new provincial *Pollution Control Act* that, Williston assured the legislature, made BC the leading Canadian province in pollution prevention. A reconstituted Pollution Control Board would have new independence from cabinet in setting standards under an appointed director. Heated debate swirled around the board's decision to allow mine tailings to be dumped in Strathcona Park's Buttle Lake during this period, and the BCRC had been drawn into that situation when the Campbell River Water District hired them to conduct a study. After the withdrawal of a first report, a second came out with findings resembling those of its Stellako study. Conceding that mine tailings could be detrimental to the lake's aquatic life, the BCRC offered no firm conclusions about their effects on Campbell River's water supply.[167]

Opposition members questioned the BCRC's scientific integrity, eliciting denials of government interference from Williston. But both the new pollution act and the BCRC's involvement in the Campbell River dispute contributed to a heightened atmosphere of unease that fed into public discourse on the Stellako issue. The NDP's Gordon Dowding expressed dissatisfaction at the dominant role civil servants would play on the new Pollution Control Board. "We need an independent board with no subservience or hint of subservience to the government," Dowding cautioned. The BCRC's Stellako report hinted at the same lack of impartiality, he went on to suggest. "To say this report is of any use to anyone is nonsense," Dowding concluded, ignoring the fact that its very ambiguity had utility for Williston. The Stellako and Buttle Lake incidents, along with rumours of a mining development for Tweedsmuir Park, were ample cause for agitation against the mounting environmental price of prosperity, declared the *Observer*.[168]

Science, even conclusive science, was rarely decisive in shaping forest practices in BC. Even when it came to sustained-yield policy, market considerations and the interest shared by major operators and the province in maximizing financial returns were primary factors in crafting and implementing regulations. Now, with the BCRC report, Williston had succeeded, at least in his own mind, in making the Stellako River log drives a matter of scientific debate. In the absence of a strong commitment by the federal government to act upon the basis of its own research, that would be enough in the end.[169] Williston implied as much in mid-March by holding up the BCRC report as justification for the 1966 drive and saying that a repeat in the summer of 1967 would depend on the federal authorities. "What on earth does this mean?" asked the *Sun*. The minister who had proclaimed the province's "sovereign jurisdiction" over rivers now implied that the ultimate decision rested with Ottawa. Perhaps Williston meant that BC would, "in keeping with current fashion," simply defy any federal objection to a 1967 drive.[170]

But would Ottawa object? Even if Robichaud did, would he follow through with enforcement of his own *Fisheries Act*? Robichaud, with his information that there were no logs to be driven, must have begun to wonder about Williston's intentions. Further cause for concern came when he and Deputy Minister A.W.H. Needler learned on April 4 that the BCFS would launch an engineering study looking at the various log transportation alternatives between Francois Lake and Fraser Lake. Data would be gathered on what river "improvements" and driving practices were needed to minimize damage to the fisheries. They would investigate the cost of a machine to debark logs and the cost of improving road access to Highway 16 so that logs could be trucked. In explaining all this to Needler, provincial Deputy Minister of Forests F.S. McKinnon admitted that previous information about the lack of logs in Francois Lake was incorrect. Apologizing, he now revealed that Fraser Lake Sawmills had about 9,439 cubic metres (4 million board feet) left over in booms from the previous year. The small operators had not been completely idle, either. Their seasonal cut would bring the total to 14,158 cubic metres (6 million board feet). "An appropriate comment on this matter escapes me," McMynn later told Department of Fisheries Regional Director W.R. Hourston. On the bright side, the BCFS seemed serious about evaluating the economics of the transportation alternatives. The BCRC, unfortunately, had focused its energies on "trying to disprove the original fisheries report."[171]

Fisheries officials were still awaiting the results of the engineering study when BC's Deputy Minister of Water Resources A.F. Paget informed Hourston on April 14 that a log drive would occur on the Stellako in June. Williston waited a week before making a public announcement, explaining that the 1967 drive would be conducted on an experimental basis by his staff, with more rigid controls than its predecessor. The 1966 drive had not taken place under optimum conditions, and while the BCRC study revealed no clear damage to spawning beds, more questions needed to be answered before rendering a final decision on the Stellako's future fate. Fin booms would be installed to minimize erosion from a small-scale drive, limited to the logs remaining from the previous year's cut. Williston made no mention of the 609,600 metres (2 million feet) of fresh logs supplied by the small operators who had, according to Shelford's campaign, been thrown out of work over the previous winter.[172]

Williston's attempt to frame the 1967 drive as another instalment in the quest for knowledge lacked the credibility needed to convince the opposition. The *Province*, contrasting the $1.8 million annual worth of the Stellako's Sockeye yield to the $200,000 earned by the Francois Lake farmer-loggers, declared the gamble not worthwhile when a "few miles of logging road would make the whole drive unnecessary." Further explanation was required. Comparing the outright opposition of the IPSFC report to the much less assertive language of the BCRC findings, the *Citizen* urged Williston to call off the drive. Subsidizing the company to maintain its viability, if necessary, was a wiser course of action than jeopardizing the salmon run. The BCWF took a wait-and-see attitude initially. Possible legal action depended on what the federal Fisheries Department had to say and on the validity of Williston's claim that the drive would involve only a few logs to be driven under controlled conditions. But if suspicions proved correct that the objective was simply cheap logs for Fraser Lake Sawmills, the Federation would "raise every possible objection," Howard Paish warned. The UFAWU's T. Buck Suzuki raised the prospect of organized picketing by conservation organizations.[173]

Williston's deputy minister, McKinnon, conveyed the Stellako engineering study results to Needler on May 1. A controlled drive could bring logs to the mill at a cost of 80 cents per cubic foot, far less than the $5.25 estimated cost of a truck haul. Debarking the logs would raise the cost to $5.30 for 1967, but carried over five years of driving that expense fell to $2.64 per cubic foot. "The figures speak for themselves," McKinnon said. Handling costs made the trucking option much more costly, therefore the Department of Lands, Forests and Water Resources would proceed with the installation of booms in preparation for the drive. These improvements, coupled with proper supervision of the log flow, would eliminate jams and reduce bark deposits to a minimum. There remained the problem of the two conflicting scientific reports, which McKinnon hoped to see resolved soon through the experts reaching a consensus. [174]

The engineering study found its way to BC's Deputy Minister of Recreation and Conservation David Turner, whose marginal notations questioned the relationship between the study's figures and McKinnon's conclusions. Debarking, in fact, raised the cost of log driving above that of trucking in the short term. The point, in any event, was moot, as there is no record of the purchase or installation of such a machine. Turner then sent the report along to McMynn, who collaborated with E.H. Vernon on a joint statement expressing the views of the Commercial Fisheries and Fish and Wildlife branches for the consideration of Turner and minister Ken Kiernan. McMynn and Vernon pointed out that the federal-provincial conflict over the Stellako had placed BC's fishery biologists in a problematic relationship with citizens who looked to them to protect the public interest.[175]

Their confidential memorandum, summarizing the professional opinion of provincial fishery biologists, condemned the Stellako drives as incompatible with salmon and trout production. The IPSFC report on the 1965 drive, "tempered by years of experience, field work and laboratory studies," left no doubt about the harmful effects of log driving in degrading habitat, reducing food supplies and creating unfavourable spawning conditions. That said, fishery agencies did not oppose the practice on all streams, but very productive ones such as the Stellako deserved special consideration. The BCRC findings, accurate with "minor exceptions," did not disagree in any fundamental way with the earlier fisheries report. It was, however, incomplete in considering only the early stage of the Sockeye life cycle and in failing to evaluate "many drastic effects on the river itself." Finally, McMynn and Vernon argued, the Forest Service's engineering study focused solely on the operator's costs, ignoring those that long-term river degradation would inflict on fisheries. The Stellako should, therefore, be protected; continued driving would inevitably cause serious damage to "precious public resources."[176]

The McMynn-Vernon statement captured the frustrations of biologists constrained by a policy that went against their professional obligations. Neither it nor the earlier critique of the BCRC report entered the public domain; however, and while the biologists carried out their intergovernmental struggle, provincial government crews got busy 'improving' the Stellako. Workers cut overhanging trees and brush from the river's banks. Logs left over from previous drives and natural debris accumulations were cleared. Most of this material was simply swept downstream, since steep terrain made it too difficult to carry away for piling and burning. Glance booms— logs cabled together—were installed at points previously shown to be especially susceptible to bank erosion and jams. Fin booms, with hinged planks for angling logs back into the stream from banks, went in at other locations. The crews made no attempt to place booms at all locations considered vulnerable to erosion and, at the falls where jams had occurred in the past, unspecified difficulties prevented boom installation.[177]

Back in Victoria, the BCWF convened in early May to consider the Stellako's meaning in its broader approach to BC resource development policy. "Persistent gentle persuasion" had failed as a tactic in convincing government that the province's recreational assets were worthy of systematic management, Paish told the delegates. The federation had undertaken its expensive legal campaign against the 1966 Stellako drive with full knowledge of its likely futility, but they had succeeded in their main goal of focusing public attention on the issue. Both Paish and federation President James C. Murray bemoaned the Department of Recreation and Conservation's lack of influence within the Socred government, and the latter used newly belligerent rhetoric in decrying Kiernan's dedication to turning fish, wildlife and recreational resources "into quick dollar earners." While Williston supported the loggers on the Stellako the previous summer, Kiernan had done nothing more than proclaim his jurisdictional helplessness and express concern over "throw away pop bottles."[178]

Praising Paish's role in raising the federation's public profile, Murray called for an end to co-operation with government, an approach that had too often found the organization "compromising on compromise." "We always should have been political without being partisan," Murray concluded. "The decision to drive logs down the Stellako was a political decision. The decisions at Buttle Lake have been political decisions all along." Political engagement came with a price tag attached, however, and the federation's legal bills had contributed to a $10,000 deficit. Members had endorsed an emergency 25-cent levy, and 1967 income paid off the previous year's bills, but a shortfall loomed. The introduction of an austerity program, membership fee increases and the raffle of a half-ton truck with camper and tent trailer kept the federation solvent. But despite a new commitment to a "watchdog" relationship to government, 1967 would bring no costly second venture into the court system.[179]

Robichaud, meanwhile, had signed a logging order prohibiting a 1967 log drive. But the federal Fisheries minister was eager to avoid a showdown, issuing public statements which seemed more conciliatory than confrontational. He told the *Citizen* that he favoured a solution that would both protect the fisheries resource and find support among forestry interests, but would fulfil his duty to oppose a drive *if* it threatened Stellako spawning beds. That implied an embrace of multiple-use thinking as Williston and Kiernan defined it—a philosophy that had opened Strathcona Park to mining, authorized the dumping of tailings into Buttle Lake and now promised to place Stellako River fish populations at further risk.[180]

Conservationists had come to view multiple use with suspicion, but it was by no means clear where the opposition to Williston's plan for the Stellako would come from in 1967. Ottawa appeared unlikely to "fight it out over jurisdiction," *Citizen* reporter Scott Honeyman observed. The Francois Lake resort owners could be counted on to protest, but their voices were few in number. The BCWF planned to oppose the drive, but its financial problems ruled out legal action. Despite the strong feelings of some of its members, the federation's Prince George Rod and Gun Club affiliate would remain silent. The UFAWU was still considering joint action with other opposition forces and had expressed its displeasure to Robichaud, but they showed no signs of taking a lead role.[181]

Honeyman had read the federal government's intentions correctly. On May 16 Robichaud informed Williston of his willingness to deal, despite the province's unilateral actions, which had left him no alternative but to sign the order prohibiting the drive. Motivated by his conviction that the fullest use should be made of rivers "as long as no single resource suffers", Robichaud wished to pursue a technical solution that would allow the Stellako's conflicting resource users to coexist. He was prepared to rescind the logging order, then, provided that Williston assured "true co-operation and joint consideration" of issues. His officers and IPSFC staff would join Williston's in supervising the drive to minimize damage to the stream and participate in the production of a joint report. This was the approach he had in mind at the March 14 Fisheries Committee meeting, Robichaud explained, and it was "not yet too late for us to get together on this problem." He later used the same language in the House of Commons, saying that his ultimate decision would be made in keeping with the fullest possible use of water resources so long as the fishery resource did not suffer.[182]

Ironically, that same day Kiernan responded to the McMynn-Vernon statement on the Stellako, telling his deputy minister that it might be possible to phase out log driving there. In pursuit of that end, McMynn and Vernon should consult with BCFS and Water Resources officials, advising Kiernan and Williston of the results confidentially. McMynn and Vernon eagerly produced their new confidential "Stellako River Log Driving and Fisheries" report, expressing regret about the adversarial atmosphere that had developed over a rather simple conflict that might be resolved if approached in a reasonable manner. They were particularly anxious to show Kiernan and Williston a film of the 1966 log drive that illustrated its impacts better than written explanations.[183]

In their report, they conceded that forestry dominated the BC economy, and some damage to resources of lesser importance could be expected. These costs, however, were justified "only to the extent that the resulting benefits to the forest industry exceed the costs borne by the secondary industry." Logging was inherently disruptive to freshwater fish habitat, with erosion, stream bank instability and sedimentation representing the unavoidable consequences of a profitable forest economy. But log driving fell into another category, they maintained, one in which the additional costs to fisheries might easily outweigh the economic benefits derived by the logging industry.[184]

McMynn and Vernon described the Stellako as one of the province's "most important salmon and trout producing rivers" and emphasized its exceptional recreational qualities. Other than those streams supporting Steelhead runs, the Stellako represented one of the province's few easily accessible, highly productive trout fishing rivers—one worth preserving on financial grounds. Estimating the Stellako's annual value from commercial, recreational and tourist contributions at roughly $1.5 million, they made the only argument with any hope of swaying Williston. Unable to calculate the precise loss in the Stellako's value attributable to habitat degradation, McMynn and Vernon put forth a conservative estimate of five per cent per year. Log driving, then, came at an annual cost of $75,000.[185]

Applying the data from the BCFS's engineering study, which put the cost of log driving at 80 cents per cubic feet, in contrast to the $5.30 per cubic foot cost of trucking, they calculated the benefits to the company of river-driving the 141.58 cubic metres (5,000 cubic feet) of logs to the mill. Fraser Lake Sawmills, they estimated, stood to reap a financial benefit of roughly $23,000 annually, but at a cost of $75,000 to the "fishing industry, the fishing resorts, and the sport fishermen." Even if one accepted the argument that the mill's survival hinged upon the log drive, a case could be made for a public subsidy to allow the operation to overcome any temporary economic difficulties. The subsidy, however, should not come in the form of damage to the Stellako's long-term productive capacity. Rather than continue log driving, they concluded, the BCFS should be asked to explore all harvesting alternatives, including re-allocation of timber rights and road improvements to allow truck hauling.[186]

McMynn and Vernon had turned the cold calculation of multiple-use management—traditionally used to justify the preference accorded the forest industry in policy-making and planning—on its head. Their argument was careful, reasoned and, unfortunately, quite irrelevant. The following day Williston communicated his response to the report, telling Robichaud that fisheries biologists remained adamant in their opposition to *any* log driving on BC streams supporting fish life. Given the conflicting studies on the 1965 and 1966 drives, he therefore faced "another case where the experts do not agree or, if they do, they do not communicate." Confronted by the biologists' outright opposition to log driving and in the absence of real data on the effects of a controlled log drive, Williston felt the Stellako represented an ideal opportunity for further experimentation. "It is our desire to determine to what extent river improvements could eliminate those elements of a river-drive that can cause trouble," he informed Robichaud. The drive would go ahead, then, but Robichaud's offer of co-operation was most welcome. Further joint study should be undertaken. Joint study, however, was not to be confused with joint supervision of the drive. That would be the BCFS's domain alone, although Robichaud's chief fishery officer should feel free to offer recommendations.[187]

Unaware that the two ministers had agreed on a third Stellako drive, Paish continued to press Robichaud on behalf of BCWF, urging him to be assertive in protecting the fisheries resource. Federation president Dick Phillips, a Prince George resident, wondered publicly if Williston's decision on the Stellako was part of a larger design for massive log drives on central interior rivers. Perhaps the goal was undisputed provincial control over water resources, involving a complete withdrawal by Ottawa? Either prospect was chilling, given BC's record, and the organization would continue opposing log drives on the Stellako. If case-by-case investigations proved that other rivers could be driven without harm, however, no objections would be raised.[188]

Commercial fishery interests were firm in their opposition to further disturbance of the Stellako runs. The UFAWU, informed by Robichaud that he had not yet issued a permit for a June Stellako drive, shared the Wildlife Federation's concern that the forest industry intended to make more general use of BC rivers. The Fisheries Association of BC, having dismissed the BCRC study as "hastily prepared" and inconclusive, was wary as well. Interior lumbermen, for their part, continued to see the Stellako drives as representing a fundamental struggle for freedom in log transportation. A Price Waterhouse report on mills belonging to the Northern Interior Lumbermen's Association (NILA) revealed that marginal profits had turned into losses in the last three years. Convening in late May, the NILA unanimously endorsed a resolution by Joe Leslie expressing support for Williston's Stellako River policy. The federal Fisheries Department "chose the battle ground," Leslie said. "Mr. Williston took the challenge. He's not just doing it for the small company involved...but for the industry."[189]

On the banks of the Stellako, as crews continued to install booms and Fraser Lake Sawmills' tugs began preparing to tow logs down Francois Lake, lodge owners could only watch. Menard Resort owner Gerry Menard, now head of the Resort Owners' Association and responsible for "gathering the opposing forces", expressed his group's sense of futility. "There's not much we can do," he said. "Williston just goes ahead and does it." Catches were down since the drives began, and the lodges might be forced to close, Menard predicted. He found it incredible that the logs could not be lifted from the lake at the bridge crossing the Stellako's outlet and trucked a few miles to the mill at less expense, given the manpower involved. Menard did note that the water level was unusually high that spring. Indeed, a deep snowpack caused flooding concerns along the Fraser in the spring of 1967. Another Francois Lake "old-timer" who declined to be identified told Scott Honeyman that the high water would protect the spawning beds. Menard conceded that high water would prevent logs from gouging the beds but insisted that bank erosion and bark deposition remained a threat.[190]

As May drew to an end, Williston and Robichaud finalized their mutually agreeable "solution", the former taking care to maintain absolute authority over the drive. Robichaud consented to rescind the federal prohibition order, but he wanted provision for consultation by his staff. A senior fisheries official could act as spokesman, Williston agreed, with McKinnon and Hourston communicating directly in upper-level discussions. McKinnon would be on-site for the drive's first few days, forecast to begin on June 19. Federal and provincial officials tied up the administrative loose ends at a June 5 meeting. The BCFS would assume sole responsibility for the drive, McKinnon confirmed, with supervisor T.N. Stringer taking federal and provincial fisheries input from a single "contact man": the Department of Fisheries' F.C. Boyd. A technical subcommittee, consisting of Stringer, Vernon and representatives from the provincial Water Rights Service and Department of Recreation and Conservation, along with a federal representative, would coordinate field studies and prepare the joint report. It was agreed that the subcommittee members should be able to concur on most conclusions, noting any areas of disagreement in the report. The possibility of a separate BCRC report came up at the technical subcommittee's first meeting three days later, but the desire for a single joint report reflecting a federal-provincial consensus ruled that out, for the time being at any rate.[191]

All that remained was for Robichaud to officially revoke his prohibition order, which he did on June 12. Ottawa and Victoria had come to a "mutually acceptable" arrangement to drive the Stellako. Political conflict had been replaced by co-operation and good will. Williston told the *Citizen* that all points of contention between he and Robichaud had been cleared up, and another study would be conducted. British Columbia was not only leading other provinces in the pollution fight, he told the Conference on the BC Environment in Vancouver in early June; it had also pulled ahead of most American states. Ironically, Cyril Shelford now told a Burns Lake public meeting on Tweedsmuir Park that truck and train transportation must put an end to log drives. Researchers would study the upcoming drive, he assured his audience, noting it was "absolutely essential to find an alternative...because the demand for logs will be so tremendous the rivers would be black with logs."[192]

British Columbians learned of Robichaud's reversal on June 10 when Williston announced that the BCFS would conduct the drive as soon as flood waters on the Stellako subsided. He said that only 2,359.7 cubic metres (1 million board feet) of logs were involved, however, and costs would be assessed against Fraser Lake Sawmills. Other reports put the amount at 9,439 cubic metres (4 million board feet). In the end, just over 7,079 cubic metres (3 million board feet) of logs went down the Stellako in 1967. He emphasized that the 1966 run had done no damage to the fishery resource, although the lack of booms had permitted scouring in "a couple" of spots. But crews had spent the last three weeks correcting those problems. Anything but surprised, Howard Paish accused Ottawa of "spinelessness". The *Province* called the entire episode a "comedy of errors", demanding that this year's study leave no room for "further doubt and acrimony."[193]

With his minister Kiernan under attack again over a second mining proposal for Strathcona Park, premier Bennett came forward with a curious take on BC's environmental awakening after a Bank of BC breakfast a few days later. "The worst pollution of the air is by people smoking, and the worst pollution of water is by polluting it with liquor," Bennett proclaimed. The *Citizen* termed the remark childish, petulant and a "foreshadowing of senility."[194] Senile Bennett was not, but he surely lacked an appreciation of the depth of feeling building in the province for a more balanced relationship to nature. In dismissing opponents of mining in parks as obstructionists with no regard for employment, the premier voiced a tried-and-true development philosophy that had lost some, but by no means all, of its appeal. In Vancouver a small group of expatriate Americans, veterans of the peace movement with an ecological worldview and links to New Left politics and the Sierra Club, would soon take a prominent role in establishing an identifiable environmental movement. The BCWF had rejected its traditional co-operative relationship with government in favour of a more aggressive "watchdog" role. Pollution was a major concern, both in metropolitan areas and the hinterland communities that hosted the new pulp mills. Faith in wise-use conservation remained, but alongside a growing conviction that the rhetoric used by its proponents masked an underlying commitment to unfettered exploitation.[195]

Amidst these cultural cross-currents, final preparations were underway for the 1967 Stellako log drive, scheduled to begin Monday, June 19. By June 14 a number of log booms had been stationed in a bay on Francois Lake, but that evening seven of the booms mysteriously opened, allowing the logs to drift away. A safety boom surrounding the entire lot was also opened, indicating a deliberate attempt to subvert the drive. Suspicion fell on the lodge owners, who had announced plans to conduct a "boat-in" or fishing derby at the Stellako's mouth Monday morning, permitting only a single log to enter the river at a time. The lodge operators hoped conservationists from Quesnel to Prince George would join the protest. "There is not much else we can do," Doug Kelly said. "We are just a small organization fighting the provincial government...and now the federal government has joined in." The Vanderhoof Royal Canadian Mounted Police detachment announced both an investigation and its intention to have officers on site Monday morning. Fraser Lake Sawmills assigned "night riders" to patrol the booms the following night.[196]

That evening the CBC's *Fisherman's Broadcast* featured an interview between Ron Tarves and IPSFC director Lloyd Royal. Although the IPSFC had advised against another Stellako drive, Royal seemed optimistic that no significant damage would result. Only about half the number of logs were to be driven as the previous year, and a substantial portion had been laying on the shore of Francois Lake over the winter, so much of their bark covering would have been removed. Finally, the unusually high water levels should prevent excessive gouging. Depth of flow was the crucial consideration, he explained; neither the IPSFC nor the Department of Fisheries had objected to driving rivers with flows sufficient to prevent the scouring of stream beds.[197]

The IPSFC had a purely advisory role, Royal cautioned, with government assuming the responsibility of making policy in light of the various economic factors. Moreover, the effects of log driving on fish life were cumulative, delayed and largely undetectable. Years of research would be required to compile convincing mortality data. In fact, Royal continued, fisheries agencies had probably invested sufficient funds investigating the Stellako problem to cover the cost of hauling the logs by truck. In the not-too-distant future, he hoped, the opening of new log markets in the Burns Lake area or west of Francois Lake might well eliminate the need to drive the river.[198]

This final act in the Stellako drama took a more alarming turn the following evening, with reports of shots being fired in the direction of a Fraser Lake Sawmills tugboat. The crew informed Joe Leslie of the incident Friday morning, saying that the shots had been fired over their heads. Leslie notified the RCMP, warning that the "situation could get worse." No accusations were made, but once again drive opponents seemed the likely culprits, said a BCFS official. Kelly, now the most vocal and determined of the lodge owners, remained defiant. He and his colleagues were committed to being on the water in their boats, "and maybe do a little trolling and maybe give them a little trouble getting the logs through." It would be risky, but the protest was "for BC and Canada." Under no illusions, though, Kelly knew that the river would be run "come hell or high water." That weekend F.S. McKinnon met with the lodge operators, threatening them with injunctions in the event of any interference. Kelly now stood alone among the lodge operators; "we" had become "I" in conversations with reporters about the boat protest. He would, nevertheless, place his boat in the direct path of the logs until presented with an injunction.[199]

Kelly, perhaps, was more alone than he knew. The Wildlife Federation, in debt and in the midst of a fundraising campaign, had become a less active ally. The Prince George and Quesnel sportsmen would not show up with their boats, either. The Stellako was a fight of the "Lilliputians of BC versus the Gullivers," observed the *Sun*. "Single platoons of fishermen, of hunters, of resort operators, of bird-watchers, of hikers, of climbers, of citizens' leagues, of local councils, of trade unions" had fought their separate battles and lost in the past years. The

Francois Lake at start of log drive. NA-23383.

Highway Bridge and Fraser Lake beyond. NA-23418.

province needed an umbrella organization, perhaps an "Outdoors Council" to bring the fish, wildlife and wilderness enthusiasts together.[200]

The 1967 Stellako drive began as intended on June 19, a week after the migration of Sockeye fry was essentially complete. The river's discharge had reached a 10-year peak on June 10, with higher than average water levels making log passage easier than in previous years. Crews were stationed at strategic points to maintain the protective booms and prevent jams, and two BCFS helicopters conducted patrols. About 8,000 logs went downriver the first day, but not without Doug Kelly making good on his promised protest. With about 70 onlookers watching from the Stellako bridge, and with fellow lodge owners

John Kost and Clarence and Enid Plowman on hand, Kelly steered his small aluminium boat into the path of the logs, tossed out a small anchor and began fishing. Several times the logs nearly swept him downstream. "A well-controlled log drive," he yelled at one point as he fought the current and the logs. "Just look at them!" F.S. McKinnon and six RCMP officers were among the observers. Expressing concern for Kelly's safety, McKinnon noted that feelings were intense, but said that any action was up to the police. "The man is endangering his own life, using his own judgement," said a staff sergeant from Prince George.[201]

Aside from Kelly's protest, the drive's first day proceeded with no major problems. A few jams developed at the falls about halfway down the river, but McKinnon pronounced his satisfaction with a first release that left the Stellako "clean as a whistle." Tuesday, though, did bring difficulties. Strong easterly winds had kicked up, slowing the progress of tugs towing logs down the lake. A large boom arrived too late for opening, but almost 12,000 logs were released. And McKinnon had his own problems. While deeper than usual, in some places the Stellako remained too shallow for the outboard motors powering the aluminium boats used for transportation. The boat carrying McKinnon and Prince George district forester Norm McRae as they performed an inspection broke down, forcing them to walk three hours back to Francois Lake; they did not arrive until 11:00 pm. Kelly stayed on shore that day, criticizing the Wildlife Federation and rod and gun clubs for not coming through with support. "It looks like a really commercial fight this way. The lodge owners against the logging companies," he told Scott Honeyman. "That's not the way it is. It's a matter of saving the fish."[202]

With the winds still strong, only 4,533 logs were in position for driving Wednesday, June 21. Despite the small release, a jam three kilometres downriver caused a delay that morning. A disgusted Kelly was back on the water, this time keeping a safe distance "in the interest of his own life and limb." Poplar Lodge owners Clarence and Enid Plowman provided the only support, pulling their boat alongside Kelly, who carried a sign reading: "We Protest This Log Drive Because It Has Been Proven Harmful To The Fish." His hopes for a large protest now gone, Kelly again bemoaned the absence of other conservation groups. On Thursday, with no logs due to the winds that continued to delay the arrival of booms, Honeyman described the drive as a "study in frustration for all concerned." The researchers, "only half jokingly" looking ahead to another study in 1968, wanted to go home. The company wanted the

Resort owner protesting at release point. NA-23381.

winds to drop. Doug Kelly wanted his supposed allies to provide the support that they had promised. BCWF President Dick Phillips and the Quesnel Rod and Gun Club had assured the lodge owners that other boats would join the naval blockade. "But they've just talked," Kelly said, "and you can't stop logs with talk." The shooting story, which he described as "pure fallacy" and a cynical attempt to discredit the lodge operators, contributed to Kelly's disen-chantment.[203]

Honeyman captured much, but not all, of the frustration mounting on the banks of the Stellako and beyond. Drive supervisor T.N. Stringer thought the 7,079–9,439 cubic metres (3–4 million board feet) of logs could have been run in four days if Fraser Lake Sawmills had organized log delivery more efficiently, making allowances for the east wind and vandalism. The release of 40 to 50 logs per minute during the first two days had proven excessive, causing the logs to pile up and creating unanticipated delays. Each time a crew had to be sent in to clear the jams, log releases came to a halt. If the jams caused consterna-tion for the Department of Fisheries, so did the lingering uncertainty about the joint scientific report. Hourston and McKinnon, who were to work together, discussed the matter on June 16, but agreed to wait until the drive's completion before deciding how to proceed with the report. Perhaps the BCRC would be called in again if the federal researchers came forward with critical findings.[204]

Top: One of the fin booms. NA-23391. **Bottom:** Clearing a jam. NA-23385.

Top: Shallow spots and control booms. NA-23429.
Bottom: Some jamming at a control point below the shoot. NA-23419.

Research Council retrieving tagged logs at Highway Bridge. NA-23446.

Driving resumed on Friday, June 23 without protest. Enid Plowman still held out hope that conservationist forces would rally the next day, but had heard no word from those who had pledged support. The Wildlife Federation had released a report documenting Williston's alleged "double cross" of Robichaud, excusing the federal department for accepting the inevitable and cooperating in the drive out of a desire to do its best in protecting the resource. The real victims were the Stellako's salmon and trout, the fishermen and all British Columbians who saw a "publicly-owned resource sacrificed to politics and single-minded commercial greed." Saturday and Sunday came and went with no federation reinforcements, although Kelly was now stationed alone on Highway 16 with his protest signs. The last logs entered the Stellako on Monday, but a crew stayed on clearing logs from the banks for a few days. High water had swept a great deal of debris from the banks into the river, demanding six weeks of additional work to keep the booms and Highway 16 bridge clear.[205]

River conditions and industrial damage-mitigation initiatives meant the 1967 drive was anything but representative. Even so, all had not gone as advertised. Of the 14 jams described by Stringer as "minor", seven occurred over or adjacent to spawning areas. Erosion to a depth of 0.5 to 1.5 metres (2 to 5 feet) damaged one stretch of productive stream bottom, and a second jam caused by logs caught up at a fin boom produced similar scouring. The installation of a glance boom contributed to extensive bank erosion at another point, but overall the booms seemed to limit erosion. Bark loss was also down from previous years; most logs had either been boomed in Francois Lake for two years or salvaged from the beach, and over half had lost all their bark prior to the drive. Those with some bark covering lost more than logs in previous years, though, because it was loose and easily dislodged. That added to the estimated 116 tons of bark divers found remaining from previous years. Post-drive investigation revealed 42 major deposits, totalling an estimated 151 tons, comparing well to the 300 tons deposited in 1966.[206]

The final report on the 1967 drive would not be completed until 1969, and in the drive's immediate aftermath Williston and the BCWF offered the usual contrasting perspectives. The minister—flush with accomplishment as the Mica and High Arrow dams on the Columbia proceeded on time and construction on the Peace River hydro-electric project sped a full year ahead of schedule—continued to frame the Stellako drive in terms of rigorous, painstaking scientific inquiry. To Williston, the BCRC study of the 1966 drive had shown it to be harmless, and the "controlled experimenting" of 1967 would contribute further insights on the future of the spawning grounds. "It really comes down to the wise philosophy of doing nothing to excess," he told readers of his regular "Northern Way" newspaper column. That meant observing conservation principles in a way that produced maximum commercial and aesthetic benefits rather than adopting the "so-called" conservationism that restricted resources for the use of the few "purely pleasure-bent" outdoor enthusiasts.[207]

For the BCWF, the 1967 Stellako drive was another chapter in a story of frustration. Avoiding federal-provincial confrontation, Robichaud had salvaged what power he could by gaining a role for his staff in the conduct of the drive. That had eliminated the possibility of another legal action, members learned in a federation *Newsletter* account and, with Robichaud's decision, "what had been both morally and legally wrong last year was now only morally wrong." The reported sabotage of the Francois Lake boom and the admittedly doubtful reports of gunfire contributed to the organization's place on the sidelines; the federation would not ally itself with those responsible for violence, if any had occurred. Rather, it would continue its "responsible" opposition to log drives considered to be harmful. Williston's pretence that the federation opposed all drives was just that, and his "short-sighted arrogance" in allowing one industry to "ride roughshod over all other interests", they said, had created the risk of permanent damage to the Stellako. In the current climate, where aggressiveness and might triumphed over passiveness and right, a federation *BC Outdoors* editorial observed, greater coordination and militancy among those interested in outdoor recreation was required. "Hand wringing, shocked expressions, and mutterings of 'oh dear'" would not save other streams from becoming industrial log chutes. From this perspective the 1967 Stellako drive represented a failure of citizen and organizational activism. Apart from the resort owners and the "virtually bankrupt" BCWF, too many had remained silent, including the commercial fisheries interests who reserved their loudest outcry for opposition to the few salmon taken by sports fishermen. The federation and everyone who valued what Howard Paish called a "quality environment" as an "essential attribute of the British Columbian way of life" needed to adopt a new attitude of belligerence.[208]

Such views, coupled with editorial condemnation and complaints from sportsmen (such as Maurice Wrixon of Victoria, who had frequently fished the Stellako and now pledged not to return to his former favourite trout river), prompted the minister to clear up the many misunderstandings that he felt clouded appreciation of his Stellako policy.[209] "I think it is about time we looked at the issue objectively," he asserted in a mid-July "Northern Way" column. Peaceful coexistence between loggers, sport fishermen and the commercial fishery was the goal, Williston explained—on the Stellako and all BC rivers. But the pre-1967 studies on log driving's effects were inconclusive; clear answers would now be forthcoming thanks to co-operation on the part of the various provincial and federal agencies and the mill operator. The logs' financial value to Crown and industry was downplayed in Williston's post-drive account, nor were the logs part of the struggle for provincial rights. Rather, they were now part of the scientific process, essential components of an experiment designed to yield firm economic data applicable to multiple-use decision-making.[210]

The first step in this process was the inquiry into transportation costs, proving that trucking was considerably more costly than river driving. Next came the matter of the drive practice, including measures to limit bark loss and erosion, along with controls on log release and protective booms—all were fundamental elements of the study design. Under these controlled conditions, Williston reported, no jams had occurred and only half a day was required to clean up after the drive. Whether this statement, at odds with actual events, was a product of information the minister had at hand or a conscious effort to misinform the public must remain a matter of conjecture. The final findings were not yet in, but if the technical subcommittee's "assessment of multiple-use feasibility" favoured the continuance of controlled drives, the sensible course of action would be to permit them, using the 1967 study as the basis for strict driving procedures. Conservationist charges of arrogance and short-sightedness were misguided, Williston concluded: "The Stellako river drive was undertaken as a responsible, professional attempt to answer a question of decided economic importance to the province."[211]

Williston's handling of the Stellako issue over the previous two years caused some critics to scoff at his commitment to dispassionate science. Wholesale Fish Dealers' Association President C.B. Shannon saw the attempts at reducing the 1967 drive's destructive effects as a "real whitewash job." The use of helicopters and a large crew to clear jams quickly merely represented the minister's endeavour to rig the study's results. The report, he predicted, would no doubt "prove Mr. Williston was right in allowing the log runs." Williston was taking no chances. In mid-September Hourston again contacted McKinnon about arrangements for the joint report. After discussions with his superior, McKinnon informed Hourston that Williston endorsed the joint report concept, but that if the BCRC objected to any of its findings, a separate report might be prepared. That would not be necessary. An interim technical subcommittee report to the March 1968 meeting of the Federal-Provincial BC Fisheries Committee pointed to an acceptable consensus. The report, McKinnon remarked, indicated "that on this particular river, under certain circumstances, log driving can be carried on." The Stellako, however, was not destined to carry another run of logs. In 1968 Fraser Lake Sawmills altered its log procurement policies, securing raw material from different areas and trucking logs to the mill. The Stellako drives had come to an end, not as a result of public outcry or scientific findings, but as a consequence of the same sort of resource and market considerations that had inspired them.[212]

Epilogue

WHEN DAVE STEWART visited the Stellako in the late summer of 1967 for some fly fishing and a conversation with Doug Kelly, bark still littered the shores of Francois Lake. But the river offered good fishing, yielding several Rainbow Trout. Kelly's reputation in the area had suffered, though, Stewart reported. Most residents of the Lakes District, connected to logging in one way or another, now worked at "making Doug Kelly's life miserable." The Stellako Lodge owner was paying the price for having "the guts to stand up for what he felt was right," and Stewart concluded that the time had come for more British Columbians to follow Kelly's example in the face of government indifference.[213]

Stewart may have overemphasized the degree of Kelly's alienation in the region, but the outdoors writer was far from alone in pondering the implications of the Stellako affair. The BCWF, having asserted its commitment to a less cozy relationship with government and industry, remained convinced that multiple use too often lent respectability to unbridled resource exploitation. By late 1968, however, the organization had become concerned about appearing too negative in its approach to issues such as the Stellako. Confrontation over single issues detracted from its ability to co-operate on other matters.[214]

The federation thus came to two conclusions. First, the province needed to adopt integrated-use legislative and administrative structures that could accommodate the diversity of interests, "rather than a chance system of trying to accommodate a variety of users after one unilateral decision had been made." Had that been in place, the Stellako controversy, taking just one example, could have been avoided. The provincial government should consider creating a single department of resources, then an umbrella agency to establish long-range priorities and coordinate the activities of specific "user oriented departments."[215]

Second, the federation should avoid becoming cast as an "opponent of progress". That goal had, perhaps, to do with the organization's membership makeup and its financial ties to both government and industry. Many of the 16,000 members affiliated through their fish and game clubs would have been resource workers; the federation drew a $5,000 annual grant from the province; and honorary corporate members included firms such as MacMillan Bloedel, Crown Zellerbach Canada and BC Forest Products, in addition to the BC Federation of Labour. After discussing the organization's future with a new advisory board that included Roderick Haig-Brown and wildlife biologist

Ian McTaggart-Cowan, directors announced that the watchdog role would be fulfilled within a more "positive" framework. Feeling a need to set the record straight, the federation claimed that its opposition to Western Mines' activities in Strathcona Park did not imply opposition to mining, just as its complaints about the Stellako log drives meant no enmity towards loggers. The maintenance of environmental quality, they said, could be reconciled with the resource development that provided economic prosperity.[216]

As the Wildlife Federation plotted its direction—wavering between its traditional moderate consensus-building relationship to government and industry and a sharper, more explicitly political approach—similar trends were evident in the American conservation movement. The Sierra Club, under the prodding of executive director David Brower, pressed for a "new militancy" that carried the organization into a less friendly relationship with the US Forest Service and US Parks Service. Brower and the Sierra Club also figured prominently in national campaigns against US Bureau of Reclamation dam projects that threatened western wilderness lands, succeeding in blocking the Marble Canyon dam initiative that would have altered the flow of the Colorado River through Grand Canyon National Park.[217]

There were lessons to be learned from such victories, Penticton's Eric Sismey concluded in 1968. Small local groups such as the Francois Lake resort owners would never muster the political strength to stop log drives on the Stellako, just as the opposition of Campbell River residents to mining in Strathcona Park and the dumping of tailings into Buttle Lake had proven futile. Not until wider public opinion mobilized and focused in a way that would be reflected in election results, Sismey observed, "will the ravishment, under the multiple use alibi, of our natural heritage end." Within a year or so Sismey's wish for new organizations to energize and direct concerns over parks, wilderness, rivers and pollution was granted.[218]

Modern environmentalism arrived in BC in 1969 with the establishment of the Society for Pollution and Environmental Control (SPEC) and the Sierra Club of BC. Greenpeace followed in 1971. Both of the former groups, Gordon Hak notes, expressed a "vibrancy and militancy" lacking in previous organizations such as the BCWF. The federation was far from static in this period, though, and while it lost prominence to the newer organizations, Jeremy Wilson and Arn Keeling are correct in highlighting the environmental leadership that sportsmen provided during the 1960s.[219]

While the provincial government saw the Stellako affair as a clear win in its struggle with Ottawa over control of water resources, the victory came with its own set of contradictions amidst an increasingly politicized discussion of provincial land and water use priorities. In a 1968 brief to a public hearing on water pollution SPEC asked: why did the Department of Fisheries permit clear violations of its own Act? The new environmental group interpreted the log drives as a "classic case" of non-enforcement, one which had seen British Columbians "incensed at the selfish and irresponsible approach by an industry and the stupidity of the provincial government's Minister of Lands and Forests." Rhetorically free of the Wildlife Federation's commitment to positive thinking (which was evident in its 1969 brief to the BC government, peppered with references to "encouraging" and "heartening" developments), SPEC sought confrontation. The Stellako drives were "tantamount to a criminal act against our natural resources" and the offenders should be prosecuted.[220]

The political and industrial elites who controlled the levers of economic progress responded to this new critical environment in two main ways. A few, like BC Hydro and Power co-chairman Gordon Schrum, simply ignored it. He told an early 1968 meeting of the Canadian Forestry Association of BC that those who desired the province's preservation as a natural paradise engaged in "buffalo thinking". Wheat had taken the place of bison on the prairies and the province's camping, hiking and fishing enthusiasts could not turn back the clock either. When mineral reserves were discovered in a park, Schrum mused, perhaps the park should be moved.[221]

The time had long passed for Ray Williston to utter such ideas, at least in public, and he was far too shrewd and capable a politician to invite further rebuke. Foresters could no longer ignore the claims of competing users, he informed a 1969 Canadian Institute of Forestry gathering in Prince George. A "broad and balanced philosophy about land use", one that accepted integrated thinking on resources and recognized the public's right of recreational access, was needed. Industry spokesmen acknowledged the pressures as well, holding to a faith that a public properly educated on the principle of multiple use would prop up a conservationism based on economic realities rather than emotion. During the summer of 1969 the Canadian Forestry Association of BC began just such a campaign, taking the "integrated forest use" terminology favoured by the Wildlife Federation for its own. Citizens would be made "fully aware of the economic values of the forest," cultivating their personal interest in the "preservation and wise use of this resource."[222]

Here, though, preservation did not mean withholding forests from exploitation. Rather, it meant protection from the demands of both a growing population clamouring for outdoor experiences and infrastructure developments that saw timber lost to dam reservoirs, power lines and highway rights-of-way. Fisheries interests—commercial, recreational and government—figured prominently in this scenario, their demands for streamside leavestrips representing a recognized threat to fibre supplies. That, indeed, was where the Williston-forestry industry view of integrated use parted ways with that of the fishers. Depriving loggers of access to streamside timber, like barring log drives from rivers, represented an "extreme insistence on single use" a *British Columbia Lumberman* editorial explained, calling for an "unemotional meeting place" where priorities could be set. Williston remained the industry's strongest ally in this context, allowing fisheries managers to provide input but tolerating no sharing of decision-making authority. Resource use, then, whether labelled "multiple" or "integrated", continued to privilege the rights of forest managers over other interests.[223]

Some thought the path to a more ecologically oriented administrative system lay in breaking down bureaucratic barriers. As noted, the BCWF supported this idea. Prince George–based provincial wildlife biologist Ken Sumanik told the Canadian Institute of Forestry's Cariboo section that the creation of a new Department of Natural Resources would ease conflict between wildlife and lumbering interests. Forestry expert Peter Pearse, who headed the Royal Commission on Forest Resources during the latter 1970s, went so far as to suggest amalgamation of the BCFS and Fish and Wildlife Branch, the prospect of teamwork and a free exchange of ideas among foresters and biologists drawing some support. Others considered the idea naïve, the equivalent of "putting David in bed with Goliath", as one sportsman put it.[224]

But amalgamation of provincial resource agencies would not have resolved the more fundamental federal-provincial tension. From Ottawa's perspective, the Stellako affair reinforced a lesson already learned in conflicts over early 20th-century immigration policy that inspired federal head taxes and other restrictions on the entry of Asians: on issues of fundamental importance to the Pacific province, Ottawa tended to let the 'Spoilt Child of Confederation' have its way, if the cost of accommodation did not run too high. In the mid-1960s,

Stellako River spawning habitat was an acceptable price to pay for political peace. That the compromise left a bitter taste in the mouths of administrators and field staff can hardly be doubted, as they endured open defiance of the *Fisheries Act* in 1966 and the implementation of what must have seemed a cynical agreement to drive the river again the next year under the guise of science.

A fuller answer to SPEC's question about the Department of Fisheries' meek approach to the Stellako drives needs to look at the forest industry's power relative to that of the commercial fishery, both in Victoria and Ottawa, as well as the department's low ministerial status in the federal government. Western issues may also not have ranked highly among Robichaud's priorities—at least, that was the impression on the west coast, where the industry welcomed his 1968 retirement. "The west's problems got short shrift during his regime," columnist Gerry Kidd observed, "and our case was not presented in Ottawa with any degree of skill or aggressiveness." Robichaud's successor, British Columbian Jack Davis, was greeted warmly. He became preoccupied with his Davis Plan of licence limitation and fortunately never had to "pass judgement on whether or not a BC cabinet minister should be able to drive logs down a salmon stream against explicit federal orders."[225]

Williston's ability to play his hole card of scientific uncertainty over the drive's damage likely contributed to Ottawa's waffling on the Stellako. The federal and provincial biologists had no doubt that the drives were harmful, but the long-term effects on the river's ecology could only be assessed through years of systematic study. Not until the 15-year Carnation Creek project, initiated in 1970 on the west coast of Vancouver Island, did BC forestry–fisheries interactions benefit from that sort of analysis. In the mid-1960s Williston could, and did, argue with a degree of legitimacy that no one knew how severely log driving disturbed the Stellako's salmon resource. The uncertain evidence played a part in another federal retreat just over a decade later at Riley Creek on Haida Gwaii, then called the Queen Charlotte Islands (see Chapter 5). That episode replayed many features of the Stellako controversy, with BC's aggression and Ottawa's willingness to back down rather than enforce its own legislation as key factors, as on the Stellako. And when expert opinion was deemed to fall short of certain proof, once again the solution to federal-provincial conflict was more study.[226]

If scientific uncertainty helped define Ottawa's lack of resolve in both instances, doubts about the constitutionality of the *Fisheries Act* may have reinforced caution. Williston certainly seemed eager to have the jurisdictional question referred to the courts. Robichaud, by contrast, opted to leave the matter in limbo, where it remained until the 1970s when logging contractor Dan Fowler was charged with depositing debris in a salmon-bearing stream. Fowler's lawyer argued that section 33(3) of the *Fisheries Act* interfered with the province's jurisdiction over forestry and was therefore *ultra vires*, winning an acquittal in provincial court. The Crown appealed, gaining a reversal in Vancouver County Court. Ultimately, the Council of Forest Industries financed an appeal to the Supreme Court of Canada in an effort to free industry from *Fisheries Act* restrictions. The court's initial 1980 judgement found section 33(3) an unconstitutional invasion of provincial jurisdiction over forests, but a second ruling on a separate case upheld a related section of the act that prohibited the dumping of harmful substances in waters frequented by fish. A fuller account is presented in the next chapter but, reading backwards to the mid-1960s, it is worth noting that, when put to the test, the federal government's jurisdiction over fisheries was by no means certain when it came to aspects of forest industry activities.[227]

After 1967 the Stellako controversy faded from public attention. By 1969 Fraser Lake Sawmills had adopted a dry-land log storage and sorting system, eliminating the need for further drives. The only remaining issue to resolve was that of the now largely irrelevant scientific report submitted to the Federal-Provincial BC Fisheries Committee in May 1969. Its findings highlighted the atypical features of the 1967 drive. Higher flows and "stream development work" involving boom installation and channel clearance had reduced the number and extent of jams. The volume of logs amounted to about half the totals driven in 1965 and 1966, and over half of those logs had little or no bark cover. That factor, coupled with controlled releases and larger crews to free log accumulations before they developed into massive jams, reduced bark deposition. Still, an estimated 230 tons of bark remained in the river after the drive, with 10 significant deposits on or adjacent to Sockeye spawning areas. An estimated 35 tons of bark remained after the 1968 spawning season.[228]

Streambed erosion resulting from jams and boom installations occurred as well, affecting about 91.44 metres (100 yards) of spawning area in two locations. Erosion elsewhere could not be attributed directly to the drive. Nor could the researchers link the drive to decreased oxygen levels in gravel bed test sites, and controlled testing of egg survival demonstrated no conclusive evidence that bark concentrations increased mortality. As for the Sockeye spawners, an estimated 50 per cent of the 90,680 that arrived in 1967 died before spawning, due to a "number of adverse conditions". There was no evidence to suggest that the 1967 drive affected the distribution of spawners along the river. Summing up, the technical subcommittee could attribute no fishery resource losses to the 1967 drive.[229]

The Stellako had received a relatively clean bill of health, but one that measured only immediate impacts. Evaluation of "long-term cumulative effects of log drives on the fishery" were beyond the study's scope. Separate laboratory studies conducted by IPSFC researchers to determine the consequences of bark deposits on dissolved oxygen levels were more cautionary. The micro-organisms responsible for bark decomposition created a quite significant demand for oxygen, reducing the amount available for eggs and young fish for two years. The process began to ease thereafter, but only the discontinuation of the drives had saved the Stellako from the inevitable tipping point of bark-induced salmon mortality. Analysis of water that flowed through the bark indicated the release of low amounts of toxic chemicals, but within acceptable limits.[230]

Related laboratory studies of egg incubation in waters representative of the Stellako's spawning grounds indicated that gravel heavily contaminated with bark did significantly increase the mortality rate, attributable to uneven inter-gravel water flows and reduced oxygen concentrations. Fry emerged later as well, a disruption of the normal life-cycle that would lessen survival potential. Fortunately, Robert Gordon and Dennis Martens concluded, termination of the drives had prevented bark deposition from reaching harmful levels, but resumption "would be ill-advised."[231]

The Stellako log drives left an inconclusive scientific legacy, but that did not affect fishery managers' convictions that the practice was inappropriate for shallow spawning rivers. As McMynn explained to an Ontario grade 13 student researching the subject, log driving and fisheries production were compatible on "larger deeper rivers which require no channelization or other protective works," but shallow, meandering streams which required "improvements" were unsuitable. Hourston drew the same distinction when questioned at the 1969 UFAWU convention about Nass River log driving and the reported use of dynamite to free jams. The Department of Fisheries knew of no spawning grounds on the main stem of the Nass, he replied, and Colcel's logging subsidiary had been authorized to blast snags from the riverbank the previous year. The Stellako, though, was "another matter"; there the logs could damage spawning grounds.[232]

On both rivers, science was hardly the decisive factor, Hourston implied. Colcel's Prince Rupert pulp mill depended on Nass-driven logs, and under the *Fisheries Act* no damage could be proven. His department had confronted the company over its use of dynamite "in pretty strong terms here a little while ago," but once agreement had been reached on drive timing and procedures, faith was required as staff levels permitted only occasional spot checks. "We have to take their word on it," Hourston admitted. The commercial fishery, in short, had to "live with log driving to some extent" and hope for regulatory compliance. Ottawa's laissez-faire approach to log driving on the Nass provided no comfort to the commercial fishery, which experienced its lowest salmon catch in a decade in 1969. Poor runs on northern rivers prompted some to wonder if log transportation practices on the Wannock and Nass, the latter "year by year declining in significance" as a salmon producer, fulfilled warnings first heard on the Stellako.[233]

Log driving may have been an unavoidable fact of life on the Nass, and on the Fraser and Quesnel Rivers used by Weldwood, but British Columbians were fast losing patience for other forest industry practices. The use of herbicides near fish-bearing rivers, yarding logs across streams and clearcutting to the edge of all waters became increasingly controversial even as the Stellako faded from prominence. But the Stellako affair had, for three years, forced British Columbians to confront the fundamental underlying issues. What were the acceptable costs of progress? Did it make sense to run logs down a vulnerable stretch of river given the existence of a road link, even if the use of that road would have doubled the company's transportation costs? Ray Williston, for reasons that surely went beyond concern for the financial health of Fraser Lake Sawmills, concluded that it did. He and the forest industry had their way on the Stellako, but in so doing helped undermine the legitimacy of their multiple-use resource management regime. Local SPEC and Sierra Club chapters spread across the province, the former cultivating tenuous links with organized labour and First Nations. Commercial fishermen grew more militant, as the Davis Plan reduced their numbers and logging and pulp mill pollution threatened freshwater habitats. New conservation organizations such as the Steelhead Society of BC and the Pacific Salmon Society joined in, adding to the discomfort of Williston and the forest industry.[234]

But in Prince George, at least, the price of progress was still being calculated after the Stellako runs. The Intercontinental pulp mill, the city's third, went into production in the spring of 1968, and air quality ranked high among residents' concerns. But the plant brought total investment in Prince George's pulp and paper economy to $216 million, employing 1,200 workers and contributing an annual payroll of $11 million. Sawmilling and logging employed another 8,000 in the Prince George forest district, generating $50 million in annual earnings. To the north, on the Peace, Williston Lake was forming behind the Bennett dam, creating a "nightmare of drowned forests, log jams and floating debris." To the west, power from the Alcan development had begun providing electricity to Terrace and Prince Rupert. Salmo continued to list the Stellako as among the best of the region's fly fishing streams, but the Nechako's Sockeye and Chinook populations were in steep decline due to the Kenny dam. The Bennett dam had a more complex impact on fisheries resources, with some species increasing, but the huge reservoir disrupted migration routes for the now endangered Mountain Caribou. Modernization's benefits and costs were giving rise to an ongoing process of weighing, and for many the rapid pace of change seemed haphazardly planned, even reckless.[235]

Doug Kelly stood largely alone in defying the 1967 Stellako drive. That he did so in defence of his own economic interest cannot be denied, but his actions represented something more than the profit-seeking of a lodge operator unwilling to sacrifice a season's income. Unable to attract outside support, in 1967 Kelly was a potential leader without a movement. But that would come. Had the Stellako drives occurred six or seven years later, Kelly would likely have enjoyed much greater support. Civil disobedience would not become a staple of environmental protest until the 1980s, but it's easy to imagine a real gathering of opposition forces at the Stellako's mouth had the drives taken place in the mid-1970s.

In the 1960s, though, Williston could still depict the north-central interior as a frontier in the early stages of its industrial development, where getting things done took priority over environmental concerns. "The people of BC are dedicated to opening up this province," he told a Prince George audience of Social Creditors at a 1968 dinner held to support the federal candidacy of Bert LeBoe. Cyril Shelford spoke that evening as well, but LeBoe, the "lumbermen's MP", lost to his Liberal opponent after serving in Ottawa for 12 years. Williston and Shelford, finally appointed to cabinet as Minister of Agriculture after holding the Omineca riding since 1952, survived in 1969 as Bennett scored his final election victory.[236]

Running for the NDP in the Omineca riding that year was Doug Kelly, but the Stellako Lodge owner polled less than half of the votes that went to the popular Shelford. Three years later Kelly ran again, campaigning on NDP promises to boost old age pensions and introduce government automobile insurance. Kelly also criticized Social Credit hydroelectric dams that destroyed farms, orchards and the province's "beautiful rivers." The pressure for industry and government to cultivate a more sustainable relationship to nature contributed to the 1972 election of Dave Barrett's NDP government, ending two decades of W.A.C. Bennett's Social Credit administration. "The support given to the NDP reflects a profound change in public attitude," Hal Griffin observed in the *Fisherman*. "No longer are people prepared to accept environmental destruction as the price of industrial development."[237]

In one of the 1972 election's shocking results, the Conservative candidate siphoned off enough of Shelford's support to allow Kelly to edge the incumbent out by just 164 votes and claim a seat in the legislature. Williston lost his Fort George race too; unionized pulp and paper workers cast ballots for the NDP candidate. Both veteran MLAs accepted defeat, having little enthusiasm for a term in opposition.[238]

It's possible Kelly saw the election as a fitting triumph over his old Stellako rivals, but the record provides no evidence that he did. But it is evident that Kelly's profile in the region owed much to the Stellako affair. Though a World War II veteran, a member of the BC Provincial Police and a Vancouver fireman for 15 years before coming north and acquiring the Stellako Lodge, Kelly was known primarily for his stand on the Stellako. More than that, with the passage of time he had become the victor, seen as the lone crusader who had brought sufficient public attention to bear on the river to have the log drives stopped. That the evidence does not support this conclusion is less important than the fact that local people, and Kelly himself, chose to remember the Stellako affair in this way.[239]

Supporting a piece of NDP forestry legislation during a late-night sitting of the legislature in November 1974, Kelly referred to his "altercation" with the BCFS. "I actually took them on single-handed in attempting to stop a log drive on the Stellako River," he told the House. "They actually had to break the law to carry out the log drive on the Stellako River, and you know, there was so much publicity created...that indeed there has been no log drive since." Remarking on Kelly's statement, the NDP's Gary Lauk joked, "that's why Cyril isn't here today." Just over a year later Kelly's career in provincial politics ended when Bill Bennett returned the Socreds to power by uniting the right. No Conservative ran in the Omineca in 1975 and Jack Kempf defeated Kelly by winning almost 60 per cent of the votes.[240]

Kelly was not alone in remembering the Stellako as an early triumph for environmental values. The BCWF also declared victory in the Stellako war. "We stopped log drives on the Stellako River," declared the federation's early 1973 *Newsletter* in a retrospective of its relationship to W.A.C. Bennett's government, emphasizing the difficulties in wringing concessions from the regime. A local history of Fraser Lake attributes the end of the drives to concern for Sockeye spawning beds. Actually, changes in Fraser Lake Sawmills' log procurement strategy put an end to the drives, but the minor myths, whether of one man's defiance in stirring public outrage, the Wildlife Federation's stalwart stance or the application of wise policy, were more palatable explanations to help the public make sense of this piece of BC history.[241]

What about the river itself, over which all the controversy raged? Fly fisherman Maurice Wrixon, after vowing never to return to his favourite river, continued to make annual trips. "That river is the closest to Heaven I will ever reach," he remarked in 1977 after enjoying the best fishing in his memory. Wrixon's hosts were Stellako Lodge operators Doug and Betty Kelly, with whom he had become friends. Wrixon thought the river's future now depended on reserving its best places for fly fishers only, and a section was later so designated. The Sockeye continued to return, up to 350,000 arriving to spawn in peak years, and their eggs provided an important source of food for the Rainbow Trout. Ironically, in 1980 the BC government moved to protect the Stellako, establishing a 127-hectare fish and wildlife reserve.[242] Today fly fishers continue to rank the Stellako as a prime trout stream, its four resorts drawing over 9,000 visitors annually. As one fisherman observed recently: "I have never seen a river as beautiful as the Stellako".[243]

As for Fraser Lake Sawmills, the company was acquired by West Fraser in 1997. Harvesting trees damaged by mountain pine beetle boosted the forest industry, albeit temporarily, and logs came by truck to a new, modern sawmill from the Ootsa Lake area. The former log drives remain of interest to scientists concerned with the environmental effects of log transportation in west coast waters, and they are remembered in the region as a colourful aspect of local history. Older conservationists still recall the Stellako conflict specifically. The long-term consequences of the drives are unknown, but clearly the river withstood the gouging of spawning beds and the bark deposits to remain productive.[244]

The river's resilience should not be taken as a vindication of those who supported the drives. Nor should drive supporters be condemned, for that only obscures understanding of the issues at play. Everyone who took a position on the Stellako log drives had a reason for doing so, though in retrospect some seem more reasonable than others. Ray Williston took the perfectly rational stance that the forest industry's needs came first and that proof of damage to the river was lacking. Whether *any* proof would have satisfied Williston is a matter worth pondering, for he had one eye on Ottawa the entire time. This was a *BC* river, to be used in a way that best suited BC's economy and demonstrated the federal government's irrelevance in provincial resource management. The operative word in multiple use was 'use' on the forest industry's terms, and to Williston a few federal fish were well worth sacrificing in the process of asserting BC's control over water.

Federal Fisheries minister H.J. Robichaud seems to have wanted nothing more than for the Stellako issue to go away, and he succeeded in making his wish come true (to his satisfaction, at least) with the 1967 agreement subjecting the much-studied Stellako to further research. For Robichaud, this small river in a thinly populated region of a distant province was not worth fighting for. Despite the unqualified conclusions of the 1966 report that the previous year's drive had sacrificed a good deal of spawning habitat—a report prepared in part by Robichaud's own department—he chose the path of least resistance. This, too, was a reasonable choice, especially given the constitutional questions that would surface a decade later at Riley Creek. If going along to get along with the fractious Pacific province meant a loss of respect for his department, there were million-dollar investments in new spawning channels to balance that out in boosting Ottawa's legitimacy as a resource manager.

The Stellako had little or no symbolic importance for Robichaud, unlike for Williston, but the river did become a symbol to British Columbians. The forest industry saw rivers like the Stellako as natural conveyor belts—raw material chutes which eliminated the expense of building and maintaining roads in a difficult terrain and climate. For Cyril Shelford and the farmer-loggers of Francois Lake the Stellako was an economic lifeline, the essential link in connecting timber to sawmill, pulpmill and the world market beyond. A way of life based on a mixed economy was seen to hang in the balance. Regional tensions came into play as well, linked to the Bennett government's reputation as a defender of the hinterland against the power of the metropolitan centres of the south coast. No benefits from the commercial fishery found their way to the Lakes District; the balance sheets of Vancouver-based BC packers and the earnings of coastal fishermen were of little concern to locals in the Stellako region.

There is no simple way to capture the perceptions of the sporting interests. Howard Paish and the BCWF seized on the Stellako drives, as did Williston, for their broader implications. Massive expansion of the pulp and paper sector placed the province's waters at risk on a scale that demanded opposition, and the Stellako represented the ideal opportunity on many different levels. Kiernan's silence, Robichaud's eagerness to leave the river to its fate, Williston's perceived arrogance and the illegitimacy of government/industry multiple-use promises formed a potent brew of discontents. Added to the mix was the seemingly illogical and reckless disregard for law, science and even basic economic calculations. For the BCWF, the Stellako drives did not make sense.

These perceptions reached from the federation's Burnaby office up the Fraser to the Quesnel Rod and Gun Club and extended to the Burns Lake-based Tweedsmuir Rod and Gun Club. But the response of the Prince George sportsmen complicates this tidy picture of conservationist outrage. There the rod and gun club withdrew after putting forth its convention resolution condemning the drive. Did occupational concerns in a community so heavily dependent upon a profitable forest industry dictate caution? Was pressure brought to bear by the logging, sawmilling and pulp interests? No answers are explicitly available, but the questions themselves caution against sweeping generalizations about the sporting interests in the Stellako issue.

Finally, there is the Stellako band's place in the controversy, and here further research is in order. Apart from a couple of *Citizen* stories and another in the *Native Voice*, First Nations' concerns played little part in the drama, at least in the published record. Sadly, that comes as no surprise, but evidence from elsewhere in the region depicts this period as one of mounting First Nations resistance to the forest industry's destruction of fisheries and wildlife habitat. Aboriginal trappers along the Skeena and Fraser systems protested, demanding compensation for lost traplines. Trapping was a frontier industry, Williston responded, its difficulties "one of the penalties of progress."[245]

It was, in the end, that notion of progress that inspired the Stellako confrontation and others of the postwar era. British Columbians grew increasingly skeptical about the ease with which political and industrial elites exchanged unspoiled land and rivers, subsistence patterns of existence and economic independence for development and wage labour in the service of large corporations. The Stellako issue, stemming from one small river, is complicated and important because it focused so many of these tensions so sharply, just at the time when nature was coming to mean more than a storehouse of resources. As a symbol, the Stellako was a river that led, in its meandering way, from a traditional BC of unbridled resource-based materialism to the one we inhabit today. And as debates over off-shore oil development, fish farming and proposed hydroelectric projects suggest, BC is a province that continues to confront the dilemmas raised on the Stellako River four decades ago.

RICHARD A. RAJALA

5

The Battle of Riley Creek
Clearcuts, Salmon and Multiple Use on Haida Gwaii, 1970–1985

Introduction

RILEY CREEK, a small stream on Haida Gwaii, is unknown to most British Columbians today. Flowing into Rennell Sound on the west coast of Graham Island, the creek drains an area of just over 28 square kilometres in a surrounding area of steep terrain rising from sea level to an elevation of about 609.6 metres (2,000 feet). A fairly substantial run of Pink Salmon spawns in its lower reaches and a few decades ago stands of Western Hemlock stood undisturbed by commercial activity. An isolated area in the archipelago formerly known as the Queen Charlotte Islands and described as "typical of small Pacific Northwest rain forest valleys", the forests around Riley Creek stood beyond the reach of industrial capital. But when a Japanese-backed company penetrated Rennell Sound in the 1970s, building roads and clearcutting the steep slopes with overhead logging technology, Riley Creek became the site of one of British Columbia's most bitter environmental conflicts.[1]

Facing page: Clearcut hillside, Rennell Sound, April 1981. Courtesy of Keith Moore.

Riley Creek's role was shaped by the forces of both nature and industrial capitalism. Here is where the strains of resource management within Canadian federalism met pressures generated by Aboriginal rights and environmental movements. The Rennell Sound area may have been typical of many sites on Haida Gwaii, but it was also typically fragile. Fully exposed to strong winds, heavy rainfall and snow at higher elevations, the slopes have a thin covering of "course textured" soil, are dissected by deep gullies and subject to landslides even with the forest cover in place. Geologists have a number of technical terms to describe the various sorts of "soil mass movement processes." For our purposes it is sufficient to note that the slopes are unstable, and logging could only exacerbate that condition as road systems disturbed drainage patterns and clearcutting eliminated forest cover.[2]

In retrospect, it's easy to depict the logging of Riley Creek's slopes as an accident waiting to happen. Landslides *did* occur, salmon habitat suffered and fingers of blame were pointed at all those who played a part. Some with a stake in the conflict—most notably, federal fisheries officer Jim Hart—warned in advance that the slopes would fail. But in a depressing replay of the Stellako River controversy (see Chapter 4) the provincial government and timber capital, with an assist from International Woodworkers of America (IWA) leaders, had their way. The ensuing slides discredited all those who endorsed the logging operations, including federal fisheries officials who did not support Hart and his colleagues in the field. But the jurisdictional point had been made again: BC's power over forests trumped Ottawa's interest in productive fish habitat.

Circumstances specific to Haida Gwaii also contributed to igniting this familiar story of environmental degradation. When QC Timber, subsidiary of a giant Japanese trading company, set off logging-induced slides in late 1978, Hart applied the authority of a recently strengthened *Fisheries Act* to issue a stop order. Amidst loud protest from the BC Ministry of Forests (MOF), industry and the IWA, the agencies seemed to agree on a plan to spare the small area covered by cutting permit 144. The consensus had a short life. The BC Forest Service (BCFS) authorized the logging, QC Timber decided to defy the ban by sending in fallers, and Hart began arresting workers. Reports suggest that Riley Creek, in the context of industry-wide concern over access to timber and the federal regulators' apparent determination to protect salmon habitat, was selected as the site for a showdown. Facing a direct threat to the corporate clearcutting regime, an MOF-industry-IWA united front ultimately forced a federal retreat. QC Timber gained authority to clearcut the slope, with some protective measures imposed; all the charges were dropped and Hart resigned. Then, when the rains and winds came in November 1979, major slides again hit Riley Creek.

Commercial fishers, First Nations and environmentalists saw these slides as a betrayal of integrated resource use promises issued in the province's 1978 *Forest Act*, as evidence of federal officials' failure to enforce their own legislation and as proof of timber capital's success in defending its freedom to abuse sensitive ecosystems. This view helped fuel the Haida and environmentalist campaign to preserve South Moresby Island from logging. Haida fisherman Charlie Bellis sought, with the backing of the Islands Protection Society, to have high-ranking MOF and federal Fisheries Service officials answer for their actions in court. The province blocked the prosecution but that merely reinforced the sense that Riley Creek had exposed the moral bankruptcy of both federal and provincial resource management. On Riley Creek, as on the Stellako, the dominant industry's practices seemed immune to regulation, to stewardship and to common sense. And in another replay of the Stellako drama, the official response to the Riley Creek debacle involved the legitimacy offered by science.

Just as the 1967 Stellako drive was conducted as a supposedly scientific enterprise, federal-provincial conflict morphed into co-operation at Rennell Sound, giving rise to the Fish/Forestry Interaction Program. Research, again, would serve to reconcile the contradictions of resource exploitation, this time by studying the applicability of heavy-lift helicopters to cutting sensitive, steep-slope sites. Logging and the protection of fish habitat would, in the tradition of technological optimism that characterizes BC forest history, go forward in compatibility, not conflict. Such, at least, was the conclusion of the official narrative. Critics told the story differently, depicting the Riley Creek slides as a glaring example of what could go wrong in the single-minded pursuit of victory in the game of federal-provincial resource politics and in giving one industry freedom to exploit a diminishing supply of timber. Multiple-use rhetoric aside, streams were disposable.

My account agrees more with the latter narrative than the former, but I hope to provide greater insight by situating Riley Creek in historical context. Whereas the Stellako controversy occurred in the flush times of the postwar boom just as the environmental movement was beginning to take shape, Riley

Creek came as the boom was sputtering to an end and the environmental movement was already well in place, with the addition of greater interest in Aboriginal rights. Whether one thought of nature in terms of resource values or ecosystems, Riley Creek brought social tensions into sharp relief as British Columbians confronted a new sense of limits.

No easy solutions to the sustainability challenge were forthcoming then, and they remain elusive today. If all of the province's streams were Riley Creeks, as Charlie Bellis would put it, how could they be saved? Many concluded that the *Fisheries Act*'s strong language offered no solution without the will to enforce. Others called for large-scale preservation of forest landscapes, but too many streams flowed through too many valleys for a preservationist solution. The 'New Forestry', an ecosystem-based model of management, captured the enthusiasm of many; others saw only a new label for a commodity-driven approach that prioritized forestry values over all others. If Riley Creek revealed problems, agreeing on the solutions and the lessons to be learned proved difficult. While Riley Creek has retained but a dim place in our collective memory, it deserves more scholarly attention than it has so far received. The implications of a century of resource management trends, achievements and faults came to a head at Riley and, as with the Stellako a decade before, the issues posed fundamental questions about capitalism, federalism and our place in nature.[3]

Clearcutting, Fish Habitat and the Regulatory Setting

CONCERNS OVER THE IMPACT OF CUTTING PRACTICES on fish habitat did not arise suddenly in the 1970s. Since the early twentieth century, fisheries managers and fishers—both commercial and recreational—had pointed to the abuse of streams that went well beyond the obvious problems associated with log driving. Streams flowed through the valley bottoms, which provided easy access for logging railways and the steam-powered yarding equipment stationed along the tracks. There the timber grew in greatest abundance and the gentle terrain offered transportation advantages relative to the hillsides. But streamside logging came with severe consequences and was the subject of frequent commentary in federal fisheries officers' reports. Enormous amounts of slash and debris entered the streams. Logs piled at landings caused bank erosion, worsened by the typical practice of yarding across and along stream beds. Clearcutting to a stream's edge reduced shade, causing water temperatures to rise above optimum levels for fish during hot summers.[4]

As the clearcuts stretched across the valleys and up the slopes, natural flow regimes were disrupted. Freshets followed heavy rains, the torrents carving new channels, shifting spawning gravels and introducing high sediment loads. In late summer and early fall water levels fell, interrupting upstream salmon migration. All of this unfolded at different times in different places, and scientific understanding was slow in coming. By mid-century, though, fisheries biologists had no doubt that logging was "a potent cause of fluctuations in the abundance of mature salmon."[5]

The most popular—and contentious—proposal among fisheries interests for the protection of aquatic habitat was the leavestrip, which retained borders of timber along streams to preserve their integrity. The BCFS and industry successfully fought that idea, essentially a challenge to their control over the land base. But fisheries managers gained something of a voice in planning with the introduction of a referral system in the late 1950s. The process was cumbersome, however, causing delays and the potential for restrictions in cutting permit language that government foresters and their industry clients disliked. A 1983 report concluded that protective clauses in cutting rights were "violated by almost every operation near a stream."[6]

The referral system prevailed despite, or perhaps in part because of, a complex regulatory structure. The federal Fisheries Service had primary responsibility for enforcing the *Fisheries Act*. As seen in the Stellako case, the legislation's wording, and therefore its power, was applied selectively and with considerable regard for the province's constitutional rights over forests. The province's Fish and Wildlife Branch, part of the Ministry of Environment in 1978, also took a role in fisheries management—quite a strenuous one at Riley Creek. But in the hierarchy of provincial institutions the MOF, created in 1976, reigned supreme. As Jeremy Wilson puts it, drawing on the words of Richard Overstall who provided critical coverage of Riley Creek at the time, "the 'imperial forest service' was timber-oriented, intolerant of dissenting ideas, disinclined to experiment, and not given to humility about its knowledge base."[7]

After passage of the 1947 *Forest Act* the BCFS pursued a sustained-yield agenda with single-minded intensity. The tree farm licence (TFL) tenure provided major firms with access to vast expanses of timber, accompanied by

Stream damage caused by logging, 1972. NA-27481.

freedom to set cutting rates and manage their holdings under loose government supervision. Smaller operators competed for timber in the province's Public Sustained Yield Units (PSYU), where government foresters took a more direct managerial role. As the intensity of environmental conflict grew during the 1960s and 1970s, industry and the BCFS responded with the rhetoric of multiple use, or "integrated resource management" to retain legitimacy. Then, in early 1972, the agency responded to mounting discontent over unrestricted clearcutting with the Coast Logging Guidelines. A moderate response that preserved the essential efficiencies of clearcutting while limiting the scale of cutblocks in a system of patch logging, the guidelines pleased no one. Industry protested the new restrictions, while fisheries interests continued to advocate for retaining continuous leavestrips.[8]

The guidelines, a half-hearted but nonetheless significant disruption of forest industry freedoms, remained in place from 1972, under Dave Barrett's NDP government, until the election of Bill Bennett's Social Credit party in late 1975. New Forests minister Tom Waterland immediately relaxed guideline enforcement, drawing industry praise for a return to "a more flexible and reasonable" approach to multiple-use forest and water management. On Haida Gwaii,[9] as elsewhere along the coast, forest practice regulation gave way to encouragement of "flexibility and site-specific management" by operators to "maximize the harvest of merchantable timber along streams." Fisheries managers had always been at a disadvantage under the referral process, an arrangement that allowed a measure of federal and provincial input into cutting plans (through the Department of Fisheries and the BC Fish and Wildlife Branch, respectively) but left final decisions on the introduction of stream-protection clauses to foresters. The consequence was a widespread disregard for fish habitat, which only grew more pronounced after 1975. Streamside timber would be cut routinely and foresters exercised ultimate approval on any road location and construction constraints. Socred Minister of Conservation Sam Bawlf also curbed the Fish and Wildlife Branch's perceived tendency to act as an "independent environmental advocate", leading the BC Wildlife Federation (BCWF) to conclude that the Socred government was "overwhelmingly sympathetic to the destroyers and to the strippers".[10]

That left the federal government to assert its jurisdiction, and here conservationists found new reason for hope during the late 1970s. After years of drawing scorn for its hesitant use of the *Fisheries Act*'s habitat provisions, in 1977 Liberal minister Romeo LeBlanc steered a strengthened act through parliament. Bill C-38's provisions included new power to actively prevent habitat deterioration, rather than penalize offenders after the fact, and much stiffer financial penalties for violations. The BCWF and UFAWU welcomed the bill, amidst much hand-wringing by forest industry executives over its implications. Particularly disturbing was section 31(1), which prohibited any undertaking resulting in "the harmful alteration, disruption or destruction of fish habitat." Section 33(2), long a feature of the act but loosely enforced, made it an offence to introduce any "deleterious substance" in salmon-bearing streams or waters that entered such streams. Another section called for the prior submission and approval of plans if a project might threaten fish habitat, giving the Fisheries Service the power to issue stop orders. Potential financial penalties rose—up to $50,000 for a first offence and $100,000 for each subsequent offence.[11]

The MOF and Council of Forest Industries (COFI), representing major firms, responded to the proposed amendments with alarm. "The potential effect on the Province's forest harvesting programs could be bad," chief forester E.L. Young informed the government. Entire watersheds might fall under the "fish habitat" designation, an analysis warned. Only if enforced with discretion could the forest sector tolerate the act. COFI considered the amendments a case of regulatory overkill, the wording so broad that "almost all forest industry operations could be held in technical violation of the new provisions of the act." Bill C-38 drew specific attention from Bill Bennett at the August 1977 Premiers' Conference as an unwelcome example of federal intrusion into provincial rights. He declared that Ottawa was seizing new powers to "constrain provincial resource management policies".[12]

Passed in September and set to take effect by the end of the year, the new *Fisheries Act* united all forest sector elements in opposition to a "frightening piece of legislation" which left the logging industry "open to paralyzing abuse", observed forest industry journalist Gray Wheeler. At their January 1978 convention, the Truck Loggers Association's (TLA), along with COFI, the Council of Marine Carriers and IWA, presented a joint brief to BC's federal Liberal caucus demanding withdrawal to allow consultation for revisions. The *BC Lumberman's* Brian Martin considered it "the most unified and determined front the forest industries of BC have ever presented." A "bear pit" session with Environment minister Len Marchand and caucus leader Senator Ray Perrault provided a forum for heated discussion. The perceived draconian power held by Fisheries Service field officers, now with the authority to carry firearms and serve arrest warrants, was denounced, as was the threat of punitive fines and the act's "vague and all-embracing terminology." The need for trade-offs between industries had not been acknowledged, complained COFI's Don Lanskail. Bert Gayle of Canadian Forest Products, denying any correlation between logging and declining fish population, said that operators already worked closely with fisheries personnel. The TLA's Dave O'Connor went further, warning that the legislation could cripple the entire coastal forest industry. Pointing directly to the conflict ahead, the IWA's regional president, Jack Munro, described the act as a regulatory burden created by those who "don't know the facts of life." His members should not be targeted, Munro continued, by legislation that ignored reality and threatened to disrupt working families and their communities. The Liberals promised to consider the need for amendments, but LeBlanc's parliamentary secretary, Comox-Alberni MP Hugh Anderson, defended the act as necessary for the survival of the fishing industry.[13]

Another key element to help develop a healthy commercial fishery was the federal-provincial Salmonid Enhancement Program (SEP), inspired by a belief that spawning channels, fishways and a new generation of hatcheries could double river and ocean productivity. Announced in 1975, SEP got underway in 1977 after two years of studies. Federal funding of $150 million would be allocated to the program's first five-year phase, with BC contributing $7.5 million. Despite concerns that emphasizing large projects and technology could not compensate for industrial devastation of spawning grounds, many were pleased by SEP, which boosted hopes for tough *Fisheries Act* regulations and rigorous enforcement. Liberal government credibility would suffer if the millions of dollars devoted to enhancement were undermined by weak habitat protection. Over time confidence in SEP would fade, replaced by increasing cynicism about a program that seemed too infatuated with artificial production methods at the expense of natural runs.[14]

Just what sort of protection those runs would receive under the new *Fisheries Act* provoked continued discussion throughout 1978. In February federal and provincial officials met in Victoria to discuss jurisdictional issues and COFI's Lanskail travelled to Ottawa for talks in early March. Federal bureaucrats pledged "reasonable enforcement", but the prospect of fisheries field officers upholding the letter of the law without regard for discretion remained high. BC's Forests minister Tom Waterland and new Environment minister Jim Nielsen reassured corporate heads at COFI's annual meeting that April, with Nielsen promising co-operation with the "true conservationists" in industry, as opposed to environmental critics who would "travel anywhere to comment as long as it was negative." The cord of red tape was strangling a hard-pressed industry, he confirmed, singling out the *Fisheries Act* for criticism as a "double permit" system. BC was capable of solving its own problems without federal interference and the Socred government would always listen to its "No. 1" industry.[15]

The rhetorical battle with Ottawa continued that spring when Romeo LeBlanc denied the validity of the forest sector brief. Certain logging practices had an undeniable impact on the fisheries resource base and he would confront non-compliance with the full use of his authority. But the forest industry had overreacted, he maintained; the legislation merely sought to encourage consultation between companies and fisheries officials in working out mutually agreeable solutions. Nor did that mean Fisheries Service veto power over logging plans, habitat protection division head Forbes Boyd assured operators. The existing referral system would continue the tradition of co-operative management. The habitat protection division's Tom Bird took a similarly conciliatory approach in remarks to interior lumbermen. True, the act did give the Fisheries Service the right to demand plans and issue stop orders, but its real intent was to plug loopholes and fine-tune fisheries-logging liaisons within a "co-operative and discretionary" atmosphere. Disinclined to accept these expressions of collaboration and compromise, the BC *Lumberman's* Brian Martin described LeBlanc's rebuttal as the "high handed" response of an "ill-informed and out-of-touch minister."[16]

Commercial and recreational fishers, on the other hand, put aside their growing differences over catch allocation in supporting what seemed to be a more serious federal commitment to habitat protection. The BCWF's executive director, Bill Otway, praised Hugh Anderson for standing his ground at the Truck Loggers' Convention and pointed to the forest industry's about-face on the exercise of resource managers' discretionary authority in the field. During the fight over compulsory leavestrips, logging operators had insisted on foresters' power to make decisions on a site-specific basis as an alternative to blanket regulation. Now the prospect of fisheries officers exerting the same sort of judgment under the *Fisheries Act* was terrifying.[17]

Given that federal statements blended seriousness of purpose with the language of co-operation and compromise, the ultimate meaning of the legislation remained very much in doubt. The skies seemed to clear in early 1979, however, when Wally Johnson, director general of the Fisheries Service Pacific Region, spoke in comforting terms at the TLA's Vancouver convention. The previous convention's atmosphere of acrimony and distrust had given way to one of ease and harmony—"more like a love-in than a panel discussion", remarked one delegate. Johnson referred to "building a bridge of mutual understanding" through the *Fisheries Act*, a measure designed to inspire not confrontation but "advance planning and accommodation." Mounting environmental concern among the public had seen the forest industry take a disproportionate amount of blame for declining fish stocks, Johnson declared. The solution lay in application of the multiple-use philosophy, meaning that loggers try to see things from the fisheries perspective once in a while. "Think about how you'd react if we sent trawlers steaming through your tree stands," he remarked.[18] In offering a truce under the multiple-use planning option, Johnson spoke in terms familiar to the forest sector.

Indeed, government and industry had marketed their practices under that heading for years and the province's 1978 *Forest Act*, Bill 14, made multiple use official policy. For the previous three years Peter Pearse's Commission on Forest Resources had given British Columbians the opportunity to express themselves on the issues. Defending the land base against encroachment by other users ranked high among forest industry priorities, even as small operators criticized the monopolistic features of the TFL system that gave major companies so much control over the forest. A diverse grouping of established organizations, like the BCWF, along with newer environmental groups such as the Sierra Club and Scientific Pollution and Environmental Control Society (SPEC), called for forest practice reforms.

Pearse himself had urged a more genuine application of multiple-use principles in his 1976 report but otherwise defended the essential tenets of industrial forestry. Conceding that annual cuts were too high in a few coastal areas, he saw no need for drastic reductions in the provincial harvest. Concerns about clearcutting lacked credibility as well. The Coast Logging Guidelines, for example, were a misguided regulatory exercise, both too costly and unsuited to the province's diverse forest conditions. True, clearcutting could alter flow regimes and affect water quality, with consequences for both watersheds and fish habitats. But with proper safeguards to prevent obstructions, stream bank deterioration and siltation the practice was "not inevitably more injurious to fisheries than other harvesting techniques." Road-building, he concluded, caused far more serious environmental problems than clearcutting. Streamside leavestrips and cutting in smaller patches merely dispersed operations, requiring more road mileage and "thereby multiplying the source of the most serious environmental damage."[19]

The multiple-use solution, Pearse advised, lay in expanding the resource folio planning system. Introduced in 1973 as an alternative to the delays associated with the referral process, folio planning meant the various agencies and companies compiled forest soil, water, fisheries, wildlife and other data for a particular watershed on a sheaf of overlay maps for consideration in the logging plan. Pearse considered the folio system "a most significant advance in integrated resource use planning", one that offered a systematic way of accommodating relevant values. Unfortunately, he acknowledged, the demand for data outstripped the capacity of agencies to provide them. The resultant delays hindered licensees in exercising their cutting rights, causing "frustrations and friction" between industry and agencies. Worse yet, in the absence

Large clearcut, 1973. NA-29197.

of data, fisheries and wildlife personnel sometimes imposed "restrictions on operations that may be unnecessary and costly."[20]

On the central issue of tenure, Pearse's recommendations acknowledged the alarming control over cutting rights exerted by a few large corporations. Considering this a matter of urgent concern, he sought to provide more opportunity for small operators without making fundamental changes to the system. Timber sale harvesting licences (TSHL) should be converted into a new form of tenure—the forest licence—when they expired, and small operators should continue to have access to timber sale licences. Pearse considered the TFL tenure a great success, having brought large expanses of unregulated forest land into sustained yield while providing integrated enterprises with the assured control over timber supplies needed to attract investment capital. TFLs had also "met, if not exceeded expectations" in resource management due to the proprietary interest they had created among holders. In a rare critical comment, Pearse noted that annual cut rates on the tenures had risen alarmingly over the years thanks to company revision of inventories, higher yield estimates and silvicultural practices. Rejecting company justifications,

Large clearcut, 1973. NA-29198.

Pearse observed that "only a very modest fraction of the increases in harvest rates can be attributed to licensees' efforts to enhance forest growth." Firmer government oversight was needed, he concluded.[21]

Waterland accepted Pearse's report and appointed a Forest Policy Advisory Committee to come up with recommendations on implementation. Ideas poured in, with even Waterland expressing disappointment at the self-interest of corporate submissions. The major firms, satisfied that Pearse had made no radical proposals, expressed some discomfort at his desire to promote more competition for timber rights. The Environment and Land Use Committee (ELUC) Secretariat—an advisory body established by the NDP—joined the Parks Branch in hoping for a multiple-use policy that would place other forest users on a more equal footing with industry. The BCWF and Sierra Club endorsed that view, seeing promise in folio planning but desiring legislative protection for environmental values in the interim. Waterland pledged that the new act would protect industry access to forests but not to the exclusion of others. The multiple-use strategy would therefore balance competing demands in a way that "sustains production and avoids environmental deterioration."[22]

COFI had faith that the forthcoming legislation would make for a healthier business climate, and Waterland did not disappoint. Bill 14 ignored Pearse's desire for a more competitive timber allocation, Jeremy Wilson relates, and economist Richard Schwindt observes that the tenure provisions served to "legitimize and thereby to entrench the concentration of harvesting rights." On all but minor points COFI found itself "in the comfortable position of agreeing with Bill 14." Under the bill, all TFLs would be converted to 25-year "evergreen" terms, after their initial renewal. All of the PSYUs were to be consolidated into 33 Timber Supply Areas (TSA), Timber Sale Harvesting Licences (TSHL) became renewable forest licences, and 10-year timber sale licences would provide small operators access to Crown timber. In requiring the chief forester to consider recreational, fisheries and wildlife values in setting harvest levels on the TSAs, multiple-use policy committed the Minister of Forests to consultation and co-operation with other ministries and with the private sector.[23]

The act's entire package, Waterland said, would promote intensive management under the concept of industry-government partnership. His new deputy minister, former COFI staffer and Forest Policy Advisory Committee member Mike Apsey, also stressed that relationship in describing the *Forest Act* after its June 1978 passage. Incentives for quality management in the form of increased allowable cuts and reduced red tape put the government "in partnership with industry in the management of the forest resources", he declared. But just who qualified for partnership proved contentious. The large, integrated companies were "very happy, indeed," Ken Drushka reported, and COFI endorsed the strengthened partnership. Small operators, on the other hand, felt left out, confined largely to the scraps offered through the timber sale licence tenure.[24]

Others worried about being left out, as well. The Coalition for Responsible Forest Legislation—comprising SPEC, the Federation of BC Naturalists, Sierra Club and Federation of BC Mountain Clubs—declared that the act provided too little recognition of fisheries, recreational and wildlife values and would undermine public participation in forest management decisions. The UFAWU, Victoria Labour Council, Campbell River and Courtenay Labour Council and the IWA's New Westminster local also wanted greater recognition of the public's right to challenge plans under the act. When the legislation was on the verge of passing in June, the IWA, having initially given cautious approval, joined the TLA in urging a delay of third reading until the fall. The union's

Tom Waterland, 1976. NA-31532.

primary objections lay in the act's failure to expand employment in manufacturing or free up excess timber held
in TFLs, and thus the lack of a public
hearing process in the renewal of those
tenures came in for criticism.[25]

The IWA had a part in building
opposition to the *Forest Act*, but much separated the opponents. Although
the need for public hearings in the renewal of TFLs seemed to provide unity
among critics of multinational dominance of the land base, the IWA worried
about too many voices clamouring for preservation. The Sierra Club had succeeded in wresting parts of TFLs held by BC Forest Products and MacMillan
Bloedel in the Nitinat Triangle for inclusion in Pacific Rim National Park.
Conflict over the Tsitika Valley threatened the TFLs of MacMillan Bloedel
and Canadian Forest Products on the east coast of Vancouver Island, a dispute that divided the UFAWU and IWA. By mid-1978 the IWA felt that "every
tree in the province grows in a forest that someone wants preserved." Public
hearings on TFL renewals should be introduced but restricted to "bona fide
public interest groups" such as SPEC, and park advocates should be required
to justify their proposals against the long-term economic benefits of timber
harvesting. The sustained-yield principle alone provided too little acknowledgement of non-timber values, but neither could it be subordinated to preservationist demands.[26]

The Socreds ignored the protests, pushing the *Forest Act* through the legislature without amendment. That hurried process left the impression that,
multiple-use promises notwithstanding, the agenda was one of uninterrupted
old-growth liquidation without due regard for agencies and groups whose
interests might contradict that goal. The stage was set, as Jeremy Wilson has
well documented, for a decade of confrontation over the legitimacy of Socred
forest policy. Nowhere would that conflict unfold with greater volatility than
on the islands of Haida Gwaii, where discontent was approaching a boil.[27]

Haida Gwaii's Forest History, Rising Dissent and the Arrival of QC Timber

BY THE EARLY 1970S many Haida Gwaii residents, Haida and non-Haida alike, were critical of a forest exploitation structure that yielded few social and economic benefits but left a harsh legacy of environmental destruction. QC Timber's arrival thus coincided with an increasingly polarized atmosphere concerning the region's future. Informed discussion flourished on the rate of cut, the disruption of salmon habitat and the behaviour of major companies in draining the islands' resources to feed mills elsewhere. QC Timber's success in securing cutting rights to a depleted forest contributed to public skepticism about the application of both sustained-yield and multiple-use principles in a setting where timber and salmon occupied a precarious relationship. Neither the *Forest Act* nor the *Fisheries Act* inspired confidence in the will and capacity of managers to maintain the health of salmon populations as clearcuts crept up the hillsides, exposing streams to erosion and sedimentation. Against a backdrop of increasing agitation for the preservation of South Moresby, QC Timber's operation on Graham Island raised a host of questions rooted in disenchantment with forest policy and practice.

The region's experience with large-scale logging began during the First World War, when the British War Office's demand for aircraft components brought value to the extensive stands of Sitka Spruce.[28] Masset Inlet and Port Clements, both on Graham Island, became temporary hives of industry, along with Skidegate and Cumshewa Inlet on South Moresby. Several camps were also established on Lyell Island and Louise Island. Over 7,924,800 metres (26 million feet) of spruce had been cut by war's end and the enormous waste that accompanied the drive set an enduring pattern.

The pace of exploitation slowed dramatically after the war, but during the 1920s the Ocean Falls, Powell River and Swanson Bay pulp and paper enterprises drew fibre from the region's forests. The islands had become, and would remain, a resource hinterland that supplied raw material for processing elsewhere. That structure prevailed through the Great Depression, and then World War II unleashed a second spruce drive. High-grading of that species in the east coast inlets of Graham and South Moresby islands again left tremendous amounts of waste with little regard for forest renewal. After the war Pacific Mills, the Powell River Company and Alaska Pine and Cellulose knitted their vast holdings into enterprises that drained the islands' timber to mainland pulp mills.

By the early 1970s Pacific Mills had been acquired by Crown Zellerbach, the Powell River Company had merged with H.R. MacMillan's interests in creating MacMillan Bloedel, and Rayonier had acquired Alaska Pine. Crown Zellerbach Canada Ltd.'s TFL 2 folded portions of Moresby Island timber near Sandspit into a licence that included lower coast and Vancouver Island holdings—the 'Moresby Block'—with an annual allowable cut (AAC) of 70,000 cunits.[29] MacMillan Bloedel's TFL 39 dominated Graham Island, with an AAC set at 430,000 cunits, and it also encompassed coastal and Vancouver Island forests. Rayonier dominated southern Moresby Island and several small adjacent islands, the AAC in its TFL 24 set at 154,000 cunits. All three firms cut less than their limit during the early 1970s, but in 1974 the total TFL cut amounted to 536,063 cunits. All of that timber left Haida Gwaii unprocessed, barged to southern pulp mills and sawmills.[30]

For decades that pattern of hinterland exploitation had disturbed islanders, and some foresters, and it would be hard to describe the region's standard of forestry as anything other than rudimentary. In 1975, for example, Crown Zellerbach did no planting at all, its silvicultural accomplishment limited to the spacing of 30 hectares to enhance growth. Rayonier had begun a resource folio for Lyell Island in preparing a five-year working plan for TFL 24, conducted an investigation of soil instability problems on the tenure and planted a grand total of 77,400 spruce seedlings. MacMillan Bloedel undertook similar landform analysis on TFL 39 and planted about 28 hectares. The BCFS, responsible for forestry on non-TFL lands in the Queen Charlotte PSYU, supervised the logging of 85,586 cunits in 1975 and planted no trees, citing the area's "exceptional natural regeneration."[31]

Contributing to the ferment of the 1970s was the Haida people's conviction that the land and resources belonged to them. The Skidegate and Old Massett bands organized the Council of the Haida Nation to advance their claim, initially targeting Rayonier's TFL 24 in 1974 when the firm began preparations to shift contractor Frank Beban from Talunkwan Island to Burnaby Island. The Skidegate Band Council took their concerns to Rayonier and the provincial government. NDP premier Dave Barrett placed Burnaby Island under a five-month moratorium, and Rayonier directed Beban to Lyell Island, producing a temporary but very uncertain resolution. Later in 1974 a group of young Haida and American activists established the Islands Protection Committee, later the Islands Protection Society (IPS),[32] calling for preservation of South Moresby and the adjacent islands. "Logging and strip mining have already desecrated the northern half of this Island," Thom Henley and Gary Edenshaw, also known as Guujaaw, explained in a plea for support from the Canadian Nature Federation. The time had come to protect the remainder from being "sacrificed on the high alter of the pulp and timber industry."[33]

Meanwhile, the Haida pressed ahead on the land claim, confronting a history of "co-ordinated exploitation" of resources by government and the three multinationals. The Skidegate Band Council seized the opportunity of Pearse's Royal Commission hearings in Prince Rupert to propose a dramatic reversal of multinational control of the islands. When the three TFLs came up for renewal, they should be placed into a village-controlled TFL, one to be run for the benefit of all islanders. Lawyer Duncan Shaw, representing Mac-Millan Bloedel, counterattacked. He defended the firm's local training and employment policies and demanded to know the author of the band council brief—which, he implied, accused former president Robert Bonner of wrong-doing. Shaw also asked if the band intended to compensate the TFL holders for roads, camps and other improvements.[34]

Particularly disturbing to the Haida, the IPS and the islands' commercial fishers was the industry's rough treatment of salmon streams. MacMillan Bloedel and its contractor, Fix Logging, had been charged with violating the *Fisheries Act* in the Hans Creek watershed in June 1974. The contractor eventually pled guilty to depositing debris in a fish-bearing stream and drew a $300 fine, but after a number of postponements the charges had been dropped against MacMillan Bloedel. The IPS demanded an explanation for this "obvious miscarriage of justice" and asked the province to reinstate the charges. "We seek justice for the creek, the fish and all else that was hurt," Guujaaw wrote in a letter of protest to BC Attorney General Alex MacDonald. Logging was a fact of life on the islands, the IPS acknowledged in advertising an early publication, but "it should not be necessary to silt rivers, create landslides, and condone excessive erosion in the pursuit of this activity."[35]

MacMillan Bloedel's Hecate division responded by sponsoring a February 1975 seminar at Sandspit's Islander Hotel, attended by about 40 people. Industry, Forest Service and Fisheries Service representatives appeared on the podium, discussing road construction, soil conditions and current research on fish-forestry interactions. Vince Hernandez and Jim Hart of the BCFS attended, Hart speaking about the referral process. In a public letter appearing in the local newspaper, Hecate division manager Bill Cafferata claimed the seminar refuted the IPS charges and put the firm's practices in a better light. Slides were inevitable on many "inherently unstable" areas of the islands even in the absence of logging, and concerted efforts were underway to identify soil problems and develop sound road construction methods. "I resent the continual characterization of logging as the root cause of all environmental evils and of loggers as a class of insentient beings," Cafferata declared. Queen Charlotte City logger Doug Aiken also responded, attributing salmon spawning problems on Hans and Sachs creeks to low autumn water levels. Aggressive ocean fishing by Russian, Japanese and Korean fleets far outranked logging in the commercial fisheries' problems, Aiken continued, and the IPS would not gain support by "putting the knock on people who provide our bread and butter."[36]

MacMillan Bloedel also met opposition over plans to log along the Yakoun River, a major Graham Island salmon producer. The Masset Rod and Gun Club initially wanted a moratorium on logging until the completion of environmental impact studies. The conflict quickly became one of patch logging along the productive steelhead river, the option favoured by government foresters, or a permanent and substantial leavestrip, advocated by federal and provincial fisheries agencies. District forester W.G. Bishop felt that this "preservation-oriented approach" ran counter to the management objectives on TFL 39. After an inter-agency agreement for a temporary 122-metre (400-foot) leavestrip was reached, MacMillan Bloedel, citing economic implications and the threat of blowdown, requested reconsideration. That led to another public meeting on forestry issues—in what would become a flurry of gatherings—on July 13, 1976. It was attended by representatives from MacMillan Bloedel, agencies, IWA, the Masset Rod and Gun Club, the Trappers' Federation and Skeena–Queen Charlotte Regional District. The Haida had been invited but could not attend, and an effort to contact the IPS failed.[37]

The forestry-fisheries conflict also loomed large at a Queen Charlotte Islands Museum meeting at Skidegate later that week, convened to consider the South Moresby wilderness proposal. Ottawa lacked the "clout" to enforce leavestrip provisions in cutting plans, some said, laying rare charges for stream damage only after the fact. Notably, ranger Jim Hart agreed, saying that the federal agency either could not or would not exercise its powers to shape logging plans. Government decisions were "company dominated", others declared. With two such meetings in a week, lawyer and Skeena-Queen Charlotte Regional District director Carey Linde urged islanders to keep it up. The July 23 meeting of the Skeena–Queen Charlotte Regional Board gave the Graham Island Advisory Planning Committee (GIAPC) the opportunity to endorse the Yakoun River leavestrip, citing Hart's support. In August, Fisheries minister Romeo LeBlanc made a brief visit to the islands and, at a Skidegate event, heard local fishermen describe his agency quite bluntly as "failures in fisheries management".[38]

Even though $1.5 million of SEP funding had been allotted for the islands, a November 15 meeting at Queen Charlotte City made it clear that the public was less concerned with enhancement than protection of wild salmon runs. Vic Bryant spoke for an hour, deploring weak enforcement of the *Fisheries Act* and criticizing the contradiction of pouring millions of dollars into hatcheries while allowing "continuing, often irreparable harm to an existing, functioning natural resource." The Masset Rod and Gun Club proposed that the logging companies be required to post bonds prior to entering watersheds rather than trying to prosecute after damage had been inflicted. The IPS also showed up, displaying slides illustrating stream and watershed damage to help advance the South Moresby wilderness proposal. The group protested the large clearcuts involved in Rayonier's Lyell Island cutting plans and urged the new Bennett government to deny any further South Moresby cutting permits until completion of an ELUC Secretariat study on the wilderness proposal. All of the meetings' voices supported the IPS's conviction that clearcutting as practised on the islands violated the principles of both multiple use and sustained yield, which challenged the Fisheries Service as negligent in enforcing the federal act. Finally, logging and its impact on salmon ranked uppermost among Haida concerns. Rather than spend vast sums to undo damage to spawning grounds, Lavina Lightbody wrote, "let us ensure that we don't have any damage."[39]

By the end of 1976, discontent with all aspects of industrial forestry festered on the islands. Wealth was being drained away, leaving a paltry legacy of regional benefit while the environmental costs mounted and social divisions deepened. When the *Queen Charlotte Islands Observer* presented a picture of MacMillan Bloedel's log barge *Haida Monarch* on the occasion of its 100th voyage, the IPS's Dan Bowditch called it "the most blatant symbol of multinational exploitation on these Islands." Doubts had also begun circulating about the rate of cut on the Queen Charlotte PSYU. After a 1967 survey had estimated the total volume at over 481 million cubic metres (17 billion cubic feet) the BCFS had begun a review with an eye to subtracting inaccessible timber and "environmentally sensitive areas" from that total, and islanders were waiting impatiently for the figures' release. Hoping to funnel all of the region's criticism into a manageable forum, the MOF established a Queen Charlotte Islands Public Advisory Committee (PAC) in the spring of 1977. About 70 attended the organizational meeting at Skidegate, nominating members from the forest industry, labour, fisheries, the Haida and the wilderness and environmental protection movement, among other interests. In the wake of the PAC's demise two years later, chairman Rick Helmer characterized the process as designed to "defuse embarrassing questioning from the IPS." The South Moresby wilderness proposal would be the PAC's "albatross" in the end, making consensus impossible.[40]

For two years, though, the PAC engaged in a serious and inevitably contentious scrutiny of forest policy and practice. Amidst some skepticism about MOF intentions, early meetings considered the ongoing PSYU inventory; the threat steep-slope logging posed to fish habitat; and the Yakoun River leavestrip, which MacMillan Bloedel continued to resist. The reserved timber would be worth $12 million, the company asserted, and much would inevitably blow down in the region's high winds. A July 24 question about leavestrips' beneficial effects on stream temperature drew a response from Jim Hart. Disenchanted with the MOF's disregard for streams, he had recently joined the Fisheries Service as a habitat protection officer. Hart said that leavestrips minimized temperature variations, helped keep streams free of debris and maintained food sources for fish. Asked about the value of stream data from southeastern Alaska, Hart said he considered it relevant to the islands but that the real issue was the extent to which damage from logging practices should be tolerated. He cited Rennell Sound as one of two sites where impacts thus far had been kept to an acceptable level, but "on small 'rearing' streams the logging operations were generally unacceptable." Keith Moore, who had recently arrived after studying the leavestrip question on Vancouver Island for the MOF, discussed the importance of planning clearcuts with prevailing winds in mind to minimize blowdown. At the meeting's conclusion the PAC issued its first official recommendation, endorsing the Yakoun River leavestrip.[41]

To this point QC Timber and Riley Creek occupied only a peripheral place in public discourse, as the Moresby Island wilderness proposal and Yakoun River leavestrip took centre stage. The firm, a subsidiary of C. Itoh and Company, third-largest of the Japanese trading companies, had acquired a TSHL at Rennell Sound in 1972. C. Itoh operated a Nanaimo sawmill through CIPA Industries and went on to open a Pitt Meadows plant in 1975, both mills cutting primarily for the Japanese housing market. QC Timber's Rennell Sound holdings, with an AAC of 32,040 cunits, would supply the new mill. Not until 1974 did the company complete its road to the sound, linking up with MacMillan Bloedel's network and providing access to Queen Charlotte City. The road passed through old-growth timber, rising in elevation before dropping sharply to the camp, which included an elementary school and recreation hall. No one at all had lived at Rennell Sound in 1966 and only 15 in 1971, but by 1976 the camp numbered 50 residents.[42]

The introduction of large-scale logging on the west coast of Graham Island drew little comment for the first couple of years, but QC Timber sowed the seeds of the coming controversy by constructing its road system hastily. Although higher construction standards to minimize environmental damage had accompanied the NDP's Coast Logging Guidelines, later studies would show that the bulldozers simply pushed rock and soil to the edges of the new roads. That sidecasting disrupted natural drainage patterns, a problem worsened by inadequate ditching and culvert installation. An area of steep slopes and thin soil already vulnerable to heavy rainfall and high winds had therefore been made much more unstable even before large-scale clearcutting operations began. QC Timber had opened up the forests of Rennell Sound to exploitation, but in a way that invited mass soil movements. Within three years of the company's arrival, inadequate road drainage provisions and poor construction methods produced six slides.[43]

QC Timber's arrival coincided precisely with growing public disenchantment over industrial forestry on the islands. In particular, as companies had left the cutover valley bottoms to access higher elevation timber, exposing streams to sedimentation from erosion and slides, residents grew increasingly worried about widespread deterioration of salmon habitat. "Slides which take the soil down to the bedrock are occurring with more and more frequency, as logging companies facing a decreasing timber supply find themselves in the steeper areas," declared an *Observer* correspondent. That concern, in turn,

Haida Monarch, self-dumping log barge. NA-31118.

fuelled doubts about the Queen Charlotte PSYU's annual cut. Withdrawing timber on sites considered vulnerable to erosion would have serious implications for the AAC. Before leaving the MOF Jim Hart had collaborated with fellow ranger Vince Hernandez on a report indicating that the PSYU's rate of harvest was excessive, including timber on many sites too sensitive to clearcut. District forester W.G. Bishop had even told Pearse's Royal Commission that uncertainty over the amount of accessible timber on the islands ruled out further allocations until completion of a new forest inventory.[44]

The so-called "Hart-Hernandez" report would come into greater prominence as time went on; meanwhile the MOF went ahead with its review of the PSYU annual cut, contemplating the exclusion of inoperable and "environmentally-sensitive" sites from the calculation. Rennell Sound, bordered by steep slopes, figured prominently in this work just as QC Timber began operations. The sound's three main creeks—Riley, Gregory and Bonanza—spawned, according to one estimate, 25 per cent of the Pink Salmon on the islands' west coast. In the spring of 1975 the MOF's Dave Wilford began fieldwork, evaluating "soil instability problems attributable to logging and road construction." That project coincided with one undertaken by the BC Ministry of Environment's Neville Alley and Bruce Thomson, who would study the geology of Rennell Sound and Naden Harbour, to the north. Both projects were intended to provide data for the NDP's Environmental Protection Area (EPA) strategy, which looked to preserve forests selected for their high fisheries, wildlife and recreational values. For the moment, though, cut calculations on the islands proceeded on the basis of a very preliminary 1974 "initial assessment" for the PSYU and the determinations made by MacMillan Bloedel, Rayonier and Crown Zellerbach on their TFLs.[45]

Amidst mounting concerns about the rate of cut, QC Timber submitted its five-year logging plan for Rennell Sound in April 1975. Both the Fisheries Service and BC's Fish and Wildlife Branch recommended that the steep slopes be withdrawn pending the completion of the soil stability studies. The area later encompassed by cutting permit 144 (CP144), destined to become the site of so much controversy, was not designated for logging in the original plan nor in a revised proposal submitted in February 1976. QC Timber followed up with a third plan in May 1977, including a request for approval of logging on the area designated CP144, owing to a storm that had caused blowdown on the tract. The Fisheries Service recommended provisional approval, with the reservation that specific soil stability data might force reconsideration. The Fish and Wildlife Branch expressed its ongoing concerns, and there the matter stood—until another development brought QC Timber's place in the islands' industrial structure into the spotlight.[46]

Already worried about the sustainability of existing operations, many islanders were shocked when the MOF put a 60,000-cunit-per-year TSHL up for tender at Naden Harbour on northern Graham Island in August 1977. Over its 12-year duration, rights to 720,000 cunits of timber would go to the successful bidder. The PAC, scheduled to discuss ongoing EPA studies at an early September meeting, focused instead on the surprising "Queen Charlotte Proposal" amidst considerable controversy. Even local foresters had advised holding off on further commitments until completion of the PSYU inventory and small operators were especially disturbed at the large offer, which exceeded their financial resources, having been told for years that requests for timber sales could not be met until the inventory was completed.[47]

Regional Director Carey Linde spoke for them in a six-page critique of the sale to Tom Waterland. Advertising the sale as one designed to meet the needs of the small operator was "a deceit and a complete falsehood," he asserted. Although the award would not be made for months, Linde sensed outside forces at work. Both QC Timber and Naden Harbour Timber, currently operating in the area, were backed by Japanese capital or sold to that market. "Foreign money, I submit, is the reason this sale has gone on the market at this time." Forester Chris Kindt explained at the PAC meeting that recent estimates indicated a surplus even with some EPA restrictions. In fact, the MOF had quietly revised the timber supply estimate on the Queen Charlotte PSYU in 1976, putting the AAC at 1,074,008 cubic metres, up from the 1965 level of 702,336. That determination, however, had made no allowance for soil stability factors. Asked to explain the rush, Kindt replied that "the Minister likes to see things get moving." Small operator Werner Funk walked out of the meeting after relating his recent inability to obtain cutting rights on the PSYU. The PAC passed a motion that the sale be put in abeyance until completed EPA mapping results had been incorporated into the new AAC calculations. "Any large TSHL proposal at this time is premature," the PAC resolved. The Skeena–Queen Charlotte Regional District's GIAPC would endorse both Linde's letter and the PAC's position.[48]

Waterland's response to the PAC, mailed the day after the closing date for bids, acknowledged that the PSYU review was ongoing but maintained that the existing inventory indicated a large, uncommitted surplus. "The industry needs more timber," Waterland declared, and additional cutting rights meant more jobs. A disgruntled PAC received information from an unidentified source about the Hart-Hernandez report at an early November meeting. Those findings—that further AAC increases would be unjustified—must be even more valid, some members thought, with expected EPA withdrawals and the South Moresby wilderness proposal unresolved. But efforts to persuade local MOF staff to release a copy were continually refused. Finally, though, the EPA maps were available for viewing at the Queen Charlotte Islands Museum, a welcome development given the growing rate-of-cut controversy. South Moresby remained relatively untouched, but some felt that the existing blocks of PSYU timber at points such as Rennell Sound and Naden Harbour would be gone within a couple of decades. Increased logging under the "QC Proposal" would only worsen the overcut.[49]

The PAC continued pressing Waterland for withdrawal of the sale until the suspected discrepancy in the AAC had been resolved. But on November 16 Waterland announced that QC Timber had outbid Doman Industries, Naden Harbour Timber and a couple of smaller companies who had submitted applications for only a portion of the timber. QC Timber's bid at $3.52 per cunit actually more than doubled Doman's, the next highest at 98 cents per cunit. In announcing the award Waterland pointed to the creation of 66 new logging jobs on the islands, with an emphasis on local hiring, as well as higher employment in QC Timber's Nanaimo and Pitt Meadows mills. The company would also make cash payments of $75,000 each to the communities of Masset and Queen Charlotte City. "The Japanese company has been a good corporate citizen on the Queen Charlotte Islands," Waterland said, noting that they had the transportation, marketing and financial backing to ensure a successful operation. Moreover, up to 20,000 cunits per year would be made available to local operators in a new timber sale program.[50]

Waterland had stressed the local benefits in justifying the sale, but the announcement only stimulated suspicions that something was amiss. The GIAPC questioned QC Timber about the reason for the cash grants to the communities, asked if the company knew of the controversy over the sustainability of cut rates on the PSYU and requested more details on local hiring commitments. A December 4 PAC meeting only added fuel to the fire. MOF staff had removed the EPA maps from the Skidegate Museum after a brief exhibit, and no further access would be permitted. The maps were unfinished, Chris Kindt explained, and he had "goofed" in releasing them without proper authority. Asked again about the Hart-Hernandez report, an MOF representative said that the confidential document could not be released either. Another official then explained that QC Timber had done its own PSYU inventory before bidding on the QC Proposal and found that the MOF had underestimated the volume of merchantable timber. When asked for a copy of that inventory, the official refused to supply it.[51]

The MOF's credibility on the islands sagged in the wake of the QC Proposal award and its failure to live up to the spirit of consultation with PAC. The PAC's support for full public hearings on the renewal of all island TFLs, a demand Waterland ignored, contributed to the climate of distrust in late 1977. Rayonier's TFL 24 was approaching its 1979 renewal date, pressure was continuing to build for the preservation of South Moresby, and the clearcutting of Talunkwan Island had earned the company a public relations black eye for the devastation of salmon habitat. In that context, islanders took more than a passing interest in the new *Fisheries Act*.

Representing local commercial fisherman on the PAC, Ed Regnery finally got to present his report on the adverse effects of logging and mining on fisheries at a December 4 meeting, after having been shunted from the agenda three times. Regnery had hoped to secure the PAC's endorsement of Bill C-38, since passed, and his delayed report stirred a strong rebuttal from Rayonier representative Frank Kutney. His company did a good job protecting the environment, Kutney said, and loggers had been subject to exaggerated claims about damage inflicted on spawning streams. Jim Hart appeared at the next meeting in mid-January, outlining the new act's features and cautioning that some of the habitat protection measures had yet to be tested in court. Even the SEP program came with contradictions. Construction of a hatchery at Pallant Creek in early 1978 caused heavy siltation, threatening eggs and fry. Siltation was a continuing hazard on the islands, Hart remarked—"part of a larger problem with which we contend all the time."[52]

Forestry-fisheries issues again dominated at the PAC's March 5 meeting. Natural erosion factors, Al Breitkreutz of the BC Fish and Wildlife Branch explained, included high winds, shallow soil, steep slopes and heavy rainfall. The islands' many small streams contributed to a viable commercial fishery, but conservation was difficult given the lack of baseline data and the inadequate staffing. Breitkreutz might review 22 cutting permit applications a month, but he never visited most of the areas for field assessment. The PAC, having already called for an increase in federal fisheries staff for the islands, passed a similar motion on behalf of the Fish and Wildlife Branch. Discussion then turned to QC Timber's new Naden Harbour operation, the PAC requesting a folio study before cutting began. The MOF took the position that folio planning would be too expensive, according to Guujaaw's report of the meeting. Leaving planning solely under company control might constitute a conflict of interest, given QC Timber's "vested interest in dollar profit," Guujaaw wrote in describing the response of some PAC members.[53]

Folio planning *was* a long and expensive process, one that continued to exceed the capabilities of the agencies involved. The resulting bottleneck forced managers back to the cumbersome and time-consuming referral process. As company plans went to the agencies for evaluation and were returned with demands for revision, delays ensued. The alternative was approval without site inspection. Industry folio submissions were often "so vague and nebulous as to be nothing more than motherhood statements" subject to infrequent field checks by resource managers, BCFS forester R.A. Johnson claimed. For its part, the forest industry deplored referral process delays and pressed fisheries agencies to provide economic justification for logging restrictions. "If industry needed support" in terms of meeting agency demands, Deputy Minister of Forests Mike Apsey told COFI directors in late 1978, "the BCFS would fight for it."[54]

This relationship of mutual support, expressed in the 1978 *Forest Act*, added to the climate of unrest. A PAC statement claimed the legislation provided no assurance that sustained-yield objectives would be met, afforded too little protection for the rights of small operators and contained no provision for public hearings in the renewal of existing TFLs. On both economic and biological grounds, then, the act failed to ensure future stability for island communities.[55]

The new *Fisheries Act* seemed equally unlikely to offer sufficient protection for aquatic resources. In a learned 1978 study for the IPS, biologist T.E. Reimchen reviewed the "failure of Federal Fisheries to deal rationally and effectively with watershed deterioration." Beginning with an overview of salmon life history, focusing on the Pink and Chum species that spawned in the lower reaches of many of Haida Gwaii's small streams between August and November, Reimchen set out the importance of undisturbed gravel beds in providing a free flow of water for egg development. After hatching, the Pink and Chum fry migrated to the ocean, but logging posed several distinct threats to this cycle. Drawing on research from Alaska and the American Pacific northwest (since no similar studies had been initiated locally and findings had only begun to emerge from the Carnation Creek project on Vancouver Island), Reimchen first summarized the hydrological impacts. In removing forest cover and leaving mosses and soil exposed, clearcutting promoted much faster movement of water across the land surface into streams during heavy rains. Logging roads exacerbated the problem of flash flooding, capturing water as it moved downslope and funnelling it into the creeks and streams. Spawning gravels might shift during such discharges, crushing eggs or preventing the emergence of alevins.[56]

Less obvious but more disruptive consequences arose from the introduction of silt to spawning beds. To meet oxygen demands, salmon eggs required a constant flow of clean water through the gravels. When fine particles of sediment settled in the gravels, eggs were deprived of oxygen, and it clogged the gills of fry. Roads probably outranked clearcuts as a contributor to sedimentation, Reimchen observed, except where cutover steep slopes caused runoff to enter streams directly. Clearcutting to the edges of streams on Haida Gwaii likely did not cause dangerously high water temperatures except during the hottest summers, but colder winter temperatures might be problematic. Turning to logging practice regulation, Reimchen acknowledged recent improvement. The agencies no longer permitted stream beds to be used as yarding roads, and road construction on steep slopes received more attention. "Overt cases of stream demolition are a thing of the past," he remarked, except in isolated areas, including Rennell Sound along with Talunkwan, Lyell, Louise and Moresby islands. But clearcuts on the islands were too large to "preserve an acceptable level of stream quality" and no uniform leavestrip policy had yet been developed.[57]

Federal regulators, Reimchen noted, could not be relied upon to enforce the "very progressive language" in the new *Fisheries Act*, an observation based on his access to files in the Fisheries Service's Queen Charlotte City office. Only about 12 charges had been filed against loggers over the previous decade. Of these cases, nine had been upheld in court, but the fines levied totalled only $4,600. Given this history, the much higher financial penalties permitted under the new legislation seemed "irrelevant." Clear violations, such as Rayonier's clearcutting to the edge of Tasu Creek on Moresby Island, resulting in "log jams, debris and massive siltation" over several months, had gone unpunished. Less drastic but routine increases in silt loads due to road construction had never been subject to charges.[58]

This reluctance to invoke the act, Reimchen asserted, lay in "a number of reasonable, though often obscure justifications." First, once the MOF and Fisheries Service had approved a cutting plan, and if practices held to the plan's spirit, the blame for any slide or other habitat disruption lay with the agencies as well as the company. Second was the inadequate number of fisheries officers, and third was the courts' tendency to dismiss cases on the basis of technicalities, which undermined enforcement. That problem, Reimchen claimed, could be attributed to the lack of baseline data on pre-logging stream conditions.

The second part of the IPS report, prepared by Reimchen and journalist Sheila Douglas, addressed that issue. The IPS hoped the data—representing a variety of watershed conditions, from virgin forest to sites where clearcutting was in progress—would provide the sort of information needed to assess the impact of logging operations. For the time being, though, the clearcutting of over 2,832 hectares on the islands went ahead annually under ineffective enforcement despite an enlightened *Fisheries Act*, Reimchen concluded. Douglas put it more directly in a *Telkwa Foundation Newsletter* summary of the report, stating that strong legislation was "worth nothing" if not invoked and pressed in the courts.[59]

Political Football: Late 1978 Slides, Jim Hart and the 'Preventative Measures' Solution

BETWEEN LATE 1978 AND THE SUMMER OF 1979 Rennell Sound, little known and isolated from major population centres, came to the forefront of environmental discourse in BC. In the midst of ongoing debate about wilderness proposals targeting the Tsitika Valley on eastern Vancouver Island, the Khutzeymateen on the north coast, the Stein Valley and South Moresby, the situation at Riley Creek raised slightly different but equally fundamental questions. But no one was clamouring for the preservation of Rennell Sound as an ecological reserve or a park. Rather, the issue here was more mundane and therefore, arguably, more pressing to the forest industry as a whole. To what extent would the new *Fisheries Act* dictate logging practices or, worse yet, deny access to sites deemed too fragile to cut? The question became more than theoretical in late October 1978, when heavy rain and high winds caused slides, which had been foreseen, at Rennell Sound.

As described above, QC Timber's Rennell Sound operation had moved closer to the spotlight at the end of 1978, with the area's steep terrain the subject of numerous inter-agency meetings and much correspondence over the previous year. The Fisheries Service's May 1977 conditional approval for a five-year logging plan was predicated on more detailed soil stability data, particularly around CP144, on the north slope of Rennell Sound, scheduled for logging that autumn. The MOF, however, pressed for authority to cut. Federal officials gave conditional approval for CP144 logging in November, and in that same month MOF soil specialists D.J. Wilford and J.W. Schwab, collaborating with Keith Moore, recommended that a troublesome branch road undergo reconstruction prior to logging, a proposal endorsed by the Fisheries Service. They also reported that stability problems could be expected to worsen as root systems on cutover slopes deteriorated but anticipated that Riley Creek would experience only minimal sedimentation. BC's Fish and Wildlife Branch continued to withhold approval and, in fact, would never sign off on the CP144 logging plan.[60]

The BCFS approved QC Timber's Rennell Sound timber sale harvesting area working plan early in 1978, requiring the submission of soil stability data with individual cutting permit applications. Authority to construct a branch road into CP144 followed that spring, and on August 1, 1978, the MOF approved the clearcutting of the slopes above Riley Creek. That decision ignored Alley and Thomson's cautionary report on Rennell Sound. Drawing on fieldwork and insights from geologist Douglas Swanston's work in the similar conditions of southeastern Alaska, they observed that heavy precipitation and saturated soil was the "triggering factor" in most landslides, associated with strong winds that caused the soil to loosen under swaying trees. Such factors had initiated slides on the islands as recently as the winter and spring of 1977. Clearcutting and road-building increased the likelihood of slope failures as drainage patterns changed and root systems deteriorated after logging. Their findings clearly agreed with Swanston's conclusions on the "acceleration of slope erosion by timber harvesting activities." Indeed, they noted that Rennell Sound was already the site of several logging-induced slides. Although the two geologists made only a brief reference to fisheries, they acknowledged that mass soil movement processes altered the aquatic environment by introducing sediment to streams, with consequences for fish populations. Concluding, Alley and Thomson asserted that forests played a critical role in stabilizing slopes and that clearcutting promoted landslides and erosion. Management alternatives included accepting the consequences, undertaking "massive stabilization controls", altering cutting practices to leave more trees or simply avoiding the areas. "Until sufficient studies can be made," they advised, "the latter alternative is probably the most practical policy at the present."[61]

The consequences of ignoring that advice were very quickly apparent. In late October and early November a massive series of storms hit the northern BC coast, producing severe flooding in several areas. The exposed west coast of Haida Gwaii took a particularly hard hit and companies across the islands reported roads and bridges washed out, along with numerous slides. Climatological stations in the Rennell Sound area recorded 135 millimetres of rainfall on October 30, and almost 150 millimetres more fell over the next two days. Winds averaged speeds of 53 kilometres per hour, with stronger gusts at times. Vi Halsey, who reported on Rennell Sound goings-on for the *Observer*, described the results of the "big blow", which produced "torrents of rain", washed out roads and reduced the QC Timber camp to "a mess." Familiar places had been obliterated, leaving "in their place piles of mud, wood and other debris." With passage over the Phantom Creek road to Queen Charlotte City impossible, food came in by plane for two weeks.[62]

In a 1983 report Jim Schwab concluded that slides, or "mass wasting", at Rennell Sound began on October 30 and continued through to November 1. Debris avalanches occurred on both cutover and forested terrain, but the former were about twice as large. Roads and logging both contributed to the total of 264 mass soil movements—126 in clearcuts, 25 attributed to roads and 113 in forested terrain. But, Schwab reported, "the rate of mass wasting on man-modified terrain is fifteen times greater than on forested terrain." Schwab's findings, again, were not released until 1983, but simple observation confirmed that Riley Creek had fared badly.[63]

In the aftermath of the storm Jim Hart and Keith Moore (now a habitat protection technician with the Fish and Wildlife Branch after working under contract with Wilford and Schwab on the CP144 soils study) inspected Rennell Sound along with other logging sites on the islands. By this time Hart and Moore were also consulting on strategy with senior Fisheries Service officials and Department of Justice lawyers in Vancouver as they contemplated applying the preventative measures of the *Fisheries Act* at Rennell Sound. Many slopes previously considered stable had suffered failures and on November 16 Hart advised newly appointed Prince Rupert district forester Jack Biickert that no further logging should be permitted in the Riley, Gregory and Bonanza creek watersheds. Moore followed up on November 29 with a specific request that the MOF withdraw approval for CP144. The PAC, also worried about the recent slides, wanted to know how much of the recent damage could be attributed to logging. Biickert, according to Richard Overstall's account, interpreted their letters as "general input into the referral system" and, sensing no urgency on the part of fisheries agencies, did not reply. Perhaps the fact that QC Timber's Rennell Sound operation had shut down for the annual Christmas break contributed to his calm.[64]

That calm came to an end on January 11, however. After a December field inspection, Hart used section 31(1) of the *Fisheries Act* to order QC Timber to curtail CP144 falling operations performed under contract by Bonanza Creek Contracting Ltd. The following day, when Hart arrived at the site and told the fallers to stop work, they complied. Despite "repeated advice and warnings" from the Fisheries Service and Fish and Wildlife Branch, Hart explained, the MOF had allowed QC Timber to continue logging, thus requiring his intervention. Ranger Ben Hanson, stationed at the MOF's Queen Charlotte City office, confirmed the story but said that until receipt of Hart's letter, the company held a valid logging contract with the Crown on the 16–20 hectares covered by the stop order—a contract that the federal department had previously agreed to through the referral process. Besides, he said, logging in such an area could not be undertaken without some silt entering streams. Having referred the matter to the regional office in Prince Rupert, he would await further events.[65]

The significance of these events reached well beyond the region. For the first time, the Fisheries Service had used the federal act's preventative mechanism, curtailing a logging operation to protect a salmon stream. While the area in question was small, the "precedent-setting move" had serious province-wide implications. It was also significant for the islands overall, as there were many similar settings facing similar pressures. Industry was "moving into the steep areas a lot now," Hart told *Victoria Times* writer Mark Hume; "it has us concerned." Slides and erosion had already occurred at Rennell Sound, one flushing out a creek to the estuary. "Debris roars down the creeks just like two or three D8 caterpillars," Hart elaborated to the Prince Rupert *Daily News*. "It scours the creek as high as twenty feet on either side right down to the rocks...fish eggs have no chance of surviving." In a subsequent statement to the paper, Hart made it clear that Rennell Sound was simply the focal point of an islands-wide problem. With most of the flat land cutover, and the loss of stabilizing root systems on the hillsides leading inevitably to slides, the time had come to "look at future ramifications, planning around problem areas and if necessary eliminate them from cut calculations."[66]

The BC Ministry of Environment, based on advice from Fish and Wildlife Branch staff, concurred with the federal position: future logging in Rennell Sound would "create extensive environmental damage to fish populations" in Riley, Bonanza and Gregory creeks. The MOF would be asked to reconsider any approvals for logging in this area. COFI monitored the situation closely, worried about a more strenuous application of the *Fisheries Act* around the province. Forests minister Tom Waterland also saw the wider consequences of a surrender at Rennell Sound. On January 13 he fired off a blunt telegram to Romeo LeBlanc protesting Ottawa's intrusion into provincial jurisdiction over timber harvesting operations. Therein lay the problem, for many islanders, with the South Moresby question always in the background. Waterland had confirmed in late 1978 that public hearings would not be part of the TFL 24 renewal process, but in an early December interview Hart told Mark Hume that logging on South Moresby would "undoubtedly spell destruction for salmon streams." The UFAWU's local No. 28 held a mid-January meeting at Queen Charlotte City prior to the union's annual convention, coming out in full support of the IPS demand for public hearings in the renewal of TFL 24. Current logging practices posed a distinct threat to the livelihoods of the islands' fishermen, president Herb Hughan wrote, and they "could no longer stay silent." By the time the TFLs reached their next renewal date in 25 years, the major companies might well have pulled out in search of timber and cheap labour in Brazil or some other similar destination, "leaving the Islands a vast stubble of stumps and destruction." The IWA would, in the process, be tossed out of their "present position in the corporate vest-pocket." The Northern Trollers Association also demanded that Waterland reverse his denial of public hearings in the renewal of TFL 24. Rayonier's clearcutting and poor road-building practices on the steep slopes of Talunkwan, and now Lyell Island, had brought the fishing and forest industries into open conflict.[67]

The Rennell Sound story only deepened divisions between loggers and fishermen. Relations between the unions had already been strained when the IWA joined industry in condemning the *Fisheries Act*, and when the UFAWU supported a moratorium on logging in the Tsitika watershed. Now the UFAWU had come out in support of the campaign for some sort of park status for South Moresby. The IWA's local 1-71, the 'Loggers Local', meanwhile, joined government and industry in campaigning hard against such measures, which contradicted "the principles and concepts of multiple use." Logging could be conducted in a way that left areas able to support wildlife, sustain watersheds and "leave behind streams and lakes where fish can spawn and reproduce as though the surroundings were untouched," Local 1-71 declared in a 1978 multiple-use policy statement. Parks and ecological reserves were one thing, president Ben Thompson said, the creation of "blanket wilderness areas" on the archipelago quite another. Careful multiple-use management would maintain jobs and communities, while preservation would ensure only the

Rennell Sound hillside after logging, summer 1977. Courtesy of Keith Moore.

creation of a "ghost town wilderness." Waterland, long on record as "favouring a multiple-use policy and generally opposed to single use or preservationist views," made common cause with the local.[68]

Multiple-use promises from government and industry had long since lost legitimacy in a province that was firmly embracing environmental values. The prospect of folio planning did little to ease concerns when Waterland announced the renewal of Rayonier's TFL 24 on January 10, 1979. Haida Chief Nathan Young, Guujaaw and the IPS would initiate legal action in February to force public hearings, supported by the PAC. The UFAWU joined the campaign, making use of Reichem's IPS "Salmon Habitat" paper in downplaying the effectiveness of resource folios in achieving true "integrated management" and "environmentally responsible" logging. Rennell Sound was far from forgotten as all interests awaited an outcome of the South Moresby controversy. Did the stop order represent a real departure from a pattern of forest exploitation that offered only token protection for fish, or was it a mere gesture, "a face-saver and rather late in the game", as conservationist Dave Orton put it in the *Fisherman*? It was hoped answers would come at a February 4 PAC meeting where

Logging to edge of Rennell Sound, summer 1977. Courtesy of Keith Moore.

Top: Cutting Permit 144 area, summer 1978. Courtesy of Keith Moore.
Bottom: Patch logging, Bonanza Creek, Rennell Sound, summer 1977. Courtesy of Keith Moore.

Keith Moore and Jim Hart would report on the recent slides and the Rennell Sound stop order. Questioning focused on how much habitat damage the MOF and Fisheries Service were prepared to accept and whether logging was simply unacceptable on some areas no matter how sophisticated the technology. The PAC, mired in controversy over membership applications from Rayonier contractor Frank Beban and three members of his Lyell Island crew, postponed a recommendation in hopes of arranging a Rennell Sound field trip.[69]

The loggers and families at QC Timber's Rennell Sound camp, having experienced the full force of late October and early November winds, were now exposed to threatening political currents. "Rennell Sound may soon be facing a battle for survival," wrote Vi Halsey in reporting that community members had organized a defence committee. "In the struggle between Logging and Fisheries," she continued, "the victims often are destroyed in the battle." Writing in more strident terms, Rennell Sound's Helen Bozovan depicted federal actions as an attack on the forest industry and its workers, one destined to make BC a welfare state. Why could the fishing, forest and mining industries not work in harmony? That, Hart maintained during this period, was precisely his objective. He told journalist Steve Whipp that the question was whether "we are consciously going to trade the trees for the fish." Both levels of government had committed to integrated resource management but the MOF had ignored invitations to work out a plan for Rennell Sound, and falling on an area identified as unstable had gone ahead with that agency's blessing, prompting the January 11 notice.[70]

MOF assertions that the agency must live up to the obligations of QC Timber's contract with the Crown were valid only to a point, Hart explained. All cutting permits contained the "P-1 clause", which prohibited the deposit of trees, logs "or any substance likely to cause stream pollution" in lakes or streams. The sedimentation caused by dirt, rocks and debris associated with "flush-out" events certainly represented a contravention of the licence. The goal was not to shut logging down, Hart emphasized, but rather to engage in a realistic assessment of sensitive sites so that both resources could be managed sustainably. Ultimately, the rate of cut would have to be adjusted as those sites were identified. Asked by Whipp if the existing rate of cut found him in a "race against time to save the fisheries," Hart replied: "Definitely. There is no question about that."[71]

Five images of slide activity on QC Timber branch road, Rennell Sound, following 1978 storm.

Courtesy of Keith Moore.

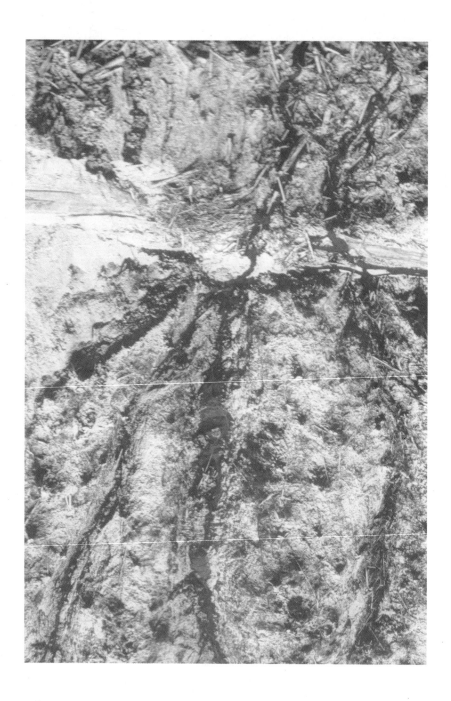

Hopes for a solution lay in meetings involving MOF, Fisheries Service and Fish and Wildlife Branch representatives set for February 15–16 in Prince Rupert. Some 60 jobs were at stake and while QC Timber had received approval for other cutting permits in the area, managers maintained that these high elevation areas could not be logged in winter. Rumours circulated of a long layoff. But QC Timber was far from idle, having hired International Environmental Consultants Ltd. of Vancouver to assess slope stability and fisheries habitat on the CP144 area. T.C. Griffing and L.A. Bayrock conducted fieldwork on January 20–21, filed their report by the end of the month, and QC Timber was anxious for a meeting with MOF officials.[72]

Griffing and Bayrock selected five slide sites for "detailed investigation" on CP144 and CP145, describing all as small. They asserted that none had deposited material in Riley Creek, no further slides of a significant magnitude were expected and any future "minor" events would probably not reach the creek. Slide areas had stabilized and they detected no root system deterioration in cutover areas. A single "debris torrent" triggered by improper road construction had swept down a gully in CP145, bringing materials to the creek, but a recurrence was unlikely. Riley Creek itself was not a prolific salmon producer, they observed, yielding "modest to low numbers" of Pinks.[73]

Concluding, Bayrock and Griffing described the potential hazards to Riley Creek salmon habitat from erosion in the CP144 area as "negligible."

They had discovered little silt in the stream and noted that further deposit of such materials was "highly unlikely." As well, the creek flowed with sufficient velocity and turbulence to prevent settling in the spawning gravels. Future openings should be planned to establish wind-firm boundaries but CP144 should, they claimed, be clearcut. Overall, the cutting plan provided "adequate safeguards" for Riley Creek fish habitat and appropriate precautions were being taken at the site. Further logging, they advised, posed no threat.[74]

Despite those findings, early signs indicated that the Fisheries Service would yield no ground in the matter of CP144. Romeo LeBlanc had waited until February 5 to respond to Waterland, perhaps an indication of where he ranked Pacific coast concerns. But after expressing his desire for negotiations to permit the logging of less sensitive sites and for continued co-operation in the referral process, he declared his steadfast commitment "to a policy of using the Federal *Fisheries Act* to protect the productive and sensitive areas of fish habitat." Pacific Region Director General Wally Johnson had spoken in similar terms at the UFAWU's 1978 convention, expressing optimism that his agency could work with the MOF in preventing logging on the crucial 16–20 hectares; his staff was "taking the strongest possible stance on that." Such assurances bolstered hopes for a multiple-use compromise that might provide some measure of satisfaction for the fishermen. The parties seemed to edge further toward some sort of a settlement at the mid-February Prince Rupert meeting, which generated proposals for the logging of alternative sites in QC Timber's Rennell Sound holdings, leaving the remaining CP144 timber in place. Maps setting out this approach went to the company and a subsequent February 22 meeting of DFO and MOF staff yielded an agreement for joint on-site assessment, also involving the Fish and Wildlife Branch. Hart had even agreed, after prodding by Biickert, to withdraw his stop order and accept whatever consensus decision came out of the joint inspection. At the conclusion of the one-day February 27 field trip —involving the agencies, QC Timber and its consultants—all parties agreed that the steep slopes of CP144 bordering Riley Creek should be spared from logging. The matter seemed to have been resolved. Agencies had stepped back from the brink of open war, preserving an uneasy peace. Vi Halsey even reported that QC Timber's rigging crew left on March 3, attributing the layoffs to both winter weather and Ottawa's "villain" role. The Bonanza Creek fallers, however, remained in camp.[75]

The peace lasted only two days. On March 2 a letter from Biickert's office went out to QC Timber revoking the MOF's commitment to the February 27 consensus. Biickert later said that his staff had agreed to leave the slopes on CP144 intact under pressure from fisheries managers at the end of a cold, wet day. "I am the boss," he would declare in explaining the reversal, "and when a decision has to be made, I must make it." For Richard Overstall, this was "a return to the days of the imperial forest service." With the agreement and all pretence of multiple-use compromise in tatters, Wally Johnson asked Mike Apsey for an explanation but received no reply. The *Colonist* predicted that the Japanese company would respect the ban, perhaps saving Waterland from "loss of face" in the "embarrassing confrontation" over a tiny patch of timber. Sources on the scene indicated that QC Timber was prepared to leave the critical area untouched, a report that proved overly optimistic. On Friday, March 16, an anonymous caller tipped the *Victoria Times* that the company intended to send fallers into the area, forcing a showdown. In fact, QC Timber had already tested Fisheries Service resolve, when fallers had defied the January 11 stop order and begun work on January 12, moving toward the steeper ground. Now, on March 16, fisheries officers Hart and Dave Schultz encountered five fallers in the restricted area, ordering them to stop under the threat of arrest and presenting manager Gary Marshall with a letter demanding that falling be halted. The fallers, Schultz told Mark Hume, had left without incident, apparently on a mission to gauge the agency's will to enforce the ban. No charges had been laid, Schultz reported, but the agency had every intention of doing so in the event of further encroachment. "We're going to be keeping a close watch from now on," Schultz said.[76]

QC Timber responded immediately. Manager Jack Sexton sent a letter to Queen Charlotte Fisheries Service supervisor Kip Slater from the firm's Vancouver head office, later releasing it to the press. The company had "an exceptionally clean environmental record," Sexton claimed, but had "been selected as a focal point for a major constitutional and jurisdictional legal fight." The wrangling had already interrupted CP144 operations, costing the 60-man crew $100,000 in lost wages and an equal loss to the company in legal expenses and log purchases to keep the Pitt Meadows mill running. Sexton went on to emphasize the operation's crucial role in providing winter work in an area troubled by high unemployment and welfare dependence, asked Slater for all government studies relating to soil stability on CP144 and countered with his consultants' findings on the minimal risk to fish habitat. Leaving the timber would actually enhance the slide hazard due to the inevitability of blowdown, he argued. QC Timber wanted to continue offering work to its employees and if that policy landed the firm in court it would contest the charges.[77]

QC Timber withheld public comment on its intentions until Monday, when Sexton portrayed the company as a victim. "We've been trying to play it very cool," he explained, "but you get tired of going to bed every night worrying about how it's going to be resolved." QC Timber had been "caught in a lemon squeezer" and Sexton hinted that the time for a showdown had arrived. "We have to face this," he said. "We have to bring things to a head." His remark suggested that QC Timber would push back in a jurisdictional struggle with industry-wide implications. Did control over forests lie with Victoria or Ottawa? He was careful to point out that the choice to defy the ban or not lay with the contract fallers.[78]

How much of subsequent events could be attributed to collaboration in Vancouver's corporate boardrooms would be a subject of much discussion in the ensuing days. Was QC Timber acting alone, or were larger forces at work, provoking a tactical skirmish in the strategic campaign against the *Fisheries Act*? Even before most news consumers read Sexton's remarks, the arrests had begun. Hart took faller Eldon Anyotte into custody on Monday, March 19, and charged him with destruction of fish habitat. The following day Maurice Gagnon, Jacques Le Francois and Jacques Bonenfon were arrested, along with logging manager Peter Pfister, the latter charged with three counts of counselling an offence. Meanwhile, about 10 placard-carrying women, some of them wives of the arrested fallers, picketed the Fisheries Service's Queen Charlotte City offices. The Rennell Sound women had cancelled their weekly whist game to present their side of the confrontation. The "Rattled Loggers' Wives" of the camp also pled for justice in letters to newspapers. "Why pick on the poor little man, just trying to make an honest living for his family?" they asked. The company highlighted the victimization of workers as well. "We're caught in an intergovernmental dispute," remarked a QC Timber spokesman, "and a lot of little people seem to be paying an awfully high price." The Sierra Club's Bob Nixon framed the affair quite differently. He believed Waterland was being misled by senior MOF officials unwilling to accept the conclusions of their own soil specialists, Wilford and Schwab, who had reversed their earlier findings and concluded that cutting above Riley Creek would trigger slides and massive erosion. This "irrational opposition" rendered the multiple-use provisions of the new *Forest Act* meaningless, Nixon said.[79]

Hart, armed with a pistol, made three more arrests Thursday, taking Ivan Anyotte, Mike Ballatti and Rocky Pelletier into custody. LeBlanc had been unsuccessful in contacting Waterland or Deputy Minister of Forests Mike Apsey, but Wally Johnson conveyed his minister's message to Waterland, expressing regrets about the Rennell Sound events. His department's actions were not part of some grand plan to take over the forest industry, LeBlanc explained; they were only seeking to prevent damage to fisheries resources. He asked that Waterland's officials prohibit further logging on CP144 but, standing firm, indicated if the MOF declined, his staff had "no alternative but to continue laying charges and making arrests." Apsey called Johnson to arrange a meeting for the 27th; however, according to an IPS chronology, he declined to stop the cutting in the interim. With the lines clearly drawn for the moment, Hart pledged to arrest every logger found attempting to cut on CP144, claiming he would arrest the entire crew if necessary. "Our instructions are to keep arresting—theirs apparently are to keep cutting," he said. Everyone at Rennell Sound understood that the company was challenging the ban, having hired additional fallers. As a result, every day a few more trees came down despite the arrests.[80]

Hart hoped for action from Ottawa in the form of an order-in-council restraining further cutting until the courts had ruled on the validity of the *Fisheries Act*. He would continue to wait, amidst chest-thumping from the forest industry, the MOF and the IWA. A "deeply disturbed" COFI informed LeBlanc that the QC Timber case confirmed the industry's worst fears about the new *Fisheries Act*. The Fisheries Service had committed a "dreadfully wrong act" in arresting loggers and the charges should be withdrawn as a prelude to discussing amendments to prevent further resource use conflict. Local 1-71 president Ben Thomson, calling the situation intolerable, telegrammed LeBlanc and Waterland demanding a meeting. "Either we get some action or we'll shut the province down until they sort it out," he threatened. IWA regional president Jack Munro also telegrammed Pierre Elliot Trudeau and Bill Bennett on Thursday, describing his arrested members as "victims of a ludicrous power struggle" between federal and provincial agencies. If it took a province-wide work stoppage to achieve a sensible resolution, one that included dropping all charges, the IWA was prepared to provide that solution.

Waterland called the loggers' arrests "completely unfair." "Ridiculous," said Bill Bennett in promising that his government would fight on their behalf.[81]

On Friday, March 23, with RCMP officers now on the scene to make more arrests, Munro sent a second telegram of warning to Trudeau and another to Governor General Ed Schreyer asking him to intercede. "We're sort of the meat in the middle of the sandwich where this thing is concerned," Munro said. "We're sure as hell not going to allow our members to be treated like this." Loggers were being arrested just for doing their jobs, Thomson remarked, deploring this un-Canadian "police-state activity." Bennett, too, drew attention to the outrage of armed federal fisheries officers patrolling BC forests.[82]

In response, federal officials maintained that they had no interest in constitutional controversy. "It's simply fish habitat versus poor logging practices," explained Kip Slater, adding that QC Timber had plenty of timber available to cut outside of the disputed area. Holding course, company spokesman Tom Carney insisted that the authority to log came from the MOF, exercising its control over a provincial resource. The firm's independent consultants had concluded that logging posed a minimal threat to Riley Creek, and the Fisheries Service had yet to provide conclusive scientific data to the contrary. Perhaps, commented the *Victoria Times*, a display of "good corporate citizenship" would have seen the company hold off on cutting the disputed trees until the two levels of government had worked out their differences. If, in the end, negotiations or a court decision authorized logging, QC Timber could be compensated for the delay. But if the result went the other way, there was "no way to bring back the trees that have already fallen." That reasoned stance by the *Times* offered a way out of the dispute, but it ignored the higher stakes of a conflict rooted in corporate and provincial government determination to break the power of the *Fisheries Act*.[83]

By the end of the week fisheries interests, established conservation groups and newer environmental organizations all staked out their positions. The Sierra Club, BCWF and Greenpeace urged Waterland to impose a moratorium on further logging. The UFAWU advised LeBlanc to drop charges against the loggers but confront corporate defiance with "full punitive measures" against the company. The 300 members of the BC Federation of Fly Fisherman, unhappy with the MOF's record in stream protection, also wanted to see charges against the company proceed. In a telephone interview with Larry Still, IPS spokesman Dan Bowditch claimed that companies had stripped the hillsides of Rennell

Sound "clear down to the shoreline" over the previous decade. For Bill Bennett, however, a Rennell Sound surrender of any sort would only strengthen Ottawa's hand in the larger jurisdictional contest. Western premiers were set to meet the following week at Prince George in their "annual opportunity to pummel federal authorities," the *Daily News* observed. A BC report on federal intrusion into areas of provincial jurisdiction, a matter of real concern to Bennett, topped the agenda. Natural resources were provincial government property, he said, and "federal meddling" would not be tolerated.[84]

That position made for a firm alliance with Jack Munro on the Rennell Sound issue. The IWA leader's strike threat conveyed a message to Ottawa that British Columbians were serious, Bennett told the *Colonist*. He and Munro would stand together in the face of federal aggression, an example of what could be accomplished "when you strip away the politics." But this was surely a classic case of "cheap politics," the *Colonist* observed. Instead of considering the best interests of all, particularly the fishermen, the province had chosen to interpret Rennell Sound as the site of a political invasion. Munro and the company had behaved badly too, the former engaging in "bully talk" while the latter kept sending fallers in to be arrested. Only about 16 hectares were involved and enough of the province's own experts now opposed the logging to justify a moratorium until all the evidence was in.[85]

Saturday brought the first day of calm to Rennell Sound after a week that had seen 16 arrests. It was unlikely more fallers would venture into the cutting permit area until after the Tuesday talks, a company official said, again with the proviso that it was up to the loggers. Bennett expressed a willingness to work things out with Trudeau if Tuesday's high level talks in Vancouver failed to produce a resolution, and some sensed a loosening of Ottawa's commitment. The *Colonist* detected "whimpering noises" coming from the nation's capital as the May 22 federal election approached. Would the Liberals stand fast and risk losing votes in BC or back down? Jack Pearsall, parliamentary secretary for Environment and MP for the Lower Mainland, expressed his desire to see all charges against the loggers dropped and a postponement of logging until Riley Creek had been studied after the spring runoff. Publicly, at least, LeBlanc still seemed willing to put up a fight. The blame lay squarely on BC's unreasonable behaviour, he insisted in the House of Commons on Monday. An agreement had been reached to preserve the critical 16 hectares of timber but, for some unexplained reason, the MOF had authorized logging. His officials' efforts to reach Apsey by phone had proven unsuccessful for six days.[86]

The NDP handled the situation carefully, condemning both the provincial Socreds and the federal Liberals whose squabbling had placed loggers in the judicial crosshairs. Early on Dave Barrett described Rennell Sound as "just the tip of the iceberg", warning that such clashes would occur with nightmarish frequency unless the two levels of government could come to an agreement over logging and environmental issues. Nanaimo-Cowichan MP Tommy Douglas asked LeBlanc to halt the arrests of loggers for simply following company orders. His colleague, Kootenay West MP Lyle Kristiansen, suggested a new law to prevent workers from being fired for refusing to carry out duties that would expose them to charges. In Victoria, NDP forestry critic Bill King accused the MOF of counselling the company to defy federal law. Whether the company or inter-governmental mismanagement was to blame, the NDP would cast itself as defender of the working man.[87]

All awaited the outcome of the meeting set for Tuesday in Vancouver, which would include bureaucrats as well as representatives from the forest industry, the UFAWU, the IWA and the BCWF. One worried federal official predicted that dropping the charges would reduce the *Fisheries Act* to a "meaningless piece of paper." Notably absent from the meeting was any representation from the BC Fish and Wildlife Branch. When the BCWF's Jack Mankelow asked about this, meeting chair Mike Apsey apparently replied that the "neutral" branch had "neither been invited nor told not to come." In a later account Richard Overstall argued that the branch was ordered not to participate. In either case, the province would present its position untroubled by internal conflict. The MOF and its industry clients emerged from the discussions as clear victors, with a press release announcing that logging of CP144 would proceed. Moreover, Wally Johnson would recommend that the charges against the loggers be dropped, although those against the company held for the time being. Habitat protection measures required QC Timber to construct settling basins at the base of the slope to prevent sediment from entering Riley Creek, and also to seed the cutover area. The adjacent CP151 would be studied closely prior to a decision on logging, and the agencies also agreed to step up research on sensitive-site logging. Commercial fisheries and conservation interests responded to the compromise with anger and dismay. UFAWU president Jack Nicol walked out of the meeting, saying that Ottawa had "absolutely caved in on the thing." QC

Timber had made an issue of the small tract, and in the face of the challenge the Fisheries Service had capitulated. "They just shot the Fisheries Act full of holes," Nicol concluded. Dave Orton of the BC Federation of Naturalists agreed, along with the BCWF, SPEC and the Sierra Club. Settling basins were "merely an excuse for poor logging practices," remarked Bob Nixon. Provincial government promises of environmental protection were patently meaningless, SPEC's Cliff Stainsby declared, and a BCWF official asserted that the Fisheries Service had "abdicated its responsibility to protect the resource".[88]

Forest industry representatives and the IWA's Munro came out delighted. According to Munro's account, when IWA representatives arrived at 1:30 pm as scheduled, federal and provincial officials had already negotiated a deal permitting the logging of CP144, with the provision for a protective settling basin. Told that Ottawa was prepared only to review the charges against his members, Munro balked. Discussions over the next three hours "got pretty god dammed warm," and in the end, federal officials agreed to recommend the charges be withdrawn. That brought the IWA into the fold, although the union remained opposed to the ongoing case against the company. Nevertheless, a QC Timber spokesman called the deal "a victory for science and proper project management." The Ottawa men scrambled to place their back-down in a positive light. Ron MacLeod, director of the federal agency's Field Services Branch, denied that any retreat had occurred. Charges against Pfister and the company remained active, subject to evaluation by the solicitor general. Better yet, CP151 had been identified as unstable and made subject to an inter-agency review. MacLeod expressed optimism that it would be exchanged for a less sensitive site, leaving the tract intact. Finally, implementation of the "safety measures" on CP144 would protect Riley Creek.[89]

LeBlanc took the same reassuring approach in response to a letter of criticism from the Prince Rupert Fish Exchange. The forestry experts had convinced his representatives that leaving the remaining timber on CP144 uncut would likely produce blowdown, and the resulting uprooting of trees would increase the danger of major slides. But the Fisheries Service had not caved in, insisting on the settling basin system and other sediment control measures. Moreover, MOF agreement that the 200 acres (81 hectares) of CP151 were unstable meant greater protection for Riley Creek than the threat logging CP144 posed. Here LeBlanc implied that affording CP151 'sensitive site' status meant its withdrawal from logging—or at least a strong role for his managers in planning.

All this, along with more research on logging techniques and erosion control and a strengthening of the referral system, ensured that the March 27 agreement fulfilled the federal mandate to protect fish habitat without imposing unnecessary restrictions on another industry, LeBlanc insisted.[90]

Face-saving press statements fell far short of insulating the Fisheries Service from withering criticism. Describing the affair as a federal sell-out of field staff, the BCWF demanded Johnson's resignation. The consequences for agency morale were indeed serious, and Mark Hume quoted an anonymous source describing federal personnel as shaken by the agreement. *Victoria Times* outdoor writer Stewart Lang noted that the "illogical and unscientific" decision by high-ranking federal officials had "a ripe aroma", exposing the *Fisheries Act* to open contempt. Unable to get a comment from LeBlanc, Lang obtained an explanation from a Fisheries Service spokesman who reiterated that previous cutting made the remaining timber vulnerable to blowdown, and therefore it made sense to clearcut. "That particular inept piece of thinking doesn't wash," Lang observed. Did the fact that loggers outnumbered fishermen in Liberal MP Iona Campagnolo's north coast riding explain this decision, which emasculated the *Fisheries Act* and left a "bitter taste" in the mouths of fisheries managers? Lang wondered: would the province have taken a different approach had it absorbed a higher share of SEP funding?[91]

Throwing a wide net of blame, the *Vancouver Express* attributed the "classic government botch-up" to "arrogance and empire-building" in both Ottawa and Victoria. LeBlanc had blundered in pushing the *Fisheries Act* through despite BC's opposition to this perceived intrusion into provincial affairs. The province, in turn, had been high-handed in provoking a showdown that left a stream damaged. The *Express* credited Jack Munro for resolving the dispute by issuing his strike threat, but environmentalists such as Victoria's Richard Krieger tended to cast Munro as the villain. Referring to a 1978 *ForesTalk* interview in which Munro had depicted loggers as "some of the best environmentalists that exist," working under stringent regulations to protect streams, Krieger called the union leader a hypocrite. The Riley Creek controversy was not rooted in jurisdictional conflict, he concluded, but poor logging practices.[92]

Steve Whipp concurred with this analysis in one of the most biting post-agreement commentaries. Rumours of a provincial election were in the air, giving Bennett a fundamental issue to campaign on, and in Alberta Peter Lougheed had recently won in a landslide, upholding that province's right to manage its natural resources. But, Whipp argued, this was less a constitutional tussle than one over land use practices. Moreover, BC's hard line lacked the support of its Fish and Wildlife Branch and the MOF's own soil specialists. Instead of acting on their advice, regional forester Biickert had accepted the findings of QC Timber's consultants, who had "spent two days in knee-deep snow examining slope stability." Then, after the late February on-site inspection which produced the apparent compromise to protect the most crucial timber, Biickert had issued the authority to clearcut. The ensuing "squeeze-play" and initial arrests had been followed by the arrival of more fallers, described as "highly-paid recruits" by Whipp.[93]

Whipp's last point raised an important question. Was this a case of a relatively small company caught up in an inter-governmental power play, or was it a coordinated industry offensive? Richard Overstall set out the case for the latter scenario, finding clues in events at QC Timber's camp, where a steady stream of fallers had arrived by plane to replace those who had been arrested. Organizing this effort, Overstall charged, was Ross Clark, a junior lawyer with Davis and Company, the province's largest law firm. And pulling the strings from Vancouver was Duncan Shaw, counsel for MacMillan Bloedel during the Pearse Commission hearings. Islanders, Overstall related, heard Shaw's voice over their CB radios "giving Clark his orders." The Rennell Sound affair, then, was the key element in a carefully planned effort to free the industry from regulatory entanglements. But Shaw had misjudged Ottawa's commitment, Overstall suggested, and as arrest followed arrest more men had to be "sent to the firing line." In this view, QC Timber's role was "high profile standard bearer in MacMillan Bloedel's fight to purge the federal Fisheries Act from the coastal forests."[94]

It seems clear that by the spring of 1979 a forest industry attack on the Fisheries Act was in full swing, and not just at Rennell Sound. In 1975 logging contractor Dan Fowler had been charged with depositing debris in a fish-bearing stream near Forbes Bay. Fowler's lawyer argued that the Fisheries Act interfered with the province's jurisdiction over forestry, and a provincial court had declared the act ultra vires. The Crown appealed, winning a 1977 reversal in Vancouver County Court, triggering a COFI-sponsored appeal to the Supreme Court of Canada in 1978, set for a hearing in the late spring of 1979. MacMillan Bloedel, charged recently with two Fisheries Act violations on Graham Island, declined to enter a plea that March in the hopes that the case would be adjourned until the Supreme Court ruling. An industry-wide "Fowler case task force", chaired by a COFI representative and members from the regional associations, oversaw the appeal. For the entire forest industry, the Fowler appeal and Rennell Sound represented two fronts in a single campaign. A Fisheries Service consultant's report released that spring showed a $2.24 per cunit (3.6 per cent) increase in logging costs to achieve compliance with *Fisheries Act* regulations, which only hardened industry resolve.[95]

With Wally Johnson's endorsement of the decision to proceed with logging on CP144, federal denials of capitulation could obscure neither the fact nor the perception that the agency had withdrawn from the first skirmish over the *Act*. That left the matter of the charges against the loggers. On March 27, the same day as the Vancouver meeting, islanders who packed the Queen Charlotte City court began hearing rumours that charges were being withdrawn even as the defence counsel concluded his lengthy argument asking Judge R.C.S. Graham to reject them as "frivolous." After a brief discussion, the judge granted a joint motion for a one-month adjournment while the Fisheries Service clarified its official position. That decision, of course, was being made, but federal officials had talked up their intent to proceed against the company. QC Timber would go on to seek dismissal of the charges, but a provincial court judge ruled them valid in late May. There the matter stood, as British Columbians contemplated Riley Creek in the context of a provincial election set for May 10 and the federal vote less than two weeks later.[96]

During the provincial campaign the Socreds received a good deal of criticism for ignoring multiple-use promises at Rennell Sound. Fisherman Harry Allen, from Quathiaski Cove on Quadra Island, saw the incident as an attempt by the Socreds to clear the way for unfettered logging of spawning areas and urged UFAWU members to vote accordingly. Bella Coola's Al Purkiss ridiculed Bennett "quivering with indignant rage" about Ottawa's treatment of the Rennell Sound loggers, "patsies" who had been "set up for a bum rap" by the province's defiance of federal law. The NDP experienced its own difficult moments. Prince Rupert riding MLA Graham Lea received rough treatment for his attitudes, "or lack of them", at early April Sandspit and Queen Charlotte City meetings. Sandspit loggers disliked his support for TFL 24 renewal hearings, and he endured persistent questioning from a Rennell Sound logger at the second meeting about his failure both to visit the camp and to take a clear stance. He had consulted with the fisheries experts, Lea responded, but lacking expertise had wanted to see "common sense prevail." Ultimately, he supported a provincial takeover of fisheries jurisdiction, an idea Bennett and other premiers had already proposed. That, Lea said, would permit the premier to adjudicate between his two ministers. Federal Skeena NDP candidate Jim Fulton, also making the rounds for the federal election, launched a direct attack on the Liberals' "sell-out" and subsequent "white wash" at Rennell Sound. But the answer did not lie in provincial jurisdiction, Fulton asserted, British Columbia having demonstrated clearly that the forest industry's needs came before fish habitat. He did not support the prosecution of workers, but the fishery resource needed protection and the Liberals had lacked "the guts to stop the destruction." The sitting Skeena MP, Liberal Iona Campagnolo, on the other hand, touted the protection offered under the March 27 agreement in her campaign stops.[97]

The Socreds' re-election left conservationists with little optimism for a more vigorous provincial commitment to habitat protection. *Western Fisheries* columnist Al Meadows hoped that the demands for better environmental management voiced during the campaign might penetrate government thinking, but he ridiculed the advertised protective measures for Rennell Sound. If built, the sediment basin would not cope with future slides, and promises of ecological monitoring amounted, he wrote, to "contemptible garbage." The recently signed SEP only exposed the "con job" being peddled in the name of conservation more starkly, as the millions being spent on "artificial fish mills" could never compensate for the loss of natural ecosystems. For Dave Orton of the BC Federation of Naturalists, Rennell Sound symbolized the emptiness of multiple-use policy as espoused by the united front of government, industry and the IWA. Timber production trumped all other concerns, the MOF "playing the role of hand-maiden" to the corporate clearcutting regime. Orton was no more optimistic that the federal election would produce land use reforms, given Ottawa's silence on the capitulation at Rennell Sound. That election brought Joe Clark's Conservatives to power, briefly. Clark's government would last only nine months, but that meant that the next phase of the Rennell Sound controversy would be James McGrath's problem as minister of the new Department of Fisheries and Oceans (DFO), created by LeBlanc just prior to the Conservative victory.[98]

Most commentators reserved their praise in the Rennell Sound affair for one man: Jim Hart. Many saw provincial politicians as captured by timber interests, and the federal government was spending millions on artificial measures to boost salmonid production while failing to enforce its own habitat protection law. Hart and his fellow officers had done their job courageously, but Hart had paid a high price, receiving threatening telephone calls and finding obscenities etched on his dusty vehicle. On June 15 he resigned for "personal reasons" to go commercial fishing, saying that he could not foresee an end to the fight over logging practices. "I just got tired of it all," he explained. Crediting local officials for their support, Hart said they had all been "sold out" by Wally Johnson. Reflecting on his time with both the MOF and Fisheries Service, he described his disdain for the province's stated multiple-use policy and what he called the "hypocrisy" of resource use on the islands.[99]

Hart's resignation coincided with the arrival at Rennell Sound of Doug Swanston, a consulting geologist with wide experience in Alaska forests. He was engaged by DFO Field Services Director J.R. MacLeod to offer an opinion on the potential for future logging-related slides at Riley Creek. Swanston conducted fieldwork on CP144 from June 11–14, devoting particular attention to the west-facing slope that inspired the dispute, felled late that spring and the site of yarding operations at the time of his visit. He began his report with a sobering observation: much of the slope was already "in an incipient state of failure even in the absence of any disrupting factors." Clearcutting the slope would only deprive the thin soil of the stability offered by the trees' root systems, "cohesive binders" that lost their strength within three to five years after logging. Wording his findings carefully, he found it "highly likely" that tree removal on the CP144 slope would "have an adverse effect on the relative stability of the site."[100]

Blowdown was an important contributor to mass soil movements in such conditions, Swanston continued, but that problem had been eliminated on CP144 "at the expense of destroying the viable root mass on the unstable upper slope." That loss increased the likelihood of slides, but he stopped short of asserting their inevitability. "This does not mean the slope will automatically fail," he concluded with emphatic underlining, although a high-intensity rainfall event in association with diminished root strength would produce the "right combination of conditions" for that outcome.[101]

Turning to the possible consequences for Riley Creek, Swanston predicted that large soil failures would carry material through the gulleys to the valley floor, "possibly" reaching the creek. At least 7.5 tons of sediment had been introduced to the creek as recently as the past winter and Swanston gave a conservative estimate that an equal amount would be flushed into the stream during the next major failure. Sediment would continue to reach Riley Creek from the slope, then, and while he called for study by a fisheries biologist, Swanston noted that "windrows of sand and fine gravel" of a size considered detrimental to fish life blanketed sections of the stream bed.[102]

Swanston concluded that the upper slope of CP144 was in an "unstable state" and that there was a high probability of "accelerated soil mass movement" in the next five years, or until the re-establishment of a stabilizing root network. The cutting permit's northeastern slope, the site of several recent debris avalanches, was also "highly unstable", as were those nearby on CP155. The latter, actually, had greater potential for discharging large volumes of sediment into Riley Creek than CP144. Nevertheless, logging of CP144's west-facing slope would "have an adverse impact" on stability, posing a risk that landslides would bring material to the valley floor and into contact with Riley Creek through at least two gullies. Yet, despite his assertive language on the likelihood, even the inevitability, of further slides that could be attributed in large part to logging, Swanston had indicated that the slope would not automatically fail, and observed that the material he had seen in Riley Creek spawning gravels was only "potentially detrimental to salmonid habitat" —conclusions with important consequences for the case against QC Timber.[103]

In mid-August it was announced that charges against QC Timber and manager Peter Pfister had been dropped, on the grounds of a Justice Department conclusion that Swanston's findings did not provide a sound basis for prosecution. The legal interpretation, new DFO Acting Field Director Al Gibson explained, forced the agency to provide "absolute proof" that an action would lead inevitably to habitat destruction. Swanston's findings provided plenty of support for the charges, Richard Overstall commented, but were "couched in terms that allowed for the small amount of uncertainty with which all scientists must view natural processes." The DFO's initial approval of the Riley Creek cutting plan also compromised the case, according to Gibson. Later verbal agreements between local DFO and MOF staff during the February field trip did not override the company's earlier written authority to proceed.[104]

The decision further undermined public confidence in both the DFO and federal regulations. UFAWU president Jack Nicol, requesting reinstatement of the charges, informed McGrath that the outcome "seriously calls into question the value to BC salmon resources of the Fisheries Act." Jim Fulton, recently elected as the MP for Skeena, likewise bemoaned the federal government's refusal to enforce its own legislation. A *Fisherman* editorial interpreted the recent events as the culmination of a successful campaign by the province's "major forest monopolies" to render statutory protection of fish habitat meaningless. The piece opined that QC Timber's operation would almost certainly destroy spawning beds, McGrath should "find another lawyer" and loggers should join with fishermen in forcing responsible forest management.[105]

Despite a torrent of criticism, the DFO declared victory in the Rennell Sound conflict. That interpretation was based on an inter-agency plan for the slopes above Riley Creek. Wally Johnson, Mike Apsey and Deputy Minister of Environment Ben Marr had agreed, drawing on the not-yet-released report of BCFS soil specialists Wilford and Schwab, to a number of requirements to be met by QC Timber. In the end, 38 acres (~15 hectares) of the most unstable area of CP144 were deleted from the logging plan upon their recommendation. The department "achieved exactly what we wanted," Al Gibson now said, citing conditions imposed on QC Timber and the province's commitment to review cutting plans on the islands as a basis for deleting sensitive areas from all of the region's cutting permits. Gibson also asserted a more co-operative approach by the MOF, giving his agency "more clout at the planning stage." Rennell Sound had been a regrettable incident, Wally Johnson admitted, a "political football" that could have been better handled. But the conflict had a positive side as well, giving rise to a "fantastic stimulation of communication" between the agencies. MOF Regional Manager Jack Biickert was similarly bullish about developments. A letter had gone out advising QC Timber of its responsibility for the special measures Wilford and Schwab thought necessary to protect the stream. In addition to reserving the unstable area, the plan called for cross-ditching roads, reseeding slopes with grass and alder, placing debris on slopes to reduce water velocities and using cementing agents on roads, all to be implemented prior to the October rains. "We are reasonably certain that the instructions...will go a long way to stabilizing the area," Biickert declared. "I'm very optimistic that we can achieve and maintain successful multi-resource use in this area through careful harvesting procedures." He too heralded a new era of co-operation, as MOF staff were now working closely with the federal and provincial fisheries agencies.[106]

Notably absent from press releases detailing QC Timber's obligations was any direct reference to the settling basin requirement that had figured so prominently as a solution in post-March 27 press releases. Wilford and Schwab had concluded that there was insufficient space at the base of the slope to permit the kinds of structures needed to cope with the sediment loads produced by major slides, confirming earlier doubts about the proposal. And slides of that magnitude could be expected on both CP144 and the adjacent CP145 in the next few years, they predicted. Withdrawal of the most problematic areas from the CP144 cutting plan was significant, but many other problems remained to be dealt with before the rainy season. Poor drainage practices, including sidecasting of soil and lack of culverts on branch roads, had contributed to recent mass soil movements, and more areas were primed to fail as roots decayed and yarding operations disturbed soil. Waiting for natural regeneration was no longer an option, they advised. Nor would better ditching of roads, positioning debris on slopes and revegetation efforts eliminate the danger. "Mass movements will occur and their impact cannot be totally eliminated," Wilford and Schwab declared.[107]

That sobering observation found no place in any of the reassuring official statements flowing from government offices in the late summer of 1979. August brought perfect weather to the islands: "blue skies, billowing clouds and sunshine each day," Alice McRea reported from Port Clements. October, though, meant the beginning of the rainy season, and local DFO officials, "gritting their teeth in anticipation", were under no illusion about what that might mean for Rennell Sound. Kip Slater, referring to the Swanston report, predicted in late September that if heavy rains came slope failure would deposit soil in Riley Creek. Anticipating trouble, Slater made it clear that Swanston, a scientist who dealt in "high degrees of possibility rather than certainties", should not be blamed. With no clear "preventative mechanism" in the *Fisheries Act*, all Slater and his field officers could do was hope for the best, wait for an offence and lay charges. Fisheries minister McGrath *could* seek an order-in-council to stop a logging operation, but that seemed unlikely given the inevitable constitutional uproar that would follow.[108]

There was no need to worry, according to QC Timber's manager Peter Pfister; the preventative measures, now nearing completion, should prevent any "major slope failure." The slopes, he said, would probably hold without any precautions—precautions which had imposed little in the way of a financial burden for the company. The MOF would extend stumpage cost offsets for silvicultural investments under the *Forest Act* to cover pollution control equipment and processes. But from Queen Charlotte City Jim Hart described the protection offered against slides as "nothing short of tokenism" and "a waste of time and money." Worse yet, CP144 was "just the start of the fiasco"; three other watersheds on the islands, with even steeper slopes, were also scheduled for logging. The UFAWU's Skidegate local shared Hart's concerns, resolving in mid-October to monitor streams for *Fisheries Act* violations after a reported Rennell Sound slide earlier in the month. Rafe Mair, now BC Environment minister, met with McGrath at Prince Rupert in early October to discuss Rennell Sound, among other issues, admitting that forestry-fishery tensions had not been fully resolved. The two had visited the site and agreed on "machinery which will prevent the situation from escalating again."[109]

The Big Blow: Late 1979 Slides, the Bellis Case and the FFIP Solution

BY THE TIME MAIR AND MCGRATH LEFT PRINCE RUPERT, autumn rains had begun to fall on the north coast, picking up in intensity as the days passed. Late October 1979 brought "the first blow of the season" to Rennell Sound, and fronts continued to saturate soils on the slopes. Then, on November 20, Swanston's high-intensity event hit, dumping over 152 millimetres of rainfall over the following 48 hours. "The Big Blow came to rattle our homes, raise the creeks to rivers, and slump the roads, making one H... of a mess," reported Vi Halsey. Massive slope failures occurred on CP144 and CP145, two of the slides actually entering Riley Creek. Kip Slater, first on the scene along with the Fish and Wildlife Branch's Keith Moore, related that the largest failure involved an area up to 60 metres across and about 15 metres deep. A second slide joined the main failure, together entering a narrow gulley and scouring it down to bare rock. At the bottom of the slope mud up to 1.5 metres deep deposited what Slater termed a "substantial amount" of silt in Riley Creek. "Now maybe the forest service will listen to us," Slater declared. "We are not in the business of writing off salmon streams." Moore's boss, Ministry of Environment regional director Don Smuin, new to the region after a transfer from the interior, had difficulty describing the scene. "Words fail me," Smuin said. "It's just a mess. I think a person would have to see it to appreciate the impact it has had on the environment."[110]

In describing the damage to Swanston a few days later, Moore related that CP144 had experienced eight separate slides, six of them on the slope facing Riley Creek. Five of the failures were quite small, having little impact on the stream. One of the three major slides, however, extended over 304 metres in length and just under 61 metres wide. "Flowing mud ran in rivulets across the forest floor and into Riley Creek," Moore explained, leaving "tremendous deposition in the stream." CP145 was also the scene of several failures, including one of about 457 metres that entered the creek, which now ran "an opaque brown colour." None of the slides appeared to have been triggered by roads; all originated in clearcuts. As for the weather, Moore considered the amount of rainfall "not unusual"—far less than the 242 millimetres recorded during the November 1978 storm.[111] Once again Riley Creek became the stuff of front-page newspaper reports.

Those who authorized the logging of the slope and developed the much-heralded preventative measures now scrambled to blame Mother Nature and Swanston while justifying their actions. Biickert cited what he called, in contrast to Moore, abnormal weather—heavy rain and "almost hurricane-force winds." He told Prince Rupert CBC radio reporters Terry Donnelly and Cam Martin that he had thought there were "unstable circumstances" to parts of the area but that the agencies had agreed that logging could go ahead with minimal damage to Riley Creek. The protective measures would have mitigated the effects under normal conditions, he implied. Responding to a question about blame, Biickert said he could not assign responsibility. Donnelly and Martin, among others, characterized the rainfall as "substantial but not unusual" and noted the MOF's tolerance for a level of "minimal damage." Was minimal damage acceptable to the DFO, they asked Wally Johnson? It depended on how one defined the term, he replied. "Man can hardly do anything in this world without changing it a little bit," but his department sought to prevent "significant change to important fish habitat." Damage *had* been done, the two reporters pointed out, to which Johnson replied that federal and provincial fisheries staff were now at the site doing everything possible. "We can't turn the clock back," he concluded. Johnson also dodged a question about responsibility then implicated his own expert, Swanston. The DFO had brought him in as a recognized authority but he too had "been fooled by the rather devious events that occurred." Perhaps, Johnson remarked, "God is accountable for the heavy rains."[112]

The attempt to shift blame to Swanston drew a swift response from an unidentified "expert" who called the Prince Rupert CBC station immediately after the broadcast. Swanston had not been fooled, the caller explained; his report had concluded accurately that slides would occur and that harm would come to the Riley Creek spawning beds. Johnson's divine intervention explanation lacked credibility even within his own agency. It was "pretty obvious" logging had caused the slides, Kip Slater observed. Failures did occur on unlogged slopes, but not with such frequency, and heavy rainfall was far from unusual on the west coast of the islands. Interviewed from Juneau, Alaska, Swanston said that he was not at all surprised at the slides in the cutover portions of CP144, allowing that their extent had something to do with the intensity of the storm. McGrath, promising to seek legal advice on the laying of charges, stressed that he had wanted to do so after inspecting the area but lawyers had told him the case could not be won. His predecessor LeBlanc, avoiding his part in the fiasco, accused the provincial government of betrayal. Tom Waterland stayed largely silent in the immediate aftermath, issuing only a promise to investigate.[113]

With DFO and MOF staff gathering at Rennell Sound to survey the site on November 28, only the BC Fish and Wildlife Branch seemed immune from criticism. Permission to clearcut the steep portions of CP144 had been granted despite the Ministry of Environment's "serious objections," Smuin declared: "we had input which was ignored." Minister Stephen Rogers, new to the post after a November 23 cabinet shuffle, stoked the fires of inter-agency acrimony by attributing the mess at Riley Creek to lax MOF regulations. QC Timber may have caused the damage, but the blame lay elsewhere. His official Smuin claimed that "many, many tons" of material had been deposited in the stream, probably ruining its productivity. Waterland called Smuin's estimate an exaggeration, conceded that some sedimentation had occurred but denied permanent harm to the spawning areas. The extent of the damage might be open to debate, but a flyover by MOF and DFO officials left Slater unimpressed. "It's not until you're up to your butt in mud that you get the real assessment," he said. "Any schoolchild could tell you that the beds must be damaged from the amount of mud deposited there on the creek bed."[114]

The blame game impressed no one, but where did the responsibility lie? QC Timber had indeed fulfilled the terms of the protective orders, all of which had been "washed away," noted the *Victoria Times*. That made prosecution unlikely, but some remained hopeful. Pressed by Jim Fulton in the House of Commons about proceeding against QC Timber, McGrath stated only that he would conduct a personal review of the situation. The Sierra Club was also anxious to see McGrath show more "intestinal fortitude" than his predecessor. The UFAWU and Native Brotherhood of British Columbia added their voices to the clamour both for prosecutions and a halt to logging at Rennell Sound. The promised protection of the federal-provincial agreement had proven illusory, Jack Nicol informed McGrath, and the agencies and company must be held responsible. The Native Brotherhood called on Bennett to halt all logging on the islands until the safety of spawning grounds had been assured, and they demanded that charges be laid against QC Timber for the "devastation in Riley Creek."[115]

The possibility of the province laying charges was beyond faint, although Rogers indicated that his ministry would make no decision until completion of a field report by Smuin. A December 5 meeting between Rogers and Waterland put an end to any speculation about charges coming out of Victoria, and to Rogers' brief flurry of assertiveness. The rift between the two ministries had been healed, the *Victoria Times* reported, and Rogers explained that the time for dwelling on responsibility for the events at Rennell Sound had passed. He and Waterland were concentrating on the lessons to be learned, and his Fish and Wildlife Branch would not proceed with prosecution. Neither would Ottawa. Johnson told a UFAWU convention audience that Swanston, when asked if he would provide expert testimony, responded that he could not say if "there was more likelihood of a slide if those last trees were cut than if they weren't." Slater gave a different explanation and referred to the publicity surrounding the slides, which made prosecution "virtually impossible." Slater also referred to improved relations with the MOF, as the agencies now forged a united front to regain public confidence. An early December MOF press release declared that foresters and DFO officials had agreed on measures to prevent a repeat of the slides that had "threatened" Riley Creek. They had also agreed that while significant sedimentation had occurred, it would not devastate the creek's productivity. The Fish and Wildlife Branch had come on board as well, following a successful meeting involving officials from all three agencies. Even the company came out looking responsible. Initial branch road construction was poor, but QC Timber had done excellent work complying with the mid-August preventative instructions.[116]

Cutting Permit 144 area, summer 1979. Courtesy of Keith Moore.

Then came reports of further large slides at nearby Bonanza Creek, on slopes logged by QC Timber in 1978. A concerned Slater believed these hit on December 6, originating on both clearcut areas and a road that had slumped. One failure, about 60 metres long, deposited material directly into the stream, considered the most productive one draining into Rennell Sound. Another 500-metre "debris torrent" dragged slash and undergrowth down the slope, avoiding the creek but creating a definite source of sediment. Many areas currently subject to logging had the potential for slides, ranger Ben Hanson admitted, but none were being cut against DFO or Fish and Wildlife Branch objections.[117]

The Bonanza Creek slides caused no serious public uproar. Then, on December 14, Joe Clark's Conservative government fell in Ottawa. McGrath, soon to lose his office in the February election that returned Pierre Trudeau's Liberals to power, put to rest any lingering hopes of a QC Timber prosecution for the November slides before departing. LeBlanc had approved the logging, and the company had complied with the conditions imposed. Until specialists better understood the landslide problem he had instructed his staff to oppose further steep-slope logging near productive fish habitats. It would be left to LeBlanc, re-appointed as Fisheries minister by Trudeau, to fulfill McGrath's promise of more aggressive habitat protection.[118]

Over the ensuing weeks, the various interests continued to sort out the meaning of Riley Creek in political, social and environmental terms. With another federal election looming, Jim Fulton took pains to clarify his position, explaining that while he and his provincial colleague Graham Lea had consistently opposed charges against the loggers, he had been equally in favour of pursuing those against the company. The failure of the federal-provincial agreement to protect Riley Creek exposed the problem of managing resources "without establishing some legal and constitutional authority for such management." Both levels of government were guilty of using workers as "cannon fodder" in the dispute, then, pitting fishermen versus loggers and obscuring the fundamental defect of "weak-kneed" policy. Rennell Sound *had* indeed troubled relations between the IWA and UFAWU and, when the slides prompted an anti-clearcutting resolution at the BC Federation of Labour's late 1979 convention, the two unions managed to avoid open conflict by agreeing on a compromise that called on governments to include their representatives in watershed planning. The final wording also condemned the arrests of IWA members and concluded that logging methods existed that would allow the industries to co-exist.[119]

The IPS's Paul George had little confidence in the will of either foresters or loggers to embrace reforms. Quoting the Association of BC Professional Foresters' code of ethics on their obligation to apply knowledge in the best interests of society, George asked in a letter to the local newspaper if the destruction of Riley Creek salmon habitat met that standard of conduct. A second clause, mandating foresters to avoid subjugating professional principles to the demands of employers and to advise the employer of any consequences arising from a course of action that did not constitute sound forest practice, drew another caustic question from the biologist: "Is permitting massive erosion sound forestry?" Foresters had approved the CP144 logging plan, George observed, confirming his opinion that they were "to blame for the forestry mess in BC."[120]

But if foresters were guilty of "ethical failure" in George's eyes, loggers and their union stood as another major obstacle to straightening out the mess. Loggers were little more than pathetic dupes, George concluded in early 1980. His contact with a "random sample of the beer drinking rank and file" left him convinced that most "would cut and cut and cut until they got over

Cutting Permit 144, Riley Creek, November 1979. Courtesy of Keith Moore.

the last hill and discovered only unready second growth." Sadly, workers had been "lulled into narcotic unawareness by both the companies they work for and their own top brass."[121]

George's perspective could only further alienate workers from the environmental movement, but it was readily apparent that land use conflict had united IWA and corporate leadership. High interest rates and a slowing North American housing market gave indications of a forthcoming recession, deepening concerns about layoffs. The prospect of economic problems coupled with tighter regulations and higher operating costs, perhaps making logging uneconomical in some areas, had Munro worried. QC Timber's recently submitted five-year logging plan for Rennell Sound was a case in point, with the Fish and Wildlife Branch taking a "harder line" on approval. Adding to the uncertainty was the upcoming federal election and the Fowler case, which had seen BC and New Brunswick join COFI in the Supreme Court appeal. The union had no desire to destroy streams, Munro told the *BC Lumberman*, wanting only to see common sense prevail in achieving reasonable multiple-use compromises. A further bogging down of the referral process by aggressive fishery agency input could only lead to delays, possible stop orders and lost jobs. Even more threatening than the fisheries officials were those environmentalists who seemed bent on putting a halt to all development.[122]

Top and Bottom: Cutting Permit 144 area, Riley Creek, November 25, 1979. Courtesy of Keith Moore.

Major slide on Cutting Permit 144, November 1979. Courtesy of Keith Moore.

Major debris torrent, 1979. Courtesy of Keith Moore.

Top: Slide on Cutting Permit 145 at point where it enters Riley Creek, November 1979. Courtesy of Keith Moore. **Bottom:** Kip Slater inspecting Riley Creek, November 1979. Courtesy of Keith Moore.

Timber capital's early 1980 framing of Riley Creek shared much in common with Munro's perspective, emphasizing the odious image of gun-toting fishery officers. Co-operation should replace confrontation, declared outgoing TLA president Dave O'Connor at the January convention. Arrest of the loggers was "reminiscent of Nazi Germany," and the technological machinery for peaceful relations on the islands was at hand in the form of spawning channels that had proven efficient on the south coast. "But guns," O'Connor concluded, "no, and never again."[123]

QC Timber developed its own public relations campaign, dispatching forest engineer Eugene Runtz, a recent hire from MacMillan Bloedel, to address a Victoria audience in late January. The event at Reynolds High School, organized by the Canadian Institute of Forestry and Camosun College, gave Runtz an opportunity to relate the Rennell Sound events to his past experience in Iran's forests, where he had never seen a firearm. The federal action had been "arbitrary and heavy-handed," he told his audience, creating a frightening experience for company personnel, treated as common criminals, and their anguished families. The senseless conflict had produced no "clearcut winner" but many losers, including the extremists dedicated to curbing or even putting an end to logging on the islands. Neither outcome could be permitted, Runtz asserted in a defence of the province's "orderly evolution of resource management and development." QC Timber, a leader in that process, took great care at all its sites to avoid stream disruption, he said. The slides, in fact, had nothing to do with logging but were "a phenomenon of nature that had its origins at the time of the violent seismic action which created the Charlottes many millenniums ago." Even so, Runtz continued, fish runs could be expected to increase in the coming years as careful road planning and new skyline and helicopter logging technologies came into use. But the "gap in regulatory inter-communications" must be closed and environmental law interpreted consistently. Make no mistake, he concluded; QC Timber intended to remain in business on the islands, fulfilling its obligations to employees, customers and governments.[124]

The company, known as CIPA Industries after an early 1980 name change, clearly had no intention of falling on its corporate sword. Others were determined to have the enterprise assume its share of the blame along with the government officials perceived to be responsible for the slides. Still hoping that the Fish and Wildlife Branch would prosecute in early December, the IPS announced its intention to go to court if no government agency laid charges. Survival of the islands' salmon fishery depended upon stopping the clearcutting of steep slopes. Calling the Riley Creek slides "a criminal destruction of salmon habitat," the IPS retained Garth Evans to prepare a case against not only the company but DFO and MOF officials as well. One potential approach was to seek a court order compelling McGrath or LeBlanc to enforce the *Fisheries Act*. The IPS soon found an ally in the UFAWU, which decided at its early February 1980 convention to take action against the company; the province, which licensed the operation; and the DFO for failing to prosecute. The resolution passed with strong support, the Skidegate local pledging $500 to support legal costs. Financial penalties were so low, said Alert Bay delegate Gilbert Popovich, "that it is profitable for the logging companies to destroy streams."[125]

Ultimately, the formal IPS and UFAWU partnership dissolved over the former group's insistence on unilateral control, but the union continued to campaign for financial support among its members. David Orton responded from Halifax, donating $10 to the Riley Creek fund, a place that had "come to symbolize all that is most rotten in BC forest land-use policy." The IPS's "Riley Creek subcommittee", headed by Margo Hearne and John Broadhead, collaborated with Masset fisherman Charlie Bellis who undertook a private prosecution under section 31(1) of the *Fisheries Act*. According to the information sworn by Bellis on May 27, CIPA Industries, Mike Apsey, Jack Biickert and Wally Johnson had acted in a way that resulted in the "harmful alteration, disruption or destruction of fish habitat." Charges were laid and summonses issued for June 25 at provincial court in Queen Charlotte City.[126]

Government officials had more pressing problems to deal with in early 1980, involving both CIPA Industries' five-year logging plan and the wider question of steep-slope logging on the islands. Mid-February saw Rogers and Waterland, accompanied by staff members, inspect the Riley Creek site. Announcements followed from both ministers that highly unstable slopes would be withheld from logging pending the development of slide control measures, Waterland's statement coming with the curious denial that this represented a change in policy. "We won't touch the obviously unstable areas until we can figure out how to do it," the Forests minister remarked, hinting at the temporary and precarious nature of the protection that might be expected. Faulty road construction rather than clearcutting had probably caused the slides, he maintained (in direct contrast to Moore's assessment), but another significant factor was the large number of deer which devoured ground cover, depriving the slopes of a stabilizing root system. That claim drew a scornful reply from Prince Rupert fisherman Stewart Brinton. "Ah, so the deer did it!" he scoffed. The "little devils were the culprits all along: herds of Bambis munching away like locusts from dusk to dawn, chewing at the trunks of trees, toppling the old growth like berserk beavers, leaving nothing but bare earth. Bambi caused Riley Creek to turn into a mud puddle."[127]

Biickert followed up later in the month, announcing that the multi-agency review of CIPA's logging plan would likely produce withdrawal of the most vulnerable areas, at least until techniques such as helicopter logging ensured safe extraction of the timber. Some sites should never be cut, though, due to their inherent instability. Such statements, along with assurances that ecological study and close monitoring of operations would lead to better decision-making, provoked cautious approval in some quarters. Striking a moderate course in keeping with the diverse composition of its membership, the BCWF hoped that the loss of Riley Creek had sparked a new recognition of non-timber values by the MOF and industry. True, the "incompetents who made the decision to create the mess" remained in their positions, but positive strides were being made. A less optimistic *BC Outdoors* appraisal by Mark Hume, titled "Death of a Salmon Stream", predicted that Riley Creek would not be the last BC stream "killed" by shoddy logging practices. Industry and MOF multiple-use promises had proven to be a "cynical public relations ploy", a "sham" and a "farce."[128]

Such perceptions demanded some concrete signs of the advertised commitment to grapple seriously with resource conflicts on the islands. An inter-agency committee tasked to develop recommendations did so that spring, setting the stage for the federal-provincial Fish/Forestry Interaction Program (FFIP) announced by Waterland, LeBlanc and Rogers on May 9. The committee's report emphasized that the natural geomorphic process of mass wasting could be accelerated by current road construction practices, although the impacts of erosion and sedimentation on fish habitat were difficult to quantify. Recommendations included a program of soil stability mapping to identify unstable slopes, recognition of the principle that some areas warranted protection, testing methods to rehabilitate damaged forest sites and streams, and investigation of helicopter and skyline logging techniques. Agencies should also refine the way they evaluate resources in "trade-off situations", weighing non-timber values more appropriately.[129]

The three ministers implemented most of the report's findings in committing to science-based decision-making through the FFIP, dedicated to investigating and rehabilitating forest sites and fish habitats on Haida Gwaii. The four-year, $800,000 program would provide research into the severity and extent of soil movements, alternatives to conventional tower logging, silvicultural treatments on steep slopes and the rehabilitation of damaged streams. In the end, LeBlanc asserted, the program would complement the one at Carnation Creek and help in resolving conflicts such as Rennell Sound. Unimpressed, UFAWU environmental coordinator Arne Thomlinson commented that FFIP represented another free ride for CIPA Industries: "They get to keep the timber, we lose the fish, and Canadian taxpayers foot the bill."[130]

CIPA Industries engaged in its own rehabilitation project on the islands that spring, one devoted to polishing the firm's image. Ron Townshend, formerly with MacMillan Bloedel and now head of Peril Bay Geotechnical Services, had been recently engaged to conduct a geotechnical study of Rennell Sound as a basis for the five-year logging plan, and he presented his findings to an appreciative audience at the firm's camp on April 6. Townshend acknowledged that conventional logging and road construction practices were "triggering mechanisms" for slides in a region prone to natural failures, but said that better planning, more careful road layout and helicopter or skyline yarding would reduce disturbance of sensitive sites and associated sediment production. Those alternative logging systems had great potential in avoiding clearcut failures and should be given top priority on the steep terrain at Rennell Sound. He went on to propose a four-level terrain stability classification model for the area based on landform, soil conditions, slope severity and vegetation, noting that on the most sensitive sites the potential for slides could be reduced but not completely eliminated. Overall, the report's tone was generally optimistic about forest managers' capacity to correct problems.[131]

Townshend's Rennell Sound speech was a prelude to a three-hour Queen Charlotte Museum meeting at Skidegate on April 27, co-sponsored by the museum and Northwest Community College. About 75 people heard introductory and concluding remarks by Eugene Runtz, prepared by writer and public relations man Paul Hurmuses. The company had come under unfair criticism, Runtz began, having made "limitless and exhaustive" efforts, at enormous cost, to manage its holdings in an orderly and productive manner. Decline of the American housing market had provoked layoffs and shutdowns around the province, but on the islands industry faced a "made-in-BC" threat mounted by hostile forces campaigning to stop all logging. The critics claimed, without supporting facts, that the company was "polluting the streams, that we are causing unnecessary slides, that we are devastating the valuable fishery, that we are...destroying the heritage of these beautiful Islands." All untrue, Runtz said, and the speakers used this forum to refute the allegations.[132]

Townshend also spoke at the museum meeting, first discussing the general principles of slide causation, then addressing the specifics of the most recent Riley Creek failures. A cat road built by a previous company in 1973, prior to QC Timber's arrival, was the problem, he and Runtz explained, coupled with heavy blowdown on the slope. Reconstruction of the road had cost $90,000 and, of the two slides discussed, one had sent "a small finger" of mud into the creek. Moreover, two days later Runtz had seen fish spawning in the water. Logging manager Ralph Torney of T.M. Thompson and Associates, a firm that provided management expertise to the industry, followed with films on helicopter and skyline logging. Addressing the fishermen in the audience, Torney promised to seek "common solutions to common problems"; the two resources "must exist in harmony, not in conflict."[133]

The exercise had a purpose that went beyond clearing the company's reputation. Its continuing operation on the islands was very much in doubt, Runtz warned, and only quick action would prevent a permanent closure. Some cutting permit application approvals had been delayed unnecessarily, some rejected outright, and in one case authority to cut had been granted and then withdrawn. Management was perplexed at such treatment, given their efforts (and expense) spent on Townshend's studies and upgrading roads. Could the company go on indefinitely in this climate of uncertainty? No, Runtz indicated. A decision to suspend operations at Rennell sound would come only after "the most agonizing deliberation", given the heavy investment and commitment to employees, but that day might come. But in that case no one would be able to claim honestly that the company had not gone "the extra mile." To do so would only add to the long list of falsehoods hurled over the past year.[134]

The museum event drew decidedly mixed reviews. *Observer* publisher D.M. Leach praised the presenters' professionalism, and the refreshments, but thought the promise to fully engage questions went unfulfilled. Asked if clearcutting created a runoff problem, Townshend said it was best not to generalize. Leach himself asked if patch logging would create less danger of slides than complete clearcutting. "Not necessarily," Townshend replied, due to the higher incidence of blowdown. Neither he nor Runtz, Leach concluded, seemed eager to answer in real depth the few audience questions. In the end, Leach wrote, the exercise failed to produce "a free exchange of information and opinions", serving instead "as a platform from which QC Timber was able to mount its 'get more wood' campaign going via the media." While the company had made a persuasive case, in Leach's view, and appeared to be making great strides, officials had failed to "lay the Riley Creek issue to rest." College sponsorship could not obscure the fact that no fisheries representative had been invited to speak, reducing the event to a one-sided, if informative, presentation.[135]

An even less impressed, Jack Miller of Port Clements ridiculed CIPA's attempt to blame the Rennell Sound uproar on environmentalists, to deny the connection between clearcutting and slides and to question the resultant sedimentation's impact on fish habitat. Nor did the speakers make any reference to preserving steep slopes, which suggested that the company had no intention of doing so. The IPS's John Broadhead, conceding that CIPA's public relations efforts were gaining sophistication, expressed surprise at the frank discussion of slope stability problems but was prompted to wonder if the "fuss in Rennell Sound" had happened at all. Runtz's claim about "a finger of sediment" in Riley Creek did not square with the press reports, and Broadhead went so far as to quote the engineer's halting and confusing explanation from his taped record of the proceedings. Finally, he considered the company's warning of an impending shutdown "nothing less than sleazy."[136]

CIPA failed to win over the hearts and minds of its critics but scored its own victories as well as celebrating industry-wide triumphs that summer. Tentative approval of the five-year Rennell Sound working plan came in June, involving a trade-off that extended rights to cut areas on nearby Hangover Creek in exchange for protection of unstable sites on Riley and Bonanza creeks. Manager Peter Pfister was pleased, but he knew that the cutting permit process would inevitably involve input from fisheries agencies. June also brought welcome news on the legal front for CIPA, the province, the forest industry at large and the government officials who had been named in the Bellis case. The first good news came in Ottawa, where Duncan Shaw headed the defence of Dan Fowler. On June 17 the Supreme Court of Canada overturned Fowler's 1975 *Fisheries Act* conviction, ruling that section 33(3) of the act was an unconstitutional intrusion into provincial jurisdiction over property rights and forestry. The blanket prohibition against the deposit of slash, stumps or debris into fish-bearing water went too far, failing to link the prohibited activity to actual harm to the fishery. "The prohibition in its broad terms is not necessarily incidental to the federal power in respect of sea coast and inland fisheries," the justices ruled, and was *ultra vires* of the federal parliament.[137]

The forest industry hailed the verdict, and COFI's Don Lanskail saw an opportunity for the negotiation of reasonable regulations allowing for the peaceful co-existence of logging and fishing. LeBlanc, however, rejected a COFI invitation to discuss amendments to the *Fisheries Act*, saying that his officials would make full use of section 31's prohibition against activities that altered, destroyed or disrupted fish habitat. That was all LeBlanc could be sure of in his regulatory arsenal that summer, as section 33(2) was also subject to a constitutional challenge in the related Northwest Falling Contractors Ltd. case, scheduled to be heard by the Supreme Court of Canada in July. In the meantime Tom Waterland praised the Fowler decision for forcing recognition of resource values other than fish, no doubt pleased with the decision that had effectively rendered a troublesome element of federal environmental law subordinate to provincial control over logging. Ottawa's defeat also came as welcome news to CIPA's Peter Pfister, who anticipated that fisheries officials would now be more reasonable in seeking multiple-use compromises. Environmentalists, on the other hand, were dismayed at the perceived setback, and DFO Enforcement Branch head Tinker Young agreed that the verdict put the agency on the defensive. Queen Charlotte DFO supervisor Kip Slater expressed surprise, admitted the wording of that section was vague, but again noted that the MOF had been much more co-operative of late.[138]

In this climate of jurisdictional uncertainty, the Bellis case against CIPA, Apsey, Biickert and Johnson began on June 25 at provincial court in Queen Charlotte City. Bellis, as a private citizen, had sworn an information that work carried out by the above had resulted in damage to fish habitat in 1979 and his lawyer, Garth Evans, expected that morning's routine hearing to produce a trial date. He was shocked when R.D. Miller, appearing for BC Attorney General Alan Williams, informed Judge J. Scherling that the matter need not be called; the Crown had directed a stay of proceedings. Evans objected, arguing that Miller had no such authority in a case involving federal law and had failed to provide notice of his intentions despite a discussion just minutes before court had been called. No notice was required, Miller responded, and he had the authority, as agent for the attorney general, to direct the court clerk to enter a stay. He had, in fact, already done so; it was a *"fait accompli."* Nor was an explanation required. Although he did not require instructions from Williams, Miller said, "he had specific instructions from the minister." "I don't need to make those available to the public," he continued. "I don't need to make those available to anybody." The case was now out of the court's jurisdiction and Evans was free to take the issue up with the BC Supreme Court.[139]

Evans continued objecting to the entire procedure when Biickert's lawyer, P.M. Packenham, entered the fray. The case was moot, he argued, given the recent Supreme Court ruling on the Fowler case, which held the relevant sections of the *Fisheries Act* to be unconstitutional. A "somewhat agitated" Evans accused Packenham of misleading the court. He explained that the Fowler case concerned section 33(3) whereas the Bellis matter involved section 33(1), which made it an offence to carry on any work or undertaking that resulted in the "harmful alteration, disruption or destruction of fish habitat." Packenham conceded the point but maintained that there was no difference between the sections. On that basis alone he supported the Crown's stay, which, in any event, had already been accomplished. "I don't know why we are going on and on," Miller said in agreement. A stay had been directed and it was out of the judge's hands: "That ends the matter today." Evans made a final objection, declared his intention to seek relief from the BC Supreme Court and promised that this was by no means the end of the matter. Scherling ruled that the Crown was within its rights to enter a stay, confirmed his court's lack of jurisdiction and concluded, in passing, that the information might be laid again, reopened, or an application to the Supreme Court might be appropriate.[140]

The Crown had gotten its stay, but in a way that struck many as heavy-handed and arbitrary. Miller had "made a mockery of the judicial process", observed the IPS's Margo Hearne. The *Fisherman* agreed that the government's handling of the case left an odour, fostering an impression that the stay was motivated by a desire to protect a high-ranking official. Justice had not been served, the *Victoria Times* agreed. The stay might have been secured legally, but doing so without notice or explanation seemed arrogant. More importantly, a private citizen's right to seek justice in the courts had been abridged. Since Apsey, a provincial government official, had been named on the charge, the court should hear the evidence. Graham Lea questioned the attorney general on the matter in the legislature on June 16, asking why Williams had instructed

Miller to enter the stay. He had not done so, Williams replied; the regional Crown counsel had exercised his own authority, applying a *Fisheries Act* clause providing for a statutory defence. Since the conduct in question had the Minister of Fisheries' approval, the case could not succeed. Dissatisfied, Lea read from the court transcript the passage quoting Miller as saying he had "specific instructions from the minister." Was Miller not telling the truth? Williams repeated his denial, prompting Lea to ask for an explanation. "I can't explain it," Williams replied, but he would ask Miller about his statement.[141]

Williams repeated his "statutory defence" explanation to the *Victoria Times*, the report coupling that with Evans' claim that the principle did not apply in a private action. Legalities notwithstanding, the *Times* asserted that Bellis had been denied his day in court and, therefore, the right to test whether federal and provincial agencies had acted with due diligence. The controversy lingered into late July, Lea declaring that if Miller had acted under direct instructions, "political power had been used to try and prevent the political embarrassment of the deputy minister of forests." Bellis would take the case to the BC Supreme Court, the IPS's Guujaaw confirmed in early August. The stay was an expensive and time-consuming stumbling block, but one that must be overcome to understand the respective roles of "government, industry and experts in the Riley Creek episode." Questions lingered, too, about the continued arrival of fallers after the stop order, the way in which interests had come together to challenge federal authority and the fact that no CIPA representatives had appeared in court on June 25. If Apsey and the others were innocent, Guujaaw asked, why had the government not allowed the case to be heard?[142]

Lea strove to keep the issue alive, hammering away at the abuse of power theme and rejecting Williams' argument that ministerial approval of logging justified the stay. Surely LeBlanc had not consented to operations of the sort that had caused the slides into Riley Creek, the very question Bellis should have been allowed to pose in court. The stay was appropriate, Williams repeated in the legislature, gaining some relief when the court reporter's office in Prince Rupert issued notification of a change in the Queen Charlotte City hearing transcript. Miller had received his instructions to enter a stay not from the "minister" but from the "ministry." Surprised yet again, Evans considered the revision of no real significance. On August 21 Bellis petitioned the BC Supreme Court for a judicial review, challenging the provincial government's power to stay a federal charge. Even if Miller had such authority,

Evans argued, he had exercised it in an inappropriate manner by failing to provide adequate notice. The challenge ended on September 5, though, when the Supreme Court dismissed the petition.[143]

The Bellis case may have reached the end of its court life but the issues it raised remained very much alive for a time. When premier Bill Bennett and his cabinet toured northern BC that autumn, the IPS took the opportunity to present a brief at a September 26 public meeting in Prince Rupert. The Bellis challenge's implications were "staggering," according to Margo Hearne. The attorney general had violated a citizen's democratic rights, and the citizens were the real owners of BC's natural resources. "We have a right to see that justice is fairly done," the brief read, and "those who destroy our resources should have to answer to the owners of that resource." The IPS then took its complaint directly to Williams, who responded with a legal overview of the Rennell Sound matter and a succinct explanation of the Crown's handling of the Bellis case. After a full report on the late 1979 slides by the Ministry of Environment, Williams explained, the question of charges against QC Timber had been given "objective consideration" and Regional Crown Counsel Peter Ewart concluded that a prosecution could not succeed. Bellis had then sworn an information "on precisely the same cause of action as that already considered by...Mr. Ewart." Since it had already been determined that a prosecution would not succeed, a stay was directed—standard procedure in the case of private prosecutions considered doomed to failure, Williams said. The Crown would have gone ahead with a prosecution in the first place had the evidence supported a conviction, and he supported both decisions.[144]

That tidy summary did not satisfy the IPS's Hearne. The information sworn by Bellis differed from the cause of action originally considered and rejected by Ewart. That had involved Hart's initial, preventative order given before the late 1979 slide, while Bellis had sworn his information *after the fact*, against senior administrators in the various federal and provincial agencies who were active in the events pertaining to Riley Creek." Williams' ministry had erred in equating the two in an effort to rationalize the stay and the matter should be reviewed. Hearne's analysis, however logical, fell on deaf ears. The questions that might have been probed in a courtroom remained unasked and unanswered, leaving suspicions that the Bellis case's quiet death was arranged to achieve precisely that end.[145]

Legal proceedings did not go entirely the forest industry's way in the summer of 1980. The Northwest Falling Contractors' case dated from 1978, when a fisheries officer had sworn information that the company had dumped oil in a stream at Loughborough Inlet on the mainland, contravening the *Fisheries Act*'s section 32(2), which prohibited the deposit of any "deleterious substance" in waters frequented by fish. The provinces of BC, New Brunswick, Manitoba and Newfoundland had joined the effort to have the section found unconstitutional, making arguments similar to those that succeeded in the Fowler case. After attempts to have the case thrown out failed, both in the BC Supreme Court and the BC Court of Appeals, an appeal had gone to the Supreme Court of Canada. In July the high court upheld the act's relevant section, finding its language within the federal jurisdiction over fish habitat and clear in defining deleterious substances. Unlike the ambiguous wording of the subsection considered in the Fowler case, 33(2) was appropriately restrictive in scope, prohibiting deposits threatening to fish. Federal officials heaved a sigh of relief at the decision which bolstered their ability to prosecute polluters.[146]

Fisheries concerns, an analyst remarked near the end of 1980, constituted the coastal forest industry's "biggest problem" in a volatile social, economic and political climate. The Supreme Court decisions in the Fowler and Northwest Contractors' cases represented a draw of sorts, and the "initial hue and cry" over Riley Creek had faded. An embarrassed MOF appeared to be catching its breath as operators contemplated the benefits of long-distance skyline and helicopter methods. The situation was murky, journalist Jim Duggleby concluded, and many had "face to save."[147]

Framing and Remembering Riley Creek

ARGUMENTS OVER THE MEANING OF RILEY CREEK persisted in the early 1980s in the context of a troubled commercial fishery, the South Moresby controversy and questions about the sustainability of logging on the islands. With adoption of the Coastal Fish/Forestry Guidelines in 1988 optimists saw a happy ending to the Riley Creek story, that interpretation fitting comfortably with reports of the stream's health. Others presented data of a stream still suffering the effects of the slides. Riley Creek, years after the conflicts that discredited both provincial multiple-use promises and federal claims to wise stewardship in defending fish habitat, remained a contested site. The South Moresby wilderness proposal sparked ongoing heated debate after Waterland approved Rayonier's TFL 24 and the PAC voted itself out of existence, citing the MOF's refusal to provide information on that company's logging plans. Thus, CIPA's Rennell Sound operation continued to generate controversy. "We in Rennell Sound have been pushed far enough," the wife of a CIPA manager told Guujaaw in reaction to his August *Observer* letter on the Bellis matter. The company itself was active in responding to critics such as Mark Hume, whose July "Death of a Salmon Stream" article in *BC Outdoors* provoked an October rebuttal to "one-sided and even misleading" reporting on the slides.[148]

Far from engaging in a "cynical public relations ploy," CIPA had complied with all laws and had pioneered improved logging techniques in adhering to the multiple-use concept while maintaining an honest and co-operative relationship with government agencies. The logging plan for CP144 had received the full approval of all those agencies before "natural and historical flooding" caused extensive landslide damage throughout Haida Gwaii and along the north coast in late 1978. The federal agency had then unilaterally withdrawn its consent in the spring of 1979, after an engineering investment of over $200,000. Still, QC Timber had agreed to defer or even abandon the cutting permits if so instructed.[149]

The CIPA narrative broke off at that point, omitting reference to the defiance of Hart's stop order, the arrests or the subsequent federal retreat. The late 1979 slides were mentioned only to deny the validity of Hume's description of Riley Creek as "mud-choked." The bulk of the "natural slide" stopped well short of the stream and, despite some runoff, salmon continued to spawn and produce fry that were observed that May. Riley Creek was "secure" then, and the firm would continue setting an example in environmental protection despite the enormous investment. The co-operation and compromise that defined multiple use was not only workable in sustaining fish and forest resources; but that bright future of co-existence was assured.[150]

CIPA was not alone in constructing a positive, even triumphant narrative of the Riley Creek events. Speaking to a friendly audience at the Canadian Institute of Forestry's November 1980 annual meeting in Vancouver, Prince Rupert forest region manager Jack Biickert gave an account that in both substance and language departed little from the CIPA script. Newspaper sources had been "misleading", "pathetically out of context" and "gross exaggerations," he began. It was "indisputable fact" that "honest and objective co-operation" was flourishing between CIPA and resource agencies and that such a relationship would ensure the continued co-existence of the islands' two key industries. Biickert repeated the story of the company receiving full approval for its CP144 plan, the arrival of the heavy rains and "heavier than usual flooding" in late 1978, the interruption of operations the following spring and the arrests.[151]

From that point, he related, "all sorts of good things started to happen," beginning with the March 27, 1979, MOF-DFO meeting that had yielded the agreement to continue logging under the protective measures. Mid-August had brought the letter of "very exacting" instructions to CIPA, all carried out by the company. Since the late 1979 slides themselves apparently did not merit inclusion in the "good things" narrative, Biickert left them out entirely, skipping to the mid-December agreement by Waterland and Rogers for closer co-operation between their agencies and the DFO. That had set the stage for the February 1980 field trip, the announcement of a deferral of operations on sensitive sites until the development of appropriate methods, and establishment of the FFIP. That initiative, Biickert concluded, expressed the sincerity of resource agencies to be "constructive, co-operative and objective", as well as their shared commitment with industry to ensure the health of fishery and forestry resources. A handwritten marginal notation at the end of Biickert's text, presumably written by a Sierra Club official, reads "could have fooled me!"[152]

Historical revisionism on the part of those who had played a part in shaping events at Riley Creek could not match the volume of critical commentary. For University of British Columbia geographer Philip Deardon the slides ranked alongside those at Hell's Gate caused by Canadian Northern Railway construction in 1913–14 as a classic case of resource abuse. With a lower commercial salmon catch giving rise to tighter regulation of fishermen in the early 1980s, Greenpeace's Michele Forest urged British Columbians to remember Riley Creek as a symbol of lax habitat protection enforcement. The Telkwa Foundation interpreted Riley Creek as indicative of the IWA's failure to develop a forest policy stance independent of the corporations. Instead of supporting their fellow workers in the UFAWU, the union had "succumbed to the old industry job blackmail line" and colluded in the arrest of loggers. Jack Miller, active in Haida Gwaii land use planning initiatives in the early 1980s, characterized Riley Creek as "merely the eruption of a long developing boil which has not yet been cured." The provincial government, in its role as "handmaiden to the forest industry," had permitted the TFL holders to clearcut the easily accessible timber, and no regulations had yet been developed for steep-slope logging.[153]

LeBlanc's appointment of Peter Pearse to head the Royal Commission on Pacific Fisheries Policy in 1981 provided further opportunity to contemplate Riley Creek's importance. Pearse was more concerned with finding a way to reduce the fleet than with habitat issues, an agenda that meshed nicely with the forest industry's position that over-fishing was responsible for declining runs. Still, both COFI and the IWA worried that resurrection of the Riley Creek story at public hearings would highlight industrial destruction of spawning grounds. The UFAWU, IPS and Northern Trollers Association all made Riley Creek prominent in their submissions to the commission, the latter organization calling on Pearse to probe the handling of the Bellis case. Trollers Association spokesman John Broadhead said that Riley Creek "epitomizes everything wrong with our present methods of enforcement. The law was deliberately broken, yet everyone involved managed to walk away from it." Pearse had no intention of being drawn into that legal quagmire but declared a willingness to study the matter as "an example of what could go wrong"—a statement that caused the forest industry some concern.[154]

COFI assured Pearse of the industry's commitment to multiple use, its recognition of the importance of commercial fishing and devotion to co-operation with fisheries managers. The FFIP and Carnation Creek studies exemplified the sort of collaboration needed to solve common problems, in contrast to the draconian *Fisheries Act*. Enacted without consultation, this "unilateral, single resource, single dimensional piece of legislation" was both too ambiguous in its definition of "deleterious substance" and too sweeping in its criminalization of offences. Accommodation would come through gathering more fish and habitat inventory data as a basis for cost-benefit analysis and from more research and consultation between operators and agencies to resolve conflicts before they reached the courts.[155]

Pearse's recommendations followed similar lines, and COFI was "clearly satisfied" with the findings. "He has identified quite clearly that the principal violation is over-fishing and inadequate management of the resource," said COFI's Lanskail. Managers needed better inventory data to assess the productivity of streams and estuaries, Pearse advised, and federal policy should tolerate no reduction in total productivity unless the damage was "fully compensated through expanded fish production elsewhere." Trade-offs were acceptable, then, and Pearse went on to challenge "superficial impressions" that placed logging in a uniformly bad light. Findings from Carnation Creek and American studies indicated that clearcutting did not necessarily have a negative effect on runoff, that large woody debris benefitted stream habitats and that higher water temperatures did not always impair fish productivity. Current logging operations were "undoubtedly less damaging than in the past" he concluded. Pearse had put logging "in a far better perspective than it has enjoyed in debates...over the past few years," a delighted Lanskail declared.[156]

For the IPS and its growing number of supporters, though, Riley Creek was the ideal symbol of why South Moresby and other areas of the islands had to be saved. The proposal for an ecological reserve at Windy Bay on the east coast of Lyell Island became one of the issues faced by the government's South Moresby Resource Planning Team (SMRPT) by 1981, with advocates arguing that even limited logging would disrupt the watershed's ecological integrity. After a visit to Windy Bay, Haida artist Bill Reid linked its fate to the campaign for South Moresby's preservation. The west side of Lyell Island had been logged in "a huge swath, miles long and nearly a hillside wide." Allowing the loggers to complete their work would leave nothing but stumps, a tangle of waste, "and the clear water of the river will be muddied by the unchecked runoff from the bare hills." As an artist, Reid conceded that he also made use of wood, but true multiple use would save some old forest for "its own regeneration, the wild-life it nurtures, and most important and most neglected, its aesthetic values." Current practices on the islands resembled "the desperate efforts of a band of brigands intent on looting a treasure house before the owners realize what's going on and take measures to stop it." Jack Miller, representing the public on the SMRPT, also advocated for an ecological reserve at Windy Bay but on scientific and financial rather than aesthetic grounds. Expressing outrage that no baseline data on the region's salmon streams had yet been accumulated by government and industry, Miller saw a need to preserve the watershed in its natural state. Soon the last of the truly productive streams would be "picked clean" and the opportunity for research would be lost.[157]

With the submission of their land claim to the federal government that year, the Haida made salmon habitat protection central to their campaign for the preservation of Windy Bay and for a sharp reduction in the rate of cut on the islands overall. Particular focus rested on TFL 24, acquired by Western Forest Products (WFP) from Rayonier the previous year. WFP had proposed a

271-hectare ecological reserve along the Windy Bay shoreline, while the Haida and IPS wanted the entire 3,000 hectare watershed protected, dictating a 5.3 per cent reduction in the TFL 24 allowable cut. John Lamb, the DFO's member on the SMRPT, admitted that the agency had little data on the area, but recent work indicated that Windy Creek supported a run of over 40,000 Pink Salmon, making it Lyell Island's most important producer. Trying to avoid taking sides, Lamb nevertheless applied the DFO's philosophy that logging could proceed without damaging the runs given the application of "normal constraints." Citing Riley Creek, the IPS and Haida had little confidence in such assurances. As Charlie Bellis put it, "they're all Riley Creeks. Riley Creek is just an example." WFP countered that a similar result could be avoided at Windy Creek, and Lamb spoke glowingly of the much improved increase in MOF co-operation post–Riley Creek. "Multiple use is all very good," a skeptical Margo Hearne observed, "but if a watershed of a creek is destroyed, there is no multiple use." University of Victoria law professor Murray Rankin also warned that clearcutting the watershed's steep slopes would lead to "a repetition of the nightmare of Riley Creek."[158]

The memory of Riley Creek remained powerful in undermining the credibility of multiple-use promises, and Windy Bay was but a small battle in a much larger war. In August 1981 the Council of the Haida Nation (CHN) asked Waterland to reduce the allowable cut on TFL 24 by 50 per cent pending completion of the SMRPT's work, their own land claims research and study of the "Fisheries-Forestry conflict." Two months later chief forester Bill Young approved WFP's TFL 24 working plan but denied the company's proposal for an increase in the annual allowable cut from 436,679 to 460,982 cubic metres. After deleting some timber from the inventory out of concerns for terrain stability, streamside protection and aesthetics, Young approved a cut of 432,375 cubic metres, a slight reduction. "The concept of multiple use has been mocked by the forest industry," a CHN brief declared shortly thereafter. Current management practices that allowed destruction of salmon habitat were unacceptable; South Moresby should be protected.[159]

While the South Moresby issue dragged on, an embattled forest industry curtailed production along the coast in response to a worsening recession. A good deal of uncertainty surrounded CIPA's Rennell Sound operation. Vi Halsey reported the departure of several families in late 1980, including the Anyottes and Pelletiers of Bonanza Creek Falling Contractors. In October

CIPA announced an extended shutdown to the following March, prompting an exodus. The Halsey family left for Richmond, returning in the spring to further uncertainty, deepened by closure of the school. A bulletin board notice in June provided assurance that CIPA's Rennell Sound division would not be shifting elsewhere, but the summer brought a province-wide IWA strike lasting six weeks. Loggers began returning after an August 24 settlement, but on October 9 CIPA announced a closure until year's end, citing poor market conditions. As Halsey reported: "The topic of this camp is 'Who is leaving and who is staying?'" The bunkhouse men would go, but for those who called Rennell Sound home it was "a time to exercise our faith in this industry and stay in a holding pattern until the storm is over."[160]

The new year came and went with no reopening. And despite a May 1982 statement that operations would begin at the end of the month, CIPA was by this time embroiled in controversy over the MOF's timber supply assessment as a basis for setting the AAC on the Queen Charlotte TSA. The MOF's first provincial Forest and Range Resource Analysis, released in 1980, had confirmed that the "falldown" effect triggered by the transition from logging old-growth to second-growth forests would occur much earlier than Pearse had anticipated in his 1976 report. Many coastal areas faced a steep reduction in the cutting rate to achieve sustainability, and the subsequent analysis for the islands revealed a particularly alarming situation. Within 30 years the allowable rate of cut would have to be reduced by over 50 per cent of the current level of 1,074,088 cubic metres. Alternatively, lowering the existing harvest by about 30 per cent would allow 60 years of logging before a 40 per cent reduction.[161]

Prince Rupert forest region personnel explained the predicament at a March 1982 public meeting at Port Clements, prompting "trenchant comments on the sorry picture." Much of the criticism involved the 1977 Davidson Creek timber sale to CIPA's predecessor, QC Timber. Together with Rennell Sound, CIPA's share of the annual TSA cut came to 49 per cent, the Davidson Creek operation taking up almost 30 per cent of the total. The licence had been awarded amidst considerable controversy over the still undisclosed Hart-Hernandez report and now, the CHN declared in one of the 20 responses to the TSA report, "our greatest fears are proven correct…. The sustained yield principle has been sacrificed for short-term profits." That record of mismanagement created the current timber supply emergency, not potential withdrawals of productive forest in proposals for the South Moresby wilderness area and a Haida tribal park at Naden Harbour on Graham Island. The CHN went even further, alleging "serious wrongdoings" in the Davidson Creek sale, demanding a royal commission to investigate and claiming that many unstable, steep-slope areas had been declared "operable" in the TSA analysis. Even more blunt in its accusations, the IPS said that the 1977 sale had been made "in knowing contradiction of the management data available at the time." Alleging that bribery and corruption were involved in the award of the TSHL, the IPS called for its repeal.[162]

After two postponements, in September 1982 the MOF set the new Queen Charlotte TSA allowable cut at 450,000 cubic metres, announcing that a further reduction would likely be in order at the next five-year review. The optimistic assumptions of years past—that technological innovations would compensate for accelerated logging—were no longer justified. The designation of new EPAs and withdrawal of timber now considered inaccessible demanded the deep cut reduction, chief forester Bill Young explained. The TSA had been run "like something in the land of Oz," IPS director John Broadhead observed in response to the announcement. The MOF's own calculations had determined an appropriate cut of just 233,000 cubic metres, he charged, and had thus done nothing more than "institutionalize" an ongoing rate of unsustainable logging.[163]

Yet to be determined was how the reduced cut would be allocated among the TSA operators. The MOF accomplished that by the end of the year in a way that maintained the volume of existing cutting rights, shifting a portion of the quotas to other coastal TSAs. In CIPA's case that involved transferring over 52,000 cubic metres of the Davidson Creek and Rennell Sound rights to the Kingcome TSA while "rolling over" the firm's island holdings into a single forest licence under the terms of the new *Forest Act*. CIPA, "pondering its future" on the islands, announced an early 1983 reopening of the Davidson Creek camp but said nothing about a Rennell Sound resumption. By early 1983 the firm had withdrawn from the sound, disrupting FFIP logging studies on Hangover Creek. Ultimately, Husby Forest Products took over CIPA's Haida Gwaii operations, transferring most of the Rennell Sound quota to Naden Harbour at the northern end of Graham Island. Heavy rains in January 1984 caused over 100 slides on the islands, 90 per cent occurring on the steep slopes of clearcut areas. Alex Grzybowski related that a FFIP inspection attributed the failures to "insufficient guidelines, unpredictable factors or insufficient enforcement of rules."[164]

But that was not the end of the slides, and one in particular revived some of the concerns that Riley Creek had inspired about the DFO's will to hold companies responsible for the destruction of fish habitat. In December 1984 a major slide that blocked Landrick Creek spawning beds occurred on the south side of Lyell Island, in an area logged by WFP contractor Frank Beban. Beban's company and ITT Industries (their name before the WFP takeover) had been charged with destruction of stream habitat on the island during the late 1970s. The case eventually went forward as the Haida and environmentalists continued their campaign for South Moresby's preservation as a national park, a status that would not infringe upon the comprehensive land claim. Within Brian Mulroney's cabinet, support for a national park gained advocates, including Fisheries minister John Fraser. In the interim, Fraser promised to use the *Fisheries Act* to "protect those streams" after an August 1985 tour of Lyell Island logging operations with Haida Nation president Miles Richardson. "Anyone who doesn't think logging won't damage those streams is whistling in the wind," Fraser told reporters.[165]

An autumn 1985 Haida blockade of Beban's logging road on Lyell Island led to arrests, national headlines and mounting national pressure for a wilderness park. The *Fisheries Act*'s utility in defending the islands' streams until the park could be achieved came into question, though, when a provincial court judge dismissed the case against Beban and ITT Industries in August 1986. The judge accepted defence arguments, ruling that the Crown had failed to link the logging and road-building activities to stream obstruction. An appeal was filed, and in the meantime federal-provincial negotiations for a South Moresby wilderness park stalled. But by the end of the year neither Bill Bennett nor Tom Waterland stood in the way; the latter forced to resign over his holdings in Western Pulp Partnerships, a corporate entity with interests in Lyell Island timber. COFI acknowledged his "service and contribution" to the province, expressing gratitude for the congenial working relationship industry had enjoyed with government during his decade as minister. Bennett resigned after opening Expo 86, Bill Vander Zalm taking over as Socred leader and premier in an increasingly volatile climate of First Nations and environmental protest.[166]

The struggle to preserve South Moresby from further clearcutting would be won in July 1987 with the establishment of Gwaii Haanas National Park. To many, decades of multiple-use promises had gone unfulfilled, and one can only speculate about the extent to which Riley Creek and other less publicized events hardened that conviction. The story of the park campaign, negotiations and ultimate financial compensation package has been told elsewhere, but that was not the end of the fish-forestry conflict on Haida Gwaii.

In 1986 federal Fisheries minister Tom Siddon introduced the "no net loss" principle of management, striving to balance habitat unavoidably lost to development with habitat replacement of equal measure. But uncertainty over the *Fisheries Act*'s power to prevent habitat destruction remained, as evidenced by the resolution of the Beban-ITT case. Scheduled for a September 1988 hearing in the Supreme Court of Canada after a BC Appeals Court ruling revived the case, the charges were stayed amidst fresh controversy, as Siddon and Justice Department officials jockeyed to shift responsibility to each other. When Skeena MP Jim Fulton demanded his resignation, Siddon attributed the decision to legal technicalities cited by the Justice Department. An official there countered that no response had come from Siddon's office for the three weeks after an initial recommendation from a "lower bureaucrat" to stay the proceedings.[167]

Romeo LeBlanc's 1977 amendments had "strengthened the Fisheries Act's environmental power," Joseph Gough maintains, but in the decade between Riley Creek and Landrick Creek too little seemed to have changed. On one hand, the act's preventative potential was underutilized; on the other, tying forest practices to habitat destruction in a way that would hold up in court, when prosecuting offenders after the fact, proved difficult. The "no net loss" policy would provide a remedy, Siddon maintained, and the Landrick Creek issue could be addressed in the $31 million compensation package offered to firms for lost South Moresby cutting rights. "We're presuming that something can be done," he concluded.[168]

Something, in fact, was being done to reconcile the conflict between logging and fish habitat. The MOF established an Integrated Resources Branch, responding to the Vander Zalm government's demand that the Forests Ministry remain dominant in land use planning. At the same time, the FFIP and Carnation Creek projects were producing research findings, with studies from the former showing that normal logging operations created stream sedimentation problems and lower egg to fry survival rates at least as serious as those caused by landslides. After examining 8,000 landslides on the islands, researchers concluded that logging was responsible for a six-fold increase over natural failures. Still, the FFIP's Vince Poulin summarized the research in hopeful terms. "We're beginning to see that forest operations can be carried out in a way that can safeguard and even enhance fisheries," he told a *BC Outdoors* writer. The key was "meaningful co-operation" between resource managers.[169]

The policy mechanism to achieve that goal was the Coastal Fish/Forestry Guidelines, introduced in 1988, after COFI complaints about their cost and complexity delayed implementation. Streams were categorized into four productivity classes upon which to base appropriate practices that would maximize the net benefits of both resources. Interdisciplinary bridge-building would replace "counterproductive spear-chucking" in the fish-forestry relationship, said former chief forester Bill Young, and the *Vancouver Sun* characterized the guidelines as a "trilateral treaty" between industry and the two levels of government. Nine years after the Riley Creek "spat", interests had come together "to resolve conflicts peacefully and manage resources in the best interests of society."[170] Such rhetoric proved overly optimistic, as a 1992 audit documenting widespread violations on Vancouver Island streams would prove. NDP Forests minister Dan Miller and federal Fisheries minister John Crosbie both promised tougher action against the industry that had helped develop the guidelines but, as the *Sun* editorial makes clear, the Riley Creek episode had an enduring legacy.

As for Riley Creek itself, and the others draining into Rennell Sound, the stream remained a contested site in terms of what it represented in the years after 1980. Early on industry and MOF spokesmen depicted Riley Creek as heading for a quick and full recovery. In a 1983 *Canadian Forest Industries* article, Vancouver Forest Region Manager Don Grant described its salmon production as "embarrassingly good", with runs of 20,000 or so, and a healthy plantation had grown up on CP144. A year later journalist L. Ward Johnson expressed the same view. "There is almost no indication that the event even occurred," he wrote. "The fish carry on their usual cycles as though nothing happened." Nature had brought the stream back to life. Logger R.L. Smith, campaigning hard against the preservation of South Moresby during these years in his *Redneck News* and frequent letters to the *Observer*, quoted Grant's article in deploring the heavy environmental burden the industry suffered under. Instead of blaming logging, he wrote, problems in the commercial fishery should be attributed to the "creek robbers", those who fished illegally on the islands.[171]

Responding with a counter-narrative, Karl Puls of Queen Charlotte City described Smith's glowing account of Riley Creek's health as "the worst kind of bad faith" reporting after checking with the DFO office there. Puls reported that post-slide Pink populations were actually down sharply, slipping to 5,200 in 1980 and just 780 in 1982, a significant decline from 1978's return of 15,700. Smith's distortions were intended to exacerbate hostility between loggers and conservationists, he wrote, asking rhetorically: "Who profits from poisoning this relationship?"[172]

That question, so central to the dynamics of land use conflict in the province, was one Mike Harcourt's NDP government tried to resolve in the 1990s. They packaged a Protected Area Strategy with the Forest Practices Code and created Forest Renewal BC, an initiative designed to provide employment for displaced woodworkers. Michael M'Gonigle has criticized the approach as sacrificing a genuine ecosystem-based forestry alternative to maintaining "the prevailing industrial paradigm", and initiatives on Haida Gwaii's steep slopes lend support for his conclusion. The development of a technological solution to the problem of accessing timber without devastating those fragile landscapes was a central FFIP mandate and Husby Forest Products had become an acknowledged leader at Naden Harbour since 1986, contracting with Erickson Air Crane Ltd. in the use of heavy-lift Sikorski helicopters to log steep slopes with minimal ground disturbance. Journalist Mike Halleran visited the operation in 1991, praising the collaboration between Husby engineers and DFO staff in planning, noting that habitat damage was "just about nil." On the return flight Halleran had the pilot take him over Rennell Sound. The clearcuts over Riley Creek had "greened up" with waist-high Sitka Spruce and Hemlock, but the major slide area had not yet stabilized. Silt and debris continued to enter the stream and a failure several weeks prior seemed to be growing in scale. Yet Halleran, a moderate and respected voice in conservation circles, drew a positive conclusion from what he had seen at Naden Harbour. "We learn by doing," he commented. "At Riley Creek, we learned to do it right."[173]

Interpreting Riley Creek as a site where things had gone right fed the technological optimism that had supposedly been discarded. For traditional conservationists who retained faith in multiple use, helicopter logging offered wish fulfillment, albeit with few jobs. Hope for the new technology ran high in industry and bureaucratic circles as well; slopes considered inoperable under traditional tower yarding and truck hauling methods could be reclassified as operable. And so industrial logging returned to Rennell Sound in 1992 after a hiatus of a dozen years, under the auspices of a FFIP arrangement with Husby Forest Products. Riley Creek was left alone, but FFIP consultant Keith Moore deemed Hangover Creek and Gregory Creek suitable for a pilot project involving conventional clearcutting, small openings and single-tree selection. All operations would conform with Coastal Fish/Forestry Guidelines, currently the topic of public consternation after the audit of Vancouver Island streams. In that context, the helicopter's potential for "environmentally-correct" selective logging became the project's centrepiece. Up to 16 per cent of the Queen Charlotte TSA annual cut was out of bounds due to unstable slopes, and similar constraints prevailed along the entire BC coast. "Hundreds of thousands of hectares" could be opened to exploitation if the Rennell Sound trials proved successful, FFIP director Steve Chatwin predicted. His colleague Ray Krag was equally clear about the study's intent: "to demonstrate that steep and unstable slopes can be logged to the satisfaction of the Forest Service and Fisheries and Oceans people." Heli-logging would increase the forest land base, an alternative to "writing off all sensitive areas." In this view of the longstanding drama, Riley Creek had been a problem area that now yielded land use solutions.[174]

Conclusion

A PERSPECTIVE that frames Riley Creek as a site of positive change should not be rejected outright, for it embodies hope that science and technology can indeed be marshalled in ways that allow us to achieve a sustainable relationship with 'non-human' nature. Mistakes were made, the story goes, conflict ensued and cooler heads eventually prevailed as the contenders achieved compromise and common ground. Lessons were learned in balancing the needs of economy and ecology, of loggers and fishers and environmentalists. Indeed, a 1998 summary of the history and status of Riley Creek by Steve Chatwin suggests that while the scars of the slides on CP144 remained, seeding and planting achieving only partial renewal, the stream itself seemed on the road to recovery. Pink returns reached an estimated 70,000 that year, the highest since the 1950s, a productivity he attributed to improved fishery regulation, restored gravel quality and the curtailment of logging. Chatwin concluded that the slides' long-term impact on salmon habitat was less severe than once thought. Moreover, the incidents at Riley Creek had given rise to better coordination among the resource agencies and the FFIP's unique research effort had real influence in crafting the Coastal Fish/Forestry Guidelines. Keith Moore shares this perspective, seeing the Riley Creek embarrassments and controversies as pivotal in later decisions to afford protection to thousands of hectares of steep terrain.[175]

That narrative around the Riley Creek slides is justifiable, placing the incidents in a context that incorporates real policy outcomes. More problematic, however, is that it can also be interpreted as offering a measure of

Clearcut hillside, Rennell Sound, April 1981. Courtesy of Keith Moore.

legitimacy to the politicians and administrators whose actions sacrificed a stream's health to federal-provincial gamesmanship. Lessons were learned at Riley Creek, but the historical forces that came to be focused there in the late 1970s can be obscured by simply treating the stream as a site of solutions to land use conflict. Ultimately, the battle of Riley Creek was rooted in the dynamic of capital accumulation, in a dominant industry's history of getting its way by virtue of its capacity to generate "fifty cents of every dollar" in BC's economy. British Columbians of my generation knew that phrase by heart, so routinely did we encounter the words.

Forests, simply put, generated more economic returns for capital and the province than did Pacific salmon. The same went for the federal state, despite its constitutional obligation to manage the fishery. BC was always intolerant of any federal effort to constrain forest exploitation in the interests of salmon and those who relied on them for subsistence, sport or commerce, and Ottawa pushed back cautiously. When it did, on the Stellako River in the 1960s and

Riley Creek just over a decade later, a hard line by the province led to a hasty federal retreat. Lack of field staff, the difficulty of meeting standards of proof in court and scientific uncertainties were all relevant factors, but they flowed from a general tolerance of a powerful industry's priorities in getting the wood out. At Riley Creek all the partners in that enterprise—companies large and small, the MOF and IWA—put aside their differences in defence of their shared freedom to exploit one resource at the expense of another. The IWA's role—guided by the "tripartism" Jack Munro pursued with government and companies to achieve the tenure security considered necessary for capital investment—was in one sense a logical culmination of a style of business unionism that left questions of resource management to technical elites employed by the province and its corporate clients. Confronted by a new social movement dedicated to wilderness preservation, one that did not go out of its way to cultivate alliances with loggers, IWA leaders lacked a tradition of independent, working-class policy advocacy. When caught between the forces of a resource in decline and environmentalism, they held the course in fighting for industry's right to the forest.[176]

Any reduction of the AAC was to be resisted, therefore, whether for parks or the protection of fish habitat, and clearcutting was defended as essential in making BC wood products competitive in global markets. Multiple use, from this perspective, meant timber production with small withdrawals for "single use" purposes tolerated in isolated cases. Left out was the UFAWU, which saw its resource's critical habitat being worn away in a manner that Riley Creek highlighted dramatically. As Scotty Neish said, in the context of the UFAWU's alliance with environmentalists to end clearcutting of the Tsitika watershed in 1979, "the government's policy is to hell with everyone else; get the logs out of the woods as cheaply as possible." That was not multiple use, as Neish understood the term, and therein lay the source of intra-class disharmony that erupted at Riley Creek. That is not to say that commercial fishers lacked a utilitarian, market-oriented approach to their own resource, only that their different relationship to forests as part of productive stream ecology lent itself to friendlier relations with environmentalism than the IWA had. When Aboriginal and non-Aboriginal fishermen rallied against DFO closures, as they did in September 1981 at Queen Charlotte City, they too were motivated by a desire for a greater share of BC's resource pie. Methods used to cut up the forest pie had implications for the size of their own slice, though, and it was only just coming to be understood that salmon played a part in the nutrient cycle of healthy forests.[177]

Multiple-use provisions in BC's *Forest Act,* folio planning and the science informing the Coastal Fish/Forestry Guidelines and Forest Practices Code notwithstanding, the federal *Fisheries Act* was the final source of protection for coastal streams. Drafted at a distance from the pressures of a political economy that made salmon expendable, it required the will to enforce. On Haida Gwaii that will existed primarily in the person of Jim Hart, but accommodation proved more appealing than confrontation at senior DFO levels. The *Fisheries Act,* Charlie Bellis observed at a 1995 Simon Fraser University forum on environmental issues, simply "does not work." Streams on the islands were being "lost" at a rate of about four per year, surveys showed. Reflecting on the Riley Creek slides and his effort with the IPS to lay charges, he praised Hart and Kip Slater for their attempts to protect the stream. But lawyers had made "a mockery out of the Fishery Act" in court, ending the battle.[178]

Others held the higher-up decision-makers responsible. Hart, for instance, blamed Wally Johnson for not standing behind his local staff. To many, the villain was Tom Waterland, who jokingly referred to his "Tom Wasteland" nickname in a 1983 meeting with small operators on the islands. Yet the salmon continued to spawn in Riley Creek, he maintained, and while the values and needs of other agencies had to be acknowledged, "somebody's got to be the boss." Waterland had fulfilled that role to his satisfaction and to that of Jack Munro and the corporate heads who had chosen Riley Creek for a showdown over the *Fisheries Act.* But Charlie Bellis and so many others felt only disgust at the single-minded crusade for corporate rights in the name of provincial rights.[179]

Bellis worried that unless habitat stewardship became a component of timber harvest rights, all the streams would be lost. In 1994 the BC Ministry of Environment reported that 485 streams and lakes had suffered significant habitat losses attributable to logging. A 1997 Sierra Legal Defense Fund audit of 1,086 BC streams logged under the Forest Practices Code found that 83 per cent had been clearcut to their banks, and in 1986 the American Fisheries Society reported that 142 BC and Yukon salmon populations were extinct. Another 624 faced a high risk of that fate. In 2000 the DFO urged the MOF and companies to increase protection for small streams by complying more fully with *Fisheries Act* regulations. Industry responded as it had in 1977, pressing the province to take an aggressive posture with Ottawa. The DFO, too, followed form, agreeing to talk the matter over. Then in 2001 Gordon Campbell's Liberal government moved to a "results-based" Forest Practices Code, easing industry's regulatory burden.[180]

Environmental organizations had little respect for the code even before it was relaxed and describe the DFO's "no net loss" policy as a failure because of administrative confusion, insufficient funding and enforcement personnel, and recent deregulation. Despite federal-provincial agreements in 1997 and again in 2001 to improve the standard of habitat protection programs, "the lack of effective habitat coordination remains," claims the David Suzuki Foundation, and the Natural Resources Defense Council notes a "systematic failure" to enforce the *Fisheries Act*.[181]

The legacy of Riley Creek is by no means unambiguous, then, and one might ask if it has any lasting legacy at all today. Inevitably, interested parties often have a self-congratulatory view of history. Some environmentalists prefer versions that cast the movement in heroic terms, and the bickering agencies would no doubt prefer that the events be forgotten except as a stimulus to the development of sound, science-based policy. A 2004 treatment of the history of forest hydrology in BC is a case in point. In this account QC Timber received approval to cut from all agencies, the late 1978 storm led to landslides and the DFO reconsidered. The company continued to log, arrests followed and a "major political impasse" resulted. Then, all parties agreed that logging could go ahead if carried out safely. In the end, "a steep portion of the block directly above a tributary stream was deleted from the cutting permit and the road was deactivated immediately after logging." Here selective memory deletes all reference to the 1979 slides and hurries to a happy conclusion about the incident's importance in shaping inspiring new research.[182]

Historians have summarized the story briefly in various sources, relying largely upon Richard Overstall's excellent contemporary coverage in the *Telkwa Foundation Newsletter*. But Riley Creek is worth more than a page or two, not as a story where we got it right, as Mike Halleran put it, but where it all went so horribly wrong. The Riley Creek story is ultimately about power and control, seeming winners and losers and, as Jeremy Wilson observes in an overview of debate from 1935–85, "those with political-economic power controlled the agenda." Charlie Bellis knew that from the inside, as a Haida fisherman who lost. Jim Hart, another loser, knew well the power he was confronting and learned a bitter lesson about the weakness of the agency he represented. Tom

Waterland undoubtedly sensed that weakness, as the official with the power to make other agencies—federal and provincial—reach an accommodation on his terms. QC Timber, backed by an entire industry and with allies in Victoria and the IWA, applied all of that power in achieving a victory over meddling fisheries officials and their act. Race and class are fundamental lines of both division and accommodation, of course, and these took interesting forms on the islands. The urban middle class allied with the Haida in bringing pressure to bear on governments for South Moresby's preservation, just as the IWA stood with the corporations and MOF at Riley Creek. In the end, one can say those partners achieved victory in a significant battle only to contribute in some measure to their own defeat in the South Moresby debate.[183]

But no one, of course, won in the end. Those with the power used it in a way that led to their own embarrassment. CIPA left Rennell Sound, Waterland earned his "Wasteland" nickname, and Jack Munro seemed less a defender of workers' rights than those of his industry and provincial state partners. Elizabeth May has written of South Moresby as a "paradise won" in a book bearing that title, but the loggers of Sandspit lost in that struggle and too few worried about their plight.[184]

My account suggests tentatively that those who thought they had won in the battle of Riley Creek actually helped assure their loss in the overall Haida Gwaii land use conflict. The entire pattern of logging on the islands, which Riley Creek helped bring to public attention, screamed of abuse. With multiple-use forestry increasingly discredited along with the sustained-yield concept, the defenders of clearcutting fuelled a public conviction that preservation was the only acceptable management option. That logic, in turn, helped legitimize a zoning approach to conflict resolution. Work, as Richard White has analyzed so well, is equated with destruction; 'nature' with leisure and human fulfillment. In terms of a lasting legacy that still speaks to us today, episodes like Riley Creek contributed to the construction of this paradigm, one that is not easily escaped. To do so requires a recognition that while drawing lines on a map to balance 'intensive forestry' zones against 'natural' areas may be politically feasible, the approach avoids the harder question of how to go about meeting the full range of human needs in a truly sustainable way.[185]

Appendices

APPENDIX 1

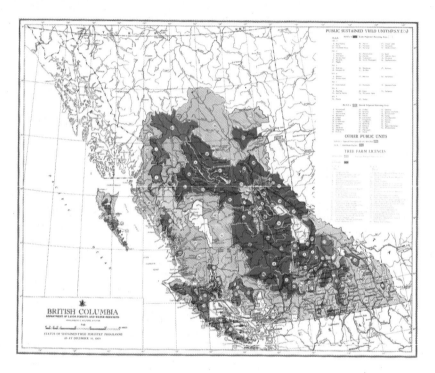

Map showing the location of Public Working Circles and Forest Management Licences.
RBCM Research Files.

APPENDIX 2

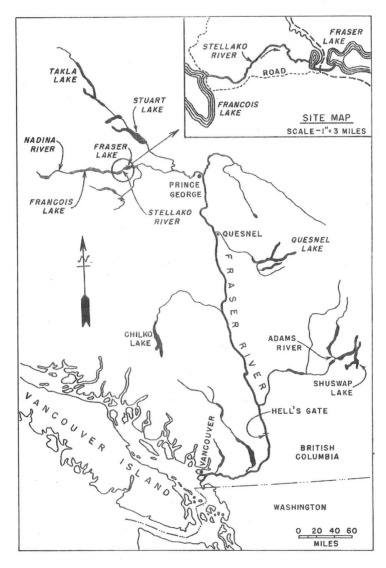

The International Pacific Salmon Fisheries Commission Progress Report No. 14: *Effects of Log Driving on the Salmon and Trout Populations in the Stellako River*, Vancouver, BC, 1966. Courtesy of the Pacific Salmon Commission.

APPENDIX 2

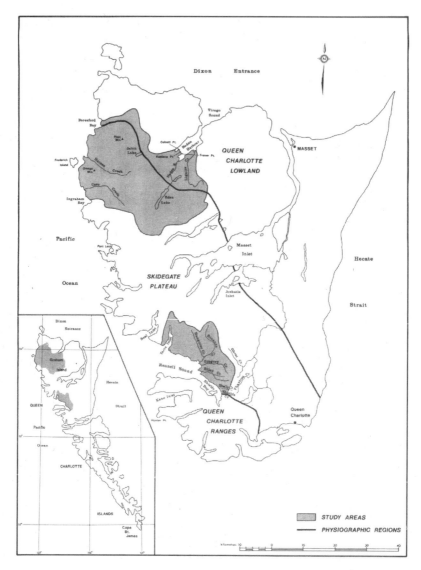

Figure 1: Outline of study areas and physiographic regions. "Queen Charlotte Islands Aspects of Environmental Geology", British Columbia Ministry of Environment Bulletin No. 2.

Reproduced with permission of the Province of British Columbia.

APPENDIX 3

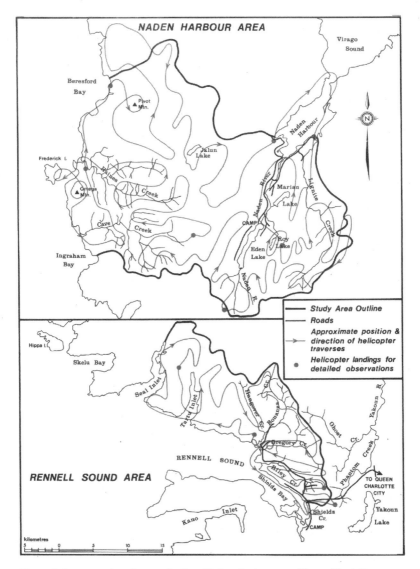

Figure 2: Access roads and generalization of helicopter traverses. "Queen Charlotte Islands Aspects of Environmental Geology", British Columbia Ministry of Environment Bulletin No. 2. Reproduced with permission of the Province of British Columbia.

Glossary of Acronyms and Abbreviations

AAC	Annual Allowable Cut
BCFS	BC Forest Service
BCRC	BC Research Council
BFWF	BC Wildlife Federation
CHN	Council of the Haida Nation
COFI	Council of Forest Industries
DFO	Department of Fisheries and Oceans
ELUC	Environment and Land Use Committee
EPA	Environmental Protection Area
FBM	Foot Board Measure
FFIP	Fish/Forestry Interaction Program
FML	Forest Management Licence
GIAPC	Graham Island Advisory Planning Committee
GTP	Grand Trunk Pacific
IPS	Islands Protection Society
IPSFC	International Pacific Salmon Fisheries Commission
IWA	International Woodworkers of America
MOF	Ministry of Forests
MLA	Member of the Legislative Assembly

NILA	Northern Interior Lumbermen's Association
PAC	Public Advisory Committee
P&T	Pinette and Therrien
PGSSA	Prince George Special Sale Area
PHA	Pulp Harvesting Areas
PHA	Pulpwood Harvesting Agreement (Chapter 4)
PSYU	Public Sustained Yield Unit
PWC	Public Working Circle
SEP	Salmon Enhancement Program
SMRPT	South Moresby Resource Planning Team
SPEC	Society for Pollution and Environmental Control
SSA	Special Sale Area
TFL	Tree Farm Licence
TLA	Truck Loggers Association
TSA	Timber Supply Areas
TSHL	Timber Sale Harvesting Licence
UFAWU	United Fishermen and Allied Workers Union
WFP	Western Forest Products

Endnotes

CHAPTER 1

1   The Honourable Gordon Sloan, Report of the Commissioner, The Forest Resources of British Columbia, Victoria, King's Printer, 1945, Q127.

2   A managed unit is an area of forest operated as a sustained-yield unit.

3   The BC Forest Service established several special sale areas where creating a sustained-yield management area was deemed too difficult. The two largest areas were from Prince George south to Quesnel and around Kamloops. The problems might result from too many existing commitments or when the area might be better suited to agriculture.

4   S.E. Marling to chief forester, December 20, 1950, Supervision, file 0187119 section 1, Ministry of Natural Resource Operations, Records Management Centre, Victoria (NRO).

5   E.W. Bassett, Vancouver, to chief forester, Victoria, December 7, 1950, Supervision, file 0187119, section 1, NRO.

6   W.G. Hughes to management, March 6, 1953, Supervision, file 0187119, section 2, NRO.

7   R.C. Telford to S.E. Marling, Victoria, December 5, 1950, file 0187119, section 1, NRO.

8   F.S. McKinnon to D.M. Carey, March 20, 1951, file 0187119, section 1, NRO.

9   L.F. Swannell to chief forester, May 10, 1951, file 0187119, section 1, NRO.

10 L.B. Boulton, Prince Rupert, to chief forester, Victoria, attention W.G. Hughes, November 16, 1951, Supervision, file 0187119, section 1, NRO.

11 D.M. Carey, Public Working Circles reports, February 1951, Supervision, file 0187119, section 1, NRO.

12 Between May 1 and July 3, 1952, R.B. Fisher was posted to Vancouver, A. Groner to Kamloops, A.L. Parlow to Nelson, W. Leesing to Prince Rupert and N. Wylie to Prince George from the Victoria working plans division. Progress report on Working Circles to F.S. McKinnon and C.D. Orchard, August 12, 1952, file 0187119.

13 H.B. Forse, district forester, Nelson, to Grant Ainscough, assistant forester in training, Victoria, January 17, 1953, Supervision 2.

14 A.L. Parlow, assistant forester, Nelson to W.G. Hughes, Victoria, January 30, 1953, Supervision, file 0187119, section 2, NRO.

15 C.D. Orchard to all district foresters, ranger school, March 4, 1953, Ministry of Forests (hereafter MOF), Supervision, file 0187119, section 2, NRO.

16 R.A. Waldie to H.G. Bancroft, April 4, 1960, Supervision, file 0187119, section 5, NRO.

17 A.L. Parlow, assistant forester, Nelson, to chief forester, Victoria, attention H.M. Pogue, forest surveys division, March 25, 1953, Supervision, file 0187119, section 2, NRO.

18 W.G. Hughes, "summary of field trip to Prince Rupert, Prince George and Kamloops," March 11- 21, 1953, Supervision, file 0187119, section 2, NRO.

19 Note on "summary of field trip to Prince Rupert, Prince George and Kamloops" districts, W.G. Hughes, March 11-21, 1953, Supervision, file 0187119, section 2, NRO.

20 W.G. Hughes, "summary of field trip to Prince Rupert, Prince George and Kamloops," March 11-21, 1953, Supervision, file 0187119, section 2, NRO.

21 L.F. Swannell, district forester, Prince George, to chief forester, Victoria, July 9, 1951, Naver, file 0189897, section 1, NRO.

22 Eric Robinson, assistant forester, Prince George, to chief forester, Victoria, September 24, 1951, Naver, file 0189897, section 1, NRO.

23 C.D. Orchard, deputy minister, memorandum to management, November 2, 1951, Naver, file 0189897, section 1, NRO.

24 C.D. Orchard, deputy minister, memorandum to management, November 2, 1951, Naver, file 0189897, section 1, NRO.

25 F.S. McKinnon, memorandum to chief forester, November 9, 1951, Naver, file 0189897, section 1, NRO. Although addressed to the chief forester, this memo actually went to Prince George.

26 D.R. Glew, assistant forester, to chief forester, attention F.S. McKinnon, November 15, 1951, Naver, file 0189897, section 1, NRO.

27 C.D. Orchard, chief forester, to F.S. McKinnon, November 20, 1951, Naver, file 0189897, section 1, NRO. Copy also sent to D.R. Glew at Prince George.

28 D.R. Glew, Prince George, to chief forester, Victoria, attention J.S. Stokes, May 4, 1954, Naver, file 0189897, section 1, NRO.

29 Basin Lumber Company to BC Forest Service, Victoria, April 29, 1955, Naver, file 0189897, section 1, NRO.

30 R.G. McKee, Victoria, to W.C. Phillips, Prince George, May 12, 1955, Supervision, file 0187119, section 3, NRO.

31 J.S. Stokes, Victoria, to W.C. Phillips, Prince George, September 22, 1954, Naver S, file 0189897, section 1, NRO.

32 LaGrace, Industrial Forestry Service, Prince George, to C.D. Orchard, deputy minister, Victoria, January 13, 1953, Naver Supervision, file 0189897, section 1, NRO.

33 A. Groner, Kamloops, to W.G. Hughes, Victoria, October 2, 1953; J. Stokes to Kamloops, October 14, 1953, Kamloops file 0218594, section 2, NRO.

34 Coast Small Operators Association to R.E. Sommers, September 29, 1953, Supervision, file 0187119 section 2, NRO.

35   C.D. Orchard to R.E. Sommers, December 3, 1953, Supervision, file 0187119, Section 3, NRO.

36   Walter Lessing, notes on trip, March 8-12, 1954, Supervision, file 0187119, section 2, NRO.

37   Walter Lessing, notes on trip, March 8-12, 1954, Supervision, file 0187119, section 2, NRO.

38   A. Groner, Kamloops, to W.G. Hughes, Victoria, September 13, 1954, Supervision, file 0187119, section 2, NRO.

39   The Public Working Circles were gradually being renamed Public Sustained Yield Units.

40   F.F. McKinnon, chief forester, Victoria, to E.S. Huestus, director of forestry, Edmonton, January 29, 1963, Supervision, file 0187119, 93-2738-1213, BC Archives.

41   F.S. McKinnon to chief forester, Victoria, May 10, 1951, Supervision, file 0187119, section 1, NRO.

42   N.A. McRae, Victoria, to L.F. Swannell, Kamloops, March 3, 1955, Supervision, file 0187119, section 3, NRO.

43   W.F.T. Battle, Backwater Timber, to J.S. Stokes, BC Forest Service management section, February 7, 1955, Supervision, file 0187119, section 3, NRO.

44   D.M. Carey to Hughes and Stokes, Victoria, August 31, 1955, Supervision, file 0187119, section 3, NRO.

45   John Stokes, deputy minister, to Ray Williston, minister, September 27, 1971, BC Archives Big Valley PSYU Supervision, GR-1110.33.213.

46   Quesnel ranger district 6, annual report, 1955, MOF, Prince George district, 110, 2, 7, p. 16.

47   G.E. Meents, Quesnel, to district forester, Prince George, December 28, 1955, BC Archives MOF, Prince George District, BC Archives, GR-1110.32.210.

48   H.G. Bancroft, Vancouver, to management, Victoria, October 9, 1956, Supervision, file 6187119, section 4, NRO.

49   S.E. Marling to district foresters, November 2, 1956, Supervision, file 6187119, section 4, NRO.

50   S.E. Marling to district foresters, November 2, 1956, Supervision, file 6187119, section 4, NRO.

51   N.A. McRae, forester, to D.B Taylor, district forester, Vancouver, August 8, 1957, Supervision, file 0187119, section 4, NRO.

52   J.S. Stokes to management, Vancouver, August 27, 1957, Supervision, file 0187119, section 4, FNRO.

53   W.G. Hughes, Victoria, to district forester, Prince George, March 19, 1959, Supervision, file 6187119, section 4, NRO.

54   For a full discussion of this incident, see Betty O'Keefe and Ian MacDonald, *The Sommers Scandal: The Felling of Trees and Tree Lords.* Victoria: Heritage House Publishing, 1999.

55 Comments on application of Eagle Lake sawmills for TFL 29, p. 6 file 19680-25/ TFL 29, NRO.

56 C.D. Orchard to the minister, November 6, 1956, file 19700-20/TFL4 "A", I.W. McDonagh, British Columbia Forest Products Ltd.

57 The BC Forest Service established close utilization as a harvesting standard. Essentially this meant that as sawmills acquired new technology suitable for smaller logs, additional timber was made available to those sawmills.

58 J.C. Payne, Kamloops, to chief forester, Victoria, May 8, 1968, file 1000-30/0272547, section 1, BC Archives.

59 A.P. McBean, chief forester, MacMillan Bloedel, to J.E. Stokes, assistant chief forester, Victoria, December 5, 1966, close utilization logging standards, 1000-30/0-268206, NRO.

60 E.L. Young to J.S. Stokes, October 24, 1966, close utilization logging standards, 1000-30/0-268206, NRO.

61 C. Highstead to W.G. Hughes, July 29, 1966, close utilization logging standards, 1000-30/0-268206, NRO.

62 Ray Williston to Joe Frolek, July 22, 1964, W. Hanbury, July 22, 1964, C.J. Bessette, July 22, 1964, Kamloops Region, file 0218594, NRO.

63 Ray Williston to Kamloops region operators, April 27, 1964, Kamloops Region, file 0218594, NRO.

64 R.G. McKee to Ray Williston, April 15, 1964, Kamloops Region, file 0218594, NRO.

65 A.F. Specht to district forester, November 5, 1957, Kamloops Region, file 0218594, NRO.

66 File note, R.G. McKee, May 10, 1963, Kamloops Region, file 0218594, NRO.

67 BC Interior Sawmills was awarded tree farm licence 35 in 1959, but only after considerable opposition from the Kamloops sawmill community. Opposition was so great that one of the earliest public hearings regarding a tree farm licence was held by then Minister of Forests Robert Sommers in Kamloops, 1954. Jamieson Creek tree farm licence, TFL 35, section 1, 19700-20 TFL 35 "A", FLNRO. The Ponderosa Pine Lumber Company was granted their licence in April 1954. http://www.for.gov.bc.ca/dmswww/tfl/TFL-49/Management-plans/MP3/00-TFL-49-Management-Plan-3.pdf, p. 33.

68 George Long, Kamloops, to Ray Williston, Victoria, November 26, 1968, Kamloops Region, file 0218594, NRO.

69 Ray Williston, minister, to Mr. Edgar Drew, October 16, 1967, file 0218594, Section 2, Kamloops Region, NRO.

70 Ray Williston to Frolek Sawmills, Kamloops, January 30, 1969, Kamloops Region, file 0218594, NRO.

71 W.C. Phillips, district forester, Kamloops, file memo, Victoria and Kamloops Region, file 0218594, NRO.

72   Management, Victoria, to management, Kamloops, January 24, 1955, Williams Lake Public Working Circle, section 1, file 006543, NRO.

73   Bill Young, former district forester, talking to BC Forest History Association, March 3, 1988, file 0250164, NRO.

74   A stud mill produced mainly stud dimension lumber (see text for dimensions) and could therefore utilize smaller logs than the standard sawlog sawmill.

75   L. Swannell to R. Williston, memorandum to the minister, administration of Special Sale Area, no date but about May 1, 1965, file 0250164, section 2, Lands, Forests and Water Resources.

76   Brief from Tubafour Sawmills' Lloyd Sword to Minister of Lands, Forests and Water Resources Ray Williston, September 10, 1963, administration of Special Sale Area, file 0250164, section 2, NRO, p 3.

77   Ray Williston, minister, to Lakeland Mills Limited, February 24, 1966, PGSSA, file 0250164, NRO.

78   W.F. Tuttle, forester in charge of management, Prince George, to chief forester, Victoria, March 15, 1966, PGSSA, file 0250164, NRO.

79   N.H. Holt, president, Atlin Sawmills, to R.G. Williston, minister, May 4, 1966, PGSSA, file 0250164, NRO.

80   Honourable R.G. Williston, minister, to N.H. Holt, president, Atlin Sawmills, May 11, 1966, PGSSA, file 0250164, NRO.

81   John Ernst, president, to R.G. Williston, minister, September 19, 1966, PGSSA, file 0250164, NRO.

82   The Chip-N-Saw was developed in Shelton, Washington in 1960. The only company interested in manufacturing it was the Vancouver engineering firm Canadian Car Pacific. It was a machine that chipped four sides of the log while at the same time splitting the remaining timber into 2-inch boards. The Logging and Sawmilling Journal, February 2005, http://forestnet.com/archives/Feb_05/sawmilling1.htm.

83   R.G. Williston, minister, to A.L. Patchett & Sons Ltd., November 17, 1966, PGSSA file 0250164, NRO.

84   Ray Williston, minister, to Ernst Lumber Company, December 1, 1966, PGSSA, file 0250164, NRO.

85   Tubafour Stud Mills to Ray Williston, minister, October 27, 1967; Ray Williston, minister, to Tubafour Stud Mills, November 4, 1967, PGSSA, file 0250164, NRO.

86   Ray Williston, minister, to Tubafour Sawmills, May 1, 1968, PGSSA, file 0250164, NRO.

87   "History of the Special Sale Area since 1965," attachment to a letter, Tubafour to Ray Williston, minister, April 8, 1968, PGSSA, file 0250164, NRO.

88 "Commissioners told 'Land use unsatisfactory'", *Prince George Progress,* May 8, 1968.

89 Report on Public Meeting–Quesnel land use policies, May 3, 1968, by F.M. Cunningham, assistant director of lands, p. 7, p. 3, PGSSA, file 0250164, NRO.

90 Tubafour Stud Mills to Ray Williston, minister, August 22, 1968, PGSSA, file 0250164, NRO.

91 E.A. McRae, Tubafour Stud Mills Limited to Ray Williston, minister, April 8, 1968, PGSSA, file 0250164, NRO.

92 Williston also received a letter from the Ernst Lumber Company requesting additional timber, although their claims were not quite as extravagant as Tubafour's. J. Ernst Lumber Company to R.G. Williston, minister, November 18, 1968, PGSSA, file 0250164, NRO.

93 E.A. McRae, Tubafour Stud Mills Limited to R.G. Williston, minister, February 14, 1969, PGSSA, file 0250164, NRO.

94 W. Young, district forester, August 27, 1970, PGSSA, file 0250164, section 5, NRO.

95 R.G. Williston, minister, to Pinette and Therrien Planer Mills, November 27, 1969, PGSSA, file 0250164, NRO.

96 R.G. Williston, minister, to J. Ernst Lumber Company, February 5, 1971, PGSSA, file 0250164, section 5, NRO.

97 J.S. Stokes, deputy minister, to R.G. Williston, minister, October 20, 1971, Narcosli 0206389, section 3, FNRO.

98 Hugh Goodman to R.G. Williston, minister, March 20, 1970, PGSSA, file 0250164, section 5, NRO.

99 Third band timber was smaller timber that previously could not be harvested profitably, but with sawmills installing chippers and gang saws the smaller timber was now included in the logs to be harvested.

100 Memorandum to the minster from J.S. Stokes, deputy minister, September 3, 1970 PGSSA, file 0250164, section 5, NRO.

101 J.S. Stokes, deputy minister, to R.G. Williston, minister, September 10, 1970, PGSSA, file 0250164, section 5, NRO.

102 W. Young, district forester, to E. Knight, management division, Victoria, September 10, 1970, PGSSA, file 0250164, section 5, NRO.

103 Note on copy of letter sent to chief forester, Victoria, W. Young, district forester to Tubafour Stud Mills, March 22, 1971, PGSSA, file 0250164, section 5, NRO.

104 Interim report on proposed schedule "X" lands in the PGSSA, M. Fenton, forester, to file, December 17, 1971, PGSSA, file 0250164, section 5, NRO.

CHAPTER 2

Author's note: *When chapters 2 and 3 were originally written the files were in the custody of the Royal BC Museum's history section. These files were subsequently transferred to the BC Archives where the files were re-sorted, re-boxed and assigned new box and file numbers. I have not tried to determine the new location and number of each file. Anyone desirous of tracking down a reference should be able to do so by using the senders name and the date. Weldwood-Westply Fonds PR-2308; Ms-3081 to Ms-3088.*

1   E.E. Gregg to Neil W. McCallum, chief engineer, Department of Public Works, August 14, 1950, Weldwood-Westply Fonds PR-2308.

2   Even prior to opening of the Quesnel plywood plant, they planned to expand into interior pulp production. The next interior softwood plywood plant, S.M. Simpson's at Kelowna, did not go into production until 1957.

3   E.E. Greg to W.J. Bowerman, district superintendent of radio, Department of Transportation, November 8, 1950, Weldwood-Westply Fonds PR-2308.

4   E.E. Gregg to Ian MacQueen, December 21, 1950, Weldwood-Westply Fonds PR-2308.

5   E.E. Gregg to Ian MacQueen, May 22, 1954, file Garner Road, Weldwood-Westply Fonds PR-2308.

6   Ian MacQueen to E.E. Gregg, October 7, 1955, file Garner Road, Weldwood-Westply Fonds PR-2308.

7   E.E. Gregg to John Bene and John Huberman, September 25, 1956, file south operations, Garner contract, Weldwood-Westply Fonds PR-2308.

8   E.E. Gregg to Ian MacQueen, May 27, 1955, and Ian MacQueen to E.E. Gregg, October 7, 1955, file south operations, Garner contract, Weldwood-Westply Fonds PR-2308.

9   Ian MacQueen to E.E. Gregg, February 16, 1956, file south operations, Garner contract, Weldwood-Westply Fonds PR-2308.

10 Bucking: de-limbing and cutting the fallen tree into the desired lengths. Skidding: dragging the log to the landing, usually by truck arches or crawler tractors, for loading onto trucks that then hauled the logs to the mill.

11 Ian MacQueen to John Bene, May 7, 1956, file south operations, Garner contract, Weldwood-Westply Fonds PR-2308.

12 John Bene to Ian MacQueen, 1956, file south operations, Garner contract, Weldwood-Westply Fonds PR-2308.

13 Ian MacQueen to John Bene, 1956, file south operations, Garner contract, Weldwood-Westply Fonds PR-2308.

14 A truck arch is a truck on which an arch has been installed behind the cab. The arch has a wire rope running over the top, which is tied to the logs, and a winch raises the end of the logs clear of the ground. The truck can then drag the logs to the desired location. These were initially developed using surplus army trucks from World War II.

15 Cat yarding is yarding by crawler tractor, the most common brand being Caterpillar, hence the name 'cat'. A winch is on the back of the cat and the wire rope is run out and fastened around the logs so they can be towed to the desired location. Sometimes the cats are used with a wheeled arch to lift the end of the logs. Cats require very little road construction compared to truck arches.

16 Annual report, Quesnel ranger district, December 29, 1950, GR1110, box 1, file 3, BC Archives.

17 Annual report, Hixon ranger district, January 15, 1956, GR1110, file 8, BC Archives.

18 Annual report, Quesnel ranger district, December 23, 1855, GR1110, file 8, BC Archives.

19 Ian MacQueen to Ken Rymer, letter, December 2, 1954, file Horsefly, Weldwood-Westply Fonds PR-2308.

20 Ian MacQueen to Mike Gregg, teletype, May 27, 1955, file south operations, Garner, Quesnel Plant, Weldwood-Westply Fonds PR-2308.

21 Ian MacQueen to Ken Rymer, letter, December 2, 1954, file Horsefly, Weldwood-Westply Fonds PR-2308. Garner's was a long-established operator at Horsefly, and Likely Sawmills was another subsidiary company of Lignum.

22 Mike Gregg to Ian MacQueen, teletype, July 17, 1956, file south operations, Garner, Quesnel Plant, Weldwood-Westply Fonds PR-2308. The pulp mill was not constructed until 1964.

23 Ian MacQueen to E.E. Gregg, report No. 3, December 22, 1954, file Quesnel Horsefly Timber Supply, Weldwood-Westply Fonds PR-2308.

24 Ian MacQueen to E.E. Gregg, letter, January 3, 1955, file Quesnel Horsefly, Weldwood-Westply Fonds PR-2308.

25 John Bene to Mike Gregg, letter, December 31, 1954, file Quesnel Horsefly, Weldwood-Westply Fonds PR-2308. Both the Vancouver and Quesnel plants were supplied from these timber sales.

26 Application to purchase Crown timber, January 5, 1955, file Quesnel Horsefly, Weldwood-Westply Fonds PR-2308.

27 Ian MacQueen to L. Swannell, district forester, January 3, 1955, file Quesnel Horsefly, Weldwood-Westply Fonds PR-2308.

28 Ian MacQueen to E.E. Gregg, letter, May 1, 1953, file Horsefly, Weldwood-Westply Fonds PR-2308.

29 Ian MacQueen to E.E. Gregg, letter, May 1, 1953, file Horsefly, Weldwood-Westply Fonds PR-2308.

30 Ian MacQueen to Mike Gregg, telegram, July 6, 1955, file Sword and Kerr, Weldwood-Westply Fonds PR-2308.

31 J. Stokes to Ahbau Forestry Association, March 31, 1959, Naver administration file, 0189897, NRO.

32 Ian MacQueen to E.E. Gregg, letter, May 1, 1953, file Horsefly, Weldwood-Westply Fonds PR-2308.

33 E.E. Gregg, Western Plywood, to Ralph Chetwynd, minister of railways, letter, March 12, 1955; R.E. Sommers, minister of forests, to Ralph Chetwynd, minister of railways, letter, May 4, 1955, Narcosli administration file, 0206389, NRO.

34 E.E. Gregg to various, June 29, 1956, file south operations, Garner, box 5, Quesnel Plant, Weldwood-Westply Fonds PR-2308.

35 E.E. Gregg to chief forester, attention R.G. McKee, March 16, 1955, Narcosli administration file, 0189897, NRO.

36 Ian MacQueen to E.E. Gregg, letter, March 1, 1955, file Horsefly-Quesnel, Weldwood-Westply Fonds PR-2308.

37 Ian MacQueen to E.E. Gregg, letter, March 1, 1955, file Horsefly-Quesnel, Weldwood-Westply Fonds PR-2308. See also Mike Gregg to Ian MacQueen, January 11, 1955, file Quesnel-Horsefly, Weldwood-Westply Fonds PR-2308.

38 E.E. Gregg described the district forester's "warped reasoning which results in our not being eligible to apply for timber in a country where we have established the biggest investment, while at the same time a rank outsider without a dollar of investment can have sales cleared in convenient locations...." E.E. Gregg to Ian MacQueen, September 14, 1955, file TS X59246, Weldwood-Westply Fonds PR-2308.

39 Ian MacQueen to E.E. Gregg, letter, March 1, 1955, file Horsefly-Quesnel, Weldwood-Westply Fonds PR-2308.

40 E.E. Gregg to district forester, Kamloops, March 16, 1955, file Horsefly-Quesnel, Weldwood-Westply Fonds PR-2308.

41 M.L. Kerr, assistant forester, Kamloops, to J.R. Murray, Western Plywood, Vancouver, September 11, 1958, file TS X67504, Weldwood-Westply Fonds PR-2308.

42 L. Swannell to Al Kilde, May 5, 1958, file TS X67504, Weldwood-Westply Fonds PR-2308.

43 Ken Rhymer to John Bene et al., telegram, July 6, 1955, file Quesnel operations, Weldwood-Westply Fonds PR-2308.

44 There was some rearrangement of Public Working Circles, especially around Williams Lake, so the naming of the Public Working Circle may not be exact, depending on the date.

45 The large number of sawmill operators working out of Prince George probably also played a role in this decision.

46 Mike Gregg to Ian MacQueen, March 20, 1951, file Quesnel operations, Weldwood-Westply Fonds PR-2308.

47 Ian MacQueen to Harold Burritt and Ivan Larter, Quesnel, March 2, 1955, Weldwood-Westply Fonds PR-2308.

48　Ian MacQueen to E.E. Gregg, Quesnel, May 30, 1955, file Sword and Kerr; Al Kilde to Al Scheller, Sardis, December 10, 1958, file Scheller Logging Co. Ltd., Weldwood-Westply Fonds PR-2308.

49　Ian MacQueen to John Bene, telegram, Quesnel, June 23, 1955, file Sword and Kerr, Weldwood-Westply Fonds PR-2308.

50　Ian MacQueen to Mike Gregg, telegram, December 8, 1955; Ian MacQueen to E.E. Gregg, inter-office memorandum, January 20, 1956, file Sword and Kerr, Weldwood-Westply Fonds PR-2308.

51　Woodpecker is a tiny community near Western Plywood's FML 5, and a source of logs for the company.

52　E.E. Gregg to John Bene, memo, May 22, 1956, Weldwood-Westply Fonds PR-2308.

53　Ian MacQueen to E.E. Gregg, letter, May 24, 1956, Weldwood-Westply Fonds PR-2308.

54　Ian MacQueen to E.E. Gregg, letter, May 23, 1956, Weldwood-Westply Fonds PR-2308.

55　*Ibid.*

56　Henry Oosterveld to Gordon M. Steele, Vancouver, inter-office correspondence, June 8, 1956, file Sword and Kerr. Weldwood-Westply Fonds PR-2308.

57　Ian MacQueen to E.E. Gregg, Quesnel, inter-office memo, August 16, 1956; George Kibblewhite to Sword and Kerr Logging Co., Quesnel, letter, August 16, 1956; Mike Gregg to E.E. Gregg, Quesnel, letter, August 14, 1956, Weldwood-Westply Fonds PR-2308.

58　Pit Desjardin to John Bene, telegram, February 13, 1957, Weldwood-Westply Fonds PR-2308.

59　John Bene to Sword and Kerr, letter, December 10, 1957, Weldwood-Westply Fonds PR-2308.

60　John Bene to Sword and Kerr, letter, December 10, 1957, Weldwood-Westply Fonds PR-2308.

61　Unknown to Don McColl, telegram, January 28, 1958, Weldwood-Westply Fonds PR-2308.

62　It was standard practice by nearly all operators in the interior to log by contract rather than use their own employees.

63　G.J. Kibblewhite to Mr. Wm. Christie, superintendent, Williams Lake Indian Agency, January 19, 1960, file Quesnel operations, Weldwood-Westply Fonds PR-2308.

64　P & T was a Williams Lake-based sawmill.

65　George Kibblewhite to Pit Desjardin, April 23, 1958, file P & T, Weldwood-Westply Fonds PR-2308.

66　A quota was the amount the Forest Service would permit an operator to cut within any given year. The size of the quota was based on the timber sales acquired.

67　Allocation ledger, Cottonwood administration file, 0190093, NRO.

68　George Kibblewhite to E.E. Gregg, teletype, April 13, 1953, file TS X59197, Weldwood-Westply Fonds PR-2308.

69 George Kibblewhite to Ian MacQueen, September 8, 1953, file TS X59197, Weldwood-Westply Fonds PR-2308.

70 George Kibblewhite to Ian MacQueen, September 8, 1953, file TS X61072, Weldwood-Westply Fonds PR-2308; George Kibblewhite to Ian MacQueen, September 28, 1953, file TS X61137, Weldwood-Westply Fonds PR-2308.

71 George Kibblewhite to E.E. Gregg, letter, July 29, 1954; E.E. Gregg to chief forester, letter, October 1, 1954, file TS X58155, Quesnel Plant, Weldwood-Westply Fonds PR-2308.

72 George Kibblewhite to Pit Desjardin, memo, Feb 7, 1959, file TS X78696, Weldwood-Westply Fonds PR-2308.

73 Bill Sterling to Al Kilde, teletype, November 7, 1958, file TS X78596, Weldwood-Westply Fonds PR-2308.

74 Bill Sterling to Al Kilde, telegram, November 7, 1958, file TS X78596, Weldwood-Westply Fonds PR-2308.

75 Bill Sterling to Don McColl, October 21, 1958, file TS X78596, Weldwood-Westply Fonds PR-2308.

76 Ian MacQueen to George Kibblewhite, June 8, 1956, file TS X78696, Weldwood-Westply Fonds PR-2308.

77 The so-called "rat-hole" agreements Sloan, Gordon, Royal Commission, 1956 Vol. 1, pp. 165–166.

78 Mike Gregg to Ian MacQueen, January 11, 1955, file Quesnel Horsefly, Weldwood-Westply Fonds PR-2308.

79 E.E. Gregg to chief forester, attention R.G. McKee, March 16, 1955, Weldwood-Westply Fonds PR-2308.

80 J.B. Martineau & Son to district forester, letter, November 30, 1955, file J.B. Martineau & Son, Weldwood-Westply Fonds PR-2308.

81 J.B. Crawford to David Tupper, letter, November 26, 1955, file Northern BC, Weldwood-Westply Fonds PR-2308.

82 Mike Gregg to Ian MacQueen, teletype, May 19, 1955, file south operations, Garner, Quesnel Plant, Weldwood-Westply Fonds PR-2308.

83 Ian MacQueen to Mike Gregg, teletype, May 27, 1955, file south operations, Garner, Quesnel Plant, Weldwood-Westply Fonds PR-2308.

84 Mike Gregg to Ian MacQueen, teletype, July 17, 1956, file south operations, Garner, Quesnel Plant, Weldwood-Westply Fonds PR-2308.

85 Mike Gregg to Ian MacQueen, teletype, July 17, 1956, file south operations, Garner, box 5, Quesnel Plant, Weldwood-Westply Fonds PR-2308.

86 John Bene to Mr. J.L. VandeVanter, letter, June 24, 1957, file Northern BC, box 19A, Weldwood-Westply Fonds PR-2308.

87 Ted R. Westrom to Al Kilde, February 1, 1958, file Northern BC, box 19A, Weldwood-Westply Fonds PR-2308.

88   Mike to Ian, Mike to Ian, Mike to Ian, teletypes, September 14, 1955. All file Horsefly Quesnel, box 19A, Weldwood-Westply Fonds PR-2308.

89   E.E. Gregg to Leslie Kerr, June 16, 1953, file TS X58149, Weldwood-Westply Fonds PR-2308.

90   E.E. Gregg to Leslie Kerr, June 16, 1953, file TS X58149, Weldwood-Westply Fonds PR-2308.

91   George Kibblewhite to E.E. Gregg, June 17, 1953, file TS X58149, Weldwood-Westply Fonds PR-2308.

92   George Kibblewhite to Ian MacQueen, June 23, 1953, file TS X58149, Weldwood-Westply Fonds PR-2308.

93   Mike Gregg to E.E. Gregg, June 17, 1953, file TS X58149, Weldwood-Westply Fonds PR-2308.

94   George Kibblewhite to Ian MacQueen, June 29, 1953, file TS X58149, Weldwood-Westply Fonds PR-2308.

95   G.J. Kibblewhite to Cascade Spruce Mills, June 29, 1953, file TS X58149, Weldwood-Westply Fonds PR-2308.

96   George Kibblewhite to E.E. Gregg, teletype, April 13, 1953, file TS X59197, Weldwood-Westply Fonds PR-2308.

97   George Kibblewhite to E.E. Gregg, teletype, April 15, 1953, file TS X59197, Weldwood-Westply Fonds PR-2308.

98   Netherlands Overseas Mills also acquired the Matheson Planer at Macalister in 1955.

99   John Bene to John Huber and Bill Sterling, teletype, April 3, 1957, file TS X59246, Weldwood-Westply Fonds PR-2308.

100   Al [Kilde?] to John Huberman, teletype, April 4, 1957, file TS X59246, box 18A, Weldwood-Westply Fonds PR-2308. In this case 'particular nuisance' was not defined by Western but it usually meant attempts to secure timber sales Western had applied for or attempts to blackmail Western into providing them with a logging contract.

101   George Kibblewhite to John Huberman et al., April 9, 1957, file TS X59246, Weldwood-Westply Fonds PR-2308.

102   George Kibblewhite to Ian MacQueen, January 20, 1955, file TS X61943, Weldwood-Westply Fonds PR-2308; George Kibblewhite to Ian MacQueen, January 31, 1955, file TS X61943, Weldwood-Westply Fonds PR-2308.

103   George Kibblewhite to Ian MacQueen, February 7, 1955, file TS X61943, Weldwood-Westply Fonds PR-2308.

104   File TS X62851, Weldwood-Westply Fonds PR-2308.

105   The whole of the region had been under timber application from large coastal operators prior to the establishment of the Public Working Circles. These applications were almost all disallowed to give local operators an opportunity to acquire the timber.

106 W.C. Phillips, district forester, Prince George, to chief forester, Victoria, memorandum, July 8, 1954, Narcosli file, 0189897, NRO.

107 Sven Gaunitz, "Resource exploitation on the North-Swedish timber Frontier in the 19th and the beginning of the 20th Centuries", in Harold K. Steen, *History of Sustained-yield Forestry: A Symposium*. Durham: Forest History Society, 1984, p. 150.

108 This is supported in Sloan's second report when he analyzes sales sold at over the upset price. Even in 1955, probably the year of greatest competition, Sloan notes that 87 per cent of all sales had no competition while only four per cent sold for over twice the upset price. The most competitive district was the Kamloops district where competitive bidding took place in 17 per cent of the sales offered in 1955, or 142 out of 808 sales. Gordon Sloan, *The Forest Resources of British Columbia, Report of the Commissioner*. Victoria: Queen's Printer, 1957, pp. 163–64.

109 See Stylianos Perrakis, *Canadian Industrial Organization*. Scarborough: Prentice-Hall Canada Inc., 1990, pp. 117–23.

110 Annual Report, Quesnel ranger district, December 29, 1950, GR 1110 file 3, and annual report, Quesnel ranger district, January 8, 1957, GR 1110, box 2, file 9, BC Archives.

111 Annual Report, Quesnel ranger district, December 30, 1959, GR1110, file 12, BC Archives.

112 H.M. Pogue, district forester to all licensees, May 4, 1972, GR1110, box 14, file 82, BC Archives.

CHAPTER 3

1 It should be noted that the Port Alberni pulp mill was not built in response to a change in government policy, even though it comes into production near the time of those mills that were built in response to the new sustained-yield policy.

2 Sommers was accused of accepting bribes for Forest Management Licences and went to jail. For the full story see: O'Keefe, Betty and Ian MacDonald. *The Sommers Scandal: The Felling of Trees and Tree Lords*. Victoria: Heritage House Publishing, 1993.

3 Mahood, Ian and Ken Drushka. *Three Men and a Forester*. Madeira Park: Harbour Publishing, 1990, p. 184.

4 A gypo was usually a smaller logging operation run on the cheap.

5 Bene to Brewer, pulp file, Weldwood-Westply Fonds PR-2308.

6 Public hearings, April 24, 1964, Williston Papers, University of Victoria, Special Collections, p. 49.

7 Public hearings, April 24, 1964, Williston Papers, University of Victoria, Special Collections, p. 73.

8   Bob Wood to John Bene and Pit Desjardins, August 21, 1964. Weldwood-Westply Fonds PR-2308. Notes on the meeting show Weldwood of Canada and Bowater were moving toward a joint proposal. Each interpreted parts of the meeting differently.

9   Public hearings, January 4, 1965, Victoria, p. 72.

10 Weldwood of Canada, a subsidiary of United States Plywood of New York, acquired Western Plywood in 1961. Western Plywood had plywood plants in Vancouver, Quesnel and Edmonton at this time.

11 Bob Wood to John Bene and Pit Desjardins, August 21, 1964, Weldwood-Westply Fonds PR-2308.

12 The Union Bay site was undoubtedly the best physical location from an engineer's point of view. It had been acquired by Weldwood when they acquired Canadian Collieries in 1964. Weldwood-Westply Fonds PR-2308.

13 Notes from meeting with Williston, August 21, 1964, Weldwood-Westply Fonds PR-2308.

14 John Bene, Vancouver, to Ken Logan, Pulp and Paper Research Institute, Montreal, July 11, 1947, pulp mill file, Weldwood-Westply Fonds PR-2308.

15 Bene to Douglas Jones, Canadian Pulp and Paper Association, Montreal, June 29, 1948, pulp mill file, Weldwood-Westply Fonds PR-2308.

16 Williston's preference for local business is evident in his awarding of a tree farm licence to Eurocan rather than MacMillan Bloedel or Crown Zellerbach, the established large operators in Kitimat. Eurocan was a consortium of Terrace sawmills and Ben Ginter of Prince George with Finnish capital.

17 Williston, Eileen and Betty Keller. 1997. *Forest, Power and Policy: The Legacy of Ray Williston*. Prince George: Caitlin Press, p. 132. Nor did Williston like the president of MacMillan Bloedel, J.V. Clyne, p. 129.

18 In several other incidents, not related to PHAs, rather heated conflicts developed between applicants and the Forest Service. The three most controversial were the Ginter-Cattermole conflict; the conflict between MacMillan Bloedel, Crown Zellerbach and Eurocan at Kitimat; and the conflict over the Canal Development proposal in the Kootenays.

19 Bene to Brewer, March 19, 1964, Brewer file, Weldwood-Westply Fonds PR-2308.

20 Memo, Geoff Tullidge to John Bene, October 7, 1947, Weldwood-Westply Fonds PR-2308.

21 Rex Vincent, Bulkley, Dunton Pulp Company, New York, to John Bene, Vancouver, April 30, 1948, October 5, 1948 and October 9, 1948, pulping tests, Weldwood-Westply Fonds PR-2308; W.D. Maxim, International Paper Company, New York, to John Huberman, Vancouver, January 19, 1949, Weldwood-Westply Fonds PR-2308.

22 W. Boyd, Campbell Pulp and Paper Research Institute of Canada, to R.W. Weldwood-Westply Fonds PR-2308, Vancouver, July 22, 1948; Thomas Fernstrom, Fernstrom Paper Mills, to Karl Benton, Western Plywood, Los Angeles, July 19, 1948. Test Samples from Stockholm, June 4, 1948. Other tests with additional companies. Weldwood-Westply Fonds PR-2308.

23 Canadian Boxes was a subsidiary of Pacific Mills, which was, in turn, a subsidiary of Crown Zellerbach. Report on the tests, author unknown, to John Bene. The tests were made June 25, 1948. The report is undated. Weldwood-Westply Fonds PR-2308.

24 Tullidge to Bene, March 25, 1948, pulp file, Weldwood Collection, BC Archives, RBCM.

25 Bene to Douglas Jones, Canadian Pulp and Paper Association, June 29, 1948, pulp file, Weldwood-Westply Fonds PR-2308.

26 *Vancouver Sun*, September 30, 1964. p. 33.

27 Bene to Brewer, May 13, 1963, Brewer file, Weldwood-Westply Fonds PR-2308.

28 On the relationship between US Plywood and John Bene and Weldwood see Robert Griffin, Success and Failure in British Columbia's Softwood Plywood Industry, 1813–1999. Ph.D. University of Victoria, 2000.

29 Bene to Brewer, July 31, 1963, Brewer file, Weldwood-Westply Fonds PR-2308.

30 Lars Bratt to K.L. Morrow, July 30, 1965, Morrow file, Weldwood Collection, BC Archives, RBCM. US Plywood did not build a pulp mill at McCloud.

31 Bene was first informed of this possible partnership in June 1964, Brewer to Bene, June 2, 1964, Brewer file, Weldwood-Westply Fonds PR-2308. The partnership possibility grew out of US Plywood's discussion with Bowater over purchase of the Bowater hardboard plant in South Carolina.

32 Bene raised his concern over the proposed partnership with Bowater in August 1964. Brewer to Bene, September 1, 1964, Brewer file, Weldwood-Westply Fonds PR-2308.

33 Brewer to Bene, December 18, 1964, Brewer file, Weldwood-Westply Fonds PR-2308.

34 Executive memo from Gene Brewer, June 7, 1964, Pulp mill transfer file #1, Weldwood-Westply Fonds PR-2308.

35 Lars Bratt to Ken Morrow, report, September 21, 1964, Weldwood-Westply Fonds PR-2308.

36 Weldwood was regularly meeting with Williston on other issues—for example, when they acquired Canadian Collieries. Even though Williston had no authority over the acquisition, Weldwood indicated to Williston that if he disapproved, they would not proceed. Bene to Brewer, March 1, 1964, Brewer file, Weldwood-Westply Fonds PR-2308.

37 Notes taken at Quesnel Lake Forest Association, October 20, 1964, CPP file. At this meeting Weldwood learned that United Pulp would offer assistance in the establishment of chipping facilities at sawmills. They also learned the arguments United Pulp was going to present to Williston in favour of the Squamish site, primarily the cost

of winterizing the construction site and a lesser effluent problem. H. Stilson to John Bene, memo, November 26, 1964, re: attendance at a meeting held by United Pulp in Squamish. Weldwood-Westply Fonds PR-2308. The questions lasted from 8:00 pm until midnight, and a brochure was handed out.

38 Disenchantment over the Squamish site was appearing in late September, primarily due to the cost of site preparation. Brewer to Bene, September 28, 1964, Brewer file, Weldwood-Westply Fonds PR-2308.

39 Bene to Brewer, August 21, 1964, Brewer file Weldwood-Westply Fonds PR-2308, summary of company position at that date: "it might be indicated to establish a second pulp mill in the Quesnel lake area in 10–15 years...."

40 Both Bene and New York considered Ellison's autocratic management style to be at odds with the corporate philosophy of Weldwood and US Plywood.

41 Lars Bratt to C.F. Farmer, Simons Engineering, October 20, 1964, advising him that the pulp mill study had been expanded to include feasibility of a pulp mill at Quesnel. Weldwood-Westply Fonds PR-2308.

42 A number of indicators had reinforced that Weldwood was more likely to succeed with the Quesnel location. For example, the Quesnel newspaper the *Cariboo Observer* ran a cartoon on October 15, 1964, showing a monstrous animal labelled "Squamish" sucking up the region's pulpwood. Premier Bennett was very pleased with the prospect of a pulp mill at Quesnel and, following a meeting with Bennett and Williston, Weldwood was assured that if they built at Quesnel they would get the timber they needed. Bene to Brewer, November 9, 1964, Weldwood-Westply Fonds PR-2308.

43 Bene to William Speare, MLA, "My associates and I were greatly encouraged by the support which we have received from so many people and associations in the Cariboo for our pulp mill project in Quesnel. It is to a very large degree thanks to you that public support has been so effectively behind this project." Weldwood-Westply Fonds PR-2308.

44 Ernst was already setting up equipment to process logs down to four inches.

45 Alex Fraser, public hearings, p. 91.

46 Bene to W. Stirling, December 21, 1964. It was actually land the company donated but they had the town buy the land and then donated the money back, as it provided a better tax benefit. Bene to Brewer, December 22, 1964, Brewer file, Weldwood-Westply Fonds PR-2308.

47 US Plywood was prepared to counter if Canfor or Northwood seemed to be getting too troublesome. A good friend of Brewer's owned a sawmill in Prince George and another at Fort St. James and would have quite happily sold his chips to Weldwood. Brewer to Bene, December 19, 1964, Brewer file, Weldwood-Westply Fonds PR-2308.

48 Brewer to Corydon Wagner, Tacoma, January 12, 1965, Weldwood-Westply Fonds PR-2308.

49 Bene to S. Antoville and Brewer, August 5, 1964, Brewer file, Weldwood-Westply Fonds PR-2308. Bene notes that he and Pit Desjardins often met with Williston to discuss forest policy and Williston's long-term aims.

50 K. Morrow to Bene, January 27, 1964; Brewer to Bene, February 23, 1965, Brewer file, Weldwood Collection, RBCM. Informed him of meeting with Dick Sandwell and then meeting with Price Brothers on Sandwell's advice. Weldwood-Westply Fonds PR-2308.

51 Price initially tried to interest US plywood in joining them at Squamish but this was clearly not going to happen. Price decided to drop Squamish and join Weldwood at Quesnel. Brewer to Bene, May 14, 1965; Brewer to Bene, June 7, 1965, Brewer file, Weldwood-Westply Fonds PR-2308.

52 Lars C. Bratt, "Trends in the Demand for Canadian Paper-Grade Sulfate Pulp: A Preliminary Analysis", April 9, 1965, Weldwood-Westply Fonds PR-2308.

53 Among the early indications is a report from Coverdale and Colpitts, April 6, 1967, Weldwood Collection, RBCM, stating there will be idle market pulp capacity by 1969 and that this will continue into 1970. This negativity is also reflected in a number of internal Weldwood and US plywood meetings.

54 Brewer to Bene, pulp file, Weldwood Collection, RBCM. The merger with Champion created other difficulties with New York, including a basic change in philosophy relating to acquisitions and growth. These nearly caused the cancellation of the Quesnel pulp project. Bene to Brewer, May 23, 1967; Bene to file notes re: conversation with Brewer, June 12, 1967; Bene to Brewer, December 22, 1967, Brewer file, Weldwood-Westply Fonds PR-2308.

55 Brewer to Corydon Wagner, Tacoma, September 24, 1965, Weldwood-Westply Fonds PR-2308. Brewer's opinion was that "Minister Williston's present thinking [is] that the expansion rush should be slowed a bit."

56 Bene to Brewer, January 18, 1966, Brewer file, Weldwood Collection, RBCM. US plywood in 1966 was prepared to begin construction in 1967, with a completion date of 1969, despite the poor economic conditions for market pulp. Brewer to Bene, February 3, 1966, Brewer file, Weldwood-Westply Fonds PR-2308.

57 Desjardins to Roger Montgomery, September 5, 1968, regarding a meeting between Brewer and Williston, Weldwood-Westply Fonds PR-2308.

CHAPTER 4

1 "Loggers Fired Upon," *Province*, June 17, 1967, p. 1; "Gunfire Heralds Stellako Drive," *Vancouver Sun*, June 17, 1967, p. 12; "Night Riders Eye Stellako Log Booms," *Vancouver Sun*, June 16, 1967, p. 1; Scott Honeyman, "Stellako Log Booms Sabotaged," *Citizen*, June 15, 1967, p. 1.

2   E.H. Tredcroft, "Water Resources Investigation Report on Stellako River" (BC Department of Lands and Forests, Water Rights Branch, 1943).

3   Canadian Council of Resource Ministers, *The Stellako River Log Drive, 1967* (Ottawa, 1967), pp. 1–3; Richard C. Bocking, *Mighty River: A Portrait of the Fraser* (Vancouver: Douglas & McIntyre, 1997), pp. 47–67; Matthew D. Evenden, *Fish versus Power: An Environmental History of the Fraser River* (Cambridge: Cambridge University Press, 2004), pp. 149–78; Bev Christensen, *Too Good To Be True: Alcan's Kemano Completion Project* (Vancouver: Talonbooks, 1995); J.E. Windsor and J.A. McVey, "Annihilation of Both Place and Sense of Place: The Experience of the Cheslatta T'en Canadian First Nation Within the Context of Large-Scale Environmental Projects," *Geographical Journal* 171 (June 2005), pp. 146–65.

4   Relevant forest histories which neglect the Stellako controversy include Gordon Hak, *Capital and Labour in the British Columbia Forest Industry, 1934–1974* (Vancouver: UBC Press, 2007); Ken Drushka, *Tie Hackers to Timber Harvesters: The History of Logging in British Columbia's Interior* (Madeira Park: Harbour Publishing, 1998). For brief accounts in the fisheries literature see Cicely Lyons, *Salmon: Our Heritage* (Vancouver: Mitchell Press, 1969), pp. 623–25; John F. Roos, *Restoring Fraser River Salmon: A History of the International Pacific Salmon Fisheries Commission, 1937–1985* (Vancouver: Pacific Salmon Commission, n.d.), pp. 180–82. Both Arn Keeling and Jeremy Wilson mention the Stellako controversy but provide little in the way of analysis. See Jeremy Wilson, *Talk and Log: Wilderness Politics in British Columbia* (Vancouver: UBC Press, 1998), p. 105; Arn M. Keeling, "The Effluent Society: Water Pollution and Environmental Politics in British Columbia, 1889–1980," (PhD Thesis, University of British Columbia, 2004), p. 295. For a brief but insightful discussion see Alan George Phillips, "Jurisdictional Conflicts in Resource Management: Perspectives on the Canadian West Coast Commercial Fishing Industry," (MA Thesis, University of Victoria, 1984), pp. 94–102. For a treatment of the 1966 drive see Richard A. Rajala, "'This Wasteful Use of a River': Log Driving, Conservation, and British Columbia's Stellako River Controversy, 1965–72," *BC Studies* no. 165 (Spring 2010), pp. 31–74.

5   See Arn Keeling, "'Sink or Swim': Water Pollution and Environmental Politics in Vancouver, 1889–1975," *BC Studies* 142/143 (Summer/Autumn 2004), pp. 69–101. Insightful works on postwar modernization and its consequences include Arn Keeling, "'A Dynamic not a Static Conception': The Conservation Thought of Roderick Haig-Brown," *Pacific Historical Review* 71 (May 2002), pp. 239–68; Arn Keeling and Robert McDonald, "The Profligate Province: Roderick Haig-Brown and the Modernization of British Columbia," *Journal of Canadian Studies* 36 (Fall 2001), pp. 7–23; Tina Loo, "People in the Way: Modernity, Environment, and Society on the Arrow Lakes," *BC Studies* 142/143 (Summer/Autumn 2004), pp. 161–96; Tina Loo, "Disturbing the Peace:

Environmental Change and the Scales of Justice on a Northern River," *Environmental History* 12 (October 2007), pp. 895-919.

6   See, for example, Angus P. MacBean, "The Integrated Use of Public Forests," *Proceedings, Western Forestry and Conservation Association* (Portland, 1960), pp. 94-97.

7   Roderick Haig-Brown, "Let Them Eat Sawdust," *Forest and Outdoors* 47 (October 1951), pp. 10-12.

8   Frank Millerd, "The Evolution of Management of the Canadian Pacific Salmon Fishery," *Digital Library of the Commons*, http://olc.dlib.indiana.edu.archive/00000999 (December 12, 2007); Douglas M. Swenerton, *A History of Pacific Fisheries Policy* (Ottawa: Department of Fisheries and Oceans, 1993), p. 12; K.R.F. Denniston, "Water in British Columbia and its Administration," *Proceedings of the Fourth Annual Game Convention* (Vancouver, 1950), pp. 115-19; V. Raudsepp, "Some Observations on Water Resource Management in British Columbia," (Victoria: Water Investigations Branch, BC Water Resources Service, Department of Lands, Forests and Water Resources, n.d.), p. 7, box 6, Ray Williston Papers, University of Victoria, Archives and Special Collections.

9   W.A. Clemons, "Some Historical Aspects of the Fisheries Resources of British Columbia," *Transactions of the Ninth British Columbia Natural Resources Conference* (Victoria: BC Natural Resources Conference, 1956), p.129; Lyons, *Salmon: Our Heritage*, pp. 476, 526-27; Wilson, *Talk and Log*, pp. 91-92; W.R. Hourston, "The Legal and Administrative Framework of the Fishing Industry," *Transactions of the Thirteenth British Columbia Natural Resources Conference* (Victoria: BC Natural Resources Conference, 1961), pp. 262-64.

10   Thomas L. Burton, *Natural Resource Policy in Canada: Issues and Perspectives* (Toronto: McLelland and Stewart, 1972), pp. 97-100; Graeme Wynn, *Canada and Arctic North America: An Environmental History* (Santa Barbara: ABC-CLIO, 2007), pp. 211-13.

11   P. Scott and W. Schovwenberg, "Environmental Foresight and Salmon: New Canadian Developments," in Derek V. Ellis, ed., *Pacific Salmon Management for People* (Victoria: University of Victoria, 1977), p. 126; Richard A. Rajala, "'Streams Being Ruined From a Salmon Producing Standpoint': Clearcutting, Fish Habitat, and Forest Regulation in British Columbia, 1900-45," *BC Studies* no. 176 (Winter 2012/13), pp. 93-132; Canada, *Fifth Annual Report of the Department of Fisheries, 1934-35* (Ottawa: King's Printer, 1935), pp. 173-75; Canada, *Sixth Annual Report of the Department of Fisheries, 1935-36* (Ottawa: King's Printer, 1936), pp.217-18; Canada, *Eleventh Report of the Department of Fisheries, 1940-41* (Ottawa: King's Printer, 1941), pp.72-74.

12   Richard A. Rajala, "'Nonsensical and a Contradiction in Terms': Multiple Use Forestry, Clearcutting, and the Politics of Salmon Habitat in British Columbia, 1945-1970," *BC Studies* No. 183 (Autumn 2014), pp. 89-127.

13   Roderick Haig-Brown, "Fish and Wildlife in the Development of BC's Future," *British Columbia Digest* (July-August 1966), pp. 32-40.

14   *Stellako River Log Drive*, Mike Poole, Dir., Canadian Broadcasting Corporation, 1966.

15 L.H. Eyres, "Address of Welcome," *Proceedings of the Fourth British Columbia Natural Resources Conference* (Victoria, 1951), pp. 1-2; *Stellako River Log Drive*, Mike Poole, Dir., Canadian Broadcasting Corporation, 1966.

16 Phillips, "Jurisdictional Conflicts," p. 102; Anthony H.J. Dorsey, Michael W. McPhee and Sam Sydneysmith, *Salmon Protection and the BC Coastal Forest Industry: Environmental Regulation as a Bargaining Process* (Vancouver: Westwater Research Centre, University of British Columbia, 1980), pp. 76-77.

17 F.W. Lindsay, "Land of the Sunset Trail," *Cariboo and Northern British Columbia Digest* 2 (Summer 1946), pp. 87-90.

18 Douglas Hudson, "Internal Colonialism and Industrial Capitalism," in Thomas Thorner, ed., *Sa Ts'e: Historical Perspectives on Northern British Columbia* (Prince George: College of New Caledonia Press, 1989), pp. 190-194; Morris Zazlow, *The Opening of the Canadian North, 1870–1914* (Toronto: McClelland and Stewart, 1971), pp. 202-07; Richard A. Rajala, *Up-Coast: Forests and Industry on British Columbia's North Coast, 1870–2005* (Victoria: Royal British Columbia Museum, 2006), pp. 56-57; Ken Drushka, *Tie Hackers to Timber Harvesters: The History of Logging in British Columbia's Interior* (Madeira Park: Harbour Publishing, 1998), pp. 102-09; Doris Ray with Grace and Roy Foote, "Ties for the Railroad," in *Deeper Roots and Greener Pastures* (Fraser Lake: Fraser Lake and District Historical Society, 1986), pp. 92-93; "Paragraphs," *Western Lumberman* 19 (October 1922), p. 44; "Notes From the North," *Pacific Coast Lumberman* 7 (February 1923), p. 32; "Northern Logging Activities," *British Columbia Lumberman* 8 (March 1924), p. 98 (hereafter *BCL*); "New Mill Replaces One Destroyed by Fire," *Western Lumberman* 23 (October 1926), p. 18.

19 Rajala, *Up-Coast*, p. 83; Drushka, *Tie Hackers to Timber Harvesters*, pp. 108-109; "Prince Rupert District," *BCL* 11 (June 1927), p. 34; G.A. Hunter, "Northern British Columbia," *BCL* 12 (October 1928), p. 32; G.A. Hunter, "Northern British Columbia," *BCL* 14 (March 1930), p. 20; "Northern British Columbia," *BCL* 17 (June 1933), p. 28; Club members, "Fraser Lake Sawmills," in *Deeper Roots and Greener Pastures*, pp. 96-98.

20 Prince George forest district, annual management report, 1945, box 1, Prince George forest district records (hereafter GR1110), BC Archives (hereafter BCA); Richard A. Rajala, "Logging British Columbia," (unpublished report, Canada Science and Technology Museum, 1999), pp. 109-11; Club members, "Fraser Lake Sawmills," *Deeper Roots and Greener Pastures*, pp. 98-100; Doris Ray with Harvey MacDonald, "Stellako River Log Drives," *Deeper Roots and Greener Pastures*, p. 102.

21 Club members, "Fraser River Sawmills," *Deeper Roots and Greener Pastures*, p. 100.

22 C.E. Stenton, "The Effects on Fresh Water Fisheries of Development Construction in British Columbia," *Canadian Fish Culturalist* 25 (October 1959), pp. 54-56; William E. Ricker, "Cycle Dominance Among the Fraser Sockeye," *Ecology* 31 (January 1950), pp. 6-26; Roos, *Restoring Fraser River Salmon*, p. 282.

23 Matthew Evenden, "Social and Environmental Change at Hell's Gate, British Columbia," *Journal of Historical Geography* 30 (2004), pp. 130-53; J. Richard Dunn, "Charles Henry Gilbert (1859-1928): An Early Fisheries Biologist and His Contributions to Knowledge of Pacific Salmon (Oncorhynchus spp.)," *Reviews in Fisheries Science* 42 (1996), pp. 133-84; Richard A. Rajala, "The West Coast Salmon Rush," *Legion Magazine* 74 (November/December 1999), pp. 25-27; Canada Department of Fisheries and the International Pacific Salmon Fisheries Commission, in Collaboration with the Fish and Wildlife Branch of the BC Department of Recreation and Conservation, *Effects of Log Driving on the Salmon and Trout Populations in the Stellako River* (Vancouver: International Pacific Salmon Fisheries Commission, 1966), p. 3 (hereafter cited as IPSFC, *Effects of Log Driving*); Hudson "Internal Colonialism," pp. 179-84.

24 "The Decline of the Sockeye," *Industrial Progress and Commercial Record* 5 (September 1917), pp. 385-90; Joseph Taylor III, "Making Salmon: The Political Economy of Fishery Science and the Road Not Taken," *Journal of the History of Biology* 31 (1998), pp. 33-59; "BC Salmon Hatcheries to be Closed," *Western Fisheries* 11 (April 1936), p. 6 ; Matthew Evenden, "Remaking Hell's Gate: Salmon, Science and the Fraser River, 1938-1948," *BC Studies* 127 (Autumn 2000), pp. 47-83; Roos, *Restoring Fraser River Salmon*, pp. 90-98.

25 IPSFC, *Effects of Log Driving*, pp. 3-5; A. Bryan Williams, *Fish and Game in British Columbia* (Vancouver: Sun Directories, 1935), pp. 94-95; W.F. Pochin, *Angling and Hunting in British Columbia* (Vancouver: Sun Directories, 1946), p. 59; Doris Ray, "Tourism and Outdoor Recreation," *Deeper Roots and Greener Pastures*, p. 125; see the Nithi Lodge advertisement in *Cariboo and Northwest Digest* 6 (May-June 1950), p. 37; Audrey Smedley, "East End of Francois Lake," *Nechako Chronicle*, May 26, 1966, p. 5; F.W. Lindsay , "Land of the Sunset Trail," *Cariboo and Northern British Columbia Digest* (Summer 1946), p. 20; Bruce Hutchison, *The Fraser* (Toronto: Clarke, Irwin & Company, 1950), p. 296.

26 "Increase in Demand and Price for District Rail Tie Cutters," *Review*, October 25, 1962, p. 1; Club members, "Fraser Lake Sawmills," *Deeper Roots and Greener Pastures*, p. 100; IPSFC, *The Effects of Log Driving*, pp. 16-17; "Sawmill Directory, Prince George District," *BCL* 40 (December 1956), p. 11; Annual management report, ranger district no. 9, 1946, box 1, GR1110, BCA; Drushka, *Tie Hackers to Timber Harvesters*, p. 147.

27 Lawrence A. De Grace, "Development of Forest Resources in the Prince George Region," *Proceedings of the Western Forestry and Conservation Association* (Portland, 1960), p. 55; "Swing to Interior Logging and Cutting," *BCL* 40 (May 1956), p. 19; Drushka, *Tie Hackers to Timber Harvesters*, pp. 164-65; Annual management report, Vanderhoof ranger district, box 1, GR1110, BCA; IPSFC, *Effects of Log Driving*, p. 17; Annual management report, ranger district no. 11, 1959, box 1, GR1110, BCA.

28 Eileen Williston and Betty Keller, *Forests, Power and Policy: The Legacy of Ray Williston* (Prince George: Caitlin Books, 1997), pp. 134-42; Ray Williston, "A Measuring Up," *British Columbia Digest* 17 (January-February 1961), pp. 12, 40-42; Robert H. Forbes, "BC Interior: Sawlog-Pulpwood Integration," *BCL* 47 (September 1963), pp. 16-20.

29 Drushka, *From Tie Hackers to Timber Harvesters*, pp. 175-79; "Prince George Pulp Licence Granted," *BCL* 46 (August 1962), p. 39; "Northwood to Build Chip Storage Area," *Truck Logger* 20 (November 1964), p. 60; "This is it—Fastest Growing City in the Province," *Citizen*, Travel Supplement, April 1965, p. 12; *Citizen*, April 28, 1965, p. 6; "Third Pulp Mill," *Citizen*, May 11, 1965, p. 1; Rajala, "Logging British Columbia," pp. 146-147.

30 "High Bidding in Pulp Chip Market," *Truck Logger* 20 (August 1964), p. 52; The *"ABC" British Columbia Lumber Trade Directory and Year Book, 1963* (Vancouver: Progress Publishing, 1964), p. 82; Club members, "Fraser Lake Sawmills," *Deeper Roots and Greener Pastures*, p. 100; IPSFC, *Effects of Log Driving*, p. 17; *Nechako Chronicle*, April 15, 1965, p. 7.

31 "Forest Road Programme," *Truck Logger* 15 (January 1959), pp. 38, 42; L.A. De Grace, "Northern Commentary: Access vs. Established Location," *Truck Logger* 16 (July 1960), pp. 14-15.

32 Roderick Haig-Brown, "Canada's Pacific Salmon," *Canadian Geographical Journal* 44 (March 1952), pp. 109-127; Roos, *Restoring Fraser River Salmon*, pp. 214-26; Dixon Mackinnon, "Man-Made Spawning Channels for Pacific Salmon," *Canadian Geographical Journal* 63 (July 1961), pp. 28-39; United Fishermen and Allied Workers Union, "Presentation to the Premier and Executive Council of British Columbia," February 21, 1962, p. 5, BC Legislative Library; Rajala, "'Nonsensical and a Contradiction,'" p. 103; Evenden, *Fish Versus Power*, pp.179-29; Roderick Haig-Brown, "Fish Hatcheries…No Substitute for Stream Protection," *BC Outdoors* 29 (July-August 1973), pp. 16-21.

33 William G. Rector, "From Woods to Sawmill: Transportation Problems in Logging," *Agricultural History* 23 (October 1949), pp. 239-44; Michael Williams, *Americans and Their Forests: A Historical Geography* (Cambridge: Cambridge University Press, 1992), pp. 97-100, 170-75; Paul R. Josephson, *Industrialized Nature: Brute Force Technology and the Transformation of the Natural World* (Washington: Island Press, 2002), pp. 69-84; Richard A. Rajala, "The Forest Industry in Eastern Canada: An Overview," in C. Ross Silversides, *Broadaxe to Flying Shear: The Mechanization of Forest Harvesting East of the Rockies* (Ottawa: National Museum of Science and Technology, 1997), pp. 129-30; Stephen Bocking, "Encountering Biodiversity: Ecology, Ideas, Action," in *Biodiversity in Canada: Ecology, Ideas, and Action*, ed. Stephen Bocking (Peterborough: Broadview Press, 2000), pp. 3-30; Anthony Netboy, *Salmon: The World's Most Harassed Fish* (London: Andre Deutsch, 1980), pp. 188-205.

34 William G. Robbins, *Landscapes of Promise: The Oregon Story, 1800–1940* (Seattle: University of Washington Press, 1997), pp. 186–87; Robert Bunting, "Abundance and the Forests of the Douglas-Fir Bioregion, 1840–1920," *Environmental History Review* 18 (Winter 1994), pp. 45–46; Henry O. Wendler and Gene Deschamps, "Logging Dams on Coastal Washington Streams," *Fisheries Research Papers, Washington Department of Fisheries* 1 (February 1955), pp. 27–38; Donald MacKay, *The Lumberjacks* (Toronto: McGraw-Hill Ryerson, 1978), p. 143; Isabel K. Edwards, "Logging in the Early Days," *Thunderbird*, November 13, 1979, p. 5; Brendan O'Donnell, *Indian and Non-Native Use of the Cowichan and Koksilah Rivers: An Historical Perspective* (Ottawa: Fisheries and Oceans Canada, 1998), pp. 43–58; Richard A. Rajala, *The Legacy and the Challenge: A Century of the Forest Industry at Cowichan Lake* (Lake Cowichan: Lake Cowichan Heritage Advisory Committee, 1993), pp. 21–22; Arnold M. McCombs and Wilfred W. Chittenden, *The Harrison-Chehalis Challenge* (Harrison Hot Springs: Treeline Publishing, 1988), pp. 10–11; Canada, *Annual Report of the Department of Marine and Fisheries, 1910–11* (Ottawa: King's Printer, 1911), p. 401. For a useful overview see Jim Lichatowich, *Salmon Without Rivers: A History of the Pacific Salmon Crisis* (Washington: Island Press, 1999), pp. 60–64.

35 Joyce Dunn, *A Town Called Chase* (Penticton: Theytus Books, 1986), pp. 91–94; "Labor Needed at Golden," *Western Lumberman* 5 (January 1908), p. 13; "New Type of Flume in the Mountains," *Western Lumberman* 11 (January 1914), pp. 36–37; Rajala, "Logging British Columbia," pp.72–73; C. Heather Allen, "Lumber and Salmon: A History of the Adams River Lumber Company," *Wildlife Review* 8 (Summer 1979), pp. 22–24.

36 Allen, "Lumber and Salmon," p. 24; Evenden, *Fish versus Power*, pp. 71–72; C. Heather Allen, "Return of the Sockeye: Can We Help Them Spawn Again in the Upper Adams?" *Wildlife Review* 9 (Spring 1982), pp. 30–31; Bocking, *Mighty River*, pp. 145–146; James R. Sedell and Wayne S. Duval, *Water Transportation and Storage of Logs—USDA Forest Service Technical Report PN–186* (Portland: Pacific Northwest Forest and Range Experiment Station, 1985), pp. 9–10; "Facts About the Adams River Sockeye Run," *Fisherman*, November 16, 1954, p. 5. For coverage of the water licence renewal controversy see "Industry to Protest License for Adams River Timber Co.," *Fisherman*, July 4, 1944, p. 1; "Huge Salmon Loss if Water License Granted," *Fisherman*, July 11, 1944, p. 1; "Adams River Log License Turned Down," *Fisherman*, August 8, 1944, p. 1.

37 Bruce S. Wright, "Effect of Stream Driving on Fish, Wildlife and Recreation," *Woodlands Review* (November 1962), pp. 433–39; Vadim D. Vladykov, "The Effects of Man-Made Changes in Fresh Water in the Province of Quebec," *Canadian Fish Culturalist* 25 (October 1959), pp. 7–12; "Fewer River Drives, Less Pollution," *Canadian Forest Industries* 85 (March 1965), p. 17; A.L. Pritchard, "The Effects of Man-Made Changes in Fresh Water in the Maritime Provinces," *Canadian Fish Culturalist* 25 (October 1959), pp. 3–6.

38   J.T. Pennell, "Effects on Fresh Water Fisheries of Forestry Practices," *Canadian Fish Culturalist* 25 (October 1959), pp. 27-31; A.J. Whitmore, "Brief on Behalf of the Department of Fisheries of Canada, Presented by the Chief Supervisor of Fisheries, Pacific Area, Regarding Certain Aspects of the Fisheries of British Columbia in Relation to the Forest Resources," box 12, BC Commission on Forest Resources, 1955, BCA; "Northern News," *BCL* 36 (November 1952), p. 107; "Annual River Drive May Be Abandoned," *BCL* 37 (October 1953), p. 19; Arthur G. Downs, "From Trees to Textiles," *Cariboo and Northwest Digest* 6 (May-June 1950), p.16; Rajala, *Up-Coast*, pp. 147-148; "Modern Tugs Ply Upper Fraser," *Cariboo and Northwest Digest* 7 (June 1951), p. 18; "New Role for Fraser," *Truck Logger* 112 (April 1956), pp. 7-8.

39   Gordon Sloan, *The Forest Resources of British Columbia, Volume 1* (Victoria: Queen's Printer, 1957), pp. 729-31; IPSFC, *Annual Report of the International Pacific Salmon Fisheries Commission, 1952* (Vancouver: Wriggley Printing, 1953), pp. 7-8; IPSFC, *Annual Report of the International Pacific Salmon Fisheries Commission, 1956* (Vancouver: Campbell and Smith, 1957), p. 5.

40   "Weaver Creek Channel Contract $200,000," *Western Fisheries* 69 (January 1965), p. 30 (hereafter *WF*); "Channels, Hatcheries and Other Fraser Fish Facilities," *WF* 73 (October 1966), pp. 18-22; IPSFC, *Annual Report of the International Pacific Salmon Fisheries Commission, 1962* (Vancouver: Wrigley Printing, 1963), p. 5; Roos, *Restoring Fraser River Salmon*, pp. 219-21; IPSFC, *Annual Report of the International Pacific Salmon Fisheries Commission, 1965* (Vancouver: Wrigley Printing, 1966), p. 5.

41   Annual management report, ranger district no. 1, 1954; Annual management report ranger district no. 2, 1957, box 1, GR1110, BCA; Thomas G. Wright, "The Canadian Spruce Forest," *Forestry Chronicle* 35 (December 1959), pp. 291-97; "Cariboo Loggers Have Rediscovered the Fraser," *BCL* 42 (May 1958), pp. 16-20; "Swenske Hot-Rod Wrangles River Logs," *BCL* 44 (July 1960), p. 56; "Productive Season," *BCL* 46 (July 1962), p. 38; Hugh Weatherby, "Western Plywood at Quesnel," *Timber of Canada* 20 (December 1959), pp. 54-58.

42   Joseph Des Champs, "Fraser Drive is Rough But Profitable," *Canada Lumberman* 82 (June 1962), pp. 24-28; Doug Colwell, "The Last Log Drive," *Forest Talk* 5 (Summer 1981), pp. 11-17.

43   Richard Wright, "Death of the Rivers," *Western Fish and Game* 4 (September 1969), pp. 20-23; "Letters," *Western Fish and Game* 4 (November 1969), pp. 6-7.

44   "BC's Nass River Opened for Logging," *Canada Lumberman* (November 1959), p. 45; "Columbia Cellulose Nass River Log Flow Resumed," *BCL* 43 (October 1959), pp. 16-18; "River Drive Going Strong," *Forest Industries* 91 (May 1964), pp. 74-75; *Canada Gazette* 99 (January 13, 1965), p. 25.

45   "Logs 'Threaten Salmon,' Oolichan," *Vancouver Sun*, July 5, 1968, p. 30; "Colcel's Log Drive Safeguard's Fish," *Vancouver Province*, August 29, 1968, p. 23; "Big Log Drive in the Works," *Canadian Pulp and Paper Industry* 21 (September 1968), p. 8; "License Plan Scored by Northern Parley," *Fisherman*, January 17, 1969, p. 11; "Nass Log Drive Research Inadequate, Says Calder," January 24, 1969, p. 6; "Hourston Reviews 1968 Fishery," *Fisherman*, February 14, 1969, p. 8; "End Log Drives, Fishermen Urge," *Vancouver Sun*, April 26, 1969, p. 32; Richard Morgan, "'Credibility Gap' Widens Over Nass Log Drives," *Western Fisheries* 77 (March 1969), pp. 44-46.

46   Lyons, *Salmon*, pp. 526-27; Rajala, "Clearcutting, Multiple Use," pp. 27-29.

47   "Francois Lake," *Review*, May 26, 1960, p. 2; "Francois Lake," *Review*, June, 15, 1961, p. 2; IPSFC, *Annual Report of the International Pacific Salmon Commission*, 1964 (Vancouver: Wrigley Printing, 1965), p. 31.

48   *Canada Gazette* 98 (May 27, 1964), p. 189; IPSFC, *The Effects of Log Driving*, pp. 1, 14-15; C.H. Clay, "Report on a Proposal to Drive Logs by Means of a Splash Dam on the Kitsumgallum River," October 12, 1954, BC Marine Resources Branch records, box 12, GR1118, BCA.

49   IPSFC, *Effects of Log Driving*, p. 16; "North Central Zone Rod and Gun Clubs Meet in Prince George," *Review*, October 22, 1959, p. 1; "Bill MacDonald Says 'Fly Fishing is for Everyone,'" *Forest and Outdoors* 52 (June 1956), p. 18; S.B. Smith, "Sport Fish of British Columbia," *BC Digest* 17 (June 1961), pp. 15, 39-42; "Tear-Drop Trailers," *BC Motorist* 2 (March-April 1963), p. 16; Jack Chestnutt, "Camping in the Grand Manner," *BC Motorist* 5 (May- June 1966), pp. 26-27; "Francois Lake," *Review*, May 19, 1960, p. 2; "Francois Lake," *Review*, June 9, 1960, p. 3; "Francois Lake-Garden of Eden," *Review*, August 30, 1962, p. 2; "More Tourists But Resort Business Down," *Review*, August 9, 1962, p. 1; "Fishing News," *Observer*, August 22, 1964, p. 1.

50   "Log Drive Stalled, to Protect Salmon," *Citizen*, March 25, 1965, p. 4; Dick Phillips, "Highway No. 16," *British Columbia Digest* 20 (November-December 1964), pp. 25-27; Dick Phillips, "Highway No. 16," *British Columbia Digest* 21 (January-February 1965), pp. 21-22; Ray Williston, "Steelhead Running in North Central BC," *Review*, October 8, 1964, p. 1; "Outdoors with Salmo," *Citizen*, March 25, 1965, p. 5; Salmo, "Fishing the Land of the Totem," *British Columbia Digest* 21 (July-August 1965), p. 39; "Outdoors with Salmo," *Citizen*, April 2, 1965, p. 9.

51   *Canada Gazette* 99 (July 14, 1965), p. 1074; Roos, *Restoring Fraser River Salmon*, p. 180; "Panel Permits Log Run in River," *Citizen*, June 1, 1965, p. 3.

52   "Northern Interior Lumbermen's Association," *Truck Logger* (April 1952), p. 8; Bob Gallagher, "Northern Interior Lumbermen's Association," *Truck Logger* (August 1953), p.22; Bob Gallagher, "Northern Interior Lumbermen's Association," *Truck Logger* (September 1953), p. 44; BCL 37 (August 1953), p. 30; "Northern Interior," BCL 38 (January 1954), pp. 14-16; "Wants Probe on Stellako," *Citizen*, July 14, 1965, p. 1.

53 "Stellako Log Drive Safe," *Citizen*, June 9, 1965, p. 1; IPSFC, *Effects of Log Driving*, p. 1.

54 IPSFC, *Effects of Log Driving*, pp. 22-34.

55 "Stellako River Resorts Angry," *Citizen*, June 10, 1965, p. 1; "Fuss Not Over Logs," *Citizen*, June 11, 1965, p. 1; "'Crazy Cyril' Does it Again," *Lakes District News*, February 14, 1967, p. 2; "Forestry Well Represented," *TL* 21 (February 1965), p. 11; "Wants Probe on Stellako," *Citizen*, July 14, 1965, p. 1; "Wants Log Run Facts," *Citizen*, June 16, 1965, p. 1.

56 IPSFC, *Effects of Log Driving*, pp. 19, 47-48, 60.

57 Howard Paish, "Requiem for a Park," *BC Outdoors* 23 (July-August 1967), pp. 39-43; Alex Merriman, "Vancouver Island," *BC Outdoors* 22 (May-June 1966), pp. 26-28; Keeling, "A Dynamic, Not a Static Conception," pp. 258-60; Roderick Haig-Brown, *The Living Land: An Account of the Natural Resources of British Columbia* (Toronto: MacMillan, 1961), pp. 189-94; Graeme Wynn and Arn Keeling, "'The Park...Is a Mess': Development and Degradation in British Columbia's First Provincial Park," *BC Studies* 170 (Summer 2011), pp. 119-50.

58 "Recreation Policy," *Victoria Daily Times* June 22, 1965, p. 4; "Fish, Game Studies Deforestation Problem," *Citizen*, April 22, 1965, p. 3; Rajala, "'Nonsensical and a Contradiction,'" pp. 110-12..

59 "Writer Detests Everything BC Stands For Now," *Victoria Daily Times*, June 22, 1965, p. 2; "Haig-Brown Attack Stuns Author Meet," *Victoria Daily Times*, June 22, 1965, p. 1; Keeling and McDonald, "The Profligate Province," pp. 8-9; Roland Arnet, "Tofino," *Western Fisheries* 71 (October 1965), pp. 45-46.

60 "Naturalist Lashes Province of BC," *Citizen*, June 23, 1965, p. 16; "Or Will They?" *Citizen* July 2, 1965, p. 2; "Stellako," *Citizen*, July 14, 1965, p. 2.

61 Dick Phillips, "Prince George-Prince Rupert," *British Columbia Digest* 21 (July-August 1965), pp. 28-29.

62 Geoff Warden, "Cariboo and Chilcotin," *British Columbia Digest* 21 (November-December 1965), pp. 29-30. For analysis of the BC Wildlife Federation's shift in focus see John Gordon Terpenning, "The BC Wildlife Federation and Government: A Comparative Study of Pressure Group and Government Interaction for Two Periods, 1947 to 1957, and 1958 to 1975 (MA thesis, University of Victoria, 1982).

63 "From Our Readers," *British Columbia Digest* 21 (September-October 1965), p. 42.

64 Ibid.

65 Ibid.

66 "Foresters Work With Nature" *Forest and Mill* 15 (October 1961), p. 8; Gordon Hak, "Populism and the 1952 Social Credit Breakthrough in British Columbia," *Canadian Historical Review* 85 (June 2004), pp. 277-96.

67 Dick Phillips, "Prince George-Prince Rupert," *British Columbia Digest* 21 (September-October 1965), pp. 4, 23.

68 Ibid.

69 Ibid.

70 "Co-ordinating Body Urged on Resource Management," *Victoria Daily Times*, June 14, 1965, p. 35; "Notes on a Meeting Held in Victoria, BC, Oct. 19, 1965, Between Representatives of the Provincial Bureau of Commercial Fisheries, the Provincial Fish and Game Branch, the British Columbia Forest Service and the Department of Fisheries, to Informally Discuss Areas of Conflict Between the Forest Industry and Fisheries," appendix 5, Federal-Provincial BC Fisheries Committee, Nanaimo, November 5, 1965, pp. 2–3, Pacific Biological Station Library.

71 "Notes on a Meeting," pp. 2–3.

72 "Notes on Meeting in Office of Chief Supervisor of Fisheries with Columbia's Cellulose Co. to Discuss Fisheries Problems Related to Proposal to Drive Logs on the Kitsumgallum River," March 10, 1955, box 12, GR1118, BCA.

73 A.J. Whitmore to G.J. Alexander, March 18, 1955, box 12, GR1118, BCA.

74 G.J. Alexander to A.J. Whitmore, March 25, 1955, box 12, GR1118, BCA.

75 Richard A. Rajala, *Clearcutting the Pacific Rain Forest: Production, Science and Regulation* (Vancouver: UBC Press, 1998), pp. 211–14; Rajala, "'Nonsensical and a Contradiction,'" pp. 116-17; "Brief to the Special Committee on Fisheries, the Legislative Assembly of British Columbia, by the Fisheries Association of British Columbia," March 14, 1963, pp. 22–23, BC Legislative Library; Angus P. MacBean, "The Integrated Use of Public Forests," *Proceedings of the Western Forestry and Conservation Association* (Portland: WFCA, 1960), pp. 94–97.

76 R.G. McMynn, "Man, Water, and Fish," *British Columbia Digest* 22 (May-June 1966), pp. 36–42; "Bigger Fisheries Role by Province One of McMynn Report Proposals," *Fisherman*, February 18, 1966, p. 3.

77 E.E. (Ted) Barsby, "Pollution and People," *British Columbia Digest* 22 (January-February 1966), pp. 41–42; Norman Hacking, "A Tragic Situation," *Vancouver Province*, June 23, 1966, p. 12. The BC Federation of Fish and Game Clubs became known as the BC Wildlife Federation in 1966 to "reflect the broader thinking of the organization." See Howard Paish, "BC Wildlife Federation Marks 10th Birthday," *British Columbia Digest* 22 (March–April 1966), pp. 12, 32–33.

78 "Hourston Urged to See Owikeno Logging Damage," *Fisherman*, July 16, 1965, p. 1; "Common Interests Far Outweigh Commercial, Sport Differences," *Fisherman*, April 1, 1966, pp. 7, 10; "Delegates Question Hourston," *Fisherman*, April 1, 1966, p. 11; "BC Wildlife Federation Welcomes First Union," *Fisherman*, April 22, 1966, p. 12.

79 "Notes on a Meeting Held in Vancouver April 18, 1966, Between Representatives of the International Pacific Salmon Fisheries Commission, the Provincial Fish and Wildlife Branch, the Department of Fisheries and Fraser Lake Sawmills Ltd. to Discuss the Subject of Proposed Log Driving on the Stellako River," p. 1, GR1118, box 12, BCA.

80 Ibid., p. 2

81 Ibid., pp. 3-5.

82 W.R. Hourston to Fraser Lake Sawmills, May 4, 1966; R.G. McMynn to W.R. Hourston, May 31, 1966, box 12, GR1118, BCA.

83 For a summary of Williston's comments see Howard Paish, "Stellako Log Drive—Resource Use or Resource Abuse," *British Columbia Digest* 22 (September–October 1966), pp. 9, 37; Rajala, "'Nonsensical and a Contradiction,'" pp. 118-120.

84 Roderick Haig-Brown, "Fish, Wildlife and Outdoor Recreation in BC Development," Proceedings, Ninth Annual Convention of the BC Wildlife Federation, Prince George, May 4-7, 1966. For the published version of Haig-Brown's address see "Fish and Wildlife in the Development of BC's Future," *British Columbia Digest* 22 (July–August 1966), pp. 32-40.

85 Salmo, "Wildlife vs. Industry," *Citizen*, May 13, 1966, p. 10.

86 For discussion of the Columbia River Treaty, the Two Rivers Project and the Peace River development see Neil Swainson, *Conflict Over the Columbia: The Canadian Background to an Historic Treaty* (Montreal: McGill-Queen's University Press, 1979); John R. Krutilla, *The Columbia River Treaty: An International Evaluation* (Washington: Resources for the Future, 1963); David J. Mitchell, *W.A.C. Bennett and the Rise of British Columbia* (Vancouver: Douglas & McIntyre, 1987), pp. 296-375; Karl Froschauer, *White Gold: Hydroelectric Power in Canada* (Vancouver: UBC Press, 1999), pp. 174-210; Martin Robin, *Pillars of Profit: The Company Province, 1934–1972* (Toronto: McLelland and Stewart, 1973), pp. 221-49. For an understanding of the PGE see John R. Wedley, "A Development Tool: W.A.C. Bennett and the PGE Railway," *BC Studies* 117 (Spring 1998), pp. 29-50. Mackenzie's development is the subject of Greg Halseth and Lana Sullivan, *Building Community in an Instant Town: A Social Geography of Mackenzie and Tumbler Ridge* (Prince George: UNBC Press, 2002); see also Williston and Keller, *Forests, Power and Policy,* pp. 212-13.

87 Paddy Sherman, *Bennett* (Toronto: McLelland and Stewart, 1966), pp. 285-301; R.M. Burns, "British Columbia and the Canadian Federation," in *A History of British Columbia: Selected Readings*, ed. Patricia E. Roy (Toronto: Copp Clark Pitman, 1989), pp. 156-73; Norman J. Ruff, "British Columbia and Canadian Federalism," in *The Reins of Power: Governing British Columbia*, eds. J. Terrence Morley, Norman J. Ruff, Neil A. Swainson, R. Jeremy Wilson and Walter D. Young (Vancouver: Douglas & McIntyre, 1983), pp. 271-304; "Ottawa Widening Gulf Premier Bennett Says" *Prince Rupert Daily News*, May 7, 1965, p. 1; "Give Up Offshore Mineral Claim, Bennett Urges Ottawa," *Prince Rupert Daily News*, June 1, 1965, p. 4; "Gaglardi Tells Ottawa to 'Behave,'" *Prince Rupert Daily News,* June 11, 1965, p. 1; "Ottawa Stands Firm in Offshore Rights Row," *Prince Rupert Daily News*, July 21, 1965, p. 1.

88   R.H. (Dick) Phillips, "Pollution Committee Report," Proceedings of the Ninth Annual BC Wildlife Federation Convention, Prince George, May 4-7, 1966, p. 2; "Process Sewage Wastes, Says Wildlife Federation," *Fisherman*, June 3, 1966, p. 2; "War on Pollution Urged," *Citizen*, May 9, 1966, p. 1.

89   Salmo, "Wildlife vs. Industry," p. 10; "Log Drive Sparks Concern," *Citizen*, May 13, 1966, p. 3; "Stellako Log Drive Still Under Question," *Citizen*, June 1, 1966, p. 3.

90   H.J. Robichaud to R.G. Williston, June 3, 1966; H.J. Robichaud to K. Kiernan, June 3, 1966, Canada, unpublished sessional papers, first session of the 27th parliament, January 18, 1966–May 8, 1967, RG 14, vol. 1805, Public Archives of Canada; "Log Drive Permit Refused," *Citizen*, June 8, 1966, p. 3.

91   Larry Emrick, "Williston Defies Federal Government," *Citizen*, June 10, 1966, p. 1; "BC Will Defy Ottawa With River Log Drive," *Victoria Daily Times*, June 11, 1966, p. 15.

92   "LeBoe Backs Mill," *Citizen*, June 10, 1966, p. 1; Dick Phillips, "Prince George-Prince Rupert," *British Columbia Digest* 22 (July–August 1966), pp. 26-27.

93   Larry Emrick, "Battle Looms Over Stellako," *Citizen*, June 13, 1966, p. 1; Larry Emrick, "Lodge Operators Lose First Round of Battle," *Citizen*, June 14, 1966, p. 1.

94   Emrick, "Battle Looms," p. 1; Emrick, "Lodge Operators," p. 1; Salmo, "Fishing in the Land of the Totem," p. 39.

95   "Ottawa Accused in Log Ban Case," *Vancouver Province*, June 15, 1966, p. 23; "An Unfortunate Incident," *Citizen*, June 14, 1966, p. 1; "Shelford Supports Federation," *Citizen*, June 14, 1966, p. 3.

96   "BC Runs Logs, Defying Ottawa," *Vancouver Sun*, June 14, 1966, p. 3; "Ottawa Accused," p. 23.

97   "BC Runs Logs," p. 3.

98   "How Much is a Salmon Worth?" *Vancouver Sun*, June 14, 1966, p. 4.

99   BC Research Council, *Progress Report No. 1: Log Driving–Stellako River, June, 1966*, table 1, Daily log release into Stellako River, June 14-20, 1966; "Resort Owners Seek to Halt Log Drive in Salmon Haven," *Vancouver Sun*, June 15, 1964, p. 14; Canada, *House of Commons Debates, First Session, 27th Parliament, vol. 6, 1966* (Ottawa: Queen's Printer, 1966), p. 6445; Scott Honeyman, "Stellako Log Drive Going Ahead," *Citizen*, June 15, 1966, p. 1.

100   "Stellako," *Citizen*, June 15, 1966, p. 2.

101   "Stellako," *Lakes District News*, June 22, 1966, p. 2.

102   Honeyman, "Stellako Drive Going Ahead," p. 1; "$50,000 Annually At Stake," *Victoria Daily Times*, June 16, 1966, p. 21; "Letters," *Citizen*, June 16, 1966, p. 2; "Mill Makes First Pulp," *Vancouver Sun*, July 6, 1966, p. 31.

103   "Resorts Hit by Slesinger," *Citizen*, June 17, 1966, p. 1.

104   "Stellako Log Drive Threat to Salmon," *Fisherman*, June 17, 1966, pp. 1, 16.

105   Canada, *House of Commons Debates, First Session, 27th Parliament, vol. 6, 1966*, pp. 6476-477; BC Research Council, *Progress Report Nov. 1*, table 1; H.J. Robichaud to R.G. Williston,

June 16, 1966, Canada, unpublished sessional papers, first session of the 27th parliament, January 18, 1966–May 8, 1967, RG14, vol. 1805, Public Archives of Canada; Scott Honeyman, "Stellako Dispute in Common," *Citizen*, June 16, 1966, p. 1.

106 Honeyman, "Stellako Dispute," p. 1; "Log Drive Fought," *Vancouver Sun*, June 16, 1966, p. 18.

107 BC Research Council, *Progress Report No. 1*, table 1; "Williston Happy at Log Fish Test," *Vancouver Sun*, June 17, 1966, p. 19; "Writ Probably Too Late," *Citizen*, June 17, 1966, p. 1.

108 "Logs and Spawning Grounds," *Victoria Daily Times*, June 17, 1966, p. 4; "Canada," *Citizen*, June 17, 1966, p. 2; Maurice Western, "Jesse Bennett Rides Again on the Stellako Spawning Grounds," *Vancouver Sun*, June 21, 1966, p. 4.

109 Larry Emrick, "The Stellako Log Drive's A Very Touchy Situation," *Citizen*, June 20, 1966, p. 4.

110 Ian MacAlpine, "Logs vs. Fish on the Stellako," *Vancouver Sun*, June 21, 1966, p. 6.

111 Ibid.

112 BC Research Council, *Progress Report No. 1*, table 1, p. 12; "Stellako Case Winds Up Today," *Citizen*, June 20, 1960, p. 1; Larry Emrick, "Log Drive Now Over," *Citizen*, June 21, 1966, p. 1.

113 "NILA Backs Stellako Drive," *Citizen*, June 20, 1966, p. 3; Emrick, "Log Drive Now Over," p. 1; "Log Drive Goes Ahead Despite Ottawa," *TL* 22 (August 1966), p. 10; "Letters to the Editor," *Nechako Chronicle*, June 23, 1966, p. 13.

114 "Salmon Spawning Dangers Voiced by Brotherhood," *Native Voice* 20 (June 1966), pp. 1–2.

115 IPSFC, *Effects of Log Driving*, pp. 8–15.

116 Ibid., pp. 17–32.

117 Ibid., pp. 32–43.

118 Ibid., pp. 43–47.

119 Ibid., pp. 47–53.

120 Ibid., pp. 47–55.

121 Ibid., pp. 55–56.

122 Ibid., pp. 57–60.

123 Ibid., p. 85.

124 "Fishing Areas Harmed by Logs," *Victoria Daily Times*, June 22, 1966, p. 6; George Dobie, "Log Drives Could Ruin Rich Fishery," *Vancouver Sun*, June 22, 1966, p. 14; "Log Drive Halt Urged," *Citizen*, June 22, 1966, p. 1; "Stellako Log Drives Harm Salmon," *Fisherman*, July 15, 1966, p. 3; "Stellako Log Drive Shocks Industry," *Western Fisheries* 72 (June 1966), p. 11; "Association Discloses Facts," *Nechako Chronicle*, July 28, 1966, p. 9; "Poor Communications," *Nechako Chronicle*, July 21, 1966, p. 4; Norman Hacking, "Log Run Ruins Spawning, Say Experts," *Vancouver Province*, June 22, 1966, p. 13.

125 "Minister Suspects Fish Report," *Victoria Daily Times,* June 23, 1966, p. 21; "Log Beef 'Hot Air–Williston,'" *Vancouver Province,* June 24, 1966, p. 2.

126 "Logs in the Millpond," *Victoria Daily Times,* June 24, 1966, p. 4; "Williston Stays Firm on Stellako Decision," *Citizen,* June 24, 1966, p. 3; Ian MacAlpine, "Painted Pebbles Tell Stellako Story," *Vancouver Sun,* June 24, 1966, p. 14.

127 MacAlpine, "Painted Pebbles," p. 14; "Gov't Probe of Log Drive Superficial, Experts Say," *Vancouver Sun,* June 29, 1966, p. 2; "Independent Study of River Just Begun, Biologist Says," *Vancouver Sun,* July 7, 1966, p. 15; R.G. McMynn to W.R. Hourston, April 11, 1967, box 3, GR1118, BCA.

128 "Where Was Mr. Kiernan?" *Vancouver Province,* June 23, 1966, p. 4; "Mining Firm Gets Townsite in Park," *Vancouver Sun,* June 7, 1966, p. 1; "In the Wilderness," *Victoria Daily Times,* June 25, 1966, p. 4; Ian MacAlpine, "Disposable Bottle Ban Foreseen" *Vancouver Sun,* June 9, 1966, p. 1; "Stellako Drive," *Vancouver Province,* June 29, 1966, p. 4.

129 Gerry Kidd, "The Fishy Eye," *Western Fisheries* 72 (June 1966), p. 58; "Robichaud Criticized for Failing Industry," *Fisherman,* July 1, 1966, p. 1; "Secure Salmon First," *Fisherman,* July 8, 1966, p. 4.

130 "Log Drive Completed so Protest Withdrawn," *Victoria Daily Times,* June 30, 1966, p. 3; "Wildlife Group Keeps Up Fight," *Citizen,* June 30, 1966, p. 1; Jim Fairley, "Stellako Skirmish to Shift," *Vancouver Province,* June 30, 1966, p. 11; "Williston Charges 'Scare Techniques,'" *Victoria Daily Times,* June 25, 1966, p. 2; Norman Hacking, "Stellako Battle Just Beginning," *Vancouver Province,* June 30, 1966, p. 9; "BC Wildlife Federation on Stellako Log Drive," *Nechako Chronicle,* July 7, 1966, p. 2.

131 "Log Drive," *Daily Colonist,* June 30, 1966, p. 4; "Acted Foolishly," *Victoria Daily Times,* June 30, 1966, p. 5; Hacking, "Stellako Battle," p. 9.

132 "River Log Row Action Studied," *Vancouver Sun,* July 4, 1966, p. 25; "Ottawa Accepts BC Challenge," *Victoria Daily Times,* July 2, 1966, p. 1; H. Paish to H.J. Robichaud, July 11, 1966, box 3, GR1118, BCA.

133 Paish, "Stellako Log Drive," p. 42; Ian Street, "Fish Forgotten," *Vancouver Province,* June 28, 1966, p. 5; "Stellako Issue to Court?" *Fisherman,* July 8, 1966, p. 4.

134 "Wildlife Federation Raps Jim Slesinger," *Citizen,* June 28, 1966, p. 3; "Club Backs Slesinger," *Citizen,* June 30, 1966, p. 1.

135 "Discuss Stellako Log Run," *Lakes District News,* July 20, 1966, p. 1; "Rod and Gun Club," *Lakes District News,* July 20, 1966, p. 1.

136 "The Stellako Fiasco," *Lakes District News,* July 20, 1966, p. 11.

137 "Stellako Farmers Join Log Dispute," *Vancouver Sun,* July 22, 1966, p. 15; "Immediate Action Asked on Log Driving Dispute," *Vancouver Sun,* July 28, 1966, p. 16.

138 "Log Dispute Hurting Farmers," *Vancouver Province,* July 22, 1966, p. 32; Lyons, *Salmon,* p. 625.

139 "Stellako Question Recalled by Log Drive 'Phase-Out,'" *Lakes District News*, September 14, 1966, p. 1; "Log Drive End Seen on Homathko, Wannock," *Fisherman*, September 9, 1966, p. 10; Norman Hacking, "Safeguards for Salmon," *Vancouver Province*, July 19, 1966, p. 14; "Look Again," *Lakes District News*, September 14, 1966, p. 2.

140 BC Research Council, Progress Report No.1, pp. 2-4.

141 Ibid., pp. 4-7.

142 Canada, *Debates of the House of Commons, First Session, 27th Parliament, vol. 9, 1966* (Ottawa: Queen's Printer, 1966), p. 8967; "Ministers' River Probe—Logs or Fish?" *Vancouver Province*, October 21, 1966, p. 11.

143 Jack Fry, "High-Level Talks Tighten Links," *Daily Colonist*, October 25, 1966, p. 1; "BC-Ottawa Fisheries Accord Sparked by Stellako Dispute," *Vancouver Province*, October 25, 1966, p. 10; "Stellako Uproar Results in BC-Ottawa Pact," *Western Fisheries*, 73 (October 1966), p. 44.

144 Gerry Kidd, "The Fishy Eye," *Western Fisheries* 73 (October 1966), p. 58.

145 BC Wildlife Federation, "Submission to a Committee of the Cabinet of the Province of British Columbia," October 25, 1966, BC Legislative Library.

146 Paish, "Stellako Log Drive," p. 42.

147 BC, *Field Manual of Sport Fish Habitat Protection* (Victoria: Fisheries Management Division, Fish and Wildlife Branch, Department of Recreation and Conservation, 1966), p. 2.

148 "Shelford Goes to Bat for South Country," *Lakes District News*, December 21, 1966, p. 7; "Uncertainty Plaguing Loggers," *Victoria Daily Times*, January 28, 1967, p. 19; "Stellako Logging Needs Phazeout," *Daily Colonist*, January 28, 1967, p. 14.

149 "Tweedsmuir R. and G.C. Writes Minister of Fisheries," *Lakes District News*, February 22, 1967, p. 5.

150 "Shelford Replies to Rod and Gun Club Pres.," *Lakes District News*, April 12, 1967, p. 2.

151 R.G. McMynn to D.B. Turner, January 24, 1967, box 3, GR1118, BCA; "'Pork Barrel Approach,' Charges BC Minister," *Citizen*, February 14, 1967, p. 5.

152 United Fishermen and Allied Workers Union, "Brief to the Premier and Executive Council of British Columbia," February 21, 1967, BC Legislative Library; "MLAs Set Straight on Stellako Log Drive," *Fisherman*, March 10, 1967, p. 8; "The Industry in 1966," *Western Fisheries* 47 (May 1967), pp. 18-19; Lorne F. Swannell, "Impact of the Forest Industry on BC Economy," *Truck Logger* 21 (December 1965), pp. 46-49; Paish, "Stellako Log Drive," p. 41.

153 "Pollution of Lakes to be Investigated," *Citizen*, February 28, 1967, p. 3; "Logging Operators Draw Fines," *Citizen*, March 8, 1967, p. 1.

154 BC Research Council, "Summary Report No. 2. Log Driving—Stellako River, June 1966, Prepared for the Honorable Ray Williston, Minister, Lands, Forests and Water Resources," J.T. Fyles Natural Resources Library; C.C. Walden to V. Raudsepp, February 6, 1967, letter attached to summary report; Larry Emrick, "Stellako Study Almost Ready," *Citizen*, February 8, 1967, p. 1.

155 "Stellako Log Report Pending Next Week," *Citizen*, March 10, 1967, p. 1. For insight into Weldwood's development at Quesnel see Drushka, *From Tie Hackers to Timber Harvesters*, pp. 182, 198, 224.

156 BC Research Council, "Final Report on the Effect of Log Driving on the Stellako River on Salmon, June 1966. Prepared for the Honorable Ray Williston, Minister of Lands, Forests and Water Resources," (February 1967), pp. 1-8.

157 Ibid., pp. 8, 12-13.

158 Ibid., pp. 15-17.

159 Ibid., pp. 17-20, 31.

160 Ibid., pp. 8-9, 29-33.

161 Bob McConnell, "Question Marks Stud Report," *Vancouver Province*, March 15, 1967, p. 2; "A Report Without Answers," *Vancouver Province*, March 20, 1967, p. 4; "Up the Lazy River," *Vancouver Sun*, April 3, 1967, p. 4; Dale Ethier, "The Babbling Brook," *Observer*, May 4, 1967, p. 20.

162 "Stellako Log Drive Not That Bad," *Truck Logger 23* (May 1967), p. 36; "General Comments—Stellako River Log Driving," March 1967, copy filed with the 1966 BCRC report, J.T. Fyles Natural Resources Library.

163 Ibid., pp. 1-3.

164 Ibid., pp. 4-6.

165 Ibid., p. 1; IPSFC, *Annual Report of the International Pacific Salmon Fisheries Commission 1965* (Vancouver: Wrigley Printing, 1966), p. 26.

166 H.J. Robichaud to R.G. Williston, May 10, 1967, Canada, unpublished sessional papers, second session of the 27th parliament, May 8, 1967–April 23, 1968, no. 217, R.G. 14, vol.1830, Public Archives of Canada.

167 Ray Williston, "The Northern Way," *Observer*, April 6, 1967, p. 4; Ray Williston, "BC Leading Way in Pollution Fight," *Citizen*, April 10, 1967, p. 19; Paish, "Requiem for a Park," p. 43; "Buttle Battle Continues," *Citizen*, April 12, 1967, p. 23.

168 "Scraping Away the Sinister Goo ...," *Citizen*, March 3, 1967, p. 15; "Pollution Control Bill Given Rough Passage," *Vancouver Province*, March 18, 1967, p. 14; "Hands Off Our Park Investment," *Observer*, April 6, 1967, p. 14.

169 Rajala, *Clearcutting the Pacific Rain Forest*, pp. 167-216.

170 "Up the Lazy River," p. 4.

171 F.S. McKinnon to A.W.H. Needler, April 4, 1967; R.G. McMynn to W.R. Hourston, April 11, 1967, box 3, GR1118, BCA.

172 H.J. Robichaud to R.G. Williston, May 16, 1967, Canada, unpublished sessional papers, second session of the 27th parliament, May 8, 1967-April 23, 1968, no.217, RG 14, vol.1830, Public Archives of Canada; Scott Honeyman, "Stellako Drive Goes Again," *Citizen*, April 21, 1967, p. 1; "They're Poles Apart," *Vancouver Province*, April 22, 1967, p. 13.

173 "Logs vs. Fish on the Stellako," *Vancouver Province*, April 25, 1967, p. 4; "Stellako," *Citizen*, May 1, 1967, p. 2; "Log Drive Worries Wildlife Federation," *Vancouver Province*, April 24, 1967, p. 23; "Log Drive Challenged," *Fisherman*, April 28, 1967, p. 1.

174 F.S. McKinnon to A.W.H. Needler, May 1, 1967, box 3, GR1118, BCA.

175 R.G. McMynn and E.H. Vernon to D.B. Turner, May 9, 1967, box 3, GR1118, BCA.

176 R.G. McMynn and E.H. Vernon, "Log Driving and the Stellako River," May 9, 1967, box 3, GR1118, BCA.

177 "The Stellako River Log Drive, 1967," (Canadian Council of Resources Ministers, 1969), pp. 8-9.

178 Howard Paish, "Executive Director's Report," *Proceedings of the Eleventh BC Wildlife Federation Convention*, Victoria, May 3-6, 1967, pp. 1-5; James C. Murray, "President's Report," *Proceedings of the Eleventh BC Wildlife Federation Convention*, Victoria, May 3-6, 1967, pp. 1-5.

179 Murray, "President's Report," pp. 1-6; "Raffle Helps Keep Group Out of Red," *Vancouver Sun*, November 1, 1967, p. 6.

180 "Robichaud Wants Stellako Solution," *Citizen*, May 5, 1967, p. 1; "Multiple Use," *Citizen*, May 10, 1967, p. 2.

181 Scott Honeyman, "Eight Troubled Miles on a Northern River," *Citizen*, May 15, 1967, p. 3; "Has Stellako Permit Been Issued?" *Fisherman*, May 12, 1967, p. 7.

182 H.J. Robichaud to R.G. Williston, May 16, 1967, Canada, unpublished sessional papers, second session of the 27th parliament, May 8, 1967-April 23, 1968, no.217, R.G. 14, vol.1830, Public Archives of Canada; "Robichaud Asks Reason for Log Run," *Vancouver Province*, May 18, 1967, p. 29; "Evidence Shows Log Drive Harming Stellako River," *Fisherman*, June 2, 1967, p. 7.

183 W.K. Kiernan to D.B. Turner, May 16, 1967; E.H. Vernon and R.G. McMynn to W.K. Kiernan, May 18, 1967, box 3, GR1118, BCA.

184 E.H. Vernon and R.G. McMynn, "Confidential: Stellako River Log Driving and Fisheries," pp. 1-2, May 1967, box 3, GR1118, BCA.

185 Ibid., pp. 5-6.

186 Ibid., pp. 6-7.

187 R. Williston to H.J. Robichaud, May 19, 1967, Canada, unpublished sessional papers, second session of the 27th parliament, May 8, 1967-April 23, 1968, no.217, RG 14, vol.1830, Public Archives of Canada.

188 H. Paish to H.J. Robichaud, May 18, 1967, box 3, GR1118, BCA; Scott Honeyman, "Stellako Drive: A Test Case," *Citizen*, May 18, 1967, p. 1.

189 "Protests Mount Against Log Drive on Stellako," *Fisherman*, May 26, 1967, p. 12; "Down the River," *Citizen*, May 19, 1967, p. 2; Scott Honeyman, "Lumber Firms' Books Tell Sad Money Story," *Citizen*, May 25, 1967, p. 1; "Stellako Decision Supported," *Citizen*, May 26, 1967, p. 1.

190 Scott Honeyman, "Loggers Set Stage for Stellako River Encore," *Citizen*, May 19, 1967, p. 1.

191 H.J. Robichaud to R.G. Williston, May 25, 1967; Williston to Robichaud, May 31, 1967, Canada, unpublished sessional papers, second session of the 27th parliament, May 8, 1967–April 23, 1968, no. 217, RG 14, vol.1830, Public Archives of Canada; R.G. McMynn, "Stellako Log Drive 1967, Highlights of Correspondence and Meetings," October 26, 1967, box 3, GR1118, BCA.

192 H.J. Robichaud to R.G. Williston, June 12, 1967, Canada, unpublished sessional papers, second session of the 27th parliament, May 8, 1967–April 23, 1968, no.217, RG 14, vol.1830, Public Archives of Canada; "Stellako Log Drive Waits for Low Water," *Citizen*, June 7, 1967, p. 3; "BC Leads Fight Against Pollution," *Citizen*, June 8, 1967, p. 1; "Shelford Predicts Demise of Drives," *Citizen*, June 1, 1967, p. 1.

193 Alex Young, "Ottawa Okays Stellako Drive," *Vancouver Province*, June 10, 1967, p. 10; Scott Honeyman, "Stellako Log Drive Gets Go-Ahead Sign From Federal Level," *Citizen*, June 14, 1967, p. 1; "Ottawa Ban on Stellako Lifted," *Vancouver Sun*, June 14, 1967, p. 17; "Log Drive Wins Ottawa Approval," *Daily Colonist*, June 15, 1967, p. 37; "Stellako Drive Adrift on Facts," *Vancouver Province*, June 14, 1967, p. 4.

194 "Are You There, Mr. Kiernan?" *Vancouver Sun*, June 15, 1967, p. 4; Iain Hunter, "Bennett Tells Mine Critics to Quit Smoking, Drinking," *Vancouver Sun*, June 15, 1967, p. 39; "Fool," *Citizen*, June 20, 1967, p. 2.

195 Frank Zelko, "Making Greenpeace: The Development of Direct Action Environmentalism in British Columbia," *BC Studies* 142/143 (Summer/Autumn 2004), pp. 197–239; Arn Keeling "The Effluent Society," pp. 295–340.

196 Scott Honeyman, "Stellako Log Booms Sabotaged," *Citizen*, June 15, 1967, p. 1; "Night Riders Eye Stellako Log Booms," *Vancouver Sun*, June 16, 1967, p. 1; "Sawmill Patrols Booms," *Daily Colonist*, June 17, 1967, p. 13; Scott Honeyman, "Log Protest Strategy Prepared by Resorts," *Citizen*, June 16, 1967, p. 1.

197 "CBC Fishermen's Broadcast," June 16, 1967, box 3, GR1118, BCA.

198 Ibid.

199 "Gunfire Heralds Stellako Drive," *Vancouver Sun*, June 17, 1967, p. 12; "Loggers Fired Upon," *Vancouver Province*, June 17, 1967, p. 1; "Injunction Threat Poised on Stellako," *Vancouver Sun*, June 19, 1967, p. 7.

200 "Wildlife Protests Costs High," *Citizen*, June 16, 1967, p. 1; "Babes in the Wilderness," *Vancouver Sun*, June 20, 1967, p. 5.

201 Canada, "The Stellako River Log Drive, 1967," pp. 11-17; Scott Honeyman, "Stellako Logs Batter Lone Operator's Boat," *Citizen*, June 19, 1967, p. 1; "BC Log Drive Buffets Resort Owner," *Daily Colonist*, June 20, 1967, p. 1; "Kelly's Boat No Match for the Logs," *Vancouver Province*, June 20, 1967, p. 1.

202 Scott Honeyman, "Deputy Forest Minister: River 'Clean as Whistle,'" *Citizen*, June 20, 1967, p. 1.

203 Scott Honeyman, "Resort Owners 'Floundering Again' in Stellako Drive," *Citizen*, 21 June 1967, p. 1; "Log Drive Blockade Abandoned," *Vancouver Sun*, 21 June 1967, p. 4; "No Drive on River Today," *Citizen*, 22 June 1967, p. 1; Scott Honeyman, "Stellako Log Drive: Frustration on Both Sides," *Citizen*, June 22, 1967, p. 1.

204 T.N. Stringer, "Stellako River Log Drive, 1967," p. 3, box 8, Ray Williston Papers, University of Victoria, Archives and Special Collections; McMynn, "Stellako Log Drive 1967, Highlights," box 3, GR1118, BCA; Honeyman, "Stellako Log Drive: Frustration," p. 1.

205 "Stellako Drive on Schedule," *Citizen*, June 23, 1967, p. 1; "Stellako Drive Coming to a Head," *Cariboo Observer*, June 22, 1967, p. 22; "Quiet Flows the Stellako," *Daily Colonist*, June 27, 1967, p. l8; Stringer, "Stellako River Log Drive, 1967," p. 3.

206 Stringer, "Stellako River Log Drive, 1967," p. 1; Canada, "The Stellako River Log Drive, 1967," pp. i-v, 25-38, 40-44.

207 "Williston Says Growth Increases Hydro Rates," *Citizen*, June 29, 1967, p. 4A; Ray Williston, "The Northern Way," *Cariboo Observer*, June 29, 1967, p. 5.

208 "Stymied on the Stellako," *BC Wildlife Federation* Newsletter 1 (July-August 1967), pp. 2-3; "Editorial," *BC Outdoors* 23 (July-August 1967), p. 2; Howard Paish, "A Quality BC," *Vancouver Sun*, July 6, 1967, p. 5.

209 For Wrixon's complaints see "Sportsman's View," *Daily Colonist*, June 29, 1967, p. 4.

210 Ray Williston, "The Northern Way: Stellako Results Favourable," *Cariboo Observer*, July 13, 1967, p. 4.

211 Ibid. For an identical version see Ray Williston, "Stellako Log Drive," *Truck Logger* 23 (September 1967), pp. 38-41.

212 "Arrogant Letter," *Vancouver Sun*, January 25, 1968, p. 5; McMynn, "Stellako Log Drive 1967, Highlights," box 3, GR1118, BCA; "Minutes of the Sixth Meeting, Federal-Provincial BC Fisheries Committee, Victoria, BC, Mar. 26-27, 1968," p. 8, Pacific Biological Station Library.

213 Dave Stewart, "This is the Stellako," *Western Fish and Game* 3 (March 1968), pp. 22-25.

214 BC Wildlife Federation, "Submission to Committee of the Cabinet of the Province of British Columbia," December 12, 1968, p. 5, BC Legislative Library.

215 Ibid., pp. 9-10.

216 Howard Paish, "BC Wildlife Federation Report," *Western Fish and Game* 3 (January 1968), p. 37; "BC Wildlife Federation in Financial Difficulty," *Citizen*, June 30, 1967,

p. 20; *BC Wildlife Federation Newsletter* 1 (July–August 1968), p. 4; "The Positive Approach," *BC Wildlife Federation Newsletter* 2 (October 1968), p. 1.

217 Stephen Fox, *The American Conservation Movement: John Muir and His Legacy* (Madison: University of Wisconsin Press, 1981), pp. 272–81; John Opie, *Nature's Nation: An Environmental History of the United States* (New York: Harcourt Brace, 1998), pp. 393–94.

218 "Letters," *Western Fish and Game* 3 (May 1968), p. 6.

219 Hak, *Capital and Labour*, pp. 168–72; Wilson, *Talk and Log*, pp. 101–05; Keeling, "The Effluent Society," pp. 293–301.

220 "Submission by the Society for Pollution and Environmental Control (SPEC) to Public Hearing on Fisheries," 1969, p. 3, box 5, Derrick Mallard Papers, University of Victoria, Archives and Special Collections; BC Wildlife Federation, "Submission to the Executive Council, Government of British Columbia," December 15, 1969, BC Legislative Library; "Federation Dissatisfied With Gov't Pollution Stand," *Fisherman*, May 16, 1969, p. 9.

221 "'Buffalo Thinking' Blasted in BC Parks Development," *Citizen*, April 10, 1968, p. 8.

222 "Single Use of Forest Called Thing of Past," *Vancouver Province*, October 10, 1969, p. 26; "Pressures Intensify on BC Timberlands," *Truck Logger* 25 (May 1969), p. 12; "Integrated Use," *Truck Logger* 25 (June 1969), p. 16.

223 "On Learning to Work Together," *BCL* 52 (May 1968), p. 35; Rajala, "'Nonsensical and a Contradiction,'" pp. 120–27.

224 "'Natural Resource' Bureau Outlined," *Citizen*, May 6, 1968, p. 5; Alex Merriman, "Editorial," *BC Outdoors* 33 (January–February 1977), p. 6; "Amalgamate the BC Fish and Wildlife Branch and the BC Forest Service? Never!" *BC Outdoors* 33 (March–April 1977), p. 80.

225 Gerry Kidd, "The Fishy Eye," *Western Fisheries* 76 (July 1968), p. 50.

226 "Fisheries Drops Logging Charges," *Fisherman*, August 24, 1979, p. 1. For a full discussion of the Riley Creek conflict see chapter 5 in this volume.

227 "Regina v. Dan Fowler," *Canadian Environmental Law News* 5 (October 1976), pp. 155–59; Jean Sorensen, "Fish and Forests," *BCL* 64 (August 1980), pp. 30–31; Bob Lee, "Top Court Cuts Power of Federal Fisheries Act," *Truck Logger* 3 (August 1980), pp. 10–12; John Clarke, "New Court Ruling Consistent with First," *BCL* 64 (September 1980), pp. 48, 69.

228 "Minutes, Seventh Meeting, Federal-Provincial BC Fisheries Committee," Nanaimo, May 28–29, 1969, p. 6, appendix 4, pp. 1–3.

229 Ibid., pp. 3–7.

230 Ibid, p. 7; Robert Gordon and Dennis Martens, "Sockeye Eggs Killed by Bark on Spawning Gravel," *Western Fisheries* 78 (September 1969), p. 41.

231 Gordon and Martens, "Sockeye Eggs Killed," pp. 42–43; see also "Log Drives Leave Lethal Bark Wastes," *Fisherman*, December 18, 1970, pp. 27–28.

232 R.G. McMynn to R. Ashby, October 31, 1967, box 3, GR1118, BCA; "Delegates Question Area Director," *Fisherman*, February 21, 1969, pp. 6–7.

233 "Delegates Question," pp. 6-7; "The Industry in 1969," *Western Fisheries* 80 (May 1970), p. 12; "Act to Save Salmon," *Native Voice* (April 1971), p. 4.

234 "2-4D Sprating Stirs Protest," *Fisherman*, August 13, 1971, p. 1; "Ucluelet Fishermen Win Action," *Fisherman*, January 19, 1973, p. 7; "Society Wires Williams: End Streambank Logging," *Fisherman*, June 8, 1973, p. 8; "New SPEC Branch Will Combat Rupert Pollution," *Fisherman*, March 6, 1970, p. 9; "Skeena Water Authority Campaign Set by Parley," *Fisherman*, June 18, 1971, p. 9. For an overview of conflict and policy during the 1970s see Richard A. Rajala, "Forests and Fish: The 1972 Coast Logging Guidelines and British Columbia's First NDP Government," *BC Studies* 159 (Autumn 2008), pp. 81-120.

235 George Inglis, "New Pulp Mill's Ill Wind Blows No Bad Health," *Citizen*, May 6, 1968, p. 3; Con Johnson, "Forest Development Booming For BC," *Citizen*, June 25, 1968, p. 1; "Bennett Dam Back Up Blights Area," *Citizen*, June 14, 1968, p. 5; "Fears Confirmed," *Citizen*, June 21, 1968, p. 1; "Outdoors With Salmo," *Citizen*, June 13, 1968, p. 18; Christensen, *Too Good To Be True*, pp. 126-27; Loo, "Disturbing the Peace," pp. 901-02.

236 George Inglis, "BC Brass Backs Bert," *Citizen*, June 17, 1968, p. 3.

237 Hal Griffin, "Protection of the Environment?" *Fisherman*, February 2, 1973, p. 4.

238 "Letters: Reader Writes on Recent NDP Party Meet," *Lakes District News*, June 28, 1972, p. 3; "New Democratic Party," *Lakes District News*, August 23, 1972, p. 1; "Douglas T. Kelly Credits Workers for Victory," *Lakes District News*, September 6, 1972, p. 1; Williston and Keller, *Forests, Power and Policy*, p. 247.

239 "Kelly, NDP Candidate," *Lakes District News*, August 9, 1972, p. 2.

240 BC, *Official Report of the Debates of the Legislative Assembly (Hansard), 1974 Legislative Session: 4th Session, 30th Parliament, Tuesday, November 19, 1974*, p. 32, http://www.leg.bc.ca/ hansard/30th4th/30p_04s_741119z.htm (September 12, 2008); "Omineca (electoral district)," http://en.wikipedia.org/wiki/Omineck_(electoral_district) (October 17, 2008).

241 "BC Wildlife Federation Newsletter," *BC Outdoors* 29 (January-February 1973), p. 58; Club members, "Fraser Lake Sawmills," pp. 100-01.

242 Maurice Wrixon, "The Stellako...Fly Fisherman's Paradise," *Daily Colonist*, October 23, 1973, p. 3, vertical files, BCA; Lewis Johnson, "Autumn on the Stellako," http://www. Thechronicflyfisher.com/STELLAKO.html (September 10, 2008); Phillips, "Jurisdictional Conflicts," p. 101; "Land Deal to Help Stellako River System," *Western Fisheries* 100 (June 1979), p. 97; "Reserve Established on the Stellako," *Nechako Chronicle*, August 7, 1980, p. 1.

243 Afshin Shams, "Fishing the Prince to Prince Corridor," http://www.fishingwithrod. com/articles/2002/0802_01.html (October 25, 2008).

244 "Vanderhoof Land and Resource Management Plan," http://ilmbwww.gov.vc/ca/slrp// rmp/princegeorge/vanderhf/plan/vanderhoof_lrmp/section2.26.html (August 15, 2008); Club members, "Fraser Lake Sawmills," *Deeper Roots and Greener Valleys*, p. 101.

245 "Northern Interior Forests Denuded," *Native Voice* 10 (June 1956), p. 6; "Skeena Committee Under Fire, Some Closure Changes Rumored," *Western Fisheries* 67 (February 1964), p. 11; "Trappers Will Seek Damage Compensation," *Citizen,* June 14, 1966, p. 3; "Howard Fights for Trapline Compensation," *Native Voice* 10 (August 1956), p. 2; Richard A. Rajala, *Up-Coast,* pp. 154-55.

CHAPTER 5

1   T.C. Griffing and L.A. Bayrock, "An Investigation of Slope Stability and Fisheries Habitat in the Vicinity of Cutting Permit Numbered 144, Riley Creek Drainage, Graham Island, Queen Charlotte Islands, British Columbia. A Report Prepared for QC Timber Ltd." (Vancouver: International Environmental Consultants, January 1979), pp. 53, 61-62.

2   Douglas N. Swanston, "Field Reconnaissance on the Relative Stability of Potential Impacts from Timber Harvesting Operations on Cutting Permit 144, Riley Creek Drainage, Graham Island, Queen Charlotte Islands, British Columbia," (unpublished report, J.T. Fyles Natural Resources Library, 1979), pp. 2-18.

3   Jeremy Wilson, *Talk and Log: Wilderness Politics in British Columbia* (Vancouver: UBC Press, 1998), pp. 162-64; Richard A. Rajala, *Up-Coast: Forests and Industry on British Columbia's North Coast, 1870-2005* (Victoria: Royal British Columbia Museum, 2006), pp. 204-06.

4   Richard A. Rajala, "'Streams Being Ruined From a Salmon Producing Standpoint': Clearcutting, Fish Habitat, and Forest Regulation in British Columbia, 1900-45," *BC Studies* No. 176 (Winter 2012/13), pp. 93-132.

5   Ferris Neave and W.P. Wickett, "Factors Affecting the Development of Pacific Salmon in British Columbia," *Proceedings, Seventh Pacific Science Congress* 4 (1949), pp. 548-55.

6   Richard A. Rajala, "'Nonsensical and a Contradiction in Terms': Multiple Use Forestry, Clearcutting, and the Politics of Salmon Habitat in British Columbia, 1945-1970," *BC Studies* No. 183 (Autumn 2014), pp. 89-127; G.F. Hartman, J.C. Scrivener, M.J. Brownlee and D.C. Morrison, *Fish Habitat Protection and Planning for Forest Harvesting in Coastal Streams of British Columbia: Some Research and Management Provisions* (Ottawa: Department of Fisheries and Oceans, 1983), p. 31.

7   Wilson, *Talk and Log,* p. 72. The Fisheries and Marine Service, previously known as the Department of Fisheries, was established in 1973. Here I will refer to the agency simply as the Fisheries Service until early April 1979, when the Department of Fisheries and Oceans comes into existence.

8   Richard A. Rajala, "Forests and Fish: The 1972 Coast Logging Guidelines and British Columbia's First NDP Government," *BC Studies* No. 159 (Autumn 2008), pp. 81-120.

9   While the Queen Charlotte Islands officially changed name to Haida Gwaii in 2010, for simplicity its current official name will be used throughout.

10   Rajala, "Forests and Fish," pp. 117-19; "Streamside Management for the Queen Charlotte Islands," (Report held at J.T. Fyles Natural Resources Library, 198-, p. 1; Gord Price, "Streamside Logging: 'Tailor-made Solutions' to Individual Problems," *ForesTalk* 1 (October/November/December 1977), p. 20; W.G. Bishop to all licensees in the Vancouver forest district, January 30, 1978, Elk River Timber Co. Records, box 4, Campbell River and District Museum and Archives (CRDMA); "Profile: Sam Bawlf, Minister of Recreation and Conservation," *BC Outdoors* 34 (February 1978), pp. 42-46; "BC Wildlife Federation Newsletter," *BC Outdoors* 33 (July-August 1977), p. 48.

11   Joseph Gough, *Managing Canada's Fisheries: From Early Days to the Year 2000* (Sillery: Les Editions du Septentrion, 2006), p. 307; BC Wildlife Federation, Vancouver Island Region, minutes of general meeting, June 12, 1977, Elk River Timber Company Records, box 4, CRDMA; Richard Morgan, "Forest, Mining Interests Zero in on Fisheries Act," *Fisherman*, June 17, 1977, p. 8.

12   E.L. Young to J. Nielsen, May 24, 1977; C.J. Highsted, "Specific Points, Bill C-38, June 1977, Referenced to Points in Chief Forester's Letter of May 24"; E.L. Young, memorandum to the Honourable the Minister, September 6, 1977, file 02003, BC Ministry of Forests Records (hereafter BCMFR); "Forest Firms Oppose Bill," *Victoria Times*, June 15, 1977, p. 11; Gerald Walsh, "New Fisheries Act Worries Industry," *Hiballer* 28 (December 1977), pp. 29-32; W.R. Bennett, "British Columbia: Natural Resource Management and Provincial Economic Development," Eighteenth Annual Premiers' Conference, August 1977, pp. 1-7.

13   "Ottawa Passes Fisheries Act Amendments," *Nature Canada* 6 (October/December 1977), pp. 19-20; Gray Wheeler, "Fisheries Act Compromises Logging," *Journal of Logging Management* 9 (February 1978), pp. 1350-52; "Bill C-38; Amending the Disaster," *Hiballer* 29 (February 1978), pp. 30-31; Brian Martin, "Loggers Lash Federal Liberals," *BC Lumberman* 62 (February 1978), pp. 32-33 (hereafter *BCL*).

14   Gough, *Managing Canada's Fisheries*, pp. 368-69; "Bill C-38 Now Law of the Land," *Fisherman*, August 12, 1977, p. 5; "Enhancement—Real Answer," *Fisherman*, July 30, 1976, p. 4; Dave Stewart, "Fishing Talk," *BC Outdoors* 34 (November 1978), pp. 11-12; Len Shaw, "Big Projects Gobble Most Salmonid Funds," *BC Sportsman* 16 (June 1980), p. 9.

15   D.A.S. Lanskail to COFI board of directors, March 7, 1978; M.F. Painter to forestry and logging sector, COFI, April 17, 1978, box 4, Elk River Timber Company Records, CRMA.

16   "LeBlanc Rebuffs Forest Demands," *Fisherman*, April 21, 1978, p. 3; "Bill C-38 Still Worries Industry," *Hiballer* 29 (May 1978), p. 12; "LeBlanc Rejects Logging Fears," *Canadian Forest Industries* 98 (June 1978), p. 14; Jim Stirling, "We Have a Long Way to Go!" *BCL* 62 (June 1978), pp. 40-41; Brian Martin, "Comment," *BCL* 62 (May 1978), p. 4.

17   "BC Wildlife Federation Newsletter," *BC Outdoors* 34 (July 1978), pp. 27–29.

18   Pat Johnson, "Truce Declared in Fishing War," *Vancouver Express*, January 22, 1979; Brian Martin, "Let's Be Friends Says Fisheries," *BCL* 63 (February 1979), pp. 36–37.

19   Peter H. Pearce, *Timber Rights and Forest Policy in British Columbia: Report of the Royal Commission on Forest Resources*, vol. 1 (Victoria: Queen's Printer, 1976), pp. 280–82.

20   Ibid., pp. 259–60, 267–69.

21   Ibid., pp. 78–81, 30–34, 90–91.

22   "Committee Gears Up for Action," *BC Logging News* 8 (January 1977), p. 664; "Waterland Plans Big Changes in BC," *Canadian Forest Industries* 97 (June 1977), p. 10; Cameron Young, "Protecting the Forest Environment: A Progress Report," *ForesTalk* 1 (April 1977), pp. 15–16; Tom Waterland, "A New Deal for the Forest Industry," *Hiballer* 28 (December 1977), pp. 25–26.

23   COFI, annual report, 1977, n.p.; Jeremy Wilson, *Talk and Log*, p. 159; Richard Schwindt, "The Pearse Commission and the Industrial Organization of the British Columbia Forest Industry," *BC Studies* 41 (1979), p. 34; Jean Sorensen, "A Perspective on Forest Policy: the New Legislation," *ForesTalk* 2 (Summer 1978), p. 21.

24   "A Few Highlights," *BCL* 62 (June 1978), p. 32; Sorensen, "A Perspective," p. 21; "Forests Minister Outlines Philosophy," *Journal of Logging Management* 10 (March 1979), p. 1883; "Revising the Forest Industry," *Hiballer* 29 (December 1979), pp. 24–26; "Notes for a Speech by T.M. Apsey, Deputy Minister of Forests, at the 72nd Pacific Logging Congress in Vancouver, November 5, 1981, p. 13, J.T. Fyles Natural Resources Library; Ken Drushka, "The Forests Act: Corporate Logging Guaranteed," *Monday Magazine*, June 26–July 2, 1978, pp. 10–11; "COFI—We're Favourably Impressed," *Hiballer* 29 (June 1978), pp. 14–15; "The Forest Act: Industry's Response," *Journal of Logging Management* 9 (July 1978), p. 1540; "Truck Loggers Association," *Hiballer* 29 (June 1978), pp. 14–16.

25   "New Act Tailored for Monopoly," *Fisherman*, June 16, 1978, p. 4; "Massive Opposition to the New Forest Act," *BC Outdoors* 34 (September 1978), p. 10; "IWA–TLA Submit Joint Request for Delay of New Forest Act," *Western Canada Lumber Worker* (June 1978), pp. 1–2.

26   "Applications for TFL Renewal Act's Most Conspicuous Failure," *Western Canada Lumber Worker* (July 1978), p. 15.

27   Wilson, *Talk and Log*, pp. 159–62.

28   The following summary of the region's logging history is drawn from Rajala, *Up-Coast*.

29   A cunit is equal to 100 cubic feet.

30   All data taken from the annual report of the Queen Charlotte Public Sustained Yield Unit, Prince Rupert forest district, 1975, Paul George Papers, box 2, University of Victoria Special Collections (hereafter UVICSC).

31   Ibid.

32   For the sake of simplicity, I will refer to the organization as the Islands Protection Society (IPS).

33 Ian Gill, *All That We Say is Ours: Guujaaw and the Reawakening of the Haida* Nation (Vancouver: Douglas & McIntyre, 2009), p. 68; Louise Takeda, *Islands' Spirit Rising: Reclaiming the Forests of Haida Gwaii* (Vancouver: UBC Press, 2015), pp. 51–54; Rajala, *Up-Coast*, pp. 187–88; Thomas Henley and Gary Edenshaw to Canadian Nature Federation, November 12, 1974, box 3, Paul George Papers, UVICSC. Gary Edenshaw is now known by his Haida name so henceforth I will refer to him only as Guujaaw.

34 "Presentation Made to Jim Lorimer, Minister of Municipal Affairs in Victoria, April 21, 1975, by Godfrey Kelly, President of the Council of the Haida Nation," *Queen Charlotte Islands Observer*, April 24, 1975, p. 10 (hereafter *QCIO*); "Proposal to be Submitted to the Forest Resources Commission," Skidegate Band Council, September 11, 1975, J.T. Fyles Natural Resources Library; BC, Royal Commission on Forest Resources, Proceedings, September 1975, vol. 12, pp. 1953–75.

35 "Withdrawal of Charge Against MacMillan Bloedel Protested," *QCIO*, February 20, 1975, p. 1; "Islands Protection Committee," *QCIO*, February 20, 1975, p. 13; Bob Dalgleish, Gary Edenshaw and Vic Bell, "Silence Means Political Consent," *QCIO*, February 20, 1975, p. 6.

36 Irene Gudlaugson, "Multi Use and Environment," *QCIO*, February 27, 1975, p. 2; "Letters to the Editor," *QCIO*, February 27, 1975, p. 6; "Letters to the Editor," *QCIO*, February 27, 1975, p. 8.

37 "Letters to the Editor," *QCIO*, January 28, 1976, p. 5; W.G. Bishop to D. Spaulding, May 20, 1976; D.J. Spaulding to district forester, Prince Rupert forest district, June 7, 1976, file 0333286, BCMFR; "Islands Resources and Local Consultation," *QCIO*, July 22, 1976, p. 6.

38 "ELUC Looks Into South Moresby," *QCIO*, July 29, 1976, pp. 1–4; "New Members Appointed to Advisory Commission," *QCIO*, August 12, 1976, pp. 1–2; "Informal Visit Wednesday by Fisheries Minister," *QCIO*, August 12, 1976, p. 1; Percy Gladstone, "Fisheries Meeting," *QCIO*, August 19, 1976, p. 3.

39 "Salmon Enhancement," *QCIO*, October 16, 1975, pp. 1–2; "Protect What We've Got—But Identify for the Future," *QCIO*, November 18,1976, pp. 1–2; "Rayonier's Clear Cutting Practices Nailed," *QCIO*, September 16, 1976, pp. 1–2; IPS, "Preliminary Brief to the Fall Symposium, Queen Charlotte Islands: Where Are We Now? What Course for the Future?" November 20–21, 1976, pp. 1–2; Lavina Lightbody, "An Open Letter to the Haida People," *QCIO*, January 20, 1977, p. 2.

40 "Pulp Not Houses," *QCIO*, January 6, 1977, p. 5; "Director Linde Persists," *QCIO*, September 9, 1976, p. 4; Carey Linde, "Multinationals Versus Environmentalists—Round 1," *QCIO*, March 17, 1977, p. 8; "Representation by Interest," *QCIO*, March 24, 1977, p. 1; Rick Helmer, "Voices in the Wilderness," *Telkwa Foundation Newsletter* 8 (October 1979), pp. 1–4.

41 "Axes to Grind," *QCIO*, June 9, 1977, p. 9; "Reprieve for an Expanded 'Cabin Set,'" *QCIO*, June 16, 1977, p. 1; "MacMillan Bloedel Five Year Plan for TFL 39 Under Review," *QCIO*, June 16, 1977, p. 16; "Dr. Helmer New Chairman of Public Advisory Committee," *QCIO*, June 30, 1977, p. 4; "One Setting Worth a Thousand Words," *QCIO*, July 21, 1977, pp. 1-2; "First 'Recommendation' by PAC to Forest Service," *QCIO*, July 28, 1977, pp. 1-2.

42 QC Timber Ltd., "Submission to the Royal Commission on Forest Resources," November 1975, BC Commission on Forest Resources Records, 1975-77, GR 347, vol.7, BC Archives; "Queen Charlotte Public Sustained Yield Unit, Prince Rupert Forest District, 1975," Paul George Papers, box 2, UVICSC; "Only Six More Miles to West Coast!" *QCIO*, July 25, 1974, p. 1; "Skeena-Queen Charlotte Regional District," *QCIO*, June 19, 1980, p. 24.

43 E.L. Young to all districts, circular letter no.2830, forest road construction and maintenance policy, September 15, 1975, Nelson forest district records, box 3, BC Archives; L. Ward Johnson, "Loggers Versus Fishermen: Is Coexistence Possible?" *Logging and Sawmilling Journal* 15 (October 1984), p. 53; D.J. Wilford and J.W. Schwab, *Identification and Methods to Reduce Sediment Sources and Transport in C.P. 144* (BC Forest Service, Research Branch, July 9, 1979), pp. 16-24; "Summary of Events—CP144," p. 1, chronology courtesy of Keith Moore.

44 Richard Overstall, "Rennell Sound: The End of Multiple Use?" *Telkwa Foundation Newsletter* 2 (April 1979), p. 2; "Queen Charlotte Public Sustained Yield Unit, 1975," p. 3; "Letters to the Editor," *QCIO*, August 24, 1978, p. 6.

45 Overstall, "Rennell Sound," p. 2; "Queen Charlotte Public Sustained Yield Unit, 1975," p. 4; Neville F. Alley and Bruce Thomson, *Aspects of Environmental Geology, Parts of Graham Island, Queen Charlotte Islands* (Victoria: BC Ministry of Environment, Resource Analysis Branch, bulletin no.2, 1978), pp. 1-2; "Description of the Annual Allowable Cut Process, Forest Inventory Statistics for All Sustained Yield Management Units on Queen Charlotte Islands, As Summarized Nov. 1976," Paul George Papers, box 2, UVICSC.

46 "Summary of Events—CP144," p. 2.

47 "Notice of Crown Timber Sale—QC Proposal," *QCIO*, August 25, 1977, p. 18.

48 "Minister Likes to Get Things Done," *QCIO*, September 15, 1977, pp. 12-13; "Allowable Annual Cut Determination—Queen Charlotte Timber Supply Area," *QCIO*, September 2, 1982, p. 2; "Commission Meets at Port Clements," *QCIO*, September 22, 1977, pp. 1-2; Bill Cowper to T. Waterland, November 22, 1977, Paul George Papers, box 1, UVICSC.

49 "Response to the PAC Recommendation," *QCIO*, October 20, 1977, p. 1; "Rayonier Brief Under Fire," *QCIO*, November 10, 1977, pp. 1-2, "New Forest Cover Maps Are Here," *QCIO*, November 10, 1977, p. 5.

50 "'QC Proposal' Bids Show Wide Variation," *QCIO*, October 13, 1977, p. 1; "Policies Change—Facts Remain the Same," *QCIO*, November 24, 1977, p. 6B; *Hiballer* 28 (November 1977), p. 7; "QC Timber Successful Bidder," *QCIO*, November 24, 1977, pp. 1-2.

51 "Letter Directed to QC Timber Vancouver Office," *QCIO*, December 8, 1977, pp. 9–10; "A Matter of Credibility: PAC Meeting—Sunday December 4," *QCIO*, December 8, 1977, pp. 1–2.

52 "A Matter of Credibility," p. 2; "Teeth for Fisheries Act," *QCIO*, December 15, 1977, pp. 16B–17; "Public Advisory Meeting," *QCIO*, February 2, 1978, p. 10; "Fisheries Alerted to Creek Siltation at Pallant Site," *QCIO*, February 16, 1978, p. 2.

53 Gary Edenshaw, "Until Next Month," *QCIO*, March 9, 1978, p. 12.

54 M.S. Wareing to W.G. Bishop, May 3, 1977; R.A. Johnson, "Resource Folio Evaluation and Monitoring," December 1, 1977, file 0333286, BCMFR; M.F. Painter, notes on meeting of directors' forestry and logging committee with T.M. Apsey, October 3, 1978, Elk River Timber Company Records, box 4, CRMA.

55 "P.A.C. Responds to New Forest Legislation," *QCIO*, June 22, 1978, p. 2; R. Helmer to D. Thompson, June 15, 1978, Paul George Papers, box 1, UVICSC.

56 T.E. Reimchen, "Salmon Habitat, Sedimentation, and Federal Fisheries," Report for Islands Protection Committee, 1978, pp. 1–7, Paul George Papers, box 4, UVICSC. The Carnation Creek project, initiated in 1970, involved a 16-year collaborative study of the effects of logging and silviculture on a Vancouver Island stream.

57 Ibid., pp. 8–14.

58 Ibid., pp. 15–18.

59 Ibid., pp. 19–21; T.E. Reimchen and Sheila Douglas, "Siltation Data for Several Watersheds on the Queen Charlotte Islands," pp. 30–45; Sheila Douglas, "Clear Cut Logging and Salmon Habitat," *Telkwa Foundation Newsletter* 1 (April/May 1978), pp. 6–7.

60 "The Rennell Sound Conflict: Chronology of Events (Prepared by Islands Protection)," *QCIO*, April 19, 1979, p. 18; Overstall, "Rennell Sound," p. 2; Henry Frew, "Confrontation, Controversy Rages Between Fisheries and Forestry on Rennell Sound Cutting Plans," *Western Fisheries* 98 (April 1979), p. 23; "Summary of Events—CP144," p. 2.

61 Alley and Thomson, *Aspects of Environmental Geology*, pp. 43–56.

62 "A Wet Week: Creeks Spill Over," *QCIO*, November 9, 1978, p. 19; J.W. Schwab, *Mass Wasting: October-November 1978 Storm, Rennell Sound, Queen Charlotte Islands* (Victoria: BC Ministry of Forests, research note no.91, 1983), pp. 3–4; Vi Halsey, "Rennell Sounds," *QCIO*, November 9, 1978, p. 15; Vi Halsey, "Rennell Sounds," *QCIO*, November 16, 1978, p. 18.

63 Schwab, *Mass Wasting*, p. V, 3–12.

64 Overstall, "Rennell Sound," pp. 2–3; Keith Moore to R. Rajala, January 3, 2012; Johnson, "Loggers versus Fishermen," p. 55; "The Rennell Sound Conflict," p. 18; Vi Halsey, "Rennell Sounds," *QCIO*, November 23, 1978, p. 12; "Public Advisory Meeting—December 3," *QCIO*, December 7, 1978, p. 2.

65 "QC Timber Served Notice," *QCIO*, January 18, 1979, p. 2.

66 Mark Hume, "Logging Ban Precedent Set," *Victoria Times*, January 16, 1979, p. 1; "Logging Co. Ordered to Stop Work," *Daily News*, January 24, 1979, p. 2; "Officials Keep Close Watch on Logging," *Daily News*, January 25, 1979, p. 1.

67 Mark Hume, "Doomed! Here's What Will Happen on Moresby," *Victoria Times*, December 6, 1978; A. Murray to W.E. Johnson, January 26, 1979, Paul George Papers, box 3, UVICSC; COFI, "Management Report," February 1979, Elk River Timber Company Records, box 5, CRMA; "Local #28 Demands Hearings," *QCIO*, January 25 1979, p. 3; "Trollers Pursue Hearings," *QCIO*, February 1, 1979, p. 2.

68 "Keep Logging Ban on Tsitika Urged," *Fisherman*, March 10, 1978, p. 11; Jack Nichol, "Unemployment and the Environment," *Fisherman*, March 23, 1978, p. 4; "Forest Monopolies Eye Moresby Riches," *Fisherman*, September 22, 1978, p. 11; "IWA Policy is Multiple Use of the Environment," *Green Gold News*, July 6, 1978, n.p.; "Local Union Petitions Minister to Allow Multiple Use of Moresby Island," *Green Gold News*, December 6, 1978, n.p.; T.M. Waterland to Ben Thompson, November 24, 1978, Paul George Papers, box 3, UVICSC.

69 Susanne Fournier, "Wilderness Area Logging Approval Fans Critics' Fire," *Vancouver Express*, January 10, 1979, p. 3; "More than Free," *QCIO*, February 8, 1979; p. 1; "Gaawa' Hanas, 1974–1979: Southern Moresby...The War is Over But the Battle Goes On," *All Alone Stone* 4 (Spring 1980), p. 23; Dave Orton, "The Moresby Wilderness Debate," *Fisherman*, February 2, 1979, p. 5; "P.A.C. Report–Ric Helmer," *QCIO*, February 15, 1979, p. 6.

70 Vi Halsey, "Rennell Sounds," *QCIO*, February 15, 1979, p. 10; "Letters to the Editor," *QCIO*, February 22, 1979, p. 5; Steve Whipp, "Steep Slope Logging on the Charlottes: An Interview with Federal Fisheries Officer, Jim Hart," *Telkwa Foundation Newsletter* 2 (February 1979), pp. 1–2.

71 Whipp, "Steep Slope Logging," pp. 2–4.

72 "QC Timber Lay-Off Likely," *QCIO*, February 15, 1979, p. 18; T.C. Griffing and L.A. Bayrock, "An Investigation of Slope Stability and Fisheries Habitats in the Vicinity of Cutting Permit Numbered 144, Riley Creek Drainage, Graham Island, Queen Charlotte Islands, British Columbia, A Report Prepared for QC Timber Ltd., Vancouver, BC, by International Environmental Consultants Ltd., Jan., 1979," p. 1.

73 Griffing and Bayrock, "An Investigation," pp. 50–60.

74 Ibid., pp. 72–73.

75 "LeBlanc on Logging Stoppage," *QCIO*, March 8, 1979, p. 3; "UFAWU 34th Annual Convention," *Fisherman*, February 19, 1979, p. 8; Overstall, "Rennell Sound," pp. 3–4; Frew, "Confrontation, Controversy," p. 23; Johnson, "Loggers versus Fishermen," p. 55; Vi Halsey, "Rennell Sounds," *QCIO*, March 8, 1979, p. 20.

76 Overstall, "Rennell Sound," p. 4; "Comment," *Colonist*, March 10, 1979, p. 4; Mark Hume, "Charlottes Logging Showdown," *Victoria Times*, March 17, 1979, p. 1; "The Rennell Sound Conflict," p. 18; "Actions and Responses Out Rennell Sound Way," *QCIO*, March 22, 1979, pp. 1, 4; "Summary of Events–CP144," p. 3.

77 "Actions and Responses," pp. 1, 4.

78 Mark Hume, "Loggers May Defy Fisheries Ban," *Victoria Times*, March 19, 1979. p. 1.

79 Mark Hume, "Four Loggers Arrested," *Victoria Times*, March 19, 1979, p. 1; "Boss Jailed, 4 Nabbed in Fish-Logs Tiff," *Daily Colonist*, March 22, 1979, p. 1; Vi Halsey, "Rennell Sounds," *QCIO*, March 29, 1979, p. 11; "Loggers in Dilemma over Arrests," *Campbell River Upper Islander*, March 28, 1979, p. 4; Overstall, "Rennell Sound," p. 3.

80 Mark Hume, "Three More Loggers Arrested," *Victoria Times*, March 22, 1979, p. 1; "Copy of Telegram from Federal Fisheries to the Hon. Tom Waterland Mar. 22, 1979," *QCIO*, April 19, 1979, p. 19; "The Rennell Sound Conflict," p. 18; "Summary of Events—CP144," p. 3.

81 COFI, management report, April 1979, Elk River Timber Company Records, box 5, CRMA; "Telegram Sent," *Daily News*, March 29, 1972, p. 1; Mark Hume, "BC to Fight for Loggers," *Victoria Times*, March 23, 1979, p. 7; "Logging Conflict Needs Sorting Out," *Daily News*, March 23, 1979, p. 1; Larry Still and Moira Farrow, "Drop Charges 'or We Strike,'" *Vancouver Express*, Mar 23, 1979, p. 1.

82 Don Collins, "British Columbia Wide Walkout Threat by IWA Over Fish-Log Fight," *Daily Colonist*, March 23, 1979, p. 1.

83 Hume, "BC to Fight"; Still and Farrow, "Drop Charges", "Intolerable," *Victoria Times*, March 22, 1979, p. 4.

84 "Rennell Sound Logging Controversy," *Fisherman*, March 30, 1979, p. 1; "Talks Tuesday in Woods Row," *Victoria Times*, March 24, 1979, p. 2; Larry Still, "BC, Feds Duel Up the Creek," *Vancouver Express*, March 26, 1979, p. 1; "Premiers Put on Show for Federal Gov't," *Daily News*, March 23, 1979, p. 3.

85 "More Arrests and Threats on the Charlottes," *Colonist*, March 24, 1979, p. 1; "Logs or Fish? It's No Contest," *Colonist*, March 27, 1979, p. 4

86 "Talks Tuesday in Woods Row," *Victoria Times*, March 24, 1979, p. 2; "Bennett Prepared to Meet with PM," *Daily News*, March 26, 1979, p. 1; "Officials Try to Settle QC Is. Logging Dispute," *Daily News*, March 26, 1979, p. 11; "Logs or Fish? It's No Contest"; "BC Blamed for Log Fuss," *Daily Colonist*, March 27, 1979, p. 39; "BC Gov't Takes Unreasonable Stand," *Daily News*, March 28, 1979, p. 18.

87 "More Arrests and Threats"; "BC Blamed"; "Log War Stand Attacked," *Victoria Times*, March 27, 1979, p. 1.

88 Larry Still, "It's 'Timber!' for Fisheries in Big Battle of Riley Creek," *Vancouver Express*, March 28, 1979, p. 1; Mark Hume, "Fishing 'Sellout' in Logging Deal," *Victoria Times*, March 28, 1979, p. 1; Overstall, "Rennell Sound," p. 5; Richard Overstall, "Rennell Sound: The Agreement," *Telkwa Foundation Newsletter* 2 (Summer 1979), p. 11.

89 Moira Farrow, "Fisheries Claims Moves to Save Salmon Streams," *Vancouver Express*, March 30, 1979, p. 5; John Clarke, "Are Loggers Pawns in Power Play?" *BCL* 63 (June 1979), pp. 40–42.

90 "'Support Fed. Jurisdiction to Full' says Rupert Exchange," *QCIO*, April 19, 1979, p. 6.

91   "Logging Dispute Sounds Death-Knell," *Daily News*, March 30, 1979, p. 2; Hume, "Fishing 'Sellout'"; Stewart Lang, "Riley Creek Decision a Big Step Backward," *Victoria Times*, March 30, 1979, p. 29.

92   "Lancing the Riley Creek Boil," *Vancouver Express*, April 2, 1979, p. 4; "IWA Chief and Fish," *Victoria Times*, April 3, 1979, p. 4; Jean Sorensen, "ForesTalk Interviews Jack Munro," *ForesTalk2* (Fall 1978), pp. 8–10.

93   Steve Whipp, "Not an Election Issue—A Land-Use Confrontation," *QCIO*, March 29, 1979, p. 20.

94   Overstall, "Rennell Sound," pp. 1–4.

95   Rajala, "Forests and Fish," p. 70; "M-B Still Stalls in Fish Case," *Victoria Times*, March 1, 1979, p. 12; COFI, "Management Reports," May 1979, Elk River Timber Company Records, box 5, CRMA; Overstall, "Rennell Sound," p. 4; COFI Members' Newsletter, April 1979, Elk River Timber Company Records, box 5, CRMA.

96   "Logging Dispute Left in Limbo," *Daily News*, March 28, 1979, p. 7; "Court Action on QC Timber," *QCIO*, May 31, 1979, p. 4.

97   "Remember Rennell," *Fisherman*, April 27, 1979, p. 6; "Bull of the Woods," *Thunderbird* [Bella Coola], April 10, 1979, p. 4; "NDP Wants to See Justice Being Done," *QCIO*, April 12, 1979, pp. 1–2; "Liberals Didn't Have the Guts Says NDP Candidate Jim Fulton," *QCIO*, April 19, 1979, p. 20; "Federal Liberal Candidate Visits All Communities," *QCIO*, April 19, 1979, p. 3.

98   Al Meadows, "Cockpit Comments," *Western Fisheries* 98 (June 1979), pp. 15–16; "Forestry Policy Needs Debate," *Fisherman*, May 25, 1979, p. 5; "Federation of BC Naturalists," *QCIO*, May 24, 1979, p. 22.

99   "One Office to Look After All Resources?" *Western Fisheries* 98 (June 1979), pp. 11, 16; "'Charlottes' Hart Resigns but New Officer Sought," *Fisherman*, July 13, 1979, p. 7; Mark Hume, "Fisheries Officer Quits Over Logging Uproar," *Victoria Times*, July 4, 1979, p. 1.

100   Douglas N. Swanston, "Field Reconnaissance Report on the Relative Stability and Potential Impacts from Timber Harvesting Operations on Cutting Permit 144, Riley Creek Drainage, Graham Island, Queen Charlotte Islands, British Columbia," (unpublished report, 1979, J.T. Fyles Natural Resources Library), pp. 1–63.

101   Ibid., pp. 13–14.

102   Ibid., pp. 14–18.

103   Ibid., pp. 19–20.

104   "Fishery Charges in Log Row Dropped," *Victoria Times*, August 18, 1979, p. 2; "Fisheries Drops Logging Charges," *Fisherman*, August 24, 1979, p. 1; Richard Overstall, "Fisheries Act—A Paper Tiger?" *Telkwa Foundation Newsletter* 2 (September 1979), p. 1.

105   "Fisheries Drops," p. 11; "Fulton: Fisheries Test Case Must Proceed," *QCIO*, August 30, 1979, p. 1; "James McGrath Needs a New Lawyer," *Fisherman*, August 24, 1979, p. 4.

106 "Fisheries Drops," p. 1; Overstall, "Fisheries Act," p. 2; "Progress at Rennell Sound," *QCIO*, August 30, 1979, p. 3; Jack Danylchuck, "ForesTalk Interviews Wally Johnson," *ForesTalk* 3 (Winter 1979), p. 10; "Charlottes Fish-Woods War Over," *Victoria Times*, August 23, 1979, p. 41.

107 D.J. Wilford and J.W. Schwab, *Identification and Methods to Reduce Sediment Sources and Transport in C.P. 144* (Victoria: BC Forest Service, Research Branch, July 9, 1979), p. 2.

108 Alice McCrea, "Port News," *QCIO*, August 30, 1979, p. 19; "Fisheries Officers Braced for Rainy Season in Rennell Sound," *Daily News*, September 20, 1979, p. 1.

109 "Fisheries Officers Braced"; "Skidegate Local to Watch Creeks," *Fisherman*, October 19, 1979, p. 1; "Ministers Discuss Many Things, but No Policy Decisions Made," *Daily News*, October 3, 1979, p. 1.

110 Vi Halsey, "Rennell Sounds," *QCIO*, October 11, 1978, p. 24; Vi Halsey, "Rennell Sounds," *QCIO*, October 18, 1979, p. 26; Vi Halsey, "Rennell Sounds," *QCIO*, October 25, 1979, p. 26; Vi Halsey, "Rennell Sounds," *QCIO*, November 29, 1979, p. 29; "Landslides in Charlottes...Warnings Come True," *Victoria Times*, November 27, 1979, p. 1; "Worst Fears of Fisheries Come True on Q.C.I.," *Daily News*, November 25, 1979, p. 1; Terry Donnelly and Cam Martin, "Fall Rains at Rennell Sound," *Telkwa Foundation Newsletter* 3 (January–February 1980), p. 8.

111 K. Moore to D.N. Swanston, November 29, 1979, courtesy of Keith Moore.

112 Donnelly and Martin, "Fall Rains," pp. 8–10.

113 Ibid., pp. 9–10; "Charges Eyed Over Slides," *Victoria Times*, November 28, 1979, p. 1; "Three Options Available to Prevent Logging Damage," *Daily News*, December 19, 1979, p. 1.

114 Charles La Vertu, "Charlottes Salmon Fishery Near Destruction?" *Victoria Times*, December 1, 1979, p. 2; "Logging Rules to Blame for Slides—Minister," *Victoria Times*, December 4, 1979, p. 35; "New Environment Minister Says Forestry Regulations Likely to Blame for Damage," *Daily News*, December 4, 1979, p. 1; "Officials Flock to Q.C.I. to Discuss Future of Creek," *Daily News*, November 28, 1979, p. 1; "Jim Fulton on His Feet Again," *QCIO*, November 29, 1979, p. 15.

115 "Nobody Can Gloat," *Victoria Times*, November 28, 1979, p. 4; "Jim Fulton on His Feet;" Shirley Duncan to James McGrath, November 29, 1979, Sierra Club of Western Canada, BC chapter, Records, box 6, UVICSC; "Landslides Devastate Riley Creek," *Fisherman*, December 14, 1979, p. 1; "Situation in Charlottes Described as 'Outrageous,'" *Western Fisheries* 99 (December 1979), pp. 19, 56; "Riley Creek Evidence Being Reviewed," *QCIO*, December 6, 1979, p. 1; "Brotherhood Wants Charges Laid," *Native Voice* (December 1979), p. 16.

116 "Log-Fish Dispute Patched," *Victoria Times*, December 6, 1979, p. 3; "Landslides Devastate," p. 1; "Slide Hits Bonanza Creek," *QCIO*, December 13, 1979, pp. 1, 3; "UFAWU 35th Convention," *Fisherman*, February 15, 1980, p. 6.

117 "More Slides in Rennell Sound," *Daily News*, December 13, 1979, p. 1; "Slides Hit Bonanza Creek," pp. 1, 3.

118 "McGrath Rules Out Action Against Logging Company," *Fisherman*, January 11, 1980, p. 6.

119 "Letters to the Editor," *QCIO*, December 27, 1979, p. 5; "BC Fed Urges Action on Herbicides, Logging," *Fisherman*, December 14, 1979, p. 14.

120 "Letters to the Editor," *QCIO*, December 13, 1979, p. 5.

121 "Letters to the Editor," *QCIO*, February 7, 1980, pp. 5, 7.

122 John Clarke, "Labor, Corporations Find Common Cause in Environmental Activities," *BCL* 64 (March 1980), pp. 42–43.

123 "Truck Loggers Tackle Timber Shortage, Monopolies," *Hiballer* 31 (February 1980), p. 13.

124 "Charlottes Battle Not Over?" *Victoria Times*, January 25, 1980; p. 7; "Guns of Riley Creek More Fearsome than Iran," *Colonist*, January 25, 1980, p. 11.

125 "News Release: Islands Protection Society Threatens Court Action Over Riley Creek Logging Devastation," December 6, 1979, Paul George Papers, box 1, UVICSC; "Charlotte Lawsuit Looms," *Victoria* Times, December 5, 1979, p. 19; George Hewison to Islands Protection Society, March 1, 1980, Paul George Papers, box 2, UVICSC; "Fighting for Fish," *Victoria Times*, February 8, 1980, p. 4; "Union Takes Up Riley Creek Battle," *Fisherman*, February 15, 1980, p. 1.

126 "Fisherman Names Johnson in Riley Creek Legal Action," *Fisherman*, May 30, 1980, p. 3; "Want to Help Fight Riley Creek Disaster?" *Western Fisheries* 100 (June 1980), pp. 9–10; "Letters," *Fisherman*, March 11, 1980, p. 5; "IPS News," *QCIO*, May 1, 1980, p. 20; "Action Brought by I.P.S.," *QCIO*, June 5, 1980, p. 6.

127 "The Visit to Riley Creek," *QCIO*, February 21, 1980, p. 4; "Letters to the Editor," *QCIO*, February 28, 1980, p. 5.

128 "Logging Plan in Charlottes Under Government Review," *Vancouver Sun*, February 27, 1980, p. 1; "BC to Curb Charlottes Logging Firm?" *Victoria Times*, February 27, 1980, p. 1; "President's Address to 1980 Convention," BC Wildlife Federation, Proceedings of 1980 Convention, Duncan, p. 1, J.T. Fyles Natural Resources Library; Mark Hume, "Death of a Salmon Stream," *BC Outdoors* 36 (July 1980), pp. 39–41, 55.

129 "Fishery-Forestry Interactions," *QCIO*, June 5, 1980, pp. 21–22.

130 "Riley Creek Re-examined," *Truck Logger* (July 1980), p. 32; "To Tackle Fishery-Forestry Conflicts," *Western Fisheries* 100 (July 1980), pp. 25–26; "Taxpayers to Foot the Bill For QC Logging Damage," *Fisherman*, May 16, 1980, p. 3.

131 "Geotechnic Study at Rennell Sound," *QCIO*, March 13, 1980, p. 2; "Public Presentation of Rennell Sound Geotechnic Study Set for Sunday," *QCIO*, April 24, 1980, p. 7; R.B. Townshend, "Geotechnic Report—Rennell Sound, Queen Charlotte Islands: A Report Prepared for QC Timber Ltd." (Peril Bay Geotechnic Services, December 1979).

132 "Geotechnic Study at Rennell Sound," *QCIO*, March 13, 1980, p. 2; "Public Presentation of Rennell Sound Geotechnic Study Set for Sunday," *QCIO*, April 24, 1980, p. 7; D.M. Leach, "Let Our Record Stand," *QCIO*, May 1, 1980, pp. 1–3; "Queen Charlotte Timber Company Public Information Meeting on Rennell Sound and Riley Creek," Paul George Papers, box 3, UVICSC.

133 Leach, "Let Our Record Stand," pp. 3, 9.

134 Ibid., pp. 3, 9-11.

135 Ibid., p. 11.

136 "Letters to the Editor," *QCIO*, May 1, 1980, p. 6; "Letters to the Editor," *QCIO*, May 1, 1980, p. 8.

137 "Riley Creek Revisited," *Truck Logger* (July 1980), p. 32; Michael J. Hardin, John E. McLatchy and Robert E. Torangeau, eds., *Fisheries and Pollution Reports, Case Law: Prosecutions Under the Pollution Control Provisions of the Fisheries Act*, vol.2 (Ottawa: Environment Canada, 1980), pp. 286-95.

138 John Clarke, "Ottawa and Victoria: The Politics of Fish," *BCL* 64 (August 1980), p. 38; Bob Lee, "Top Court Cuts Power of Fisheries Act," *Truck Logger* 3 (August 1980), pp. 10-11; "No Help Needed," *Truck Logger* 3 (September 1980), p. 36; "Fisheries Act Ruling Greeted With Anger," *Victoria Times*, June 18, 1980, p. 1; "Logging Controls 'Unconstitutional,'" *Fisherman*, June 27, 1980, p. 9.

139 John E. MacLatchy and Robert K. Timberg, eds., *Fisheries Pollution Reports Prosecutions Under the Pollution Control and Habitat Protection Provisions of the Fisheries Act* (Ottawa: Environment Canada, 1984), pp. 52-54.

140 Ibid., pp. 55-57; "Riley Creek Hearing Stayed by Province," *QCIO*, July 3, 1980, p. 3.

141 "Province Halts Rennell Suit," *Fisherman*, July 11, 1980, p. 5; "Letter to the Editor," *QCIO*, July 3, 1980, p. 5; "Unusual Justice," *Victoria Times*, July 7, 1980, p. 4; BC, Official Report of the Debates of the Legislative Assembly (Hansard), July 16, 1980, afternoon sitting, pp. 3331-32. Available at https://www.leg.bc.ca/documents-data/debate-transcripts/32nd-parliament/2nd-session/32p_02s_800716p; "Bellis Case Could Not Be Successful Says Minister," *QCIO*, July 31, 1980, p. 3.

142 "Still Unusual Justice," *Victoria Times*, July 16, 1980, p. 4; "Letters to the Editor," *QCIO*, August 7, 1980, p. 6.

143 "Attorney-General Tramples Citizen Rights, says MLA," *QCIO*, August 14, 1980, p. 15; "From the Debates of the Legislative Assembly," *QCIO*, August 21, 1980, p. 10; "Stay Challenged," *QCIO*, August 28, 1980, p. 4; MacLatchy and Timberg, *Fisheries Pollution Reports*, vol.3, p. 58.

144 "A Brief to Premier Bennett," *QCIO*, October 2, 1980, pp. 25-26; "Before and After the Facts and Actions," *QCIO*, March 5, 1981, p. 3.

145 "Before and After," p. 3.

146 "Fish Habitat Ruling Perplexes Rogers," *Victoria Times*, July 19, 1980, p. 3; "New Ruling Puts Fishery First," *Victoria Times*, July 21, 1980, p. 1; Hardy, MacLatchy and Tourangeau, eds., *Fisheries Pollution Reports*, vol.2, pp. 296-303.

147 Jim Duggleby, "Coastal Logging—New Era, New Issues," *BCL* 64 (November 1980), p. 11.

148 Wilson, *Talk and Log*, p. 289; Joyce Jefferd to Gary Edenshaw, August 8, 1980, Paul George Papers, box 3, UVICSC; "From QC Timber Riley Creek 'Secure,'" *BC Outdoors* 36 (October 1980), p. 8.

149 "From QC Timber," p. 8.

150 Ibid., p. 8.

151 J.A. Biickert, "Riley Creek—The Lessons Learned," address to the CIF meeting, Vancouver, November 18, 1980, pp. 1-2; Sierra Club of Canada, BC Chapter Records, box 6, UVICSC.

152 Ibid., pp. 2-10.

153 Philip Deardon, "Pacific Salmon: Can Old School Ties be Preserved?" *Nature Canada* 10 (January/March 1981), p. 47; "Must Protect Fish Habitat," *Campbell River Upper Islander*, February 25, 1981, p. 4; "Who Should Manage the Trees?" *Telkwa Foundation Newsletter* 5 (June 1982), pp. 11-12; Jack Miller, "'Major' Concerns," *QCIO*, January 8, 1981, pp. 6-7.

154 "Pearse to Head Fisheries Inquiry," *Western Fisheries* 101 (February 1981), p. 32; John Clarke, "Fisheries, Logging and the IWA," *BCL* 65 (June 1981), pp. 48-49; "No Accountability Root of Fisheries' Woes, Pepper Tells Pearse," *Western Fisheries* 102 (June 1981), pp. 31-32; "The Pearse Commission," *Fisherman*, August 7, 1981, p. 1.

155 John Clarke, "Facing the Rapids Together," *BCL* 65 (September 1981), pp. 77, 81; Clarke, "Fisheries, Logging," pp. 48-49; Susan Cardinal, "DFO Under Fire at Vancouver Hearing," *Western Fisheries* 102 (September 1981), pp. 39-41; "The Pearse Commission," *Truck Logger* 4 (October 1981), pp. 11-12.

156 John Clarke, "Ironing Out the Problems," *BCL* 66 (November 1982), pp. 14, 24.

157 "Letters to the Editor," *QCIO*, September 4, 1980, pp. 6, 8; Jack Miller, "Windy Bay—One Position," *QCIO*, April 23, 1981, p. 9; Jack Miller, "Windy Bay—An Ecological Reserve," *QCIO*, February 19, 1981, p. 5.

158 Scott Mowbray, "'Remember Riley Creek': Fisheries, Forestry Clash over Moresby Island Ecological Reserves," *Western Fisheries* 102 (June 1981), pp. 56-60; Murray Rankin, "Logging, Fisheries and Wilderness: Paradise Lost?" p. 9, Paul George Papers, box 3, UVICSC.

159 "Windy Bay—Another Position Paper," *QCIO*, May 7, 1981, pp. 1-2; "AAC Reduction Requested by Council of Haida Nation," *QCIO*, August 27, 1981, p. 2; "Plan for Tree Farm Licence 24 Approved by Government," *QCIO*, October 22, 1981, p. 2; "Information Brief of the Council of the Haida Nation," *QCIO*, November 12, 1981, pp. 22-23.

160 Vi Halsey, "Rennell Sounds," *QCIO*, September 4, 1980, p. 14; Vi Halsey, "Rennell Sounds," *QCIO*, September 11, 1980, p. 13; Vi Halsey, "Rennell Sounds," *QCIO*, October 23, 1980, p. 8; Vi Halsey, "Rennell Sounds," *QCIO*, November 6, 1980, p. 15; Vi Halsey, "Rennell Sounds," *QCIO*, November 13, 1980, p. 22; Vi Halsey, "Rennell Sounds," *QCIO*, March 12, 1981, p. 16; Vi Halsey, "Rennell Sounds," *QCIO*, June 4, 1981, p. 11; Vi Halsey, "Rennell Sounds," *QCIO*, June 18, 1981, p. 13; Vi Halsey, "Rennell Sounds," *QCIO*, October 1, 1981, p. 20.

161 "How Goes It?" *QCIO*, May 27, 1982, p. 1; Wilson, *Talk and Log*, pp. 160-61; "Less Timber Predicted for Queen Charlotte TSA," *QCIO*, April 1, 1982, p. 1.

162 "Forest Ministry Blamed for Predicament," *QCIO*, April 1, 1982, p. 4; "TSA Report Unsubstantiated and Public Unable to Interpret It," *QCIO*, April 1, 1982, p. 16; "Submission on TSA Not to be Misconstrued, Says Council of the Haida Nation," *QCIO*, April 29, 1982, pp. 8-9; "Islands Protection Society Submission," *QCIO*, April 29, 1982, p. 10.

163 "Allowable Annual Cut Determination—Queen Charlotte Timber Supply Area," *QCIO*, September 2, 1982, pp. 2-4; "Allowable Annual Cut Reduced," *QCIO*, September 2, 1982, p. 12; "Queen Charlotte TSA is Cut Back," *Logging and Sawmilling Journal* 14 (March 1983), p. 7; "Charlottes' Annual Cut Reduced but Still 'No Timber in 25 Years,'" *Vancouver Sun*, September 1, 1982, p. 7.

164 "Queen Charlotte TSA Apportionment," *QCIO*, December 23, 1982, pp. 1-2; "MB Still Aims for the 17th," *QCIO*, January 6, 1983, p. 1; V.A. Poulin, "Progress Report: Fish/Forestry Interaction Program in Areas of Mass Wasting in the Queen Charlotte Islands, Prepared for the Steering Committee," March 17, 1983 (unpublished report, J.T. Fyles Natural Resources Library, 1983), p. 2; Jim Doyle, "Logging the Profile," *Truck Logger* 15 (October/November 1992), p. 28.; "More Slides," *QCIO*, February 16, 1984, p. 24; Ron Nelson, "At the Root of Landslides," *BC Outdoors* 40 (August 1984), pp. 22, 31; Alex Grzybowski, "The Fate of the Queen Charlottes," *Alternatives* (Spring/Summer 1985), p. 60.

165 "Fisheries Minister Assures Action to Protect BC Salmon Streams," *Toronto Star*, August 20, 1985, p. 11.

166 Rajala, *Up-Coast*, p. 207; "Charges Dropped Against Logging Firms," *Globe and Mail*, August 13, 1986, p. 4; J.C. Kerr, "Chairman's Report, Council of Forest Industries of BC," *Loggers' Handbook* 46 (1986), p. 12; Elizabeth May, *Paradise Won: The Struggle for South Moresby* (Toronto: McClelland & Stewart, 1990), pp. 142-44; Wilson, *Talk and Log*, pp. 216-30.

167 Terry Glavin, "Siddon's Resignation Demanded," *Vancouver Sun*, November 4, 1988, p. 7; Terry Glavin, "Stall on Charging Logging Firm Claimed by NDP MP Fulton," *Vancouver Sun*, November 5, 1988, p. 2.

168 Hough, *Managing Canada's Fisheries*, p. 384; Terry Glavin, "Minister Mystified by Barriers to Restocking Spawning Creek," *Vancouver Sun*, December 6, 1988, p. 8.

169 "Chief Forester, Ministry of Forests and Lands," *BC Sportsman* (Special Convention Issue, 1987), pp. 8-9; D.B. Tripp and V.A. Poulin, *The Effects of Logging and Mass Wasting on Salmonid Spawning Habitat in Streams on the Queen Charlotte Islands* (Victoria: BC Ministry of Forests and Lands, 1986), pp. 25-26; Tom Wood, "Fish and Chips," *BC Outdoors* 43 (March 1987), pp. 70-71, 90.

170 Wood, "Fish and Chips," p. 90; "Good Government!" *Vancouver Sun*, January 9, 1988, p. 4. For a general treatment see Dave Toews and Eugene Hetherington, "A Brief His-

tory of Forest Hydrology in British Columbia," *Streamline* 8 (Fall 2004), pp. 1-5.; "Government Orders Stream Rehabilitation on Vancouver Island", BC Ministry of Forests News Release, July 30, 1992, J.T. Fyles Natural Resources Library.

171   Don Grant, "Guilty 'til Proven Innocent," *Canadian Forest Industries* 103 (April 1983), p. 9; L. Ward Johnson, "Report Urges Protection of Unstable Slopes," *Logging and Sawmilling Journal* 15 (November 1984), p. 18; "Letters to the Editor," *QCIO*, June 2, 1983, pp. 7-8.

172   "Letters to the Editor," *QCIO*, July 7, 1983, p. 6.

173   R. Michael M'Gonigle, "The Political Ecology of Biodiversity: A View from the Western Woods," in Stephen Bocking, ed., *Biodiversity in Canada: Ecology, Ideas, and Action* (Peterborough: Broadview Press, 2000), p. 394; Mike Halleran, "Logging With Lucille," *BC Outdoors* 47 (Winter 1991), pp. 22-23.

174   Doyle, "Logging the Profile," pp. 32-33; Paul Wilson and *Truck Logger* staff, "Airborne Solutions," *Truck Logger* 16 (August/September 1993), p. 36.

175   Steve Chatwin, "The Short but Dramatic History of Riley Creek, Queen Charlotte Islands," copy courtesy of Keith Moore; personal communication, Keith Moore.

176   "Munro's Forestry Article," *West Coast Lumberworker* (March 1979), pp. 11-12; Scott Prudham, "Sustaining Sustained Yield: Class Politics, and Post-War Forest Regulation in British Columbia," *Environment and Planning D: Society and Space* 25 (2007), pp. 258-83.

177   "Talks Planned with IWA," *Fisherman*, February 19, 1979, p. 7; "Carey Linde Reports on Fishery Confrontation," *QCIO*, October 1, 1981, p. 4.

178   Patricia Gallaugher, ed., *Getting the Missing Fish Story Straight, Forum Proceedings* (Vancouver: Simon Fraser University, Public Forums on Environmental Issues, March 1995), p. 65.

179   D. Leach, "Some Things They Do Better," *QCIO*, July 28, 1983, p. 20.

180   Gallaugher, ed., *Getting the Missing Fish*, p. 65; *Sierra Legal Defence Fund, Stream Protection under the Code: The Destruction Continues* (Vancouver: SLDF, 1977), pp. 1-3; Jeffrey Young and John Werring, *The Will to Protect: Preserving BC's Wild Salmon Habitat* (Vancouver: David Suzuki Foundation, 2006), p. 3; "Failure to Enforce: How Canada Allows BC Logging Companies to Destroy Salmon Habitat: A Report of the Natural Resources Defense Council" (April 2001), p. 4; http://www.bcssp.ca/letters/nrdc_FN.pdf (August 5, 2010).

181   Young and Werring, *The Will to Protect*, p. 7; "Failure to Enforce," p. 2.

182   Toews and Hetherington, "A Brief History of Forest Hydrology," p.2.

183   Jeremy Wilson, "Forest Conservation in British Columbia, 1935-85: Reflections on a Barren Political Debae," *BC Studies* 76 (Winter 1987-88), p. 32.

184   May, *Paradise Won*.

185   Richard White, "'Are You an Environmentalist or Do You Work for a Living?': Work and Nature," in William Cronon, ed., *Uncommon Ground: Rethinking the Human Place in Nature* (New York: W.W. Norton, 1995), pp. 171-85.

Select Bibliography

PERIODICALS

All Alone Stone
British Columbia Digest
BC Logging News
British Columbia Lumberman
BC Outdoors
BC Sportsman
B.C. Wildlife Federation Newsletter
Canadian Forest Industries
Canadian Geographical Journal
Cariboo and Northern British Columbia Digest
Citizen
Daily Colonist
Daily News
Fisherman
Forest and Outdoors
ForesTalk
Globe and Mail
Green Gold News
Hiballer
Journal of Logging Management
Lakes District News
Logging and Sawmilling Journal
Native Voice
Nature Canada
Nechako Chronicle
Pacific Coast Lumberman
Province
Queen Charlotte Islands Observer

Telkwa Foundation Newsletter

Truck Logger

Vancouver Express

Vancouver Sun

Victoria Daily Times

Victoria Times

Western Canada Lumber Worker

Western Fisheries

Western Fish and Game

Western Lumberman

BOOKS

Andrews, Ralph Warren. *Glory Days Of Logging.* New York: Bonanza Books, 1956.

——. *Redwood Classic: Panorama of a Century.* New York: Bonanza Books, 1958.

——. *This was sawmilling.* New York: Bonanza Books, 1957.

Ault, Richard, Richard Walton and Mark Childers. *What Works: A Decade of Change at Champion International.* San Francisco: Jossey-Bass Publishers, 1998.

Apsey, T. M. *What's All This Got To Do With The Price Of 2x4s?.* Calgary: University of Calgary Press, 2006.

Armson, Kenneth A. and Marjorie McLeod. *The Legacy of John Waldie and Sons: A History of the Victoria Harbour Lumber Company.* Toronto: Natural Heritage Books, 2007.

Bacher, John. *Two Billion Trees and Counting: The Legacy of Edmund Zavitz.* Toronto: Dundurn Press Ltd., 2011.

Bacig, Tom and Fred Thompson. *Tall Timber: A Pictorial History of Logging in the Upper Midwest.* Bloomington: Voyageur Press, 1982.

Baikie, Wallace. *Rolling With the Times.* Campbell River: Kask Graphics, 1985.

Baldwin, Catherine. *Making the Most of the Best.* Portland: Willamette Industries, Inc., 1982.

Baptie, Sue. *First Growth: The Story of British Columbia Forest Products Limited.* Vancouver: British Columbia Forest Products, 1975.

Barrow, Susan H.L. and J. Allan Evans. *Green Gold Harvest: A History of Logging and its Products.* Seattle: Whatcom Museum of History and Art, 1969.

Bates, Marion. *Memories: Honeymoon Bay, 50 years.* NP, 1997.

Batory, Dana M. *Vintage Woodworking Machinery: An Illustrated Guide to Four Manufacturers.* Mendham: Astragal Press, 1997.

Beaulieu, Albert E. *Applied Lumber Science.* Vancouver: Clarke & Stuart, 1934.

Belcher, C. Francis. *Logging Railroads of the White Mountains.* Boston: Appalachian Mountain Club, 1989.

Bentley, Peter J.G. *One Family's Journey.* Vancouver: Douglas & McIntyre, 2012.

Bergen, Myrtle. *Tough Timber.* Vancouver: Elgin Publications, 1979.

Bernsohn, Ken. *Cutting Up the North.* North Vancouver: Hancock House, 1981.

Bocking, Richard C. *Mighty River: A Portrait of the Fraser.* Vancouver: Douglas & McIntyre, 1997.

Boyd, Kenneth C. *When the Ship Comes In: An Autobiography.* Duncan: Wester A.R.P. Services Ltd., 1998.

Bradley, Lenore K. *Robert Alexander Long: A Lumberman of the Gilded Age.* Durham: Distributed by Duke University Press, 1989.

Bradley, R. Ken. *Historic Railways of the Powell River Area.* Victoria: British Columbia Railway Historical Association, 1982.

Bradley, R. Ken and Karen Southern. *Powell River's Railway Era.* Victoria: British Columbia Railway Historical Association, 2000.

Bradshaw, Gordon, M. Bradshaw and T. Chisholm. *Tall Timber Tales: Reid, Collins Recollections: 1951 to 2002. NP, 2004.*

Brasnett, N.V. *Planned Management of Forests.* London: George Allen & Unwin, 1953.

British Columbia. *Field Manual of Sport Fish Habitat Protection.* Victoria: Fisheries Management Division, Fish and Wildlife Branch, Department of Recreation and Conservation, 1966.

Brown, Nelson Courtlandt. *Forest Products.* New York: John Wiley & Sons, 1950.

——. *Forest Products.* 2nd Ed. New York: John Wiley & Sons, 1927.

——. *Logging.* New York: John Wiley & Sons, 1949.

——. and James S. Bethel. *Lumber.* 2nd Ed. New York: John Wiley & Sons, 1947.

Burch, Gerry, Art Walker and Peter A. Robinson. *The Working Forest of British Columbia.* Madeira Park: Harbour Publishing, 1995.

Burch, Gerry and John Parminter. *Frederick Davison Mulholland, P. Eng., B.C.R.F.* Victoria: Forest History Association of BC, 2008.

Burton, Thomas L. *Natural Resource Policy in Canada: Issues and Perspectives.* Toronto: McLelland and Stewart, 1972.

Cail, Robert Edgar. *Land, Man, and the Law.* Vancouver: University of British Columbia Press, 1974

Canada Department of Fisheries and the International Pacific Salmon Fisheries Commission, in Collaboration with the Fish and Wildlife Branch of the B.C. Department of Recreation and Conservation. *Effects of Log Driving on the Salmon and Trout Populations in the Stellako River.* Vancouver: International Pacific Salmon Fisheries Commission, 1966.

Canadian Woods: Their Properties and Uses. 2nd ed. Ottawa: Forestry Branch, 1951.

Carroll, Charles F. *The Timber Economy of Puritan New England.* Providence: Brown University Press, 1974.

Cash, Gwen. *Off the Record: The Personal Reminiscences of Canada's First Woman Reporter.* Langely, BC: Stagecoach Publishing Company, 1977.

Chappell, Gordon S. *Logging along the Denver & Rio Grande*. Golden: Colorado Railway Museum, 1971.

Chemainus, Then and Now: A Pictorial History. Chemainus: Milltown Publishing, 2003.

Childers, William T. *Echoes From The Millpond*. Columbia: Caldwell Parish Library, 1987.

Clark, Donald H. *18 Men and a Horse*. Bellingham: Whatcom Museum of History and Art, 1969.

Clarkson, Roy. *On Beyond Leatherbark: The Cass Saga*. Parsons: McClain Printing Company, 1990.

Clyne, J.V. *Jack of All Trades: Memories of a Busy Life*. Toronto: McClelland & Stewart, 1985.

Coady, Howard. *Sheet Harbour History*. Hansport: Lancelot Press, 1988.

Coman, Edwin T. and Helen M. Gibbs. *Time, Tide & Timber: Over a Century of Pope & Talbot*. Portland: Pope & Talbot, 1978.

Coney, Michael. *Forest Ranger, Ahoy!* Sidney: Porthole Press, 1983.

Connor, Mary Roddis. *A Century with Connor Timber: Connor Forest Industries, 1872–1972*. 2nd ed. Laona: Camp Five Museum Foundation, 1997.

Conway, Steve. *Logging Practices*. San Francisco: Miller Freeman Pubs, 1976.

Corrigan, George A. *Calked Boots and Cant Hooks: One Man's Story of Logging the North*. Ashland: Northword, 1986.

Cox, Thomas R. *Mills and Markets: A History of the Pacific Coast Lumber Industry to 1900*. Seattle: University of Washington Press, 1974.

Crawford, Leonard W. *The way it was*. Campbell River: Ptarmigan Press, 2007.

——. Leonard and Rose. *The Changing Times: the life of an Independent Logger*. Campbell River: Ptarmigan Press, 2008.

Crittenden, H. Temple. *The Company: The Story of the Surry, Sussex & Southampton Railway and the Surry Lumber Company*. Parsons: McClain Print Co., 1967.

Dargavel, John. *Sawing, Selling & Sons*. Canberra: Centre for Resource and Environmental Studies, 1988.

Davis, John and et. al. *The outlook for Canadian Forest Industries*. Ottawa: Royal Commission on Canada's Economic Prospects, 1957.

Davis, Kenneth P. *Forest Management: Regulation and Valuation*. 2nd Ed., New York: McGraw-Hill, 1966.

DeMont, J. *Citizen Irving: K.C. Irving and His Legacy – The Story of Canada's Wealthiest Family*. Toronto: Doubleday, 1991.

Devitt, Bruce. *Forest Practice, Policy and the Profession*. Vancouver: Association of BC Professional Foresters, 1998.

Drobney, Jeffrey A. *Lumbermen and Log Sawyers: Life, Labor, and Culture in the North Florida Timber Industry, 1830–1930*. Macon: Mercer University Press, 1997.

Drushka, Ken. *Canada's Forests*. Durham: Forest History Society, 2003.

——. *HR: A Biography of H.R. MacMillan*. Madeira Park: Harbour Publishing, 1995.

——. *In The Bight*. Madeira Park: Harbour Publishing, 1999.

——. *Stumped*. Vancouver: Douglas & McIntyre, 1985.

——. *Tie Hackers to Timber Harvesters: The History of Logging in British Columbia's Interior.* Madeira Park: Harbour Publishing, 1998.

——. Bob Nixon, and Ray Travers, eds. *Touch Wood*: Madeira Park: Harbour Publishing, 1993.

——. *Working in the Woods: A History of Logging on the west Coast.* Madeira Park: Harbour Publishing, 1992.

Erickson, Harry. *Hills to Harbour: A British Columbia Forest Industry Story.* Harry Erickson: Ladysmith, 2010.

Erickson, Kenneth A. *Lumber Ghosts: A Travel Guide to Historic Lumber Towns of the Pacific Northwest.* Boulder: Pruett, 1994.

Evenden, Matthew D. *Fish versus Power: An Environmental History of the Fraser River.* Cambridge: Cambridge University Press, 2004.

Farrow, Moira. *Nobody Here But Us.* Vancouver: J.J. Douglas, 1975.

Felt, Margaret Elley. *Gypo Logger.* Caldwell: Caxton Printer, 1963.

Fenson, K.G. *Expanding Forestry Horizons.* Vancouver: Canadian Institute of Forestry, 1972.

Fernow, B.E. *A Brief History of Forestry.* 3rd Revised Ed. Toronto: University Press, 1913.

Ficken, Robert E. *The Forested Land: A History of Lumbering in Western Washington.* Seattle: University of Washington Press, 1987.

Fickle, James. *Mississippi Forests and Forestry.* Jackson: University Press of Mississippi, 2001.

Flavelle, W. Guy. *A Cedar Saga: And the Man Who Made it Possible.* Vancouver: Agency Press, 1966.

Forester, Jeff. *The Forest for the Trees.* St. Paul: Minnesota Historical Society, 2004.

Forestry Images of Lunnenburg County. Bridgewater: Lighthouse Publishing, 1996.

Fossum, Jack. *Mancatcher.* Comox: Lindsay Press, 1990.

Fox, Stephen. *The American Conservation Movement: John Muir and His Legacy.* Madison: University of Wisconsin Press, 1981.

Fox, William F. *A History of the Lumber Industry in the State of New York.* Washington: Government Printing Bureau, 1902.

Fries, Robert F. *Empire in Pine.* Ellison Bay: Wm. Caxton, 1989.

Garner, Joe. *Never Fly Over An Eagle's Nest.* Nanaimo: Cinnabar Press, 1987.

——. *Never Under the Table.* Nanaimo: Cinnabar Press, 1991.

——. *Never a Time to Trust.* Gordon Soules Book Pub, 1984.

——. *Never Chop Your Rope: A Story Of British Columbia Logging And The People Who Logged.* Nanaimo: Cinnabar Press, 1988.

Gatenbury, Steve. *Once, To Learn It: A Lighthearted Account Of A Fifty Year Adventure In The B.C. Lumber Industry.* Delta: Sedge Pub, 1989.

Gibson, Gordon with Carol Renison. *Bull of the Woods.* Vancouver: Douglas & McIntyre, 1980.

Gibson, J. Miles. *The History of Forest Management in New Brunswick.* The H. R. MacMillan Lectureship in Forestry, 1953. Vancouver: University of British Columbia, 1953.

Gill, Ian. *All That We Say is Ours: Guujaaw and the Reawakening of the Haida Nation.* Vancouver: Douglas & McIntyre, 2009.

Gillis, Peter and Thomas Roach. *Lost Initiatives: Canada's Forest Industries, Forest Policy and Forest Conservation*. New York. Greenwood Press, 1986.

Gold, Wilmer. *Logging As It Was*. Victoria: Morriss Publishing, 1985.

Gough, Joseph. *Managing Canada's Fisheries: From Early Days to the Year 2000*. Sillery: Les Editions du Septentrion, 2006.

Gould, ED. *Logging*. Saanichton: Hancock House Publishers, 1975.

Gow, Mary A. and Kitty Werner. *Draw Logs from Dowsvill: The History of the Ward Lumber Company*. Waitsfield: Distinction Press, 2011.

Grainger, M. Allerdale. *Woodsmen of the West*. Toronto: McCelland and Stewart, 1968.

Great Central Book Project Committee. *When the Whistle Blew*. Duncan: Firgrove Publishing, 2002.

Green, Harvey. *Wood: Craft, Culture*. New York: Viking, 2006.

Gregory, G. Robinson. *Forest Resource Economics*. New York: John Wiley and Sons, 1972.

Griffiths, Bus. *Now you're Logging*. 35th anniversary edition. Madeira Park: Harbour Publishing, 2013.

Gruell, George F. *Fire in Sierra Nevada Forests*. Missoula: Mountain Press Pub. Co., 2001.

Hak, Gordon. *Capital and Labour in the British Columbia Forest Industry, 1934–1974*. Vancouver: University of British Columbia Press, 2007.

——. *Turning Trees into Dollars: The British Columbia Coastal Lumber Industry, 1858–1913*. Toronto: University of Toronto Press, 2000.

Haley, David and Harry Nelson. *British Columbia's Crown Forest Tenure System in a Changing World: Challenges and Opportunities*. Vancouver: BC Forum on forest economics and policy, 2006. Synthesis Paper: SP 06-01.

Halleran, Mike. *Loggers and Lumbermen: The Evolution Of The Forest Industry In The Southern Interior Of British Columbia*. Kelowna: Interior Lumber Manufacturers' Association, 1994.

Hanft, Robert M. *Red River: Paul Bunyon's Own Lumber Company and its Railroads*. Chico: Center for Business and Economic Research California State University, 1980.

Hauff, Steve and Jim Gertz. *The Willamette Locomotive*. Portland: Binford & Mort, 1977.

Hartman, G.F., J.C. Scrivener, M.J. Brownlee and D.C. Morrison. *Fish Habitat Protection and Planning for Forest Harvesting in Coastal Streams of British Columbia: Some Research and Management Provisions*. Ottawa: Department of Fisheries and Oceans, 1983.

Hartwick, John M. and Nancy D. Olewiler. *The Economics of Natural Resource Use*. 2nd ed. Reading: Addison-Wesley, 1998.

Hawley, Ralph C. *The Practice of Silviculture, With Particular Reference to Its Application in The United States*. York: John Wiley & Sons, 1921.

Hayter, Roger. *Flexible Crossroads*. Vancouver: University of British Columbia Press, 2000.

Heal, S.C. *Tying The Knot: Consolidations And Mergers: In The B.C. Coast Forest Companies And The Tug & Barge Industry*. Vancouver: Cordillera Books, 2003.

Hidy, Ralph Willard, Frank Ernest Hill and Alan Nevins. *Timber and Men, the Weyerhaeuser Story*. New York: Macmillan, 1963.

Hindle, Brook. *America's Wooden Age: Aspects of its early Technology*. Tarrytown: Sleepy Hollow Restorations, 1975.

Holbrook, Stewart H. *A Narrative of Schafer Bros. Logging Company's Half Century in The Timber*. Aberdeen: Dogwood, 1945.

Howlett, Michael, Ed. *Canadian Forest Policy: Adapting to Change*. Toronto: University of Toronto Press, 2001.

Hughson, John W. and Courtney C.J. Bond. *Hurling Down the Pine*. Old Chelsea: Historical Society of the Gatineau, 1964.

Hutchison, Bruce. *The Fraser*. Toronto: Clarke, Irwin & Company, 1950.

Huth, Robin. *Guardians of the Forests: the First Hundred years*. Silverton: Wombat Press, 2002.

It's What's Inside that Counts: The Story of West Fraser's First 50 Years. Vancouver: West Fraser Timber Co. Ltd., 2005.

Jackson, W.H. with Ethel Dassow. *Handloggers*. Anchorage: Alaska Northwest Pub. Co., 1974.

Jamieson, Stuart Marshall. *Times of Trouble*. Task Force on Labour Relations Study No 22. Ottawa: University of British Columbia/Privy Council Office, 1968.

Johnson, Kevin. *Early Logging Tools*. Atgeln: Schiffer Publishing, 2007.

Johnson, Ralph S. *Forests of Nova Scotia: A History*. Halifax: Department of Lands and Forests, 1986.

Jones, Paul. *Out of the Rain*. Surrey: Hancock House Pub Ltd., 2003.

Josephson, Paul R. *Industrialized Nature: Brute Force Technology and the Transformation of the Natural World*. Washington: Island Press, 2002.

Kahn, Charles and Chris Hatfield. *Forgotten Cusheon Cove, Salt Spring Island*. Salt Spring Island: Salt Spring Press, 2007.

Kamholz, Edward J., Jim Blain, and Gregory Kamholz. *The Oregon-American Lumber Company*. Stanford: Stanford University Press, 2003.

Kaufman, Herbert. *Forest Ranger: A Study in Administrative Behavior*. Baltimore: John Hopkins University Press, 1960.

King, Frank Alexander. *Minnesota Logging Railroads*. Minneapolis: University of Minnesota Press, 2003.

Koch, Michael. *Steam & Thunder in the Timber*. Denver: World Press, 1979.

Koroleff, A. *Logging Mechanization in the U.S.S.R*. Montreal: Pulp and Paper Research Institute of Canada, 1952.

Krieg, Allan. *Last of the 3 Foot Loggers*. San Marina: Golden West Books, 1987.

Krygier, James T. *Handbook of Forest Protection*. Corvalli: O.S.U. Books, 1963.

Labbe, John T. and Vernon Goe. *Railroads in the woods*. Berkley: Howell-North, 1961.

Lala, J.B. *Forest Management: Classical Approach & Current Imperatives*. Dehradun: Natraj Publishers, 2007.

LaLande, Jeffery M. *Medford Corporation*. Medford: Klocker Print Co., 1979.

Lambert, Richard S. with Paul Pross. *Renewing Nature's Wealth*. Toronto: Ontario Dept. of Lands and Forests, 1967.

Lee, David. *Lumber Kings & Shantymen: Logging and Lumbering in the Ottawa Valley*. Toronto: James Lorimer & Company, 2006.

Leiren-Young, Mark. *The Green Chain: Nothing Is Ever Clear Cut*. Victoria: Heritage House Publishing, 2009.

Lembcke, Jerry and William M. Tattam. *One Union in Wood: A Political History of the International Woodworkers of America*. Madeira Park: Harbour Pub Co., 1983.

LeMonds, James. *Deadfall: Generations of Logging in the Pacific Northwest*. Missoula: Mountain Press Publishing Company, 2000.

Lichatowich, Jim. *Salmon Without Rivers: A History of the Pacific Salmon Crisis*. Washington: Island Press, 1999.

Lloyd, Donald L. *Algonquin Harvest: The History of the McRae Lumber Company*. Hitney: Robert D. McRae, 2006.

Lower, Arthur and Reginald Marsden. *Great Britain's Woodyard: British America and the Timber Trade, 1763–1867*. Toronto: McGill-Queen's University Press, 1973.

Luckert, Martin K., David Haley and George Hoberg. *Canada's Forests: Tenure, Stumpage Fees and Forest Practices*. Vancouver: University of British Columbia Press, 2011.

Lyons, Cicely. *Salmon: Our Heritage*. Vancouver: Mitchell Press, 1969.

MacCleery, Douglas W. *American Forests: A History of Resiliency and Recovery*. Durham: Forest History Society, 1993.

Macfie, John. *Parry Sound Logging Days*. Erin: Boston Mills Press, 2003.

MacKay, Donald. *Empire of Wood*: Vancouver: Douglas & McIntyre, 1982.

——. *The Lumberjacks*. Toronto: McGraw-Hill Ryerson, 1978.

Mackie, Richard Somerset. *Island Timber*. Victoria: Sono Nis Press, 2000.

MacMillan, H.R. *The Profession and Practice of Forestry in Canada, 1907–1957*. Toronto: University of Toronto, nd.

Mahood, Ian and Ken Drushka. *Three Men and a Forester*. Madeira Park: Harbour, 1990.

Management of Second-Growth Forest in the Douglas Fir Region. Portland: Pacific Northwest Forest and Range Experiment Station, 1947.

Marchak, M. Patricia, Scott L. Aycock and Doreen M. Herbert. *Falldown: Forest Policy in British Columbia*. Vancouver: David Suzuki Foundation and Ecotrust Canada, 1999.

Marchak, Patricia. *Green Gold: The Forest Industry in British Columbia*. Vancouver: University of British Columbia Press, 1983.

——. *Logging the Globe*. Montreal: McGill-Queens, 1995.

Marshall, Denis. *Sawdust Caesars and Family Ties in the Southern Interior*. Salmon Arm: Salmon Arm Branch, Okanagan Historical Society, 2003.

Maser, Chris. *Sustainable Forestry: Philosophy, Science, and Economics*. Delray Beach: St. Lucie Press, 1994.

Mason, Gary and Keith Baldry. *Fantasyland: Inside the Reign of Bill Vander Zalm*. Toronto: McGraw-Hill, 1989.

Matthews, Trevor, ed. *British Columbia's Future In Forest Products Trade In Asia And The Pacific Area*. Vancouver: The University of British Columbia, 1965.

Mayo, Joan. *Paldi Remembered: 50 Years In The Life Of A Vancouver Island Logging Town*. Duncan: Paldi History Committee, 1998.

Mayor, Archer. *Southern Timberman: The Legacy of William Buchanan*. Athens: University of Georgia Press, 1988.

May, Elizabeth. *Paradise Won: The Struggle for South Moresby*. Toronto: McLelland & Stewart, 1990.

McCombs, Arnold M. and Wilfred W. Chittenden. *The Harrison-Chehalis Challenge: A Brief History of the Forest Industry around Harrison Lake and the Chehalis Valley*. Harrison Hot Springs: Treeline Pub, 1988.

McElhanney, T.A. and Associates. *Canadian Woods: Their Properties and Uses*. Ottawa: King's Printer, 1935.

McGeer, Pat. *Politics in Paradise*. Toronto: Peter Martin Associates, 1972.

McGoldrick, Jim. *The McGoldrick Lumber Company Story, 1900–1952*. Spokane: Tornado Creek Publications, 2004.

McKillop, William, ed. *Timber Policy Issues In British Columbia*. Vancouver: University of British Columbia Press, 1976.

McKnight, George A. *Sawlogs on Steel Rails: A Story of the 45 Years Of Railway Operations In The Logging Camps Of The Port Alberni Area*. Winnipeg: Port Alberni Seniors' History Committee, 1995.

McPhee, Michael W. and Sam Sydneysmith. *Salmon Protection and the B.C. Coastal Forest Industry: Environmental Regulation as a Bargaining Process*. Vancouver: Westwater Research Centre, University of British Columbia, 1980.

Meggs, Geofff and Rod Mickleburgh. *The Art of the Impossible: Dave Barrett and the NDP in Power, 1972–1975*. Madeira Park: Harbour Publishing, 2012.

M'Gonigle, Michael and Ben Parfitt. *Forestopia: A practical Guide to the New Forest Economy*. Madeira Park: Harbour Publishing, 1994.

Milke, Mike. *Barbarisms in the Garden City: The BC NDP in Power*. Victoria: Thomas & Black Publishers, 2001.

Mills, Jenny. *The Timber People: A History of Bunnings Limited*. Perth: Bunnings Limited, 1986.

Mitchell, Bruce, ed. *Resource and Environmental Management in Canada: Addressing Conflict and Uncertainty*. 3rd ed. Don Mills: Oxford University Press, 2004.

Mitchell. David J. *WAC Bennett and the Rise of British Columbia*. Vancouver: Douglas & McIntyre, 1983.

Moore, John Hebron. *Andrew Brown and Cypress Lumbering In the Old Southwest*. Durham: Louisiana State University Press, 1967.

Morgan, Murray. *The Mill on the Boot: The Story of the St. Paul & Tacoma Lumber Company*. Seattle: University of Washington Press, 1982

Morton, James. *The Enterprising Mr. Moody, the Bumptious Captain Stamp*. North Vancouver: J.J. Douglas, 1977.

Motherwell, Andy. *Life At The Little Zipper Sawmill*. Quesnel: A. Motherwell, 2010.

Munro, Jack and Jane O'Hara. *Union Jack: Labour Leader Jack Munro*. Vancouver; Douglas & McIntyre, 1988.

Munro, John A. *Pitprops and Pulpwood: A History of Export Wood Operations in Newfoundland and Labrador 1898–1992*. St John's: Government of Newfoundland and Labrador, 2001.

Nawitka Resource Consultants. *FRDA Report 121: Increasing the Utilization Level of British Columbia's Timber Harvest*. Victoria: Forestry Canada, 1990.

Neufeld, Andrew and Andrew Parnaby. *The IWA in Canada, the Life and Times of an Industrial Union*. Vancouver: IWA-Canada, 2000.

Newman, Roger. *A Century of Success*. Winnipeg: Western Retail Lumbermen's Association, 1990.

Nikiforuk, Andrew. *Empire of the Beetle*. Vancouver: Greystone/David Suzuki Foundation, 2011.

Oakleaf, H.B. *Lumber Manufacture in the Douglas Fir Region*. Chicago: Commercial Journal Co., 1920.

Our First 100 Years, 1898–1998. Cranbrook: Crestbrook Forest Industries, 1998.

Opie, John. *Nature's Nation: An Environmental History of the United States*. New York: Harcourt Brace, 1998.

Panshin, A.J. et.al. *Forest Products*. New York: McGraw-Hill, 1950.

Parent, Milton. *Caulkboot Riverdance: Working the Columbia: Canada's Wildest Log Drive*. Nakusp: Arrow Lakes Historical Society, 2006.

Parfit, Ben. *Forest Follies: Adventures and Misadventures in the Great Canadian forest*. Madeira Park: Harbour Publishing, 1998.

Parker, Mike. *Woodchips & Beans Life in the early Lumber woods of Nova Scotia*. Halifax: Nimbus, 1992.

Patterson, Rosemary I. *Timber Sale: A British Columbia Literary History about Alexander Duncan McRae, Maillardville, The Comox Valley and the Canadian Western Lumber Company 1907–1916*. BookSurge, 2008.

Paulik, Max. *Reforestation Policy of British Columbia*. Vancouver: Foresta Publishers, 1948.

——. *The Truth about Our Forests*. Vancouver: Foresta Publishers, 1937.

Pearce, J. Kenneth and George Stenzel. *Logging and Pulpwood Production*. New York: Ronald Press, 1972.

Pearse, Peter H. *Introduction to Forestry Economics.* Vancouver: University of British Columbia, 1990

——. *Timber Rights and Forest Policy in British Columbia: Report of the Royal Commission on Forest Resources, Volume 1.* Victoria: Queen's Printer, 1976.

Peel, A.L. *Forest Resources Commission: The Future of Our Forests.* Victoria: Forest Resources Commission, 1991.

Perlin, John. *A Forest Journey: The Role of Wood in the Development of Civilization.* Cambridge: Harvard University Press, 1989.

Perrault, E.G. *Wood & Water: The Story of Seaboard Lumber and Shipping.* Vancouver: Douglas & McIntyre, 1985.

Petersen, Keith. *Company Town: Potlach Idaho and the Potlatch Lumber Company.* Moscow: Latah County Historical Society. Pullman: Washington State University Press, 1987.

Pinchot, Gifford. *A Primer of Forestry Part I the Forest.* Washington: Government Printing Office, 1917.

Plecas, Bob. *Bill Bennett: A Mandarin's View.* Vancouver: Douglas & McIntyre, 2006.

Polkinghorn, R.S. *Pino Grande: Logging Railroads of the Michigan-California Lumber Co.* 4th enlarged edition. Union City: R/Robb Ltd., 1984.

Pratt, Larry and Ian Urquhart. *The Last Great Forest: Japanese Multinationals and Alberta's Northern Forests.* Edmonton: Newest Press, 1994.

Price, Colin. *The Theory and application of Forest Economics.* Oxford: Basil Blackwell, 1989.

Raphael, Ray. *Tree Talk: The People and Politics of Timber.* Washington: Island Press, 1981.

Rajala, Richard A. *Clearcutting the Pacific Rain Forest: Production, Science and Regulation.* Vancouver: University of British Columbia Press, 1998.

——. *The Legacy and the Challenge: A Century of the Forest Industry at Cowichan Lake.* Lake Cowichan: Lake Cowichan Heritage Advisory Committee, 1993.

——. *Up-Coast: Forests and Industry on British Columbia's North Coast, 1870–2005.* Victoria: Royal British Columbia Museum, 2006.

Ramsey, Bruce. *Rain People: The Story of Ocean Falls.* 2nd Ed. Ocean Falls Library Association, 1997.

Radforth, Ian Walter. *Bushworkers and Bosses: Logging in Northern Ontario, 1900–1980.* Toronto: University of Toronto Press, 1987.

Reader, William Joseph. *Bowater: A History.* Cambridge: Cambridge University Press, 1981.

Reed, F.L.C. and Associates. *The British Columbia Forest Industry: Its Direct and Indirect Impact on the Economy.* Victoria: The British Columbia Forest Service, 1975.

Reierson, ed. *The Thrill of the Deal.* Quesnel: E.W. Books, 1999.

Rees-Thomas, David M. *Timber Down the Capilano.* Victoria: The British Columbia Railway Historical Association, 1979.

Reventlow, C.D.F. *A Treatise on Forestry.* Originally printed in 1805. Horsholm: Society of Forest History, 1980.

Richmond, Hector Allan. *Forever Green*. Lantzville: Oolichan Books, 1983.

Robbins, William G. *Hard Times in Paradise*, Coos Bay Oregon, 1850–1986. Seattle: University of Washington Press, 1988.

Robinson, A.B. *Witch Hunt in the B.C. Woods*. Kamloops: Sagebrush Book Pub, 1995.

Rohe, Randell Eugene. *Ghosts Of The Forest: Vanished Lumber Towns of Wisconsin*. Vol I. Wisconsin Rapids: Forest History Association of Wisconsin, 2002.

Roos, John F. *Restoring Fraser River Salmon: A History of the International Pacific Salmon Fisheries Commission, 1937–1985*. Vancouver: Pacific Salmon Commission, 1991.

Ross, John R. and Margaret Byrd Adams. *The Builder's Spirit a History of the Stimson Lumber Company*. Portland: John R. Ross, 1983.

Ross, Monique. *Forest Management in Canada*. Calgary: University of Calgary, 1995.

Ross, P.S & Partners. *A Study of Manpower in the Logging and Sawmilling Industry of British Columbia*. Vancouver: P.S. Ross & Partners, 1973.

Rouse, Park Jr. *The Timber Tycoons: The Camp Families of Virginia and Florida, and Their Empire, 1887–1987*. Richmond: The William Byrd Press, 1988.

Rudin, Bo. *Making Paper: A Look into the History of an Ancient Craft*. Vallingby: Rudins, 1990.

Salazar, Debra J. and Donald K. Alper. *Sustaining the Forests of The Pacific Coast: Forging Truces In The War In The Woods*. Vancouver: University of British Columbia Press, 2001.

Sandberg, L. Anders and Peter Clancy. *Against The Grain; Foresters and Politics in Nova Scotia*. Vancouver: University of British Columbia Press, 2000.

Sandberg, L. Anders. *Trouble in the Woods: Forest Policy and Social Conflict in Nova Scotia and New Brunswick*. Fredericton: Acadensis Press, 1992.

Satterfield, Terre. *Anatomy of a Conflict*. Vancouver: University of British Columbia Press, 2002.

"Sawmill Manufacturing and Lumber Recovery Seminar Booklet." Vancouver: Council of Forest Industries, nd.

Sensel, Joni. *Traditions Through The Trees: Weyerhaeuser's First 100 Years*. Seattle: Documentary Book Publishers, 1999.

Shakespeare, Mary and Rodney H. Pain. *West Coast Logging 1840–1910*. Ottawa: National Museum of Man Mercury Series, History Division Paper No. 22, 1977.

Shelford, Cyril. *From Snowshoes to Politics: A British Columbia Adventure*. Victoria: Orca Book Publishers, 1987.

Simpson, Sharon J. *Boards, Boxes, and Bins: Stanley M. Simpson and The Okanagan Lumber Industry*. Kelowna: Manhattan Beach Pub, 2003.

Sitton, Thad and James H. Conrad. *Nameless Towns: Texas Sawmill Communities, 1880–1942* Austin: University of Texas Press, 1998.

Sloan, Gordon. *The Forest Resources of British Columbia, Volume 1*. Victoria: Queen's Printer, 1957.

——. Chief Justice. *Report of the Commissioner relating to the Forest Resources of British Columbia*. 2 Volumes. Victoria: Queen's Printer, 1957.

Smith, David C. *History of Papermaking in the United States (1691–1969)*. New York: Lockwood Publishing Co., 1970.

Smith, David Martybn. *The Practice of Sivilculture*. 7th ed. New York: John Wiley and Sons, 1962.

Smith, Kenneth L. *Sawmill: The Story of Cutting The Last Great Virgin Forest East Of The Rockies*. Fayetteville: University of Arkansas Press, 1996.

Soucoup, Dan. *Logging in New Brunswick: Lumber, Mills, & River Drivers*. Halifax: Nimbus Publishing, 2011.

Spector, Robert. *Family Trees: Simpson's Centennial Story*. Bellevue: Documentary Book Publishers Corporation, 1990.

———. *Shared Values: A History of Kimberly-Clark*. Lyme: Greenwich Publishing Group, 1997.

Steen, Harold R. Ed. *History of Sustained-Yield Forestry: A Symposium*. Durham: The Forest Society, 1984.

Stein, Harry H. *Old Growth, New directions: 150 years of Pope & Talbot*. Seattle: Documentary Book Publishers, 2005.

Stephens, Kent. *Matches, Flumes, and Rails: The Diamond Match Company in the High Sierra*. Corona del Mar: Trans-Anglo Books, 1981.

Stevenson, Susan K. et. al. *British Columbia's Inland Rainforest: Ecology, Conservation and Management*. Vancouver: University of British Columbia Press, 2011.

Strobel, Larry. *When the Mill Whistle Blew: The Way it was in Coeur D'Alene Country 1888–1955*. Coeur D'Alene: Museum of North Idaho, 2010.

Studier, Donald D. and Virgil W. Binkley. *Cable Logging Systems*. Corvallis: O.S.U. Book Services, 1974.

Swanson, Robert. *Whistle Punks and Widow-Makers: Tales of the B.C. Woods*. Madeira Park: Harbour Publishing, 1993.

Swenerton, Douglas M. *A History of Pacific Fisheries Policy*. Ottawa: Department of Fisheries and Oceans, 1993.

Tall Timber Tales: Reid, Collins Recollections: 1951 to 2002. NP, ND.

Taylor, Wilf and Alan Fry. *Beating Around the Bush*. Madeira Park: Harbour Pub, 1989.

The Merchandising of Lumber. Chicago: National Lumber Manufacturers Association 12th Annual Convention, 1914.

Thompson, Dennis Blake. *Logging Railroads in Skagit County*. Seattle: Northwest Shortline, 1989.

Tollefson, Chris, ed. *The Wealth of Forests*. Vancouver: University of British Columbia Press, 1998.

Toumey, James W. *Seeding and Planting: A Manual for the Guidance of Forestry Students, Foresters, Nurserymen, Forest Owners and Farmers*. New York: John Wiley & Sons, 1916.

Transactions of the British Columbia Natural Resources Conference. Victoria: The British Columbia Natural Resources Conference 1 to 19, 1948–1970.

Trinnell, John Ross. *J.R. Booth: The Life and Times of an Ottawa Lumberking.* Ottawa: TreeHouse Publishing, 1998.

Turner, Robert D. *Logging by Rail the British Columbia Story.* Victoria: Sono Nis Press, 1990.

——. *Vancouver Island Railroads.* Victoria: Sono Nis, 1973.

Twining, Charles E. *Downriver: Orrin H. Ingram and the Empire Lumber Company.* Madison: State Historical Society of Wisconsin, 1975.

Uhler, Russell S., ed. *Canada United Trade in Forest Products.* Vancouver: University of British Columbia Press, 1991.

Vaillant, John. *The Golden Spruce: A True Story of Myth, Madness, and Greed.* New York: W.W. Norton & Company, 2005.

Vogel, John N. *Great Lakes Lumber on the Great Plains.* Iowa City: University Of Iowa Press, 1992.

White, Frank. *Milk Spills & One-Log Loads; Memories of a Pioneer Truck Driver.* Madeira Park: Harbour Publishing, 2015.

Williams, Bryan A. *Fish and Game in British Columbia.* Vancouver: Sun Directories, 1935.

Williams, Michael. *Americans and Their Forests: A Historical Geography.* Cambridge: Cambridge University Press, 1992.

——. *Deforesting The Earth: from Prehistory to Global Crisis.* Chicago: University of Chicago Press, 2003.

Wilkerson, Hugh and John Van Der Zee. *Life in the Peace Zone: An American Company Town.* New York: Collier Books, 1971.

Williams Ricard I. *The Loggers.* Time-Life Books Old West Series. Alexandria Time-Life Books, 1976.

Williston, Eileen and Betty Keller. *Forests, Power and Policy: The Legacy of Raw Williston.* Halfmoon Bay: Caitlin Books, 1997.

Wilson, Jeremy. *Talk and Log: Wilderness Politics in British Columbia.* Vancouver: University of British Columbia Press, 1998.

Witherelll, Jim. *Log Trains Of Southern Idaho.* Denver: Sundance Books, 1989.

Wynn, Graham. *Canada and Arctic North America: An Environmental History.* Santa Barbara: ABC: CLIO, 2007.

Young, Jeffrey and John Werring. *The Will to Protect: Preserving B.C.'s Wild Salmon Habitat.* Vancouver: David Suzuki Foundation, 2006.

Zhang, Daowei and Peter H. Pearse. *Forest Economics.* Vancouver: University of British Columbia Press, 2011.

Zimmerman, Adam. *Who's In Charge Here Anyway?* Toronto: Stoddart, 1997.

ARTICLES

Allen, Heather C. "Lumber and Salmon: A History of the Adams River Lumber Company". *Wildlife Review* 8 (Summer 1979): 22–24.

Burns, R.M. "British Columbia and the Canadian Federation". In A History of British Columbia: Selected Readings. Edited by Patricia Roy. Toronto: Copp Clark Pitman, 1989.

Colwell, Doug. "The Last Log Drive". *Forest Talk* 5 (Summer 1981): 11–17.

Douglas, Sheila. "Clear Cut Logging and Salmon Habitat". *Telkwa Foundation Newsletter* 1 (Apr/May 1978): 6–7.

Dunn, J. Richard. "Charles Henry Gilbert (1859-1928): An Early Fisheries Biologist and His Contributions to Knowledge of Pacific Salmon (Oncorhynchus spp)". *Reviews in Fisheries Science* 42 (1996): 133–84.

Evenden, Matthew. "Remaking Hells Gate: Salmon, Science and the Fraser River, 1938-1948". *BC Studies* 127 (Autumn 2000): 47–83.

——. "Social and Environmental Change at Hells Gate, British Columbia". *Journal of Historical Geography* 30 (2004): 130–53.

"Forest Community Sustainability". *The Forestry Chronicle*. Volume 75 No. 5. September/October 1999.

Gray, Stephen. "The Government's Timber Business: Forest Policy and Administration in British Columbia, 1912-1928". *BC Studies*, No. 81 (Spring 1989) pp. 24–49.

Haig-Brown, Roderick. "Canada's Pacific Salmon". *Canadian Geographical Journal* 44 (Mar. 1952): 109–27.

——. "Fish Hatcheries…No Substitute for Stream Protection". *BC Outdoors* 29 (July – Aug. 1973): 16–21.

——. "Fish and Wildlife in the Development of B.C.'s Future". *British Columbia Digest* (July – Aug. 1966): 32–40.

——. "Let Them Eat Sawdust". *Forest and Outdoors* 47 (Oct. 1951): 10–12.

Hak, Gordon. "Making Sense of Forestry: A Review Essay". *BC Studies*. No. 122 (Summer 1999) pp. 89–92.

——. "Populism and the 1952 Social Credit Breakthrough in British Columbia". *Canadian Historical Review* 85 (June 2004): 277–96.

Helmer, Rick. "Voices in the Wilderness". *Telkwa Foundation Newsletter* 8 (Oct. 1979): 1–4.

Hudson, Douglas. "Internal Colonialism and Industrial Capitalism". In *SA TS'E: Historical Perspectives on Northern British Columbia*. Edited by Thomas Thorner. Prince George: College of New Caledonia Press, 1989.

Hume, Mark. "Death of a Salmon Stream." *BC Outdoors* 36 (July 1980): 39–41, 55.

Keeling, Arn. "'A Dynamic not a Static Conception': The Conservation Thought of Roderick Haig-Brown". *Pacific Historical Review* 71 (May 2002): 239–68.

——. "'Sink or Swim': Water Pollution and Environmental Politics in Vancouver, 1889–1975". *BC Studies* 142/43 (Summer/Autumn 2004): 69–101.

——. and Robert McDonald. "The Profligate Province: Roderick Haig-Brown and the Modernization of British Columbia". *Journal of Canadian Studies* 36 (Fall 2001): 7–23.

Loo, Tina. "People in the Way: Modernity, Environment, and Society on the Arrow Lakes". *BC Studies* 142/143 (Summer/Autumn 2004): 161–96.

M'Gonigle, R. Michael. "The Political Ecology of Biodiversity: A View from the Western Woods". In *Biodiversity in Canada: Ecology, Ideas, and Action*. Edited by Stephen Bocking. Peterborough: Broadview Press, 2000.

McMynn, R.G. "Man, Water and Fish". *British Columbia Digest* 22 (May–June 1966): 36–42.

"Men of the Forest". *Sound Heritage* (VI, 3). 1977.

Millerd, Frank. "The Evolution of Management of the Canadian Pacific Salmon Fishery". *Digital Library of the Commons*. http://olc.dlib.indiana.edu. archive/00000999 (12 Dec. 2007).

Neave, Ferris and W.P. Wickett. "Factors Affecting the Development of Pacific Salmon in British Columbia". *Proceedings, Seventh Pacific Science Congress* 4 (1949): 548–55.

Norris, Pat Wastell. "Time & Tide: A History of Telegraph Cove". Raincoast *Chronicles* 16 1998.

Overstall, Richard. "Rennell Sound: The End of Multiple Use?" *Telkwa Foundation Newsletter* 2 (Apr. 1979): 1–3.

Paish, Howard. "Stellako Log Drive – Resource Use or Resource Abuse". *British Columbia Digest* 22 (Sept. – Oct. 1966): 9, 37.

Pennell, J.T. "Effects on Fresh Water Fisheries of Forestry Practices". *Canadian Fish Culturalist* 25 (Oct. 1959): 27–31.

Pritchard, A.L. "The Effects of Man-Made Changes in Fresh Water in the Maritime Provinces". *Canadian Fish Culturalist* 25 (Oct. 1959): 27–31.

Prudham, Scott. "Sustaining Sustained Yield: Class Politics, and Post-War Forest Regulation in British Columbia". *Environment and Planning D: Society and Space* 25 (2007): 258–83.

Rajala, Richard A. "Forests and Fish: The 1972 Coast Logging Guidelines and British Columbia's First NDP Government". *BC Studies* 159 (Autumn 2008): 81–120.

——. "'Streams Being Ruined from a Salmon Producing Standpoint': Clearcutting, Fish Habitat, and Forest Regulation in British Columbia, 1900–45". *BC Studies* 176 (Winter 2012/13): 93–132.

——. "The Forest Industry in Eastern Canada: An Overview". In C. Ross Silversides, *Broadaxe to Flying Shear: The Mechanization of Forest Harvesting East of the Rockies*. Ottawa: National Museum of Science and Technology, 1997.

——. "'This Wasteful Use of a River': Log Driving, Conservation, and British Columbia's Stellako River Controversy, 1965–72". *BC Studies* 165 (Spring 2010): 31–74.

Ray, Doris with Grace and Roy Foote. "Ties for the Railroad". In *Deeper Roots and Greener Pastures*. Fraser Lake: Fraser Lake and District Historical Society, 1986.

——. with Harvey MacDonald. "Stellako River Log Drives". In *Deeper Roots and Greener Pastures*. Fraser Lake: Fraser Lake and District Historical Society, 1986.

Rector, William G. "From Woods to Sawmill: Transportation Problems in Logging". *Agricultural History* 23 (Oct. 1949): 239-44.

Scott, P. and W. Schouwenberg. "Environmental Foresight and Salmon: New Canadian Developments". In *Pacific Salmon Management for People*. Edited by Derek V. Ellis. Victoria: University of Victoria, 1977.

Sorensen, Jean. "ForesTalk Interviews Jack Munro". *ForesTalk* 2 (Fall 1978): 8-10.

StanBury, W.T. and M.R. McLeod. "The Concentration of Timber Holdings in the British Columbia Forest Industry, 1972". *BC Studies* No. 17 (Spring 1975). Pp. 57-68.

Stewart, Dave. "This is the Stellako". *Western Fish and Game* 3 (Mar. 1968): 22-25.

Taylor, Joseph III. "Making Salmon: The Political Economy of Fishery Science and the Road Not Taken". *Journal of the History of Biology* 31 (1998): 33-59.

Vladykov, Vadim D. "The Effects of Man-Made Changes in Fresh Water in the Province of Quebec". *Canadian Fish Culturalist* 25 (Oct. 1959): 7-12.

Whipp, Steve. "Steep Slope Logging on the Charlottes: An Interview with Federal Fisheries Officer, Jim Hart". *Telkwa Foundation Newsletter* 2 (Feb. 1979): 1-2.

White, Richard. "Are You an Environmentalist or Do You Work for a Living? Work and Nature". In *Uncommon Ground: Rethinking the Human Place in Nature*. Edited by William Cronon. New York: W.W. Norton, 1995.

Wilson, Jeremy. "Forest Conservation in British Columbia, 1935-85: Reflections on a Barren Political Debate". *BC Studies* 76 (Winter 1987-88): 3-32.

Wright, Bruce S. "Effects of Stream Driving on Fish, Wildlife and Recreation". *Woodlands Review* (Nov. 1962): 433-39.

Wright, Richard. "Death of the Rivers". *Western Fish and Game* 4 (Sept. 1969): 20-23.

Zelko, Frank. "Making Greenpeace: The Development of Direct Action Environmentalism in British Columbia". *BC Studies* 142/143 (Summer/Autumn 2004): 197-239.

UNPUBLISHED DOCUMENTS

Aylen, Peter G. "Sustained Yield Forestry Policy in BC to 1956: A Deterministic Analysis of development". MA thesis, University of Victoria, 1984.

Benskin, Henry J. "Financial Implications and Some Costs and Benefits of Logging Guidelines in the Chilliwack Provincial Forest". MF thesis, University of British Columbia, 1975.

Bixby, Miriam E. "Evaluating Social Welfare Implications of Forest Policies When Economic and Environmental Values Matter in a British Columbia Context". PhD thesis, University of British Columbia, 2008.

Bronson, Elizabeth Anne. "Openings in the Forest Economy: A Case Study of Small Forest Operators in the Bulkley Valley, BC, Canada". PhD thesis, University of British Columbia, 1999.

Byron, Ronald Neil. "Community Stability and Regional Economic Development: The Role of Forest Policy in the North Central Interior of British Columbia". PhD thesis, University of British Columbia, 1976.

Cashore, Benjamin William. "Governing Forestry: Environmental Group Influence IN British Columbia and the U S Pacific Northwest". PhD thesis, University of Toronto, 1997.

Clark, Glen David. "Timber Allocation Policy in British Columbia to 1972". MA thesis, Simon Fraser University, 1985.

Cottell, Phillip L. "The Influence of Changing Logging Technology upon the Economic Accessibility of the Forest". MFor thesis, University of British Columbia, 1966.

Dellert, Lois Helen. "Sustained Yield Forestry in British Columbia: The Making and Breaking of a Policy (1900–1993)". MES thesis, North York, 1994.

Grass, Eric. "Employment and Production: The Mature Stage in the Life Cycle of a Sawmill: Youbou British Columbia". PhD thesis, Simon Fraser University, 1971.

Gray, Stephen. "Forest Policy and Administration in British Columbia, 1912–1928". MA thesis, Simon Fraser University, 1982.

Griffin, Robert B. "Success and Failure in British Columbia's Softwood Plywood Industry, 1913–1999". PhD thesis, University of Victoria, 1999.

Hak, Gordon Hugh. "On the Fringes: Capital and Labour in the Forest: Economies of the Port Alberni and Prince George Districts, British Columbia, 1910–1939". PhD thesis, Simon Fraser University, 1986.

Haley, David. "An Economic Appraisal of Sustained Yield Forest Management for British Columbia". PhD thesis, University of British Columbia, 1966.

Keeling, Arn Michael. "Ecological Ideas in the British Columbia Conservation Movement, 1945–1970". MA thesis, University of British Columbia, 1998.

——. "The Effluent Society: Water Pollution and Environmental Politics in British Columbia, 1889–1980". PhD thesis, University of British Columbia, 2004.

Kelly, Elizabeth Fay. "Aspects of Forest Use Policies and Administration in British Columbia". MA thesis, University of British Columbia, 1976.

Lawrence, Joseph Collins "Markets and Capital: A History of the Lumber Industry of British Columbia (1178–1952)". MA thesis, University of British Columbia, 1951.

McRoberts, Mary Lillian. "The Emergence of a Corporate Structure in the Williams Lake District Lumber Industry, 1947–1956". MA thesis, University of Victoria, 1986.

Marris, Robert Howard. "'Pretty Sleek and Fat': The Genesis of Forest Policy in British Columbia, 1903–1914". MA thesis, University of British Columbia, 1979.

Metcalf, Cherie Maureen. "Resources and Regional Economy: An Historical Assessment of the Forest Industry in British Columbia. PhD thesis, University of British Columbia, 1998.

Mikolash, Jacqueline V.A. "The Roots of Forest Policy Issues: The 'Conservation-Preservation Conflict' and its Role in British Columbia's Forest Policy". MPA thesis, University of Winnipeg, 1999.

Minunzie, Natalie. "'The Chain-saw Revolution' Environmental Activism in the B.C. Forest Industry". MA thesis, Simon Fraser University, 1993.

Moreira-Munoz, Simon. "Timber Supply and Economic Impact of Mountain Pine Beetle Salvage Strategies". MASc thesis, University of British Columbia, 2008.

Mullins, Doreen Katherine. "Changes in Location and Structure in the Forest Industry of North Central British Columbia, 1909-1966". MA thesis, University of British Columbia, 1967.

Nagle, George. "Economics and Public Policy on the Forestry Sector of British Columbia". PhD thesis, Yale University, 1971.

Ottens, Johannes. "The Use of Regional Economic Techniques to Analyze Forest Policy Impacts: The Case of the Impact of Close Utilization Policy on the Level of Employment within the Kamloops Region". MF thesis, University of British Columbia, 1973.

Parchomchuk, William. "Truck, Rail and Water Transport of Raw Wood in the British Columbia Forest Industry". MBA thesis, University of British Columbia, 1966.

Phillips, Alan George. "Jurisdictional Conflicts in Resource Management: Perspectives on the Canadian West Coast Commercial Fishing Industry". MA thesis, University of Victoria, 1984.

Rajala, Richard. "The Rude Science: A Social History of West Coast Logging, 1890-1930". MMa thesis, University of Victoria, 1987.

Reyden, Jeff D. "Is it time to change the Tenure System of BC to More Accurately Address the Needs of Communities?" BScF thesis, University of British Columbia, 2012.

Rowen, Marco. "Mitigating the Mid-term Timber Supply Gap; Potential Silvicultural Solutions in the Prince George TSA?" Graduating Essay for FRST 497, University of British Columbia, 2012.

Terpenning, John Gordon. "The B.C. Wildlife Federation and Government: A Comparative Study of Pressure Group and Government Interaction for Two Periods, 1947 to 1957, and 1958 to 1975". MA thesis, University of Victoria, 1982.

Tuomala. Maurice Frederick. "The Evolution of Logging on the Pacific Coast". BScF thesis, University of British Columbia, 1960.

Vance, Eric Carter. "The Impact of the Forest Industry on Economic Development in the Central Interior of British Columbia". MA thesis, University of British Columbia, 1981.

Wagner, William Leroy. "Exercising the Common Wealth? A Study of public Sector Intervention in the British Columbia Forestry Sector 1980-1996". PhD thesis, University of Victoria, 2001.

Wagner, William. "Privateering in the Public Forest? A Study of the Forest Industry's Expanding Role in the Management of British Columbia's Forest Lands". MA thesis, University of Victoria, 1987.

Wildeman, Jesse. "Technological and Managerial History of Innovation in British Columbia's Forest Industry". FRST 497, University of British Columbia, 2011.

Yerburgh, Richard Eustace Marryat. "An Economic History of Forestry in British Columbia". MA thesis, University of British Columbia, 1931.

Young, Eric Carl. "The Evolution of a British Columbia Forest Landscape, as Observed in the Soo Public Sustained Yield Unit". MA thesis, University of British Columbia, 1976.

Zietsma, Charlene Ellen. "Determinants and processes of Institutional Change in the B.C. Coastal Forest Industry". PhD thesis, University of British Columbia, 2002.

ROYAL COMMISSION SUBMISSIONS

"Regulation of the Rate of Timber Harvesting in British Columbia." Victoria: Policy Background Paper Produced by the Royal Commission on Forest Resources, 1975.

Schwindt, R. *The Existence and Exercise of Corporate Power: A Case Study of MacMillan Bloedel.* Ottawa: Royal Commission on Corporate Concentration, 1977.

ARCHIVAL COLLECTIONS

BC Forest Branch, Report of Intensive Reconnaissance of Watershed of Horsefly River, 1932.

BC Forest Service Circular letters

British Columbia Ministry of Forests. O Series Correspondence Files, Ministry of Forests Office, Victoria, BC.

Derrick Mallard Papers. University of Victoria, Archives and Special Collections.

Elk River Timber Company Records. Campbell River and District Museum and Archives.

File 081228, Sayward Public Working Circle (PWC), 1948-1958.

File 0187119, Supervision, 1950-1964.

File 0187734, Sechelt Public Sustained Yield Unit (PSYU), 1948-1965.

File 0189897, Naver PSYU, 1951-1970.

File 0190093, Cottonwood PSYU.

File 0206389, Narcosli PSYU, 1954–1971.

File 0206543, Williams Lake PSYU, 1955–1968.

File 0206554, Quesnel Lake, PWC, 1955–1973.

File 0212165, Stum PSYU, 1956–1964.

File 0212166, Taseko PSYU, 1956–1969.

File 0212167, Big Bar PSYU.

File 0212679 Bowron PSYU.

File 0212680 Big Valley PSYU.

File 0212726, Thompson PSYU, 1956–1964.

File 0218594, Kamloops Region 1960–1964.

File 0219900 Hecate PSYU 1958–1964.

File 0234016, Fort Nelson PSYU, 1960–1966.

File 0250164, Prince George Special sale Area, 1961–1989.

File 0268206, Close Utilization.

File 0272554, Narcosli PSYU 1973–1974.

File O272547, Lac La Hache, 1968–1972.

File 0272555, Nechako, 1967–1974.

File 0272557, Okanagan PSYU, 1967–1975.

File 0272567, Salmon Arm PSYU, Planning File, 1969–1973.

File 19700-20/102547F TFL 35, BC Interior Sawmills.

File 19700-25/10854F, TFL4, 1954–1956.

File 19680-25, TFL 29, Eagle Lake sawmills. 1952.

File 19680-25, TFL 30, Sinclair Spruce Lumber Co, 1945–1957.

File 19680-25 TFL 31, Upper Fraser Sawmills, 1945–1952.

File 19680-25 TFL 34, Church Sawmills, 1953–1954.

Forest Branch, Extensive Reconnaissance Upper Nechako Watershed, 1928.

Forest Branch, Reconnaissance Between Quesnel & Barkerville, 1923.

Forest Branch. Reconnaissance Bowron & Willow Rivers. 1914.

Forest Branch, Cruise Report Quesnel Lake, 1925.

Forest Branch. Reconnaissance Willow River. 1934.

Forest Branch, Report on Reconnaissance of Quesnel River Watershed, 1923.

Forest Resources Commission, Background Papers, Vol 3, A History of Forest Tenure in British Columbia 1858–1978, 1990.

Forest Surveys and Inventory Division, Forest Resources Bulletin No. 33, Cottonwood Public Working Circle, 1956.

Forest Surveys and Inventory Division, Forest Resources Bulletin No. 32, Naver Public Working Circle, 1956.

Forest Surveys and Inventory Division. Forest Resources Bulletin No. 31, Willow River Public Working Circle, 1956.

GR-110, British Columbia. Prince George Forest District, Operation Records. Boxes 1-6, 23-27, 29-48, 65-74.

GR-347, British Columbia. Commission on Forest Resources Records, 1975-77. British Columbia Archives.

GR-668, British Columbia. Commission on Forest Resources Records, 1955. British Columbia Archives.

GR-1110, British Columbia. Prince George Forest District Records, British Columbia Archives.

GR-1118, British Columbia. B.C. Marine Resources Branch Records. British Columbia Archives.

GR-1191, British Columbia. Kamloops Forest District, Operational Records, Boxes 45-74.

Management Annual Reports, Prince George Forest District, 1953, 1958-1966, 1968. Paper copies on file in the History Section, RBCM.

Management Annual Reports, Kamloops Forest District, 1953-1956 paper copies on file in the History Section, RBCM: 1959-1977 digital copies on file in the History Section, RBCM.

Ministry of Forests, Forest Range

Paul George Papers. University of Victoria Archives and Special Collections.

Pulp Harvesting Area Licences, No 1-7. Digital files History Section, RBCM.

Ray Williston Papers. University of Victoria Archives and Special Collections.

Sierra Club of Western Canada. B.C. Chapter, Records, University of Victoria Archives and Special Collections.

Tree Farm Licences at https://www.for.gov.bc.ca/dmswww/tfl/

Pulp Harvesting Area No 1, Agreement between the Minister of Lands, Forest and Water and Prince George Pulp and Paper Company, November 22, 1962.

Pulp Harvesting Area No 3. Agreement between the Minister of Lands, Forest and Water and Northwood Pulp Limited, October 30, 1964.

Index

East End Francois Lake Resort
Association, 139, 156, 172

economic development
failure of multiple use planning,
123-24
Pacific Great Eastern Railway line, 96
revenue from fisheries, 161
revenue from forestry, 123-24, 128,
161, 164

Edenshaw, Gary. *See* Guujaaw

environmental issues. *See also* fish spawning
habitat; logging practices
expert opinion disagreement, 129,
201-3, 206, 228, 285
failure of multiple use planning,
123-24
on Haida Gwaii, 254-59
impact of logging protests, 320-30
lack of conservation, 123
pollution control, 202, 211, 225-26
public awareness of, 123, 126-27, 161,
164-66, 231
and road construction, 249
and social movements, 241, 249, 285,
320, 332
watershed deterioration, 260, 261,
280-81, 293

Environmental Protection Area (EPA), 261

Ernst Lumber Company, 41-44, 48, 49, 113

First Nations
Carrier people, 120, 121, 131, 136, 139
Haida people, 241, 255-56, 273, 322-23,
326
Stellako people, 123, 173

fish spawning habitat
and clear cuts, 242-43, 244, 266-67,
322, 327
and leavestrips, 244, 257, 259
and log drives, 124-25, 143-48
salmon, 120, 128, 134-39
study results, 322, 327
trout, 120, 131, 139, 154, 183, 234

fisheries. *See also* salmon fishery;
sport fishing
federal-provincial committee, 162-63
impact of court cases, 318
joint management referral process,
243, 245, 265-66
jurisdiction dispute, 123-25

Fisheries Act (Canada)
1977 provisions, 245-48
and Fowler decision, 290-91, 313-14,
315, 318
IPS report on, 266-68
and Stellako River log drive, 123-25,
129, 173, 178, 197, 228-29
use to stop logging operation, 271

Fisheries Association of BC, 156, 185, 210

Fish/Forestry Interaction Program (FFIP),
241, 310-11, 325, 327, 329-30

Forest Act
1948, 91, 141
1961 amendment, 94, 96, 141
1978, 241, 248-49, 251-53

forest industry
access to timber, 25-26
associations, 37
competitive bidding, 77-79
demand for timber, 10-11, 14-16
operator agreements, 76, 79-82

road construction, 11–13

small operators, 26, 250

use of political influence, 21, 33, 67–68

forest management licence (FML), 22, 24

Fowler, Dan, court case, 290–91, 313–14, 315, 318

Fraser Lake Sawmills

1965 log drive, 128–29, 152–62, 165–66

1966 log drive, 167, 171–77, 188, 191

1967 log drive, 195, 203

history of, 127, 131, 134, 139, 141, 142, 229

seizure of logs, 128, 171–77

Fraser River

basin, 120

canyon area, 21–22

construction of fish ladders, 135–36, 146

river-driven logs, 58–59, 148–49

salmon spawning habitat, 128, 134–39, 148

freshwater ecosystems. *See* fish spawning habitat

Frolek, Joe, 34, 36–37

Garner Brothers, 61–62, 72, 75, 81

Graham Island, 239, 254, 260. *See also* Riley Creek controversy

Graham Island Advisory Planning Committee (GIAPC), 258, 263, 264

Grand Trunk Pacific Railway (GTP) construction, 121, 130, 131

Gregg, E.E., 60, 68

Guujaaw, 256, 265, 273, 316, 319

Gwaii Haanas National Park, 326

Haida Gwaii. *See also* Riley Creek controversy

1978 storms, 269–70

environmental issues, 254–59

impact of logging protests, 320–30

Haida Monarch, 258–59, 261

Haida people

land claims, 255–56, 322–23

and Lyell Island blockade, 326

and Riley Creek, 273, 322–23

and South Moresby Island, 241, 326

Haig-Brown, Roderick, 123, 125, 126, 158–59, 169, 170, 224

Hans Creek watershed, 256

Hart, Jim

aftermath, 293, 297, 333

on leavestrips, 257–58, 259

on new *Fisheries Act*, 265

overview of role, 240–41

stop operations order, 270–72, 276, 282–84

Hart-Hernandez report, 261, 263, 264, 324

harvest amounts. *See* annual allowable cut (AAC)

Hernandez, Vince, 261

hewn-tie industry, 131

Hixon Creek area, 17–19

Howard, Frank, 157, 195

Hughes, W.G., 5, 10, 12–13, 21, 28–29, 163

hydroelectric projects, 125, 128, 143, 148, 169–70, 178, 182, 232

integrated resource use. *See* multiple use planning

International Pacific Salmon Fisheries Commission (IPSFC), 136, 139, 143, 147–48, 153, 167, 213